Small Business

Small Business

an entrepreneur's plan

Fourth Canadian Edition

Ron Knowles
Algonquin College

THOMSON
NELSON

Australia Canada Mexico Singapore Spain United Kingdom United States

THOMSON
NELSON

Small Business: An Entrepreneur's Plan, Fourth Canadian Edition

by Ron Knowles

Editorial Director and Publisher: Evelyn Veitch

Acquisitions Editor: Anthony Rezek

Marketing Manager: Bram Sepers

Developmental Editor: Elke Price

Production Editor: Bob Kohlmeier

Production Coordinator: Julie Preston

Copy Editor: Sarah Robertson

Proofreader: Susan Broadhurst

Creative Director: Angela Cluer

Indexer: Dennis Mills

Interior-Design Modifications: Peter Papayanakis

Cover Design: Angela Cluer

Cover Image: Allan Davey/Masterfile

Compositor: Janet Zanette

Printer: Webcom

Adapted from *Small Business: An Entrepreneur's Plan*, 4th edition, published by Harcourt Brace & Company, © 1996.

Printed and bound in Canada
1 2 3 4 06 05 04 03

For more information contact Nelson, 1120 Birchmount Road, Scarborough, Ontario, M1K 5G4. Or you can visit our Internet site at http://www.nelson.com

National Library of Canada Cataloguing in Publication Data

Knowles, Ronald A.
Small business : an entrepreneur's plan / Ronald A. Knowles. — 4th Canadian ed.

Includes bibliographical references and index.
ISBN 0-17-622462-9

1. New business enterprises—Planning. 2. Small business—Planning. I. Title.

HD62.5.K568 2003 658.1'141
C2002-905306-4

Brief Contents

Contents

Chapter 4

PROFILING YOUR TARGET CUSTOMER 61

Chapter 5

LEARNING FROM THE COMPETITION 81

Chapter 6

MARKETING STRATEGIES AND PROMOTION: CONNECTING WITH THE CUSTOMER 97

Chapter 7

LOCATION 121

Preface

Welcome to the fourth Canadian edition of *Small Business: An Entrepreneur's Plan*. This book was created for you and thousands of dreamers like you who want to start your own business. Most first-time entrepreneurs start out with little more than an idea. *Small Business* lets you combine your vision with the practical approach, and shows you how to make your idea into a functional business plan.

Every great adventure begins with a map. This book serves as your map and your navigator. The Business Plan Building Blocks and Action Steps provide you with direction and tasks to accomplish along the way, while the vignettes and case studies give you a firsthand look at the trials, tribulations, and successes of other entrepreneurs.

By following these Building Blocks and Actions Steps, you learn how to develop a business plan from the inception of the idea, how to find your target customers, and how to market to them successfully.

Fasten your seatbelt, and prepare to embark on your great entrepreneurial adventure!

Target the Chapters That Call to You

The Action Steps and Building Blocks are apportioned across 17 chapters, from Chapter 1, "Your Great Adventure—Exploring Your Options," to Chapter 17, "Fast-Start Business Plan."

- Chapters 1, 2, and 3 help you focus on yourself and your ideas; they explain how to develop and test your ideas in the marketplace before you spend your money. If you are just exploring entrepreneurship, concentrate on these chapters and the accompanying Action Steps. You are designing not only your business but also your life.
- Chapters 4, 5, and 6 help you locate the key to your success in small business—your target customer.
- Chapter 7 helps you find a location—on the street or at the crossroads in cyberspace.
- Chapter 8, "Protecting Your Business from Costly Surprises," starts you thinking about protecting yourself and your business. It considers matters such as insurance, health and safety, employee fraud, and the basic principles of patents, copyrights, and trademarks.
- Chapters 9 and 10 plunge you into the world of finance. You learn how to formulate a personal financial vision and how to determine how much money you need to start your business and finance it. By the time you finish Chapter 10, you'll understand financial statements and be able to put together a financial plan to start and run your business.
- Chapter 11 helps you deal with the legal red tape of starting and running a business. We help you decide which legal form (sole proprietorship, partnership, or corporation) is best for you and your business, help you understand bankruptcy and its danger signals, and show you how to find the right lawyer.
- Chapter 12 starts you thinking about the organizational structure of your business and helps you begin building a winning team.

- Chapter 13 offers tips and advice to those who want to buy an existing business. If your goal is to be the "happy franchisee," turn to Chapter 14. Franchisees are on every corner, but, as we caution you, not all of them are happy with their lot.
- In Chapter 15 we encourage you to become export-ready. Exporting your product or service is an adventure you'll want to think about before you start your business.
- Chapter 16 asks you to gather all of your Action Steps to form the basis for your business plan. If your business concept is very simple or short-term, perhaps you don't need a fully developed business plan. If so, Chapter 17 helps you write a fast-start business plan—one that enables you to respond quickly to an opportunity and to show yourself that the venture is viable.

Features That Help

The Business Plan Building Blocks; Action Steps; and Checklist Questions and Actions to Develop Your Business Plan help you determine what belongs in your business plan.

BUSINESS PLAN BUILDING BLOCKS

Each chapter of the book is designed to help you complete one or more of the parts of your business plan. You will notice that a building-blocks illustration appears at the beginning of each chapter. The blocks show which part (or parts) of the plan that chapter addresses in its Action Steps. The blocks also help you track your progress as an entrepreneur. When all the blocks are in place, your business plan is complete and you're ready to open your doors.

ACTION STEPS

Our road to success in small business is marked by 86 Action Steps. Completing these steps should significantly help your chances of reaching your business goals. If the world of business is like a maze—a series of challenges and obstacles—then the Action Steps are designed to lead you through. Each Action Step is an exercise that accompanies our explanation of a particular portion of the maze.

OPENING WINDOWS

In each chapter, figures and tables provide useful information and concepts to illustrate the text. Examples include Internet databases (throughout the book), tips for developing strategic alliances (Chapter 4), the best places to set up your booth at a trade show (Chapter 6), and a strategy for selecting your mentor (Chapter 12). All of these offer the new entrepreneur windows onto the world of small business.

ENTREPRENEURIAL VIGNETTES

Throughout the text we present you with brief case studies full of strategies and real-world applications that provide insight into entrepreneurial minds and ventures. We have modified the stories for simplicity and clarity. Some vignettes are composites of several case studies and others are purely fictional.

STAYING ON TRACK

Other features help you stay on track and focus on the task at hand. Learning Opportunities at the beginning of each chapter identify the educational goals of the chapter. Margin definitions help you build your business vocabulary.

New Features

We have also included in this new edition a number of improvements designed to make *Small Business* the most exciting, current, comprehensive, and useful small business and entrepreneurship textbook available.

E-EXERCISES AND BOOKMARK THIS BOXES

As we move through the book, we offer many links to the Internet. We encourage linking to the web in our E-Exercises. Here you can test your entrepreneurial acumen through personal assessment, trend analysis, number-crunching, and even preparing your business plan. We also highlight key sites in our "Bookmark This" boxes. These boxes provide you with the most up-to-date information on small business. All the links included in the text are listed on this book's web page, at www.knowles4e.nelson.com

VIDEO SUPPORT

This fourth edition is supported by a series of small business case studies on video. These videos are supported on our website with a brief summary and a case study questions and answers.

THE *SMALL BUSINESS* WEBSITE

New to this Fourth Canadian Edition is the comprehensive book website (www.knowlessmallbusiness4e.nelson.com) to support you as you begin your entrepreneurial trek. Here you'll find online quizzes, e-exercises, student questions and answers, and a test bank for each chapter. We also provide you with key Internet sites. A note of caution. Because of the web's great volatility, you may type in a web address and come up empty. We will be continually updating these links to reduce frustration.

This Book Is for You

TO DREAMERS AND BEGINNING ENTREPRENEURS

This book can be used on at least two levels. One is a fast-track approach for the action-oriented entrepreneur who wants to get on with the start-up. The other is a step-by-step process for the creative dreamer who can afford to take the time to savour the atmosphere of the business arena.

As you're reading the book, keep your computer or pencil and paper close by so that you can take notes or jot down ideas. Get used to brainstorming. Also, it's not a bad idea to carry a cassette recorder in your car so that you can record ideas that occur to you while you're driving. The inspiration that you get from a highway billboard 400 kilometres from home might be the seed from which your winning business grows.

Our point is that this is *your* book. Use it in whatever way suits your needs. Make notes in the margins, mark it up with a highlighting pen. Use the book as a handbook, a textbook, or both. It's designed for a wide range of creative, energetic people who want to own their own business, and someplace in that range of people is *you*. Good luck!

Instructor's Resource Material

INSTRUCTOR'S MANUAL AND TEST BANK

The Instructor's Manual includes teaching aids such as learning objectives, lecture outlines, suggestions for guest speakers and class projects, a detailed outline for a business plan, and a comprehensive entrepreneurial profile questionnaire. The Test Bank is full of true/false, multiple-choice, and short-answer questions.

POWERPOINT® SLIDES

New to this Fourth Canadian Edition are the more than 200 images provided with it. Most of these creatively prepared visuals highlight concepts central to each chapter of the textbook. All you need is Windows to run the PowerPoint® viewer and an LCD panel for classroom display.

COMPUTERIZED TEST BANK

The computerized version of the printed Test Bank enables instructors to preview and edit test questions, as well as add their own. The test and answer keys can also be printed in scrambled formats.

VIDEOS

Video segments include coverage of themes featured throughout the text. Instructors are provided with a short summary of the segment in addition to a questions-and-suggested-answers segment.

SMALL BUSINESS WEBSITE

Visit the Knowles website at www.knowles4e.nelson.com to access a complete instructor- and student-support package. It includes online testing, case studies, success stories, Internet links, and e-exercises.

Acknowledgments

We couldn't have written this book without significant contributions from a number of people. The book is built on a foundation of case studies, and the Action Steps are taken from real-life tactics in the marketplace. Many entrepreneurs have succeeded in the real world, and we've just tried to tell you how they've done it.

I am truly indebted to our colleagues who graciously devoted their time to review and improve this Fourth Canadian Edition—especially:

Tony Bishop
Northern Alberta Institute of Technology

Al Ersser
Mohawk College

George Kennedy
College of New Caledonia

Geoff Malleck
Wilfrid Laurier University

Tom McKaig
Ryerson University

David Orr
Lethbridge Community College

Danielle van Druenen
St. Lawrence College

A special thanks goes to Shelley Ann Budd—small business student, Algonquin College—who took the time to read and critique this edition from the student's perspective.

Of course, this new edition could not have been completed without the endless help, guidance, and advice of the Nelson staff, notably Anthony Rezek, Acquisitions Editor; Bob Kohlmeier, Production Editor; and Mary Stangolis, Editorial Assistant. A special thanks to Elke Price, Developmental Editor, whose excellent work helped shape the manuscript into a book we're all proud to publish, and to Sarah Robertson, whose insightful copy edit improved the manuscript in countless ways.

Thank you, and we hope you enjoy your small business adventure.

Ron Knowles, Algonquin College, Ottawa

A Note from the Publisher

Thank you for selecting *Small Business: An Entrepreneur's Plan*, Fourth Canadian Edition, by Ron Knowles. The author and publisher have devoted considerable time and care to the development of this book. We appreciate your recognition of this effort and accomplishment.

We want to hear what you think about the book. Please take a few minutes to fill in the stamped reader reply card at the back of the book. Your comments and suggestions will be valuable to us as we prepare new editions and other books.

chapter 1

Your Great Adventure: Exploring Your Options

BUSINESS PLAN BUILDING BLOCK

At the end of each chapter, you will begin a preliminary draft of what will become a complete and free-flowing business plan.

LEARNING OPPORTUNITIES

After reading this chapter, you should be able to:

- Identify the role, skills, and characteristics of successful Canadian entrepreneurs.
- Discover why you might want to become an entrepreneur.
- Understand what it takes to be an entrepreneur.
- Identify your entrepreneurial quotient.
- Use mind maps to help you decide on the life you want.
- Discover what success means to you.
- Understand the rationale for a business plan and list the main components.
- Improve your research and information-gathering skills.

ACTION STEP PREVIEW

1. Compile your 24/7 Adventure Notebook.
2. Find out why you want to be an entrepreneur.
3. Assess your interest and abilities.
4. Expand your self-assessment.
5. Picture the future.
6. Interview entrepreneurs.
7. Take your "new eyes" into the marketplace.

"If life is a tree, find the passion to play on the ends of the branches and beyond. That's our passion. It has kept my husband and me going and made us successful." So says Adrienne Armstrong, owner of Arbour Environmental Shoppe, a small business that just keeps on growing.

Armstrong's business goal is to help others respect the earth with planet-friendly products—an idea that took shape in the mid-1990s. "While studying in France, I saw many small stationery stores selling recycled paper. These were little stores with pride and strong ties to the environment. I felt at home in these businesses. Even back then, I knew where I belonged and what I wanted to do. I kept a diary. I called it my 24/7 Adventure Notebook. I would wake up at night and mind-map my ideas like crazy. I remember writing letters to a friend—now my husband and business partner. The idea of protecting the environment consumed me and I could not wait to get started. Fortunately, I married a man who shared this same vision."

Today, Arbour Environmental is a successful retail outlet boasting a host of environmental and community service awards. "I'm very proud of these awards," says Armstrong. "They remind all of us at Arbour Environmental that we are making a difference". "We display all our achievements behind the cash desk for everyone to see. We call this our 'Eco Wall of Fame.'"[1]

Before you begin to write your business plan, explore your options.

Life is short, and you go around only once. You want to make sure you're achieving what you desire, having fun, making money, and being the best person you can be.

How do you do that?

Some people, like Adrienne Armstrong in the opening vignette, do it by going into business for themselves. If you are thinking about taking control of your life and owning your own business, this book is written for you.

Try this line of thought: What do you want to be doing in the year 2010? In 2015? What's the best course of action for you right now? What might be the best business for you? What are your strengths? What are your dreams and passions? In this chapter, we will help you address these types of questions.

We'll also try to persuade you to start your own business. If you travel this entrepreneurial route, a business plan is a must. We'll encourage you to look at some plans, and help you to get started on your plan to join some two million Canadians who now own their own business.

Building Your Road Map

This book, with its Action Steps and Business Plan Building Blocks, can be your personal road map to success in small business. Beginning with Action Step 1, the book will guide you through the bustling marketplace—through trends, target customers, and promotion; through shopping malls and hushed, grey bank buildings; through franchise opportunities and independent businesses that are for sale—all the way to your own new venture.

Along the way you will meet fascinating people, and have fantastic adventures and fun. Furthermore, by completing the Action Steps and Building Blocks, you'll be drawing a customized road map for your small business success. The Action Steps will give you direction and the Building Blocks will provide the foundation. The complete business plan you develop will clearly evaluate and illuminate your opportunity for entrepreneurial success.

You will start your journey by taking a careful look at yourself and your skills. What kind of work pleases you? What internal drive makes you believe that you are an entrepreneur? What do you value? What do you like to work with? Who do you like to work with?

Next, you'll step back and look at the marketplace. What's hot? What's cooling down? What's going to last? Where are the long lines forming? What are people buying? What distinguishes the up-and-comers from the down-and-outers?

You'll position yourself to take advantage of market opportunities. We'll encourage you to brainstorm a business that will fit into an industry niche, toss around numbers to get a feel for how they turn into money, and keep having fun.

Then it will be time to profile your target customer, assess the competition, figure out clever promotional strategies, scout locations, chart your business future with numbers, address your legal concerns, and form a winning team.

Along the way, we'll investigate three major doorways to small business ownership: buying an ongoing business, franchising, and—our favourite—starting a new business from scratch. We'll even help you check out exporting opportunities. By the time you reach Chapter 16, you will have gathered enough material to write a complete business plan for showcasing your business to the world—that is, to bankers, vendors and lenders, venture capitalists, credit managers, key employees, your family and friends.

We believe strongly that without passion you will not succeed. If you are not passionate about your business, you will have trouble coping with 10- to 14-hour workdays, no vacations, stress and tension, employee problems, misplaced cash, bank loan turndowns, and countless other frustrations. Throughout the text, we have profiled entrepreneurs like Adrienne Armstrong (in the opening vignette) who are passionate about what they do. Read their stories, and learn from their experience. Believe in yourself and the passions that will help you achieve entrepreneurial success. Now enjoy your journey as an entrepreneur!

BOOKMARK THIS

We'll be connecting to the Internet as we move through the phases of this book—personal assessment, trends, location, number crunching, legal issues, and writing the business plan.

We'll highlight key websites in the "Bookmark This" boxes. A note of caution: you may type in a web address and come up empty. Our "Bookmark This" sites were active as this book went to press. Unfortunately, as most of you know, many websites come and go at warp speed; so persevere, and you will find the desired site or one that replaced it.

It's time to get started. To get your creative juices flowing, go to Box 1.1 and visit the websites of the Canadian Youth Business Foundation and *PROFIT* magazine. Meet others like yourself who have decided to investigate the entrepreneurial option.

Box 1.1 Bookmark This

Key Websites

- **Canadian Youth Business Foundation**
  www.cybf.ca
- ***PROFIT* magazine's PROFITguide.com**
  www.profitguide.com/magazine

Interested in becoming more involved with the entrepreneurial community? Want tips from the experts on how to start a small business? Looking for sources of information help and/or inspiration? Then visit the websites of the Canadian Youth Business Foundation (even if you are over the age of 30) and *PROFIT* magazine. Dedicated to developing, supporting, and promoting entrepreneurs in Canada, these key sites are a great place to start your entrepreneurial adventure.

The Age of the Entrepreneur

Small business entrepreneurs are the fuel of our private enterprise system. They provide the competitive zeal; create jobs, new ventures, and opportunities for others; and improve our economic growth and social fibre. They are visionary self-starters who love the adventure of a new enterprise. They have chutzpah, providing a spirit of energy, initiative, and potential for progress. Above all, they are agents of change—doers who see a market need and satisfy that need by translating it into a successful business.

SMALL BUSINESS ENTREPRENEURS
agents of change—doers who see a market need and satisfy that need by translating it into a successful business

The hours for business entrepreneurs are often long and lonely. But just in case you think entrepreneurs are not a happy bunch, here is what Peter Sagar, director-general of the entrepreneurship office of Industry Canada has to say: "Surveys show that people with the highest life satisfaction levels are people who own their own businesses." Supporting this, a survey of Canadian entrepreneurs by Padgett Business Services found that 75 percent said they would take the route all over again.[2]

Hundreds of research studies have attempted to determine the common skills, personality, and behavioural traits of successful entrepreneurs. The simple deduction from all this research is that entrepreneurs cannot be cloned. They tend to defy stereotyping and broad-brush labelling. "I have seen people of the most diverse personalities and temperaments perform well in entrepreneurial challenges," concludes business guru Peter Drucker.[3]

Nevertheless, if generalizations must be made, we can say that most of our entrepreneurs possess the following characteristics:[4]

- *Visionaries.* Successful entrepreneurs have learned to visualize. They have a complete mental picture of where they and their ideas are going.
- *Passionate.* Entrepreneurs are driven by a compelling vision.
- *Independent thinkers.* Entrepreneurs have a need for freedom—a need to control their own destiny and "be their own boss."
- *Sharing.* Old-fashioned as it sounds, entrepreneurs believe in sharing.
- *People-oriented.* Entrepreneurs are not loners. They have to like people—after all, people are what drives business.
- *Goal-oriented.* Entrepreneurs set short-term and long-term goals and are committed to meeting objectives.
- *Creative.* Entrepreneurs have a great capacity to dream up and carry out projects. They see problems as opportunities to create solutions.
- *Persistent.* Entrepreneurs don't give up easily when things look bleak.
- *Agents of change.* Entrepreneurs invariably identify their primary motivations as "seeing a need and acting on it."
- *Moderate risk-takers.* Successful business entrepreneurs are moderate risk-takers. They gather as much information and support as possible before making a move. In this way, they build a safety net for themselves and decrease the amount of risk involved.

In a groundbreaking PROFIT 100 study of successful Canadian business entrepreneurs, Rick Spence, editor of *PROFIT* magazine, concluded that most of the above entrepreneurial traits represent behavioural characteristics "that can be learned, as opposed to inherited abilities (an affinity for math, say, or an outgoing personality) that confer ongoing advantages on just a lucky few."[5] According to this research of successful growth firms, most entrepreneurs are *made*, not born. This is good news for the thousands of Canadians who don't think they have the innate abilities to start up on their own.

Rev Up

If you're thinking about owning your own business, come along with us! We'll help you accomplish your vision by showing you how to build a road map. In order to decide which road to take, you are going to have to do some research and define your personal goals.

You can start the process by getting organized. Some people believe that getting organized stifles creativity. "No way," says Adrienne Armstrong, owner of Arbour Environmental. "It was and still is the place where I can organize and channel my thoughts. As a matter of fact, I woke up one night thinking 'why are we not on the web?' In my new ideas section, I started scribbling down all the things I'd need to do. It's been a while since that night. I even had to take a course at a local college. But we did it. Arbour Environmental is now on the web (www.arbourshop.com). E-commerce has given our small business tremendous

24/7 ADVENTURE NOTEBOOK

a storage place in which to organize your personal and business ideas global exposure and has resulted in new sales. Just over 10 percent of our retail sales is Internet-generated. And it's growing every year."

Now it's your turn to get organized. Complete Action Step 1.

WHY DO YOU WANT TO BE AN ENTREPRENEUR?

After racing for Canada in the Summer Olympics and winning 150 times worldwide, cyclist Louis Garneau realized it was time to do something else: "I said, 'I need a job.' I didn't want to travel any more after all that global travelling. So with my experience in sports and art, I started my own company."

As with most small business start-ups, the launch was modest. Garneau began the business as a sole proprietorship, working out of his father's garage. When the time was right, he moved out of the garage and incorporated. Today, Louis Garneau Sports Inc. (www.louisgarneau.com) is a multimillion-dollar company with over 500 employees.[6]

For some, like Adrienne Armstrong, becoming an entrepreneur is a lifelong dream. For others, like cyclist Louis Garneau, it's buying a job. Still others choose to become an entrepreneur because they want to earn a potentially huge income, to be their own boss, to build a legacy, or to experience the thrill of developing an innovative service or product. There are all kinds of motivations for taking the entrepreneurial plunge. Discover your own entrepreneurial motives. Complete Action Step 2 (see page 6).

WHAT DOES IT TAKE TO BE AN ENTREPRENEUR?

Although we concluded earlier that entrepreneurs cannot be cloned or replicated, certain characteristics are associated with entrepreneurial success. Action Step 3 (see page 7) will help you discover if you have what it takes to make it in small business.

To expand your personal profile, complete the short questionnaire in Box 1.2 and the E-Exercise in Box 1.3. As you work your way through these exercises, remember that you won't be a perfect "E" fit, because there's no such thing.

File the results of the questionnaire and the E-Exercise in your 24/7 Adventure Notebook. What did you learn about yourself? Armed with all this self-knowledge, you are ready to try your hand at Action Step 4 (see page 8).

Box 1.2 Test Your Entrepreneurial Quotient

If you really have what it takes to be an entrepreneur, you should be able to answer each of the following 20 questions with a resounding "yes!"

1. Do you prefer to go shopping for a major (expensive) purchase alone? Yes ❑ No ❑
2. Do you tend to speak up for an unpopular cause if you believe in it? Yes ❑ No ❑
3. Do you feel you can determine your desire to earn a decent living? Yes ❑ No ❑
4. Do you know that if you decide to do something, you'll do it and nothing can stop you? Yes ❑ No ❑

ACTION STEP 1

Compile your 24/7 Adventure Notebook.

If you're the typical aspiring entrepreneur, you probably write 90 percent of your important data on the back of an envelope. That might have been OK in the past, but now that you're doing this for real, get yourself some kind of container (a shoebox, a briefcase, a folder) to put those envelopes in. Even better, compile a **24/7 Adventure Notebook**, ideally using something with pockets so that you can keep track of small items like brochures. Some of you may wish to use a notebook computer or a personal digital assistant (PDA) to organize data.

Your 24/7 Adventure Notebook should include:

- a 12-month calendar
- an appointment calendar
- a priority list of things you need to do
- your name, phone number, and e-mail address (at the front, in case you leave it somewhere)
- a new ideas section (continue to add ideas to this section throughout your search)
- a mind-map section to help you picture new opportunities
- a "new-eyes" list for keeping track of successful and not-so-successful businesses you come across, plus notes about the reasons for their success or failure
- a list of possible team members (Who impresses you and why? What are their key attributes?)
- a list of possible experts to serve as resource people when you need them, such as a lawyer, an accountant, some bankers, successful businesspeople, and so on
- articles and statistics you gather that serve as supportive data
- a "Bookmark This" list of helpful websites
- a list of potential customers

ACTION STEP 2

Find out why you want to be an entrepreneur.

In your 24/7 Adventure Notebook, make a list of all your reasons for wanting to become an entrepreneur. Think about your personal and professional lifestyle, as well as your social, spiritual, financial, and ego needs.

Prioritize the items in your list. Spend a few minutes now and many more hours in the next few months reviewing how several businesses would fit into your prioritized list. What fits? What doesn't fit? If you have a job, review your current situation. Is your job secure? Are you happy and/or excited about going to work each day? Is there something else you'd rather be doing"? If you did not need the money, would you quit your job? As you explore various businesses, use these lists and questions to determine whether or not your selected business ideas meet your entrepreneurial focus and passion.

Next, make a list of all your reasons for not wanting to become an entrepreneur—your roadblocks. Review the list and think about what you can do to minimize the roadblocks. When you honestly review the advantages and disadvantages of being an entrepreneur, you'll discover they are the flip side of each other. For example, many people want to become entrepreneurs in order to be their own boss, only to discover they will have many bosses—customers, suppliers, and investors! Be as realistic as possible as you work to refine these lists during your exploration of different businesses.

5. If you want something, do you ask for it rather than wait?	Yes ☐	No ☑
6. Have you ever implemented the basic principles of marketing?	Yes ☐	No ☑
7. Do you often find yourself getting bored, especially at meetings?	Yes ☑	No ☐
8. Do you like trying new food, new places, and new experiences?	Yes ☑	No ☐
9. Can you walk up to a stranger and strike up a conversation?	Yes ☑	No ☐
10. If you are frightened of something, do you try to conquer the fear?	Yes ☑	No ☐
11. Have you ever gone on a date with someone you did not really know?	Yes ☑	No ☐
12. Have you ever, on your own, obtained a job for which you got paid?	Yes ☑	No ☐
13. Do you normally wake up "excited" in the morning? Do others describe you as "enthusiastic"?	Yes ☐	No ☑
14. Have you ever implemented the basic principles of management operations?	Yes ☑	No ☐
15. Have any of your friends ever started a business, even if it was just very small?	Yes ☑	No ☐
16. Do you see problems as potential opportunities?	Yes ☑	No ☐
17. Has an experienced businessperson ever talked to you about what it is like to own a business?	Yes ☑	No ☐
18. Is your financial situation stable?	Yes ☐	No ☑
19. Do you find it a challenge to sell your self and your ideas?	Yes ☑	No ☐
20. Have you ever implemented the basic principles of accounting or finance?	Yes ☐	No ☑

Box 1.3 E-Exercise

Are You a "Type-E" Personality?

If you are thinking about starting your own business, online self-assessments are a great place to test your entrepreneurial quotient. To learn more about yourself, check out the following web pages:

- **Take a Self-Employment Quiz**
  http://worksearch.gc.ca/english/index.pl?tid=99
- **National Entrepreneur Test**
  www.profitguide.com/quizzes
- **How Entrepreneurial Are You?**
  http://realm.net/wayofthinking/quizzes/index.cfm
- **Personality Test**
  http://haleonline.com/psych

"Inc." Yourself

So far you have explored why you want to be an entrepreneur. You've reviewed your skills, accomplishments, and passions. It is now time to think about what success means to you. Think of yourself as a product you want to create. To help you think of yourself as a business—to "Inc." yourself, figuratively speaking—we are going to introduce you to a technique called mind mapping. A **mind map**—also known as a spoke diagram, a thought web, or a clustering diagram—is a sketch that features circled words connected by lines to form units. Mind mapping is a form of doodling, only it has a purpose—to generate ideas. It works like this:

MIND MAP
an idea-generating sketch—also known as a spoke diagram, a thought web, or a clustering diagram—that features circled words connected by lines to form units

1. In the centre of a page, you write your main theme (e.g., your vision or goal), then draw a circle around the word.
2. Every time you get an idea related to your main theme, you write it down, circle it, and draw a line connecting it to the theme.
3. You keep adding new ideas to your mind map. Before you know it, you have a gigantic spider web or idea tree full of opportunities.

Most entrepreneurs do mind mapping naturally. Entrepreneurs are visionaries and mind maps help them picture what they want to become. A mind map that might have been devised by Adrienne Armstrong, owner of Arbour Environmental, is presented in Figure 1.1. To create your own mind map, along with a success

Figure 1.1 Arbour Environmental Mind Map

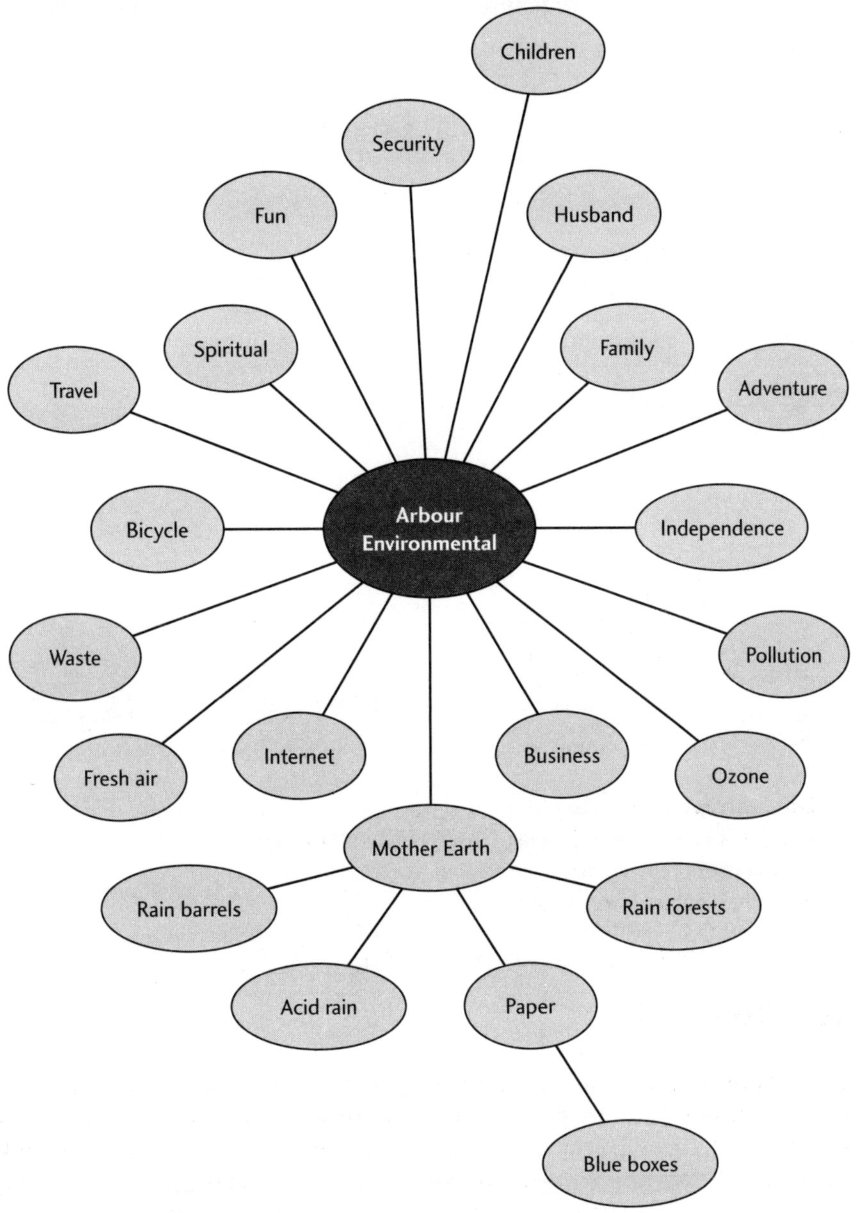

This mind map displays ideas that could have been generated by Adrienne Armstrong, owner of Arbour Environmental.

ACTION STEP 3

Assess your interest and abilities.

Do you have what it takes to make it in small business? To find out, profile yourself as an entrepreneur. You won't be a perfect fit, because there is no such thing. Nonetheless, you will get much more out of this book if you fantasize yourself in the role of a successful entrepreneur. Keep your mind open and your pencil sharp. Opportunities are unlimited. This Action Step will help you assess your abilities and interests and get your creative juices flowing. You will probably come back to this step several times.

- How would your best friend describe you?
- How would your worst enemy describe you?
- How would you describe yourself?
- How much money do you need to survive for six months? For a year?
- How much money can you earn in your present position in three years? Five years? What is the maximum potential of your earning power?
- Are you comfortable taking moderate risks?
- Are you constantly looking for newer and better ways to do things?
- What can you do better than most people?
- Where do you live now? (Describe your home, residential area, geographical area, amenities, etc.)
- In what way would you like to change any of the above?
- Do you enjoy being in control?
- How do you spend your leisure time?
- Do you look forward more often than backward?
- How important is winning to you?
- Do you know anyone whose strengths complement some of your weaknesses?

Make sure you file this information in your 24/7 Adventure Notebook.

checklist, go to Action Step 5. Once you have completed the first five Action Steps, you will be ready to enter the small business arena of entrepreneurism—the engine of our economy.

ACTION STEP 4

Expand your self-assessment.

Build on your self-assessment by compiling a list of:

- things you love to do
- skills you have acquired through the years
- things you are good at
- the times you were happiest in your life
- your achievements and failures
- your passions
- your past dreams and dreams for the future

What Is Small Business?

If entrepreneurs are the fuel or driving force of the third millennium, **small business** is the engine. About 16 percent of our labour force is self-employed—that is, they earn an income directly from their own business as opposed to a salary or wage from an employer. According to Statistics Canada, about 150 000 new corporations are established each year.[7] As shown in Table 1.1, there are about two million employer businesses in Canada; almost 60 percent of these firms, the so-called micro businesses, have 1–4 employees. Most small businesses provide services.

SMALL BUSINESS

any venture with spirit, any business you want to start, or any idea you want to bring into the marketplace

BUSINESS PLAN

a blueprint or road map for operating your business start-up and measuring progress

Table 1.1 Business Establishments by Firm Size (Number of Employees), December 2000

No. of Employees	Cumulative Percent of Employer Business Total	No. of Business Establishments: Total	Goods-Producing Sector	Service-Producing Sector
Indeterminate*		982 304	276 425	705 879
Employer Business Total	100.0%	1 042 204	249 215	792 989
1–4	58.0%	604 445	155 861	448 584
5–9	74.8%	175 140	35 079	140 061
10–19	86.4%	121 267	24 239	97 028
20–49	94.8%	86 655	19 096	67 559
50–99	97.7%	31 081	7 972	23 109
100+	100.0%	23 616	6 968	16 648
Grand Total		**2 024 508**	**525 640**	**1 498 868**

*The indeterminate category consists of incorporated or unincorporated businesses without employees. The Business Register classifies a business as "indeterminate" when it cannot determine through payroll data that the firm has paid employees. The firm may well provide work under contract.

Source: Statistics Canada, Business Register, retrieved from Industry Canada, Strategis website (http://strategis.ic.gc.ca/SSG/rd00385e.html#two).

So exactly what is a small business? Strange as it may seem, there is no standard Canadian definition of small business. Here are four different interpretations.[8]

- According to Industry Canada, a small business is any firm with fewer than 100 paid employees in the goods-producing or manufacturing sector and fewer than 50 paid employees in service-producing firms.
- Our major banks generally agree that small businesses are those that have loan authorizations of less than $500 000.

- The Small Business Loan Act, one federal government small business program, defines an eligible small business as one that has an annual revenue of less than $5 million.
- The Export Development Corporation defines small businesses or "emerging exporters" as firms with export sales under $1 million.

We tend to like the rather open definition provided by the Canadian Federation of Independent Business, which describes a small business as "a firm that is independently owned and operated and is not dominant in its field of endeavour." A typical small business owner, according to this description, would employ anywhere from 1 to 20 employees. This represents about 85 percent of all businesses in Canada today.

The small business we are talking about is any venture with spirit, any business you want to start, or any idea you want to bring into the marketplace. It may be part-time, something you do at home, something you try alone, or something you need a team for. The ideas for a small business are almost limitless.

You'll Need a Business Plan

About 70 percent of firms in *PROFIT* magazine's list of Canada's 50 Hottest Startups (2001) have one thing in common: they started out with a business plan (see Box 1.4). The result? These turbo-charged firms, founded in 1997 or 1998, grew their sales 17 times over a two-year period.[9]

Entering the world of small business demands a carefully designed **business plan**—words and numbers on paper that will guide you through the gaps, the competition, the bureaucracies, the products, the services. A business plan is a written summary of your business goals, what resources you need, and how you intend to organize these resources to meet your personal and business objectives. It is the road map for operating your business start-up and measuring progress. Your finished business plan will provide an overview of your industry, attract potential investors, demonstrate your competence as a thoughtful planner, and serve as a means of channelling your creative energies.

Box 1.4 They Said It

Here is what three of our entrepreneurial leaders have to say about business plans:

"Build a business plan, and have it tested by people other than friends and family."
Gary Darychuk, President, Funeral Directors' Choice (The Night Shift Answering Service)

"Listen to people you admire. Write a business plan. Network."
Ann Kaplan, President and CEO, Medicard Finance Inc.

"It's important not just to have a plan, but to go through the planning process."
Brian Mergelis, President, The Pressure Pipe Inspection Company Ltd.

Source: Adapted from Canada's Hottest Startups, *PROFIT* magazine (http://www.profitguide.com/hottest/2001/index.asp).

ACTION STEP 5

Picture the future.

It's time to create your own mind map—one that depicts the kind of life you want. Start by reviewing your 24/7 Adventure Notebook and your responses to Action Steps 2–4. Then draw a circle in the middle of a piece of paper, and write your name inside the circle. Close your eyes for a few minutes, and allow your imagination to take over. Think of yourself as a product. Ten years from now, where and what do you want to be? What are your personal, spiritual, and material needs and wants? As you attempt to predict your future, remember that there is no such thing as a right or wrong direction. If you find yourself running out of ideas, stop the process and revisit your mind map later on.

By meshing your personal desires with you business desires, you are more likely to find success. Complete the Success Checklist below to find out what success means to you.

Success Checklist
How do you measure success?

1. Being able to enjoy a certain lifestyle Yes ❑ No ❑
2. Earning a high income Yes ❑ No ❑
3. Dealing with friendly customers who appreciate the service Yes ❑ No ❑
4. Power Yes ❑ No ❑
5. Being able to live and work where I want Yes ❑ No ❑
6. Providing employment for others Yes ❑ No ❑
7. Owning the best business in my area Yes ❑ No ❑
8. Time to enjoy my children and hobbies Yes ❑ No ❑
9. Participating in teamwork Yes ❑ No ❑
10. Building a legacy Yes ❑ No ❑
11. Early retirement Yes ❑ No ❑
12. Fame Yes ❑ No ❑
13. Making people's lives safer Yes ❑ No ❑
14. Recognition Yes ❑ No ❑
15. Helping others Yes ❑ No ❑

CREATING A BUSINESS PLAN—WHY BOTHER?

By the time you reach Chapter 16, you will have gathered enough material to write a personal business plan to showcase your business to the real world. Your completed plan will be a blueprint for your business, whether it's a start-up or expansion. Here are a few other reasons why a business plan is important:

- *Lays out goals.* A written business plan provides an orderly statement of goals for ready reference at all times. It clarifies what you want to achieve and helps you work toward these goals.
- *Provides an organizing tool.* A plan, when completed, will provide you with the guidance to manage your business and keep it on track.
- *Acts as a financial guide.* You will know before you start your business how much money you'll need and how much you are going to earn.
- *Helps obtain advice.* A plan will provide you with a structure and format to get advice.
- *Helps secure investment.* A well-written plan will help you get the much needed start-up capital.

SO WHAT DOES A PLAN LOOK LIKE?

The particular format and content of a plan all depend on a number of factors, such as the kind of business you want to start, how much time and patience you have, and who is going to be involved with your business—that is, your target customer. If you are planning to go into business alone, or if you're in a hurry or can afford to lose a small investment, you may want to consider the fast-start plan provided in Chapter 17. If, on the other hand, you have some time to think about it and other people (such as bankers, investors, and advisers) are involved with your business, you will very likely have to write a comprehensive plan like the one shown in Chapter 16. Our template for this kind of detailed plan is provided in Box 1.5.

Although we have provided you with one particular format—one that has worked for us over the last 10 years—there are all kinds of business plan varia-

Box 1.5 Business Plan Outline

When you start a business, you must create a business plan. Your plan should contain the following broad components:

Cover Sheet

Table of Contents

Executive Summary

Description of the Business

- A. The Product or Service
- B. The Market and the Target Customer
- C. The Competition
- D. Marketing Strategy
- E. Location
- F. Management and Form of Ownership
- G. Personnel

Financial Section

- H. Projected Cash Flow (monthly, first year)
- I. Projected Income Statement
- J. Projected Balance Sheet

tions. For example, the major chartered banks and accounting firms provide their version of a business plan to their customers. To find a format that suits your particular needs, check out the web pages listed in Box 1.6.

Box 1.6 Bookmark This

Business Plan Resources

The following online resources will help you prepare your business plan:

- **Business Plans Planning Guide** (Royal Bank of Canada)
  www.royalbank.com/sme/bigidea
- **Interactive Business Planner** (Canada Business Service Centres)
  www.cbsc.org/ibp/home_en.cfm
- **Business Plan Guide** (Canada Business Service Centres)
  www.cbsc.org/english/search/display.cfm?CODE=4001&Coll=FE_FEDSBIS_E
- **Developing a Business Plan** (Human Resources Development Canada)
  http://worksearch.gc.ca/english/index.pl?&tid=97
- **Do I Want to Be My Own Boss?** (Human Resources Development Canada)
  http://worksearch.gc.ca/english/index.pl?tid=4
- **Your Roadmap: The Business Plan** (Canadian Bankers Association)
  www.cba.ca/en/viewPub.asp?fl=6&sl=23&docid=40&pg7
- **Preparing a Business Plan** (CBSC Online Small Business Workshop)
  www.cbsc.org/osbw/busplan.html
- **Virtual Business Plan** (BizPlanIt)
  www.bizplanit.com/vplan.html
- **Writing a Business Plan** (Bplans.com)
  www.bplans.com/dp
- **Scotiabusiness Plan Writer** (Scotiabank)
  www.scotiabank.com/cda/content/0,1608,CID400_LIDen,00.html

Your Chances of Success

Do some small businesses fail? Of course they do—just like some students fail a course. Failure is a part of life. During the early 2000s, about 2700 bankruptcies occurred in Canada every year.[10] Many of these involved small companies. Studies have shown that 65 percent of new businesses survive their first year; 30 percent their first five years; and only about 15 percent make it for ten years. The cold, hard fact is that there is a chance that your idea may flop. That's why we want you to work through the chapters of this book. If you prove your business idea on paper first—in your business plan—there's a good chance you'll be successful. This is where conducting a lot of primary, secondary, and new-eyes research comes in handy.

Conducting Research

Research opens doors to knowledge. There are three approaches to research. You'll need a combination of all three to make it big in small business.

PRIMARY RESEARCH
interacting with the world directly by talking to people

SECONDARY RESEARCH
reading about someone else's primary research

ACTION STEP 6

Interview entrepreneurs.

Successful entrepreneurs love to tell the story of how they made it. Interview at least three people who are self-employed. If possible, one of them should work in your own area of interest.

Make appointments with your interviewees at times and places convenient to them. Taking notes during the interview is a good idea. If you want to use a cassette recorder instead, be sure to ask permission first. Don't worry about evaluation at this stage. The information will fall into patterns sooner than you think.

Open-ended questions are best because they leave room for embellishment. Here are some suggestions to start you off:

- When did you decide to start your own business?
- What was your first step?
- Do you remember how you felt?
- If you had it to do all over again, what would you do differently?
- How large a part does creativity play in your particular business?
- Are your rewards tangible or intangible?
- What was your best advertisement or promotion?
- What makes your business unique?
- How important is price in your business? Would a price war increase your customer base?

Think of these first interviewees as sources of marketplace experience. Depending on how you hit it off, you might be able to turn to one or more of your entrepreneurs for advice when you start to assemble your team—your lawyer, accountant, banker, and so on.

PRIMARY RESEARCH

Primary research is carried out by interacting with the world directly or by talking to people, perhaps interviewing them. This includes talking to people "virtually" over the Net. You might ask small business owners questions like: Where were you when the entrepreneurial bug bit? Whom do you bank with? How did you choose your lawyer? Your accountant? What would you do if you started up tomorrow, knowing what you know today? Customers can be asked questions like: Is there something we don't carry that you need? How else can we be of help to you? How did you learn about our business? Vendors and suppliers may be asked questions like: What advertising works best in a business like ours? What products are hot? What services are being offered?

Throughout this text, we'll be encouraging you to practise your primary research skills. Why? Because this is the way most entrepreneurs stay informed and keep on top of their business. Action Step 6 will help you get started.

SECONDARY RESEARCH

When you read second-hand what someone else has discovered, you're carrying out **secondary research**. You switch on your computer and surf the Net. In fact, the Internet may be your main source of secondary information. You go to the library and look up "small business" in the Business Index. You locate and read magazine and newspaper articles that contain information you think will be helpful. Databases and information from trade associations are also good secondary sources of information. You find data on sales that will help you project how much money you can make in small business. Good techniques here will save you lots of footwork.

NEW-EYES RESEARCH

New-eyes research provides a variety of fresh ways to look at a business. In carrying out this type of research, you use your intuition and observation to learn about the marketplace. Many successful entrepreneurs have conducted new-eyes research. Claire Davenport, president of Blue Dog Bagels in Waterloo, Ontario, for example, visited about 150 different bagel shops to observe customers and the way the business is run before she opened her shop.

In new-eyes research, you play detective. You might become a "mystery shopper" to check out your competition. When **target customers** appear, you observe them so that you can profile them later. You may stand in a supermarket and, trying not to look nosy, watch what people put in their shopping carts. For example:

Steak + Beer + Veggie tray + Twelve-pack of cola = Party time

Cereal + Dog food + Diapers + Baby food = Family with young children

New-eyes research is fun. Doing it along with using the Internet, studying books, magazines, trade journals, and publications like *PROFIT* magazine, and talking to people, you will be able to develop a credible and valuable business plan. Remember, however, the business plan may become your guide to success—or it may show you that your idea isn't worth any more of your time. That's why research is so important.

It's time to practise new-eyes research. Complete Action Step 7.

In a Nutshell

It is the age of the entrepreneur. Small business entrepreneurs are the fuel of our private enterprise system. The goal of this textbook is to encourage you to join the ranks of some two million self-employed Canadians. To begin, we want you to get organized by creating a 24/7 Adventure Notebook. Next, we want you to test your entrepreneurial quotient. To find out if you are prepared to live the life of an entrepreneur, we encourage you to take a good hard look at your dreams and passions, your interests and abilities, your strengths and weaknesses. Ultimately, we want you to think of yourself as a future product—that is, to "Inc." yourself.

If you take the entrepreneurial highway, there can be wonderful personal and financial rewards. But you'll also pay a price. You'll work long hours and you will run into your share of disappointments. Are you prepared to take this roller-coaster ride? Or do you need a 9 to 5 job and some semblance of security? We help you come to grips with these kind of questions.

If you decide that becoming a small business entrepreneur is the right option for you, you will need to develop a business plan that is backed up by primary, secondary, and new-eyes research. While your success as an entrepreneur cannot be guaranteed, a business plan will improve your chances of success. This book will provide you with a business plan road map and the ideas and tools to succeed ... but the challenge is yours!

NEW-EYES RESEARCH

the use of intuition and observation to learn about the marketplace

TARGET CUSTOMERS

customers with the highest probability of buying your product or service

Key Terms

24/7 Adventure Notebook	secondary research
business plan	small business
mind map	small business entrepreneurs
new-eyes research	target customers
primary research	

ACTION STEP 7

Take your "new eyes" into the marketplace.

Your community is a marketing lab. To discover what this means for you and your business, go to a local mall and observe what's going on.

What's on sale? What's dusty? What's wilted? Where are the lineups? What are the stores promoting? Who has the most workers? The highest prices? Check out some big box stores. What products are moving fast? Try to come up with a basket of products that are in demand.

This exercise will get you thinking about market trends—the subject of Chapter 2.

Think Points for Success

- ✓ Change is accelerating everywhere, and that includes the world of business. Change creates problems. Problems are opportunities for entrepreneurs.
- ✓ To find your doorway into your own business, gather data and keep asking questions.
- ✓ Be creative on paper, organize your ideas, test your assumptions, and develop your business plan for the marketplace. Create and maintain a 24/7 Adventure Notebook. Mind map. Confirm your venture with numbers and words before you enter the arena.
- ✓ Even though you may not be in business yet, you can intensify your focus by writing down your thoughts about the business you think you want to try. Stay flexible.
- ✓ Be clear on who you are and what you want to become.
- ✓ Develop a business plan.
- ✓ Get out and talk to people. That's the way most entrepreneurs learn.
- ✓ Always be on the lookout for opportunities.
- ✓ Above all, follow your passions.

Business Plan Building Block

WHERE AM I NOW?

From the point of view of the potential readers of your business plan (bankers, loan officers, rich relatives, close friends with money, venture capital professionals), the most important part of the plan is information on you, the entrepreneur who wrote the plan.

Your goal, from the very first sentence on the very first page, is to inspire confidence. Before you write your business plan, study how you look from some of your old résumés. What picture do the résumés present? Who are you? Where have you been?

Since the résumé work is for your eyes only, jot notes to yourself about strengths and weaknesses. To trigger your brain to perform this task, review the seven Action Steps in this chapter as you search for ways to transfer your skills and aptitudes to an entrepreneurial situation. If you already have a business up and running, use this same start-up energy to improve it.

No one is perfect. Recognize your own shortcomings and make a list of people who have talents that you might lack. It's never too early to think about team building. With hard work and an honest look at your own skills picture, you'll be able to fine-tune this information when you showcase your founding team in your final business plan.

WHERE AM I GOING?

Now that you have looked at the past and present, think about where you are going. How do you see yourself in the future? How do you want to be known? Take a closer look at your personal goals. What are your likes and dislikes? Are you passionate about what you want to do? Are you ready to put in the long hours?

Checklist Questions and Actions to Develop Your Business Plan

YOUR GREAT ADVENTURE—EXPLORING YOUR OPTIONS

- ❑ Are you organized? Do you have a central deposit for all your ideas?
- ❑ Do you have what it takes to be an entrepreneur?
- ❑ Have you assessed your interests, abilities, and weaknesses as they relate to owning a business?
- ❑ Have you assessed your past accomplishments and shortcomings?
- ❑ Do you have a list and a plan of new skills you will have to work on?
- ❑ Is your family or those you live with "on board"?
- ❑ Are you prepared to take the time and do the necessary research before writing a business plan?
- ❑ Have you interviewed entrepreneurs to see what it is really like to be in business for yourself?
- ❑ Do you have any business ideas that you are passionate about?

NOTES

1. Networking interviews with Adrienne Armstrong, Arbour Environmental Shoppe (www.arbourshop.com).
2. Industry Canada, Advertising Supplement, "Small Business Tomorrow's Giants," *PROFIT*, December/January 1998, p. 49.
3. Peter Drucker is quoted in Louis E. Boone, David L. Kurtz, and Ronald A. Knowles, *Business*, 1st Cdn. ed. (Toronto: Dryden, 1998), p. 113.
4. Ron Knowles and Debbie White, *Issues in Canadian Small Business* (Toronto: Dryden, 1995); Rick Spence, *Secrets of Success from Canada's Fastest-Growing Companies* (Toronto: John Wiley & Sons Canada, 1997), p. 228; and Human Resources Development Canada, Entrepreneurial FAQ, retrieved from http://worksearch.gc.ca/english/index.pl?tid=93&sid=EUhsYowldvyizu
5. Spence, *Secrets of Success*, p. 135.
6. Boone, Kurtz, and Knowles, *Business*, pp. 105–106.
7. Industry Canada, Small Business Research and Policy, Frequently Asked Questions, retrieved from http://strategis.ic.gc.ca/SSG/rd00254e.html
8. Industry Canada, Small Business Research and Policy, Frequently Asked Questions, retrieved from http://strategis.ic.gc.ca/SSG/rd00254e.html#definition
9. PROFITguide.com, Canada's Hottest Startups, retrieved from www.profitguide.com/hottest/2001/index.asp
10. Industry Canada, Small Business Research and Policy, retrieved from http://strategis.ic.gc.ca/SSG/rd00388e.html

SUGGESTED READING

Books

Beck, Nuala. *Excelerate: Growing in the New Economy*. Toronto: HarperCollins, 1995.

Bridges, William. *Creating You & Co.* Reading, MA: Addison Wesley Longman, 1997.

Carey, Elaine. "Many More Working for Themselves. Stats Can." *The Toronto Star*, October 25, 1997, p. C7.

Covey, Stephen R., et al. *First Things First*. New York: Simon & Schuster, 1994.

Edwards, Paul, and Sarah Edwards. *The Practical Dreamer's Handbook: Finding the Time, Money, and Energy to Live the Life You Want to Live*. New York: J.P. Tarcher, 2000.

Gorman, Tom. *Multipreneuring*. New York: Simon & Schuster, 1996.

Gray, Douglas A., and Deanna L. Gray. *The Complete Canadian Small Business Guide*, 2nd ed. Whitby, ON: McGraw-Hill Ryerson, 1997.

Kushell, Jennifer. *The Young Entrepreneur's Edge: Using Your Ambition, Independence, and Youth to Launch a Successful Business*. New York: Random House, 1999.

Lewin, Marsha D. *The Overnight Consultant*. New York: John Wiley & Sons, 1995.

Norman, Jan. *What No One Ever Tells You About Starting Your Own Business: Real Life Start-up Advice from 101 Successful Entrepreneurs*. Chicago: Upstart Publishing, 1999.

Roberts, Wayne, and Susan Brandum. *Get a Life*. Toronto: Get a Life Publishing House, 1995.

Spence, Rick. *Secrets of Success from Canada's Fastest-Growing Companies*. Toronto: John Wiley & Sons Canada, Ltd., 1997.

Spence, Rick, and Richard Wright. "Canada's Hottest Startup." *PROFIT*, September 1997, pp. 34–37.

Tapscott, Don. *Growing Up Digital: The Rise of the Net Generation*. Toronto: McGraw-Hill, 1998.

Tarkenton, Fran. *What Losing Taught Me About Winning*. New York: Simon & Schuster, 1997.

Worzel, Richard. *The Next Twenty Years of Your Life*. Toronto: Stoddart, 1997.

Journals and Magazines

Canadian Business (www.canadianbusiness.com), 21 issues/year, Canadian Business Subscriber Service, 777 Bay Street, 8th Floor, Toronto, ON M5W 1A7.

The Canadian Invention and Innovation Newsletter (www.innovationcentre.ca); free by calling 1-800-265-4559.

Entrepreneurbusiness Startups, Entrepreneur Media Inc. (www.entrepreneur.com), 2445 McCabe Way, Irvine, CA 92614, (850) 682-7644.

Home Business Report (www.homebusinessreport.com), 2625a Alliance Street, Abbotsford, BC, V2S 4G5.

Inc. Magazine (www.inc.com), 12 issues, 38 Commercial Wharf, Boston, MA 02110.

PROFIT—The Magazine for Canadian Entrepreneurs (www.profitguide.com/magazine), 777 Bay Street, 8th Floor, Toronto, ON M5W 1A7, (416) 596-5523 or 1 (800) 465-0700.

chapter 2

Spotting Trends and Opportunities

BUSINESS PLAN BUILDING BLOCK

This chapter will help you describe the industry and market trends—the big picture—for your business. It will show you how to expand your knowledge of customer needs and your market niche, and how to begin writing the description of your business.

LEARNING OPPORTUNITIES

After studying this chapter, you should be able to:

- Use mind mapping and brainstorming to discover business opportunities.
- Identify trends and market signals that will create opportunities.
- Discover market forces that underlie the trends.
- Understand how to analyze the potential for small business success by applying the life-cycle yardstick to industries, products, services, and locations.
- Use diagrams and mind maps to explore market segmentation.
- Determine what business you're really in.
- Select helpful information sources and launch your industry research.

Back in the early 1990s, the Pacific Western Brewing Co. closed its doors. This small brewing company, located in Prince George, British Columbia, could not compete with the likes of Labatt and Molson. That's when Kazuko Komatsu, a seasoned businessperson with 20 years of successful marketing, brewing, and exporting experience, came to the rescue. Kazuko bought the company and began by retraining the staff and improving the quality of the beer. By the mid-1990s, Pacific Western became the first brewery to achieve the certification of ISO 9002 (the highest level of excellence) from the International Standards Organization, the most respected quality assurance program in the world. Then, in the late 1990s, Pacific Western became the first Canadian brewery to produce a 100 percent certified organic beer.

Today, Pacific Western produces 13 different types of beers to satisfy a diverse range of tastes, and exports to markets that include China, Taiwan, Argentina, Brazil, Russia, France, and the United States; its beer is the third most popular imported beer in Japan, behind the giant Budweiser and Heineken brands. Pacific Western

ACTION STEP PREVIEW

8. Travel back in time and observe a marketplace of the past.
9. What's new? What's hot? What's cooling down?
10. Compile a list of trends and opportunities.
11. Match trends with life-cycle stages.
12. Have some fun with segmentation and gap analysis.
13. Define your business and test your definition.
14. Assess the lifestyle of your potential target customer by walking his or her neighbourhood.
15. Launch your industry research.

Chapter 2 will help you prepare part A of your business plan, "The Product or Service."

adheres to a to a few carefully chosen guiding principles: quality of ownership, quality of product, quality of service.[1]

"Today is the most exciting thing. We're going to exploit opportunities and pursue new growth. We live in the future, not the past," says Ryan Kalt, the twentysomething founder, president, and CEO of NuMedia Internet Inc.

Kalt's been riding the technology wave for the past seven years. Revenues at NuMedia, one of his latest ventures, grew from $232 000 in 1998 to $3.5 million in 2001—a whopping 1400 percent increase. Kalt started NuMedia with a $3000 loan from the Business Development Bank and went on to assemble an award-winning management team that has led the company to profitable and stable growth, with 90 percent of its business coming from the export market.

NuMedia's major products are focused on the Internet-based information and technology sector—one of its hottest web properties, HostIndex.com, is used to locate web host providers. NuMedia's target customers are deep-pocketed blue chip global companies, such as Dell Computer, Sprint, and Reader's Digest, who need online information-based products and e-learning services. Says Kalt: "I'm very much about doing, not being."[2]

Chapter 2 is designed to help you recognize business trends and opportunities. We'll help you to brainstorm and to keep mind mapping and researching your ideas. We'll encourage you to always be on the lookout for emerging trends in exporting, technology, the Internet, changing demographics, and consumer values. After we have persuaded you to be a trend spotter, we'll introduce you to the life-cycle concept, segmentation, and gap analysis, all of which will help you to focus on specific industry opportunities. Then we will encourage you to step back and refine your business idea. Finally, we will get you started on conducting your own primary and secondary research.

Recognizing Opportunities

What are the best business ventures to pursue today? Where can you find a business that will really pay off? One that will make you rich? One that you will enjoy?

Only you can answer the question, because the best business for you is one that you enjoy. The best business for you uses those experiences, skills, and aptitudes that are unique to you. The early Action Steps in this book are designed to help you discover what is unique about you. Who are you? What are your skills? What excites you? What do you already know that distinguishes you from others?

As a consumer, you know, for example, that restaurants have a high failure rate. One week you're having dinner at The Hound and Glove; the next week it's locked up with a "Closed" sign on the door. You don't want that to happen to your business. That's why you do **market research**. That's why you're going to make sure your business serves a need. This means that you will enter the marketplace from a position of strength.

MARKET RESEARCH

collection and analysis of data pertinent to an existing or potential market

Let's back up and get the big picture. Before the Industrial Revolution, most people were self-employed. In this so-called agricultural or first wave, farmers and sheepherders were risk-takers because they had to be. There were few other options. The second wave, or the industrial age, began with the Industrial Revolution and was characterized by machine power and mass production.

We are now firmly entrenched in the so-called information wave. Some have termed these times the knowledge-based era. We like to think about it as the entrepreneurial age. These times, to a large extent, are marked by the growth of a new craft economy distinguished by quality; small, customized quantities; technology; and service. As in the first wave, working from home has again become both popular and common.

The existence of the megacorporation in the new millennium should not be considered a threat to the small entrepreneur, but an opportunity. First, most large corporations depend on small business to produce support products and services. This outsourcing is going to continue in the years ahead. They know that this is the most efficient and effective way to do business. Second, bigger isn't better, and many small businesses—even those whose markets are expanding rapidly—are barely noticed by the large corporation.

The exploding need for specialized products and services from beer and vacuum cleaners to coffee brewing and personal fitness training is mind-boggling. You may see as much change in the next 10 years as your parents have seen in their lifetime. Such change creates opportunities for fast, flexible, and focused firms. If you stay in touch with change and the exploding market niches that change creates, you will always see more opportunities than you can pursue. Action Step 8 will give you some perspective on change. Now we want to introduce you to brainstorming—a powerful entrepreneurial technique for discovering opportunities that are right for you.

ACTION STEP 8

Travel back in time and observe a marketplace of the past.

Place yourself in a time warp and take a look at a marketplace of the past. What was selling 25 years ago? 50 years ago? 100 years ago?

To get this picture, look at old magazines, old catalogues, old movies, old TV shows, old high-school yearbooks, and old family photographs. What do you see? Are all of the people dressed alike? Does everyone have the same smile, the same frown, the same serious look? How small is their world? How small is their horizon?

Study the advertisements in old magazines and newspapers and then:

1. List the products that are still around today.
2. List the products that are no longer on the market.

Which list is longer? What does this tell you about the changing marketplace?

Brainstorm Your Way into Small Business

Pete and Geoff loved to snowboard. For seven years, they looked for opportunities to make a living from doing what they loved.

At a local college, Pete and Geoff discovered the technique of mind mapping—a method of note-taking that involves using clusters and bubbles, letting the information float along its own course. They just knew they could mind-map their way into the snowboarding business!

In the centre of a large sheet of paper, they wrote "snowboarding." In a bubble next to "snowboarding," they wrote "segments," which led to bubbles with the words "skateboarders," "teens," "families," and "adults." "This is fun," Pete said, as the momentum built up. "This smells like money and fun," Geoff added.

The two friends kept on mapping until they developed an idea for their business: Snowboard Express, which would provide roundtrip weekend bus transportation to various mountain ski resorts from five local pickup points. Pete and Geoff's completed mind map is shown in Figure 2.1.

BRAINSTORMING TECHNIQUES

The point of this example is to show what can result from **brainstorming**—a free and open exchange of ideas. If you gather people around you with wit, spark, creativity, positive attitudes, and good business sense, the synergy will almost always surprise you, and could lead to new ideas, company growth, expanded profits, or perhaps the information for a new industry. The possibilities are limitless, but the trick is to structure brainstorming sessions in a way that maximizes creativity. A few suggestions follow.

BRAINSTORMING

a free and open exchange of ideas

Figure 2.1 Snowboard Express Mind Map

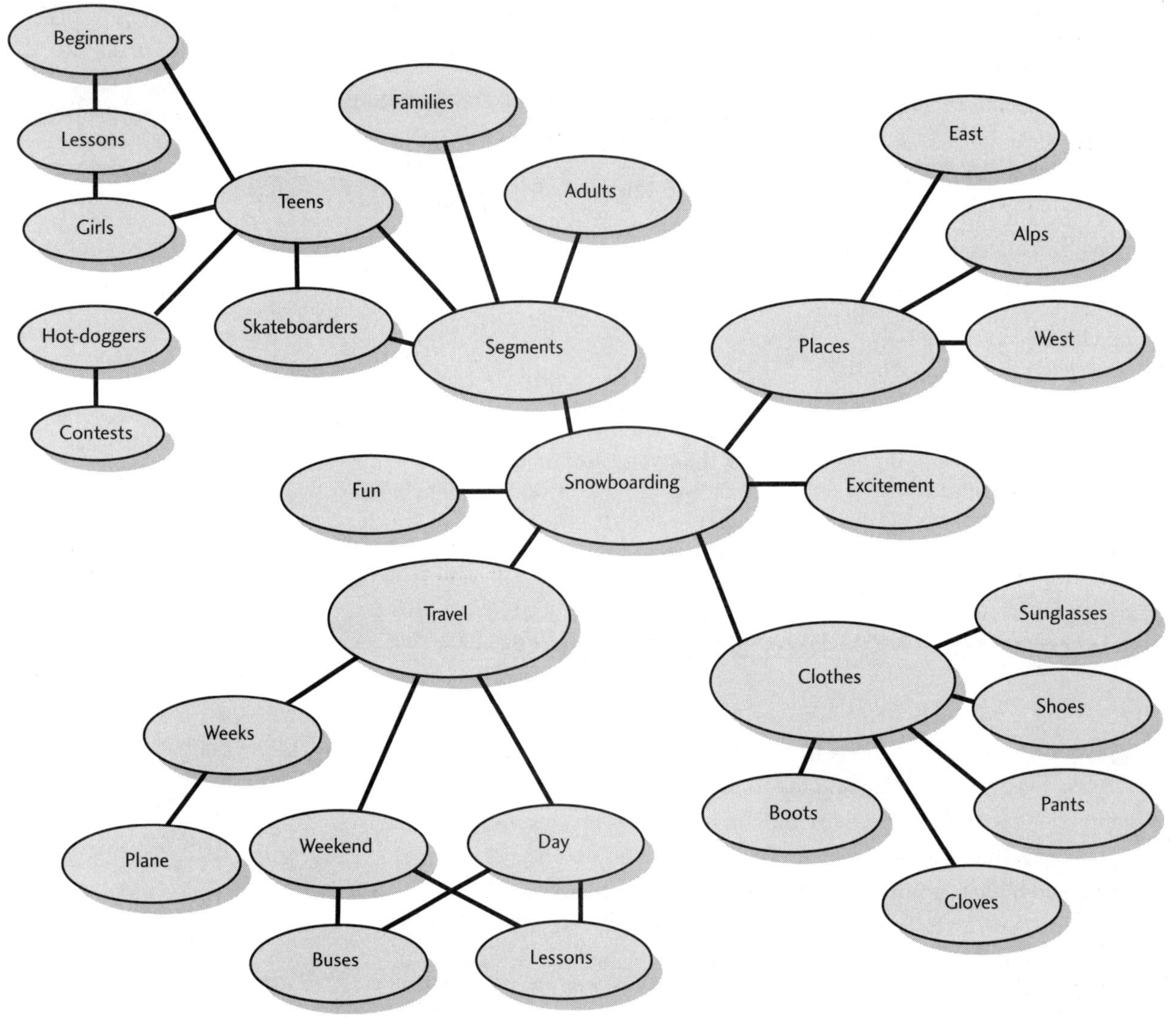

1. Pick a Saturday, Sunday, or a day when everyone has some free time.
2. Find a site where you'll have few interruptions.
3. Invite 10–15 people (some will drop out and you want to allow for the no-shows).
4. Schedule the starting time at 9:00 a.m., serve coffee and doughnuts, and really begin at 9:30.
5. Allow time for self-introduction. Tell participants not to be modest. They're getting together with winners. Have them talk in terms of accomplishments.

Tips:

- Have everyone arrive with a potential business idea.
- Before the close of the first meeting, select one or two hot ideas (cast a vote) and ask participants to prepare a one-page checklist summary and analysis of the ideas.

- Get together again within two to four weeks and brainstorm the hot ideas. Make it clear that the basic purpose is to spin ideas off one another, not to form a huge partnership.
- The best brainstorming sessions occur when you come brain-to-brain with other creative, positive people. Brain energy is real and you need to keep tapping it.

When gathering participants and planning your meeting:

- Try to find imaginative people who can stretch their minds, and who can set their competitive instincts aside for a while.
- Remember that in brainstorming sessions, there's a no-no on no's. You're not implementing yet, so don't let skepticism kill an idea.
- Find a neutral location.
- Try to focus on one problem or opportunity.
- Encourage the members of a group to reinforce and believe in each other.
- Use helpful equipment, such as a cassette recorder and flip chart. And don't forget to bring a supply of paper and pencils.

Be a Trend Watcher

Industry or market trends reflect our economy's response to change. And change creates entrepreneurial opportunities. As an entrepreneur, you will want to make sure that your business serves a need. A knowledge of market trends will help you identify growth opportunities. Ten major trends that will affect Canadians into the 21st century are shown in Box 2.1.

Box 2.1 Major Trends in the New Millennium

1. **The ecological movement toward sustainable development.**
2. **Downsizing, delayering, and outsourcing.** Large corporations will continue to shed their corporate fat. A "free agent" movement toward just-in-time employment will grow as large corporations subcontract and contract out everything they can.
3. **Alternative energy sources.** Solar power and fuel cells are two well-known examples.
4. **Media change.** The digital shift from broadcast (e.g., television) to interactive media (e.g., the Internet) will continue.
5. **Demographic changes.** As they prepare for retirement, those in the over-50 age group will assume a growing importance as they do everything in their power to push back the aging process.
6. **Democratization of information.** The Internet will gradually give small businesses and individuals access to the same information available to large firms.
7. **Telecommuting and home-based business.** The number of people working out of their homes will continue to grow, increasing the presence of so-called electronic cottages.
8. **Cocooning.** Outside stresses will be reduced as people spend more leisure and work time at home.
9. **Poverty of time.** Increasingly, people will find it harder to do it all.
10. **Home and Internet security.**

GLOBAL ECONOMY

The export market accounts for about 45 percent of Canada's gross domestic product (GDP). Today, one-third of Canadians owe their livelihood to the strength of the country's global economy. Increasingly, "new breed" Canadian small businesses are seeking to participate in this export trend. According to *PROFIT* magazine, more than 50 percent of Canada's fastest-growing start-ups tapped the export market in 2001. Pacific Western, the award-winning brewing company profiled in one of the opening vignettes, is a good example of a small business that has been able to take advantage of the export market.

KNOWLEDGE- AND TECHNOLOGY-BASED ECONOMY

> Brenda, the owner of Tomorrow Travel Inc., has convened from her home office a "virtual" meeting with her colleagues from around the world. From her "electronic cottage," she pushes a button on her computer, and one by one, the televised images of meeting participants pop up on her screen. Everyone exchanges greetings before getting down to business.[3]

Welcome to the age of technology and the electronic cottage. Increasingly, many Canadians like Brenda will work and play out of their homes, connecting with their friends and business associates at the speed of electronic mail (e-mail). According to Don Tapscott, author and Canadian cyberguru, our new economy has three main components:

- a knowledge economy made up of knowledge workers and knowledge consumers;
- a digital economy in which physical things can become virtual; and
- a networked economy in which producers and consumers operate directly through digital networks.[4]

Nuala Beck, another influential Canadian thinker, estimates that about 60 percent of our economic activity and 70 percent of our jobs are now tied up in new industries such as telecommunications, computer hardware and software, and pharmaceuticals.[5] Smart entrepreneurs will have to take advantage of this new knowledge-based, technology-driven economy. The good news is, you don't have to have a Ph.D. in computer science to take advantage of this new networked economy. Take a look at what Nuala Beck has to say in Box 2.2.

Box 2.2 Small Business Tips

"It's not what you study," says Nuala Beck, "it's where you apply what you've learned—that is the key. And you'll be further ahead if you apply your special talents in an industry that has a future, rather than in one that doesn't." For example:

- If you study English, think about starting a business in the fast-growing software industry, editing manuals or new product literature.
- If your interest is photography, think about starting a business taking photographs for media journals and pharmacology journals.

Source: Adapted from Nuala Beck, *Excelerate: Growing in the New Economy* (Toronto: HarperCollins, 1995), pp. 16, 18.

INTERNET ECONOMY

> As a pragmatist, you try to fit products into the market instead of always trying to invent, invent, invent. With the advent of Internet technology, paper-based recruitment methods are all but obsolete as they are expensive and inefficient. We have developed user-friendly tools that enable job seekers to search for jobs efficiently, while recruiters can instantly target thousands of job seekers at a fraction of the cost of traditional methods.
>
> —Matthew von Teichman, President, JobShark Corporation

Matthew von Teichman is a shrewd entrepreneurial twentysomething who knows that market trends create opportunities. Having successfully owned and operated several small businesses in the food service and home decor industries, in addition to working as a marketing consultant for a major Canadian winery, von Teichman, along with other visionary partners, turned his attention to the Internet and the online recruiting trend. His company, JobShark Corporation, has been recognized by *PROFIT* magazine as one of the 50 fastest-growing Canadian companies. JobShark's rapid growth, from 6 to 75 employees, mirrors the explosive growth of the online recruiting industry, which is expected to grow by 300 percent to about $2 billion in 2005. JobShark has pursued the lucrative international market by expanding its operations into England, Ireland, Mexico, Chile, Argentina, Brazil, Peru, Colombia, Mexico, and Venezuela.[6]

Today, the Internet is a ubiquitous part of Canadian business and culture. According to Statistics Canada, over 51 percent of Canadian households and 71 percent of all businesses are connected to the Internet. About 18 percent of Canadian households made purchases over the Internet[7] (see Figure 2.2). Despite

Figure 2.2 Canadian Households Purchasing over the Internet

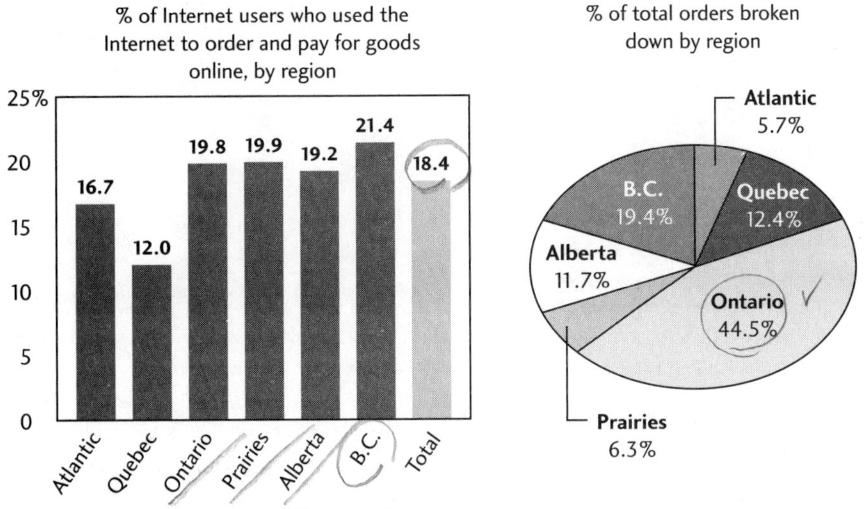

Source: Statistics Canada, 2000, retrieved from http://ecom.ic.gc.ca/english/research/b2c/regional/sld002.htm

the growth in consumer and business use of the Internet, the majority of Canada's small businesses have been slow to use the Internet for online sales. As Figure 2.3 indicates, e-mail is by far the most popular form of Internet usage among small and medium-sized enterprises. Over the next decade, however, online sales are expected to grow at a rapid pace. A website that allows you to sell your products or services over the Net should be an integral part of your own small business (see Box 2.3).

THE SPLINTERING OF THE MASS MARKET

Today's consumers are informed, individualistic, and demanding. Their buying habits are often difficult to isolate because they tend to buy at several levels of the market. For instance, a materials management person may buy the office copier from Xerox but the paper from a discount office supply warehouse. Some high-fashion, high-income consumers patronize the upscale boutiques and yet buy their household appliances at discount outlets.

For the consumer, three key factors have splintered the mass market: (1) a shrinking middle class—there are both more high-end, affluent consumers and more consumers who live at or near the poverty level; (2) shifting sizes of age groups; (3) new living arrangements, including smaller houses, smaller furniture, enclosed patios, and twin master suites for working roommates. If you look around with new eyes, you can see major market segments emerging that were not here a decade ago: **baby boomers**; vigorous, healthy over-50-year-olds; **echo boomers**; teens; single parents; and affluent over-80-year-olds. Action Step 9 will take you out into your community to conduct some trend research.

BABY BOOMERS

those born between 1947 and 1966 (about 10 million Canadians)

ECHO BOOMERS

those born between 1980 and 1995 (about 5.5 million Canadians)

E-COMMERCE

the process of conducting business operations over the Internet

Figure 2.3 **Types of Internet Usage Among SMEs**[1]

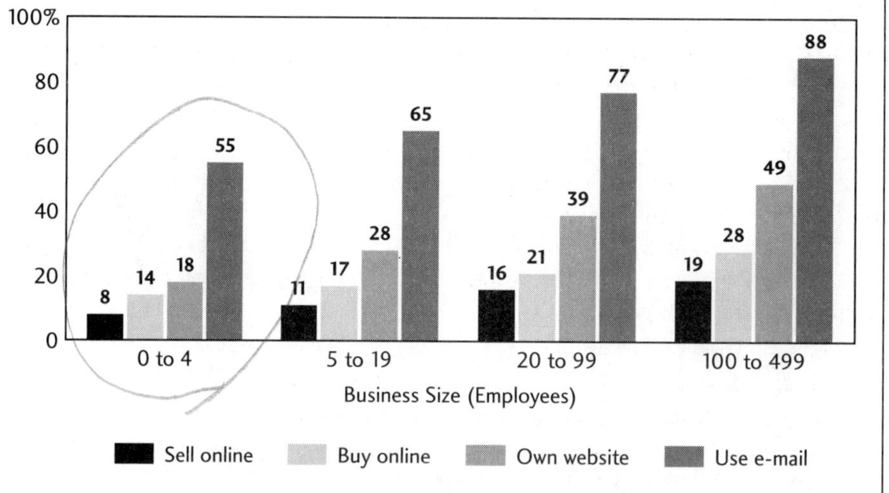

[1] Small and medium-sized enterprises.

Source: Canadian Federation of Independent Business, Q2 2000, retrieved from http://e-com.ic.gc.ca/english/research/b2b/connectivity/sld003.htm

Box 2.3 Bookmark This

E-commerce

E-commerce, also known as electronic business, e-business, or ebiz, is the process of conducting business operations—including selling products or services—over the Internet. More information on e-commerce issues and opportunities can be found at:

- **ebiz.enable** (Industry Canada)
  http://strategis.ic.gc.ca/sc_indps/ebiz/engdoc/homepage.php

  Designed to guide you through the issues and options you will encounter in implementing e-business strategies, this comprehensive online resource provides:
  - case studies and success stories
  - tips on conducting online market research
  - tools for assessing your current state of e-business readiness
  - a variety of e-business diagnostic tools.
  - advice on marketing and selling online

For further assistance, you can consult the following CBSC (Canada Business Service Centres) Business Information Guides:

- **Doing Business on the Internet**
  www.cbsc.org/english/search/display.cfm?code=4062&coll=FE_FEDSBIS_E&DispMenu=Guides
- **E-Business Info-Guide**
  www.cbsc.org/english/search/display.cfm?code=2842&coll=FE_FEDSBIS_E&DispMenu=Guides
- **E-Commerce—Exploring Your Options**
  www.cbsc.org/english/search/display.cfm?code=4021&coll=FE_FEDSBIS_E&DispMenu=Guides

TRENDS CREATE OPPORTUNITIES

Change creates market trends that lead to opportunities for enterprising entrepreneurs. Let's look at the aging trend, for example. The 50+ age group—the front end of the boomers—represented about 19 percent of the population in 1961. By the year 2011, it will represent over 33 percent of our total population (see Table 2.1). We also know that about 55 percent of disposable income and about 80 percent of the savings account dollars are controlled by the 50+ group. Therefore, knowing the needs of this growing demographic force can reap huge benefits for the imaginative entrepreneur.

Scrutinize boomers carefully to determine if you can develop products or services that will make money. The following list of opportunities should help you get started:

- Hair—toupees, hair implants, wigs, great hats, special sunscreen for bald spots
- Eyes—eye drops, cool magnifiers, trifocals, eye surgery
- Face—plastic surgery, skin creams, skin cancer checkups, facial exercise classes, facial messages, makeup for men

Now, think about where some other opportunities might exist. Let's say you like taking care of people and you have worked for 10 years in an infant daycare centre. However, the neighbourhood is aging, affluent families have moved away, and the daycare is closed. You decide to go into business for yourself. What business do you choose? How about a care centre for elderly people?

ACTION STEP 9

What's new? What's hot? What's cooling down?

1. Take your new eyes out into the marketplace and observe what's happening at the local (or regional) level. Your community is a marketing lab. To discover what this means for you and your business, prowl around a supermarket and analyze what's going on. A locally owned store will give you a clearer picture than a chain will, because it serves the needs of your area. Chains normally show you what the country is buying, and that's not much help for an entrepreneur.

   What's on sale? What is the store promoting? What conclusions can you draw about the store's marketing strategy? Which department has the most space? The longest customer lines? The most workers? The highest prices? What products must move fast? Can you guesstimate how quickly or slowly a product moves from shelf to customer in the various departments? Move on to the other locally owned stores—hardware stores, drugstores, restaurants, gift shops, and others.
2. Give your new-eyes research a database by going to the local newspaper. Visit the display advertising department and ask to see research they've completed on the area.
3. Go to the public library and study Statistics Canada's *Market Research Handbook* (Catalogue No. 63-224). Note:
   - the total dollars spent on clothing and housing
   - the percentage of households with incomes above the national average
   - the total city/province population

How do your new-eyes research findings correlate with what you found in the secondary sources?

ACTION STEP 10

Compile a list of trends and opportunities.

It is now time for you to start developing a list of trends. Review this section (including Boxes 2.4 and 2.5). Brainstorm with your friends. Form a focus group of your friends or colleagues and ask them about their wants or needs. Do some electronic research. Visit your local malls.

We want you to write down five or six trends that appeal to you, then list a few opportunities arising from those trends. Here are a few examples to get you started:

TREND	OPPORTUNITY
Information	Information broker
Cocooning	Home security
Home-based business	Networking home computers
Internet	Online shopping
Downsizing	Downsizing consultant
Dual-income earner	Pet-sitting services

Now it's your turn!

TREND	OPPORTUNITY
1. ________	________
2. ________	________
3. ________	________
4. ________	________
5. ________	________
6. ________	________

Add your trend/opportunity list to your 24/7 Adventure Notebook.

Table 2.1 Canada's Changing Population Profile (Millions)

Age	1996	2001	2011
0–4	1 991.5	1 924.3	1 980.1
5–9	2 036.9	2 082.2	2 016.6
10–14	2 035.2	2 124.8	2 104.8
15–19	1 996.3	2 124.5	2 259.2
20–24	2 027.0	2 115.2	2 332.3
25–29	2 217.5	2 177.7	2 392.8
30–34	2 615.4	2 366.4	2 416.1
35–39	2 657.3	2 723.4	2 443.0
40–44	2 377.8	2 716.3	2 544.5
45–49	2 146.6	2 399.6	2 801.9
50–54	1 667.4	2 140.1	2 722.0
55–59	1 327.3	1 651.4	2 362.2
60–64	1 209.4	1 300.9	2 063.6
65–69	1 129.7	1 154.0	1 544.5
70–74	980.4	1 027.1	1 142.5
75–79	704.9	831.9	906.1
80+	842.9	1 017.7	1 398.1
Total	29 963.7	31 877.3	35 420.3

Source: Statistics Canada, "Canada's Changing Population Profile," adapted from "Population Projections for Canada, Provinces, and Territories, 1996–2011," Cat. No. 91–520. Reprinted with permission.

Obvious business opportunities to meet the needs of dual-income families and single parents include child care, home security systems, home pet care. Those caught up in the "poverty of time" trend are also likely to be favourably disposed to easy-to-fix meals, fast food, teleconferences, feel-good products for stressful times, and in-home services. Here are three other trends and corresponding business opportunities:

- Canadian society is more ethnically diverse than ever before. *Opportunity*: helping schools and business integrate.
- People are exercising for fitness and health, and they want to look good while sweating. *Opportunity*: attractive sports clothes.
- People must change jobs, and they need retraining. *Opportunity*: education.

Action Step 10 will help you come up with your own list of trends and opportunities.

The Life-Cycle Stages

LIFE CYCLE

four stages, from birth to death, of a product, business, service, industry, or location

When you have produced a long list of trends, divide them into four groups according to the stage of their **life cycle.** See Figure 2.4 on page 28. If a trend is just beginning, label it *embryo*. If it's exploding, label it *growth*. If it's no longer growing and it's starting to cool, label it *mature*. If it's beyond maturity and is feeling chilly, label it *decline*. Think about these life-cycle stages often. Everything changes: products, needs, technology, neighbourhoods.

Looking at the life-cycle diagram, you can see, for example, that the auto industry as a whole is very mature. Nonetheless, some of its segments are promising—for example, minivans, sports models, and upscale imports.

Box 2.4 Small Business Tips

What is the future of consignment clothing? Computer repair? Women's classic ready-to-wear? Videocassette rentals, cyberspace, direct response retailing, coffee bars?

Use your marketplace radar to identify an emerging trend, and ride the crest of the wave. Be sure to get off before the trend cools down. Choosing the hot-growth sector is usually the right strategy, but occasionally things turn sour—witness the fate of the dot-coms.

How times change. What do you see in the following list that you didn't see much of 10 years ago? Brainstorm with your friends. What marketplace items can you add to this list?

- Personal computer repair
- Downsizing consultant
- Communication systems consultant
- Theme tours
- Adventure travel
- $200 tracksuits
- Personal digital assistance
- Electric cars
- Online databases for home users
- Information broker
- Chip cameras
- Ceramic engines
- CD-ROM entertainment
- Wireless technology
- In-home services
- Direct satellite TV
- Cellular communication
- Computer networking for home business
- Auto repair
- Intranet

Convertibles are back, and in the suburbs you see young mothers driving around in Jeep 4-by-4s. Despite traffic jams, people are still driving. But the cars they drive reflect changing lifestyles. What you have with this example is a growth segment in a mature industry.

How do consumer habits determine trends? Well, people are keeping their cars longer, so one growth segment in the auto industry would be the **aftermarket.** Examples of business in that segment would be paint, detailing, electronic accessories, and engine rebuilding. If you're interested in the auto industry, consider the aftermarket.

AFTERMARKET
the marketplace where replacement items can be purchased, such as auto tires and sewing machine belts

Box 2.5 E-Exercise

Market Trends Create Opportunities

- **Entrepreneurship (Atlantic Canada Opportunities Agency [ACOA])**
  www.acoa.ca/e/business/entrepreneurship/ideas/sectioniv.shtml

  Looking for a business opportunity? Visit the "Entrepreneurship" page on the ACOA website. Read the article titled "Some Market Trends to Watch" and then answer the following questions:
  - What is the difference between a trend and a fad?
  - What is meant by the term "trend tracking"?

  Complete this exercise by listing an opportunity for each of the 14 trends identified in the article.

Discontinuity Trend Analysis

- **Trends (BrainReserve)**
  www.brainreserve.com/trends/trends.htm

  If you have an idea for a business, you can complete an exercise called discontinuity trend analysis. Visit the "Trends" page on Faith Popcorn's website, BrainReserve. Review the listed trends and decide if your business idea "fits" with each trend. If your idea fits at least 50 percent of the listed trends, you are on the right track.

Figure 2.4 Life-Cycle Stages

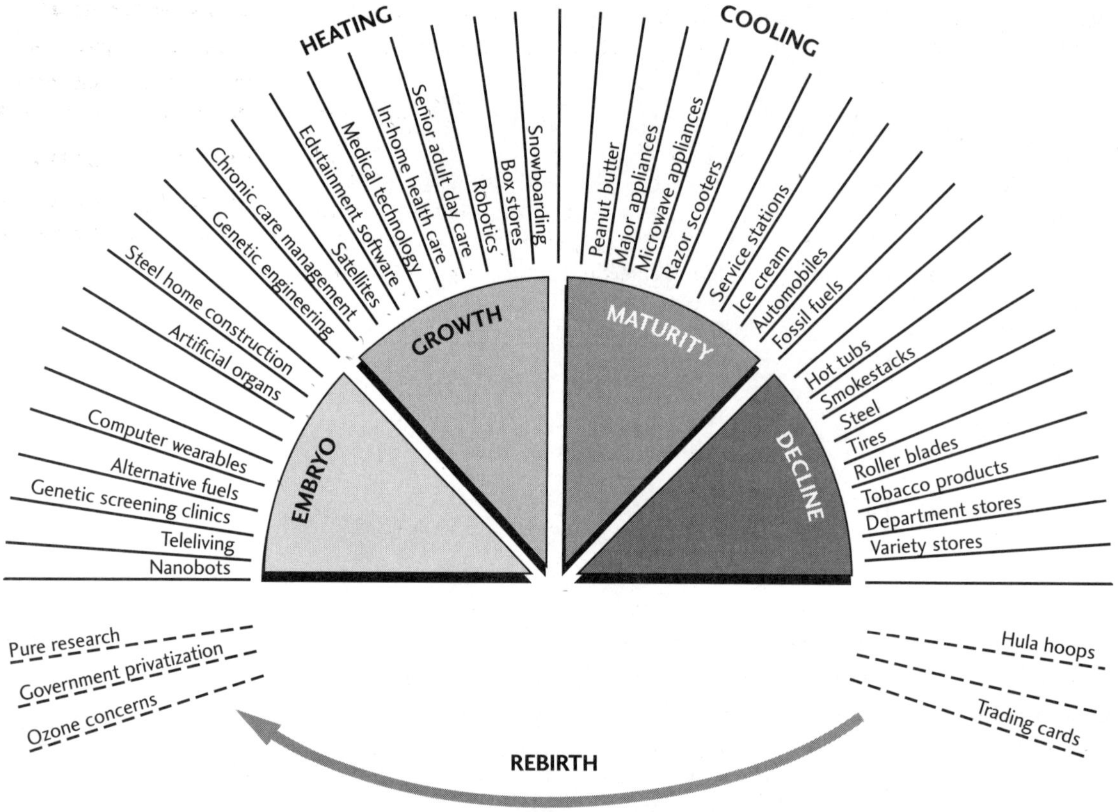

ACTION STEP 11

Match trends with life-cycle stages.

By now, you will have identified a number of emerging market trends. Review Figure 2.4 and determine where the trends that you've discovered belong on the life cycle. How many of your listed trends belong in the embryo stage? The growth stage? The maturity stage? The decline stage?

Next, try to discover opportunities that exist within the relevant stages. If you're entering the embryo stage, be prepared to "beat the pavement" for new business. If you're entering the mature or decline stage, you must be ready to meet—and beat—the competition head on!

Where can you find gaps in the life-cycle diagram? Where is your business in its four-stage cycle? Action Step 11 will get you to match the life-cycle stages with trends you have discovered.

WATCH FOR MARKET SIGNALS

Market signals are everywhere—on the Internet, in electronic display bulletin boards, in the newspaper (classified ads, bankruptcy notices, display ads), in the lines at the theatre, in the price-slashing after Christmas, in discount coupons, rebates, store closings, grand openings. With practice, you can follow a product in the market right through its life cycle.

For example, consider designer jeans. In the early 1980s, massive ad campaigns convinced otherwise-sane Canadians they should pay $40 and up for jeans carrying designer labels. The jeans were available only in the posh stores. A year later, designer jeans had reached the discount stores. Jeans that had sold for $55 were now selling at deep discount, like $9.99. A bargain? Yes, and also a trend. But what has now replaced that trend? Custom-fit jeans with over 440 combinations to ensure the exact fit.

What items have you seen go through their life cycle, from upscale to deep discount?

Now go back to the life cycle and see if you can add some products and industries to it.

HOW DEEP IS DEEP?

When merchandise slides into deep discount, the profit party is over. The air is cool. The market is flooded; sinking is likely, and drowning is possible. The product is at the end of the life cycle. If that's happened to your job—or to your business—it's time for you to find a **growth segment** of a **growth industry**.

GROWTH SEGMENT

an identifiable slice of an industry that is expanding more rapidly than the industry as a whole

GROWTH INDUSTRY

an industry whose annual sales increase is well above average

Experts tell us that the average worker will have at least seven kinds of jobs in his or her lifetime and several careers. No one's job is completely secure. Rhonda Van Warden thought hers was, until the school system eliminated her position. When that happened, she started to look at the trends in her community and in the country. Rhonda has some great assets, including intelligence and being a good listener, and she has the flexibility to see herself in a totally new role when opportunity knocks.

> After being downsized from her job as a school counsellor, Rhonda started to attend seminars, read books about job hunting, surf the Internet, and network with her friends for leads. One day she was talking to two friends, and their conversation turned to lingerie.
>
> "What I wish," said Kary, "is that I could buy some of that semi-sexy stuff without having to go into Le Sex Shoppe to buy it."
>
> "There're always the catalogues," Marsha pointed out, "and there are ads in the back of every magazine I subscribe to."
>
> "I don't trust those catalogues," Kary replied. "When I pay that much money for something that small, I want to see what I'm getting!"
>
> Marsha turned to Rhonda. "You're sitting there not saying a word, Rhonda. What're you thinking about?"
>
> "I think," Rhonda said, "I've just discovered the business I want to be in."
>
> Rhonda's idea was to tap her women friends for potential target customers who would like to come to her home for a private showing of women's intimate undergarments. Rhonda named her business Private Screenings, and had letterhead stationery printed. Then she began to contact suppliers and manufacturer's reps. They were interested in her idea.
>
> Her first "private screening" was well attended. Only women were present, and Rhonda sold almost a thousand dollars' worth of merchandise. The women loved what they saw, and they had fun. Ten years earlier they probably wouldn't have considered buying the things they bought that night, but times and people change.
>
> Rhonda went on from her success in selling to develop a line of products that she sells through her own catalogue and on her web page. Her husband has joined her in the business, and she has hired a woman to present her intimate merchandise through seminars. (The seminars also are held in private homes.) Rhonda spends most of her time recruiting personnel and developing new products.
>
> "When I started in this business," Rhonda admits, "I thought it might help to supplement my husband's income. But it's expanded so much that we have to scramble to keep up with orders. We travel a lot, talking to manufacturers about trends, picking up ideas. This business is a full-time job for *both* of us."

Rhonda was a sharp reader of market signals—the trends that reflect changes in how people think. What trends have helped to make Rhonda's business successful?

1. *Specialized consumer tastes.* Rhonda's target customers are discreet middle-class women in their forties and fifties, many of whom would be uncomfortable walking into a specialty shop to see intimate lingerie. When Rhonda brings the merchandise to them, they feel comfortable, special, and adventurous.
2. *High-tech/high-touch.* We can't stop the entry into our lives of computers and the information age. But we all try to balance the electronic effects of whirring machinery with human responses—just look at EST, dance, the arts, feeding our fantasies. Private Screenings capitalizes on the desire for softness in these high-tech times.
3. *Relaxing attitudes about sex.* Private Screenings was founded in the 1990s, a time when attitudes toward sex were becoming much more relaxed.

What other trends do you see contributing to the success of Private Screenings?

Segmentation and Gap Analysis

MARKET SEGMENTATION

breaking down potential markets into homogeneous groups with similar characteristics and qualities

The idea of **market segmentation** is to keep breaking down potential markets into as many similar subsegments as possible. The more you learn about an industry, the better informed you will be to write your business plan. This procedure will help you identify opportunity gaps and see combinations of gaps that may constitute markets. Segmenting the consumer market can be done geographically (e.g., by province), demographically (e.g., by age under 20, 20–30), psychographically (e.g., concern for safety), by benefits sought (e.g., sports utility in cars), and by the rate of product/service usage (e.g., one-time purchase for a number of years of a vacuum cleaner or weekly purchase of dry cleaning service). Figure 2. 5 illustrates a mind map that dissects one segment of the health-care industry into subsegments. This is the kind of thinking we want you to do in Action Step 12. It's another brainstorming activity, so have fun with it.

ACTION STEP 12

Have some fun with segmentation and gap analysis.

Form some of your friends into a focus group and poll them about gaps in the marketplace. Ask them to respond to the following questions:

- What frustrates you most about your daily life? Shopping? Banking? Dating? Living? Buying a car? Grocery shopping? Shopping?
- What products do you need that you can't get?
- What products or service would enhance your quality of life?
- How could you increase your productivity without working more hours?

Make a list of the gaps that the group identifies. Then project the list out as far as you can, and follow the wants and frustrations of your friends into the marketplace. Are any of the needs they mentioned national in scope? Global?

Know Your Real Business

Watch a carpenter framing a new house, working close to the wood, nailing with quick hammer strokes. But to get a view of the total house—the structure that will become someone's home—the carpenter must step back from the detailed work, cross the street, and examine the shape of the whole.

What business is the carpenter in? The nail-driving business? The framing business? The home-building business? Or the business of satisfying the age-old "nesting" need?

Only by stepping back can you answer the question of what business you are in. Once you know who your customers are and what satisfies their internal and external needs, you can move forward. Mary Clark's experience illustrates the importance of understanding what business you are really in.

Mary Clark was a 40-year-old teacher who had always been more interested in riding her prize-winning saddle horses than in teaching school. When her grandmother died and left her $200 000, Mary made a down payment on a boarding stable and left teaching forever, or so she thought.

Figure 2.5 A Mind Map

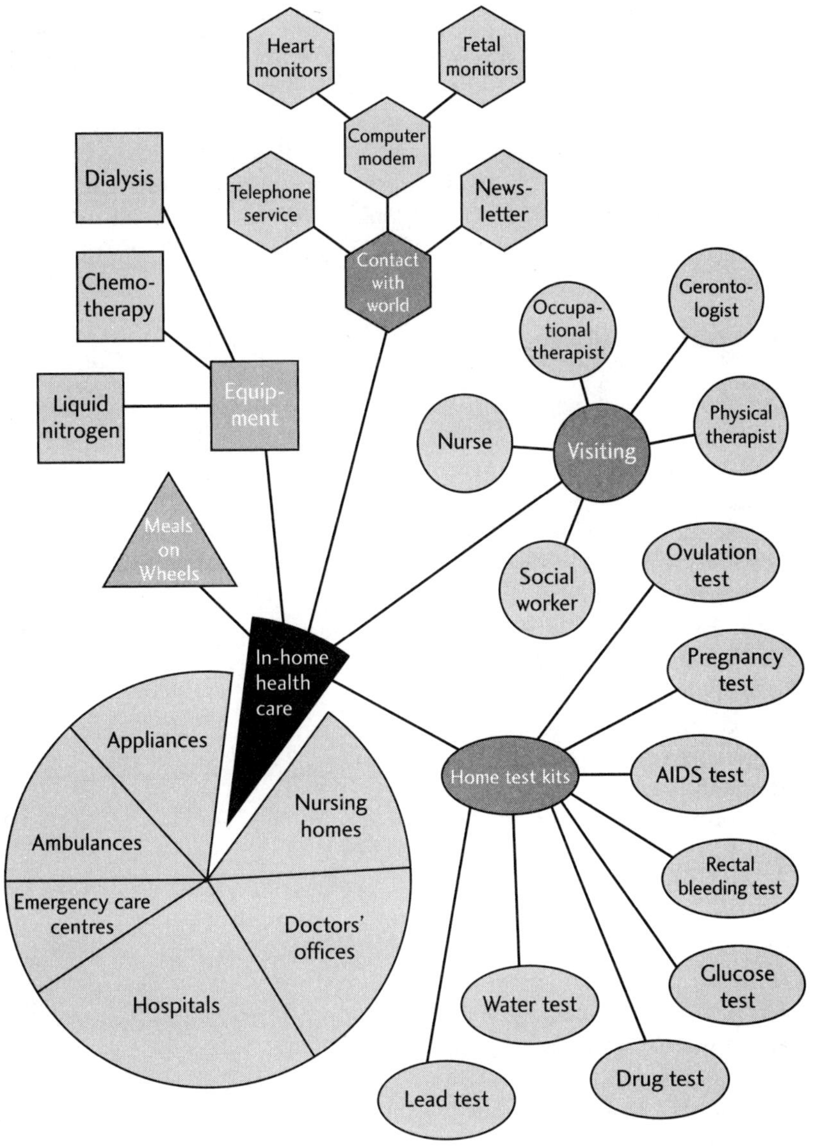

A mind-map analysis of just one segment of the health-care industry. Use mind maps to explore your industry.

The boarding stable was run down. It had stalls for 100 horses, but only 40 were occupied. Mary did everything she could think of to make the place better for horses. The $57 000 she spent on rebuilding, painting, and grading made Clark's Stables a very attractive place. She bought the highest quality of feed and gave the horses the best care money could buy.

When owners began to move their horses to other stables, Mary couldn't understand. She had not increased her fees, and she treated the horses like friends. In six months, only three customers remained. In nine months, she was behind on her mortgage payments. In her tenth month, Mary had to sell the stables.

Mary had made the simple mistake of thinking horses were her target customers. Her real target customers were girls between the ages of 7 and 14. Mary thought she was in the business of stabling horses. In fact, the business she was in was providing service for girls who rode horses. The girls wanted recreation, training, and social activities. Mary's customers left because other stables were providing lessons, trail rides, barbeques, and a fun experience. Today, Mary is back in the classroom, wondering why people don't care more about their horses—and why they didn't care about the quality of her stables.

DEFINE YOUR BUSINESS

Having defined a specific industry segment, you are ready to define what you do. Naming anything is a game of words, and a small business is no exception. If you're hesitant about defining it at this early stage, remember what happened to Mary Clark's stable.

When defining your business, keep in mind that people do not buy products or services—they buy what the product or service will do for them (for example, make their lives easier, safer, or more fun). Cosmetics firms frequently say they are in the business of selling "hope in a jar." The examples in Table 2.2 can help you define your business.

Now complete this sentence:

I'm in the business of: ____

Explain why you chose this definition and how it relates to your target customer (include benefits).

Keep honing your definition of your business. Once a month is not too often to redefine it, especially before the start-up. Check your definition against the signals you get from your potential target customers, since they may perceive your business differently. You may have new letterhead stationery printed after you talk to them, but as business expenses go, that's a small price to pay to prevent customer confusion. By developing a questionnaire about your business idea and getting feedback from a number of potential customers, you will be able to redefine the business you are in.

Now you're ready to do Action Step 13.

ACTION STEP 13

Define your business and test your definition.

Follow these steps:

1. Brainstorm what business you're really in. Let your mind play at this. Try to keep negative statements to a minimum.
2. Once you've decided what business you're in, visit your printer and order some one-colour business letterhead stationery. (One colour is cheaper, so you save money right from the start.)
3. Next, go to the library and look for a thick publication called *Associations Canada*. Locate the name of a trade association your business would be a part of. Write down the address, phone number, and name of a contact person.
4. Before you leave the library, check the *Gale Directory of Publications and Broadcast Media* for a trade journal that covers your industry. Try to find one that's not connected to the association you found listed in *Associations Canada*. Write down the name of the publication; the publisher's name, address, and phone number; and the cost (if any) of a subscription.
5. Look in the *Dun & Bradstreet Key Business Directory* or the *Robert Morris Annual Financial Statements* of similar companies to see how they have performed.
6. Finally, write or telephone the publications and trade associations that are in your area of interest. Ask them for a rate card and for demographic studies. It's free because you are a prospective advertiser. The trade association will tell you about itself and provide membership details.

You will soon have a wealth of information for your research.

Table 2.2 Defining Your Business

If you're in:	Try saying:
Software sales	"I'm in the problem-solving business."
Small business teaching	"I'm in the dream-to-reality business."
Personal financial planning	"I'm in the peace-of-mind business."
Personal fitness training	"I keep you young and buff."
Auto manufacturing	"I'm in the ego-gratification business."
Mattresses	"I'm in the sound sleep business."
Cameras/camcorders	"I'm in the happy memory business."
Gourmet cookware	"I bring fun back into the kitchen."
Locksmithing	"I'm in the security business."
Badge manufacturing	"I'm in the recognition business."

Information Is Everywhere

To discover the right opportunity for you, you will need market research, creativity, and intuition. This is a good time to walk the neighbourhood to observe clues to lifestyle first-hand. Action Step 14 will get you out into the neighbourhood of your target customers, allowing you to use your intuition and observation to learn about the marketplace—your new-eyes research.

PRIMARY RESEARCH SOURCES

It is also time to conduct some primary research. For instance, you could develop a questionnaire for potential customers on your product or service. Other ways you can conduct primary research include talking to successful and not-so-successful entrepreneurs who are operating businesses similar to yours. Talk to potential suppliers and a banker to get their perspectives on your endeavour.

SECONDARY RESEARCH SOURCES

Now we're going to introduce you to some valuable secondary research sources that you can use for gathering hard data.

Hard Data

Newspapers Study the local newspaper, starting with the classified and display ads. For a bigger picture, read *The Globe and Mail*, the *National Post*, or the business section of your local paper.

Magazines There is almost an endless list of great magazine reads—*PROFIT, Maclean's, Canadian Business, Inc., Success, Omni,* and so on. Remember to study the ads. They tell you what's hot and where the money is flowing. In Chapter 4, you'll read a case study about Mina Cohen who found a niche in the travel business. Her idea germinated from a great deal of soul-searching and reading *Equinox*. The point is, keep reading with your new eyes. Look for articles on new trends, new ideas, and new opportunities.

Trade Journals These are a valuable source once you know what industry and business you're in. Use your new business letterhead to write trade associations. You can find these listed at your local library. You might also want to try, for example, *Associations Canada*, the *Encyclopedia of Associations*, or the *Gale Directory of Publications and Broadcast Media*.

Banks Banks are in the business of lending money. Banks have economists, marketing experts, and individuals who evaluate trends and research and write forecasts and reports of economic trends. Ask to see those reports. Most major banks also have a number of publications and brochures on starting and operating a small business.

Planning Offices Cities and regional municipalities employ planners to chart the future and plan for growth. Check the city and regional offices listings in the phone book to find out where these offices are. For the best service, however, you'll need to visit the office, make friends with the staff, and be pleasant and patient. Ask for a copy of the profile on your city.

ACTION STEP 14

Assess the lifestyle of your potential target customer by walking his or her neighbourhood.

The best time to walk a target neighbourhood is on the weekend, when people are home and the garage doors are open. What you're looking for are clues to lifestyle.

How many cars do you see? What makes and models? How old are they? What's their condition? Sports cars and low-slung two-door hatchbacks indicate owners who are young, or trying to be. Station wagons suggest families. Trucks, four-wheel drive vehicles, and luxury cars tell you other things.

Do you see any sports or recreation equipment? Any tools? Any pets, doghouses, stables?

What's the maintenance level of the homes? Are they patio homes, condos, townhouses, or single-family dwellings? Estimate the average number of bedrooms, bathrooms, square feet, and so on.

Visit a real-estate office and get a ballpark figure on housing costs in the neighbourhood. Use these costs to estimate household income. (If the average price for a home in your target neighbourhood is $300 000 and buyers can finance $150 000, the household income is probably $60 000–$90 000.)

If you don't have time to walk the neighbourhood, bike it or drive it.

Commonly available secondary information can help you confirm your observations. See what data your community newspaper or cable station has already gathered. Also, review information from the latest census tract. It's all free!

Reports from Colleges, Universities, and Investment Firms Many colleges and universities publish annual and semi-annual reports on economic conditions in the province. You can probably get copies of these by writing to the university public relations office. Reports are also published by private institutions of higher learning with special interests in business.

Real-Estate Firms Large commercial and industrial real-estate firms have access to developers' site research. The more specific you can be on your requirement, the easier it will be for them to help you. Familiarize yourself with the dynamics of the area. What firms are going into business? What firms are leaving business? (For more details on this, see Chapter 7.) They can supply you with a listing of rental space in your community.

The Business Development Bank of Canada (BDC) The BDC publishes all kinds of materials of interest to small business. The BDC also provides a wide range of financial alternatives (see Chapter 10) and sponsors numerous seminars on small business. For information, call or visit your nearest BDC office. You can also write to Business Development Bank, 5, Place Ville-Marie, Suite 400, Montreal, QC, H3B 5E7; or visit the BDC website (www.bdc.ca).

Industry Canada Industry Canada (http://info.ic.gc.ca) has been given specific federal responsibilities in the area of small business. The Canada Business Service Centres of Industry Canada should be one of your first stops for small business information. There are 11 CBSCs—one located in each province and the Northwest Territories. Key activities of each centre include toll-free telephone help; CBSC websites (see discussion below); CBSC resource and information with in-person service, directories, publications, and access to external databases; a toll-free, fax on-demand service; and "Pathfinders"—brochures, organized by topic, with overviews of services and programs.

Statistics Canada Statistics Canada (www.statcan.ca) produces a large volume and variety of statistics that are available to all Canadians. For most subjects, Statistics Canada will probably be one of your major sources of secondary information. How reliable is this information? *The Economist* asked a panel of experts from various countries to rank statistical agencies. All agreed that Canada has the best statistics in the world. Yes, our number crunchers were ranked number one. If you haven't used Statistics Canada before, you may find it a little overwhelming. Persist, for it's well worth the effort. You might want to start with its Catalogue No. 11-204, which provides a guide listing over 1000 reports and documents, as well as numerous electronic databases. It's even available on diskette or CD-ROM. Their annual publication, *Market Research Handbook* (Catalogue No. 63-224), is also a useful starting place. In Chapter 7, we will introduce you to Census of Population data.

Computer Databases

As you know by now, we are bound up in the knowledge-based economy. Unique databases are cropping up daily. A discussion of this new generation of information would be a book in itself; however, there are five Industry Canada data sources and one Statistics Canada source that warrant special mention.

Industry Canada

- *Canadian Company Capabilities.* This database of over 40 000 Canadian company profiles allows you to search for a firm by product, geography, or activity. You can also register your company and promote your products or services worldwide in cyberspace.

- *Trade Data Online.* This source provides reports and graphs on 6000 exports and imports to and from over 600 countries, as well as five-year trends. You can also use the information to help forecast domestic and foreign market opportunities.
- *International Business Information Network.* Contacts, country information, and trade fair venues from the world are provided here.
- *dISTCovery.* Here you will find a list of over 35 000 worldwide technologies that can be licensed and are ready for use. You can use the technologies to solve a problem in your manufacturing process or increase your sales through innovation by acquiring the rights to license a technology in Canada.
- *Contact! The Canadian Management Network.* This is a source of Canadian contacts for business management advice, skills development, software tools, services, and useful management publications. *Contact!* also hosts online forums where businesspeople and experts can get together electronically to discuss topics of mutual interest. What a great way to do your primary research!

Statistics Canada

Another useful Statistics Canada source is CANSIM II (Canadian Socioeconomic Information Management System), a massive fee-based data retrieval system that provides access to all kinds of economic and demographic information, along with tailored data analysis packages, graphics, and a bibliographic search service. More information on CANSIM II is available at http://cansim2.statcan.ca.

In today's knowledge-based world, the list of secondary data sources just keeps growing. The point is, there's massive information out there. All you have to do is start looking, and we suggest that you start at your local public, college, or university library.

Internet Sources and Databases

In the last few years, the Internet has become a predominant source of secondary business information. There are literally hundreds of websites that can help you start and run your business. Some major sites include:

- **Strategis**
  http://strategis.ic.gc.ca
  Industry Canada, in partnership with the business community and universities, has created the largest, most comprehensive business information website in Canada. It contains over 75 000 reports, 600 000 pages of text, and 2 gigabytes of statistical data. You can also get updated information ranging from business diagnostic and benchmarking data to all the government forms you need to incorporate.

- **Online Small Business Workshop**
  www.cbsc.org/osbw/workshop.html
  This online site covers all the basics in "how-to," from fashioning the initial product idea to marketing, research, sales forecasting, financing, planning, and everything in-between.

- **Contact! The Canadian Management Network**
  http://strategis.ic.gc.ca/sc_mangb/contact/engdoc/homepage.html
  This is the primary Canadian source on the Internet for business management information and advice. It gives access to a full range of small business support organizations in Canada, and provides a wide range of educational materials and tools to help entrepreneurs start a business.

ACTION STEP 15

Launch your industry research.

1. To locate the names of trade associations in your area of interest, consult the *Gale Encyclopedia of Business and Professional Associations* or *Associations Canada*, or visit the following online sources:
   - Canadian Industry and Professional Associations (Industry Canada index) http://strategis.ic.gc.ca/scdt/businessmap/engdoc/2.2.html
   - Associations Canada http://circ.micromedia.on.ca/hotlinks/associations/main.htm
   - AssociationCentral.com www.associationcentral.com

   Make note of the addresses, phone numbers, and websites. Contact the associations that interest you and request information and membership details. If you mention you're a student conducting research, they may be surprisingly helpful. You can go further on this assignment by contacting associations your potential suppliers and customers may belong to.
2. Locate a chapter of a national association and attend a meeting as a guest.
3. Visit www.mediafinder.com to locate (a) magazines or journals associated with your selected industry, (b) magazines or journals that reach your potential customers, and (c) magazines or journals directed at your suppliers. Spend some time on the Net or at the library researching your list and delving deeper into the information.
4. After completing your industry research, select at least one magazine or journal from each of the categories and request a media kit. The media kits will help you fine-tune your research.

- **Canadian Technology Network**
  http://ctn.nrc.ca
  Here is a site that helps Canadian businesses look for technological assistance. Advisers work with individual entrepreneurs to identify needs and to find the right source of assistance for almost every technology imaginable.
- **Business Development Bank of Canada (BDC)**
  www.bdc.ca
  According to the BDC, this is a cyber-destination that small and medium-sized Canadian businesses can call their own. The website includes more than 300 hyperlinks to small business resources, coast to coast.

Other secondary research online sources include:

- **Associations Canada**
  www.silverplatter.com/catalog/daca.htm
- **Canadian Industry and Professional Associations** (Industry Canada index)
  http://strategis.ic.gc.ca/scdt/businessmap/engdoc/2.2.html
- **ACNielsen Canada** (tracks retail store sales movement to consumers)
  www.acnielsen.ca
- **Canadian Innovation**
  www.innovationcentre.ca

Following are some online government databases:

- **Canadian Company Capabilities**
  http://strategis.ic.gc.ca/sc_coinf/ccc/engdoc/homepage.html
- **Federal Corporations Data Online**
  http://strategis.ic.gc.ca/cgi-bin/sc_mrksv/corpdir/dataOnline/corpns_se
- **Strategis, Business Information by Sector**
  http://strategis.ic.gc.ca/sc_indps/engdoc/homepage.html
- **Strategis, Canadian Industry Statistics**
  http://strategis.ic.gc.ca/sc_ecnmy/sio/homepage.html
- **Trade Data Online**
  http://strategis.ic.gc.ca/sc_mrkti/tdst/engdoc/tr_homep.html
- **Canadian Importer's Database**
  http://strategis.ic.gc.ca/sc_mrkti/cid/engdoc/index.html
- **Statistics Canada, Merchandise Trade Database**
  http://www.statcan.ca/trade/scripts/trade_search.cgi

Now is a good time to start researching your chosen industry. Complete Action Step 15.

In a Nutshell

A trend is a direction of movement. For example, the trend of our present civilization is away from the smokestacks of the industrial age and toward the computers and the Internet of the entrepreneurial age. An easy way to start studying trends it to step back in time and observe a marketplace of the past. Then move on to your own arena—the neighbourhood, nearby shopping malls, Main Street, your trade association, your supermarket.

Two tools will help you chart trends: looking around with new eyes, playing marketplace detective, and applying the life-cycle yardstick to products, industries, and so on. As you learned earlier in this chapter, a life cycle has four phases: embryo, growth, maturity, and decline. Before you open the doors of your small business, you need to be aware of what phase your product is in. For example, if you think there's easy money in selling microcomputers, you need to know that this industry is now maturing. If you want to install security products, you need to know that this industry is in the growth stage. If you're thinking about opening a toy store, you need to know that the toy industry is mature and may be on the decline, and that you may be forced to steal customers from other people.

Just for fun, select three to six businesses at random—for example, a foreign auto repair business, a restaurant-bar, a flower shop, a bedding manufacturer, a travel agent, and a computer school—and determine their life-cycle stages. While you're doing that, remember how the old post office had to adjust. Is the same thing happening to some of the smaller firms you know because they're failing to see what business they're really in?

Information on trends is all around you: on the highways, in the stores in mid-December and after Christmas, in the headlines and classifieds, at government agencies, in the many trade associations. This information can give you the big picture if you know how to seek it out.

Key Terms

aftermarket
baby boomers
brainstorming
echo boomers
e-commerce
growth industry
growth segment
life cycle
market research
market segmentation

Think Points for Success

- ✓ A valuable tool you can use for charting trends is the four-stage life-cycle yardstick.
- ✓ The life-cycle yardstick helps you find a growth industry, decide what business you're really in, and discover gaps and segments that are promising.
- ✓ Once you know what segment you're in, you can focus on market research with new eyes.
- ✓ Try to latch onto a trend that will help you survive (in style) for the next 10 to 15 years.
- ✓ Trends don't develop overnight. The signs are out for all to read, months—even years—in advance.
- ✓ Develop and circulate your primary research customer questionnaire to your target customer.

Business Plan Building Block

INDUSTRY OVERVIEW

You need to demonstrate your knowledge and understanding of the business opportunity you want to pursue. How big is the total industry? How old is it? Is it growing, and if so, in what direction?

What segment have you chosen? It is vital that you present a comprehensive understanding of who your customers are and why they will buy from you. Get on the Internet. Use some of the secondary sources provided in this chapter and definitely do some primary research.

CURRENT POSITION AND FUTURE OUTLOOK

Example:
This is what you learn about Big Wheels, a growing bike shop in town: The two owners are well-known trail bike riders who, for the past two years, have been repairing and servicing all kinds of bicycles out of the oversized garage of one of their partners. In the past 12 months, this part-time venture grossed $161 000 without the benefit of advertising or a retail location.

The market for high-quality and custom-made bicycles has grown over 10 percent per year for the past 10 years, and industry observers expect the trend to continue into the next century. The new retail store will have 5000 square feet in showroom space and another 3000 square feet for doing repairs and stocking goods.

The bicycle industry in North America sells two dollars' worth of accessories and clothing for every one dollar spent on bicycles. The store conservatively expects sales to at least double the first year (they previously had not sold clothing) and to reach $1 million in three years.

It's your turn again. Develop your section on the current situation and future outlook. It's important to demonstrate an understanding of growth problems (such as choosing the right location and attracting customers), as well as cash management, gross margins, inventory control, and vendor sources. Ready or not, start writing down what you already know and what you need to know. You will have many opportunities to upgrade this section as you gather data. Your primary research, when complete, will help.

MANAGEMENT AND OWNERSHIP

Needed now is a mini-résumé of the key player (or players) you'd like to have on your founding team. Lenders, capital firms, and vendors consider the founding team to be the most important factor in a business plan.

At this point, keep the résumés brief, focusing on the past experience that will give this start-up a competitive edge. (Save the full-blown résumés of the management team for the appendix at the back of the plan.) Explain your business form (that is, corporation, partnership, or sole proprietorship) and, if you have more than two people on the team, include an organizational chart.

Your turn again: Who are the players?

____

____

____

____

____

DESCRIPTION OF YOUR BUSINESS

Think of yourself riding up 50 floors in an express elevator. You have 30 seconds to explain to a stranger what your business is about.

Example:

My partner and I retail high-end bicycles from our store in Halifax. We repair, service, and modify off-road bikes for the serious trail rider. Ninety percent of our customers are from Halifax and they see us as a valuable resource in helping them to achieve a healthy and enjoyable exercise lifestyle.

Note that this description is not only short and to the point, but it also includes important customer benefits.

Now it's your turn.

My business is:

____

____

____

____

____

Checklist Questions and Actions to Develop Your Business Plan

SPOTTING TRENDS AND OPPORTUNITIES

- ❑ What trends will influence your small business?
- ❑ What business are you really in?
- ❑ What segment of the market will be your niche?
- ❑ Is it a growth segment in a growth market?
- ❑ Initially define your target market, and determine how large that customer base is.
- ❑ Identify the secondary sources you will use as part of your market research.
- ❑ Does this business fit your vision and values?
- ❑ Other than making money, what are the goals of your proposed venture? (You should be able to establish four to six over the next three years.)
- ❑ For your business, what objectives do you wish to achieve this next year?

NOTES

1. Pacific Western Brewing Co., About Us, retrieved from http://pwbrewing.com/about_us.html; and Daphne Bramham, "Japan Taps into Pacific Western Beer: The Various Brands Are Brewed to Suit Japanese Tastes, Entrepreneur Says," *The Vancouver Sun*, March 7, 1997.
2. Canadian Youth Business Foundation, Success Stories, retrieved from http://www.cybf.ca/en_success.html#fastestgrowing; "NuMedia Internet," retrieved from www.profitguide.com/winner/issues_article.asp?id=769; and "Success and Sacrifice," retrieved from www.profitguide.com/hottest/2001/index.asp
3. Catherine Swift, "It's a Small World After All," *Post 2000*, Issue 8, November 15, 1997, p. 4.
4. From an interview with Don Tapscott, "Cyberwhiz Don Tapscott Is Mapping the Digital Frontier," *Royal Bank Business Report*, November 1996, p. 21. See also Louis E. Boone, David L. Kurtz, and Ronald A. Knowles, *Business*, 1st Cdn. ed. (Toronto: Dryden, 1998), p. 245.
5. Nuala Beck, quoted in Colin Campbell with Carole Hood, *Where the Jobs Are* (Toronto: Macfarlane Walter & Ross, 1997), p. 9.
6. Job Shark Corp. website (www.jobshark.com); and "Best Businesses to Go into Now," retrieved from www.profitguide.com/magazine/issues_article.asp?ID=731
7. Household Internet Use Survey (2000), retrieved from www.statcan.ca/Daily/English/010726/d010726a.htm; and 2001 Survey of Electronic Commerce and Technology, retrieved from www.statcan.ca/Daily/English/020402/d020402a.htm

SUGGESTED READING

Campbell, Colin, with Carole Hood. *Where the Jobs Are*. Toronto: Macfarlane Walter & Ross, 1997.

Celente, Gerald. *Trends 2000*. New York: Wagner Books Inc., 1997.

Cork, David, with Susan Lightstone. *The Pig and the Python: How to Prosper from the Aging Baby Boom*. Toronto: Stoddart Publishing, 1996.

Feather, Frank. *Future Consumerism.com*. Toronto: Warwick Publishing, 2000.

Gates, Bill. *The Road Ahead*. New York: Viking Press, 1996.

Harris, Lesley Ellen. *Digital Property, Currency of the 21st Century*. Whitby, ON: McGraw-Hill Ryerson, 1997.

Helzel, Leo. *A Goal Is a Dream with a Deadline*. New York: McGraw-Hill Professional Book Group, 1995.

Hise, Phaedra. *Growing Your Business Online: Small Business Strategies for Working the World Wide Web*. New York: Henry Holt, 1996.

Peters, Tom. *The Circle of Innovation*. New York: Knopf, 1998.

Thurow, Lester C. *The Future of Capitalism*. New York: William Morrow & Co., 1996.

chapter 3

Positioning Yourself as an Entrepreneur for Market Opportunities

BUSINESS PLAN BUILDING BLOCK

This chapter will help you align your personal vision and values with your business mission, goals, and objectives, and guide you as you start to develop your strategy. It will also help you collect data that will allow you to focus on the most promising unmet needs, and identify the industry or market trends—the big picture—for you and your business.

LEARNING OPPORTUNITIES

After reading this chapter, you should be able to:

- Mesh your personal business objectives with one of the many opportunities in the marketplace.
- Understand that your business objectives provide a positive and unique thrust to your business.
- Narrow your industry research until viable gaps appear.
- Gain insight into hidden pockets of the life cycle by using an industry chronology.
- Understand how problems can be turned into opportunities.
- Combine demographic (population) data with psychographic (picture of a lifestyle) data to produce a customer profile.
- Identify heavy users of your product or service.
- Brainstorm creatively.
- Use a matrix grid for blending your objectives with your research findings to produce a portrait of a business.
- Create a mission statement for your business.

The voice at the other end of the telephone was gritty and determined. Its owner, Beverly MacIntyre, is talking from Dieppe, which is just outside Moncton, New Brunswick. "I have always wanted to make a difference, whatever I do," she says. "That's my vision and it's very important to me."

In 1990 MacIntyre and an associate, Terry Miller, started BKM Research & Development Inc. (www.bkm.ca), a company that talks to employers, figures out what skills they're looking for, then creates a training program for its clients. Since then, they have trained over 10 000 clients. They began the business with bricks-and-mortar classrooms, but today deliver training to educational, corporate, and human resource organizations via the Internet. BKM's mission is to align training solutions with organizational standards and performance objectives. The company's eLearning technologies can

Chapter 3 will help you prepare part B of your business plan, "The Market and the Target Customer."

ACTION STEP PREVIEW

16. List your business goals for the next three years.
17. Collect secondary data on your favourite industry segment.
18. Identify three or four market gaps that look promising.
19. List problems that need solutions.
20. Brainstorm for solutions.
21. Mesh possible solutions with your goals and objectives, using a matrix grid.
22. Narrow the gaps and see your target customer emerge.
23. Draft your mission statement.

determine whether employees or students are complying with their clients' organizational standards and training objectives, as well as with industry standards. This compliance data can be benchmarked to job attainment, job performance, certification success rates, and job succession to measure return on training investment.[1]

Edmonton-based Kinnikinnick Foods Inc. is an award-winning bakery that specializes in gluten-free foods. Its target customers are people who are allergic to wheat, barley, rye, or oats; people who are dairy/lactose intolerant; people who are on a special diet for the biological treatment of autism; or people who simply want to expand, balance, or rotate their diet.

Founding partner Ted Wolff von Selzam had a background in environmental education and teaching programs when he started the company as a home-based business in 1991, selling his homemade products at a local farmer's market. A specialized bakery was a natural extension of his love for food and his personal vision to help people live in harmony with their environment.

The first retail location of 500 square feet opened in February 1992. In the space of 10 years, the company has grown from a mom-and-pop operation to a corporate structure that can meets the demands of a growing North American market. Kinnikinnick now boasts over 120 brand products, including a wide variety of breads, buns, bagels, donuts, cookies, muffins, cereals, easy-to-use mixes, soups, sauces, and snack foods.

Kinnikinnick owes its success to the following:

- **A compelling vision:** To be a leading producer of alternative foods.
- **A focused mission:** To provide people with celiac disease, people with autism, and people with special dietary requirements with an uncontaminated, risk-free source of food products. And to provide our customers with food that actually looks and tastes good.

An e-commerce enabled website is the third key to Kinnikinnick's success. Since the site (www.kinnikinnick.ca) was launched in 1998, sales have grown by nearly 500 percent. Much of this growth is attributable to online sales. "Our U.S. sales account for at least 50 percent of our business," says Marketing and IT Manager Jay Bigam, "and a very large portion of that 50 percent is driven by the Internet."[2]

In Chapter 1, we asked you to step back, take a good hard look at your strengths and weaknesses, and think about your personal vision, values, and goals. In Chapter 2, we encouraged you to be on the lookout for industry trends that signal entrepreneurial opportunities. Now we want to help you align your personal vision and values with the market opportunities. Think for a minute: this "alignment" was a major factor contributing to the success of Beverly MacIntyre of BKM and Ted Wolff von Selzam of Kinnikinnick Foods. MacIntyre had a personal vision, "to make a difference, whatever I do." She positioned her business in the growth markets of education, training, and technology. Her business mission "to align training solutions with organizational standards and performance objectives" guided her along the lifelong path to make a difference. In the same fashion, Wolff von Selzam's personal vision—"to help people live in harmony with their environment"—was in keeping with the healthy-eating trend and his resulting business mission.

As you work your way through this self-assessment chapter, you will better understand what type of business best suits you. The sky is the limit on ideas for your small business. On the other hand, you may already have very firm ideas about what type of business you plan to start. If you are not sure, keep your options open at this stage. As you assess your vision and values, establish your mission, goals, and objectives and let your ideas percolate. In the final analysis, you want to match your business idea with your interests. Box 3.1 diagrams the flow of the thought process from your vision to your strategy. As was the case for Beverly MacIntyre and Ted Wolff von Selzam, your best business opportunity will be where your personal vision and values meet your business mission.

Your Values

"I believe that the owner and/or president of a company determines its culture. His or her personal qualities of doing business and treatment of others are disseminated through the rest of the organization: the company ends up with the reputation of its leader." So says Alex Tilley, owner and chairman of Tilley Endurables Inc.[3]

Art Coren, instructor at Kwantlen University College, agrees with Tilley. "A business reflects the values and personality of the people that own and operate it. If, for example, your core values are respect for others and upholding the traditional family structure, could you start an escort service? As a small business owner, your business must embody your values. Starting a business that violates one or more of your core values could lead to chaos and misery."[4]

So you need to ask yourself what intrinsic **values** guide your day-to-day activities, behaviour, and decision making. Think about what things in life are really important to you. You may not die for them, but they are principles that mean a great deal to you. Now make a list. The following is a cross-section of both personal and business values one may have. Use this as a guide, but don't just incorporate them as yours unless you firmly believe that they are important to you.

VALUES
the things in life that are important to you

- Customer service
- Quality
- Family
- Friends
- Money
- Material items
- Trust of others
- Security
- Benefits of a socially aware community
- Confidence in others
- Work ethics
- Desire for ownership
- Desire for power
- Desire for affiliation
- Desire for achievement
- Desire for recognition

Box 3.1 It Is All Connected

YOUR VISION
is
Based on YOUR VALUES and beliefs.
It is spelled out in
YOUR MISSION statement
fleshed out in
YOUR GOALS and OBJECTIVES
and accomplished through
YOUR STRATEGY.

What does your list look like? Which are business values and which personal values? You may find, as you develop your list, that it will consist of values and priorities. If one of your values is security, then think what this means to you. Does it mean being able to take care of others and provide opportunities? If to your spouse it means having a small business that allows flexible time, is close to home, enables weekends off, and does not involve travel, then you'll find your business choices are limited. Don't ignore your spouse's values and personal priorities or choices.

Values serve as guideposts for your actions. They help you deal with problems you have never seen before. As Alex Tilley points out, a business reflects the values and personality of the people that own and operate it. If you believe in treating people fairly, chances are your business will too. If you are socially aware, you may want your business to embody the same values. For example, you may budget an annual financial contribution to a charity in your business plan. Values, once crystallized, become the basis of your mission statement and goals (Figure 3.1). Now that you've had a chance to think about your values, it's time to focus on market opportunities that support these values.

Welcome to Opportunity Selection

Think of the process for selecting the right opportunity for you as a huge funnel equipped with a series of idea filters. You pour everything into this funnel—your visions, values, long-term goals, short-term objectives, personality, problems, hopes, fears, and primary, secondary, and new-eyes research—and a valuable business idea drains out at the bottom. This opportunity selection process contains seven steps. It is a method to help you find market segments that match with your personal vision and goals (see Boxes 3.1 and 3.2). It connects your skills to your research, and shows you the skills you need to develop. It aims the power of your mind at the particular segment of small business that suits you (see Figure 3.2 on page 46).

Figure 3.1 Vision, Mission, and Need

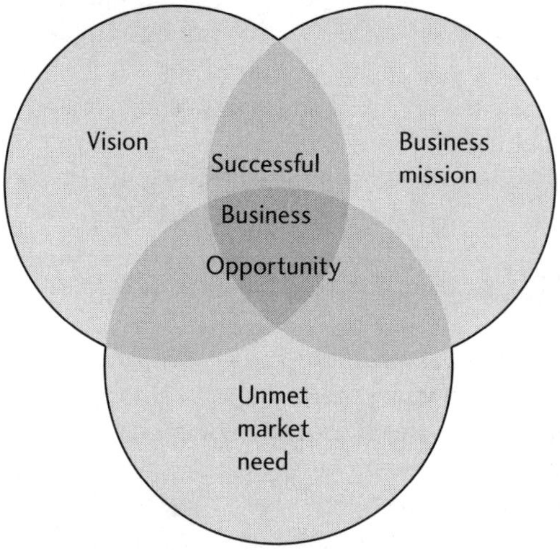

Success is where your personal vision, based on your values, connects with your business mission and matches with an unmet need in the marketplace.

Box 3.2 The Power of Vision

Five percent of the workforce—some 670 000 Canadians—is affected by depression every day. Depressive disorders cost Canadians more than $3 billion annually. Over the late 1990s and early 2000s, downsizing—"laying off employees across the board without changing the basic corporate structure"—was a major source of stress for thousands of Canadians.

If your personal vision is to help people understand and deal with depression, then the downsizing trend and the resulting stress factor are problems that can translate into a real business opportunity. CHC-Working Well, a Financial Post "50 Best Managed Private Companies," is one of Canada's leading firms that has taken advantage of the downsizing trend. "We help people understand the early signs and symptoms, so they can be aware of depression before it becomes a serious problem. We're part of the solution," says Jack Santa-Barbara, head of CHC-Working Well. This Mississauga, Ont., firm started out small in the 1980s and has since grown to a $20-million medium-sized company with over 700 employees.

Source: Rod McQueen, "Canada's 50 Best Managed Private Companies: CHC-Working Well," *The Financial Post*, December 13, 1997, p. 17.

Here is a quick preview of the seven steps to opportunity selection:

1. Identify your business goals.
2. Learn more about your favourite industry.
3. Identify promising industry segments.
4. Identify problems that need solutions.
5. Brainstorm for solutions.
6. Mesh possible solutions with opportunities in the marketplace.
7. Take stock of, and focus on, the most promising opportunities.

To understand how this process works, let's see how Steve and Anne found their business opportunity. Steve, a graduate from a technical school, had been bounced from job to job over the last few years. Anne graduated with a major in marketing and still hadn't found a real job—but then she'd not been looking that hard. They weren't too sure whether they wanted to start a business together, so they took a night course in small business to help sort things out. Both had a good handle on their personal visions and goals, and now it was time to see if they could come up with a good business idea.

We'll show you how they worked through their idea using the seven steps of opportunity selection. This case study also introduces another important concept: teamwork. Let's start with Steve and Anne's business goals.

STEP 1: IDENTIFY YOUR BUSINESS GOALS

Anne and Steve's first step was to develop a list of business goals. Their small business professor had asked, "If you were to start a business, what would your goals—in relation to your values—be? Security, money, independence, control?" She added that eventually these general goals would have to be refined as short-term objectives and made much more specific and measurable (as noted in Box 3.3).

It took a few days—more time than they thought—but Steve and Anne finally came up with a list of broad goals that sounded like heaven:

1. *Psychological rewards.* They wanted to plant a seed and watch it grow into a business that they and their future family would be proud of.

Figure 3.2 Opportunity Selection

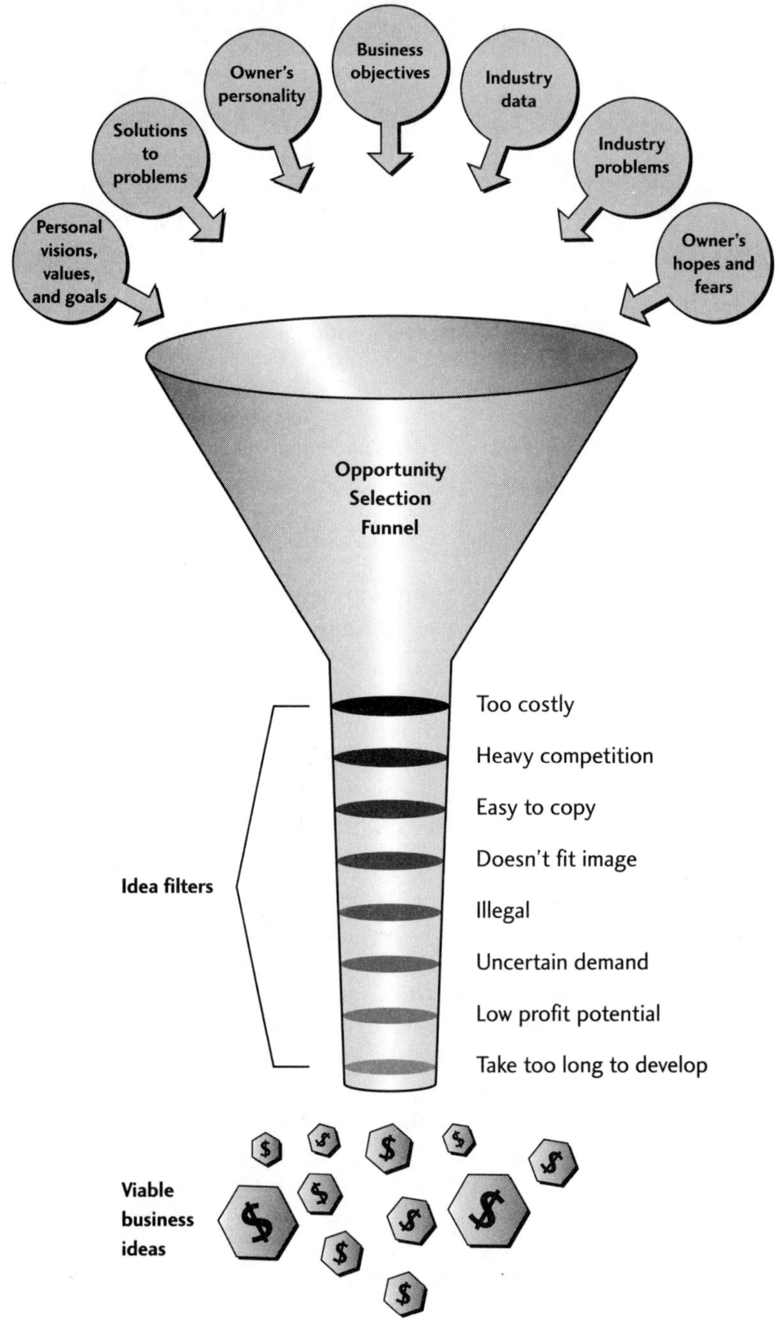

Think of the opportunity selection process as a huge funnel that contains a series of idea filters.

2. *Teamwork.* All their lives they had planned to work together to build a strong family unit. Now they wanted to practise these teamwork skills in business. They wanted their business to be something bigger than they could accomplish as individuals—the value of synergy. As a team, both Anne and Steve had listed their strengths and weaknesses. They wanted to build on their strengths.

Box 3.3 Small Business Tips

In the final analysis, each of your broad goals will boil down to a set of specific business objectives. These objectives should be S M A R T:

Specific
Measurable
Action-based
Realistic
Time-framed

3. *Money*. They wanted to earn a respectable family income—a minimum of $50 000 per year.
4. *Safety*. There was no way they wanted to lose money now. They had a family to think about.
5. *Growth industry*. They wanted to find a booming segment of a growth industry (an industry whose annual sales growth is considerably above average).
6. *Time*. They knew that getting a business up and running could take a year at the very least. They wanted to define and develop their business so that they could make a little money the first year, get their feet wet, and then go bigger in the next two to four years, once they knew what they were doing and what the market really wanted.
7. *Key people*. They wanted to operate the business themselves for the first year. But as the business grew over the next four years, they wanted to be able to attract the best people to work with them.
8. *Fun, adventure, excitement*. They knew that starting a small business, even in a growth or glamour industry, would involve hassles, problems, and surprises. So they decided to make sure their business would be one with which they would have some fun.

Now it's your turn. Why would you want to start your own business? What are your goals? Action Step 16 will help you work through this.

ACTION STEP 16

List your business goals for the next three years.

What do you want from small business? Money? Fame? Job security? To be your own boss? Freedom to explore the marketplace? Control of your own destiny? Just want to be a president?

Think back to the forces that made you interested in small business in the first place. What were those forces? Where were you when you first thought about owning the store? How have circumstances changed your goals?

List everything you want, even if it seems unreasonable or embarrassing to you. This is your personal list, after all, and you will sift through the ideas later.

STEP 2: LEARN MORE ABOUT YOUR FAVOURITE INDUSTRY

As you searched for trends in Chapter 2, you probably found a dozen industries that seemed interesting. Now it's time to explore one of them in more depth. The industry should be the one that interests you most and about which you have at least some knowledge, whether it's genetics, robotics, entertainment, food service, travel, education, publishing, retailing, construction, manufacturing, information, or whatever.

As you move into your selected industry, collect information from previous Action Steps. For secondary data, the Internet is probably the best place to start, but you need to sift through a lot of information. Be sure to check out Strategis; it's a very useful source of industry research (see Box 3.4). Visit a resource centre or library, study periodicals like *The Globe and Mail*, *Canadian Business*, the *National Post*, *PROFIT* magazine, and other general business or news sources. Most libraries have computer databases to help you search. In addition, the Canadian Business Index and other such sources will point you to dozens of articles in your field. Is there a trade show you can attend? What you're looking for is an accurate picture of trends in the industry that interest you. You need to learn what's breaking, what's cresting, and what's cooling down.

Box 3.4 Bookmark This

Strategis

As we noted in the last chapter, the Industry Canada, Strategis website (http://strategis.ic.gc.ca) is a great source of secondary research. It is devoted to providing information, resources, contacts, and hard-to-get information in a prearranged, easy-to-use format. On its "Researching Markets" page you will find the following industry information for foreign and domestic markets.

Foreign

Dynamic Market Research Reports. Build your own comparison from the topics listed within one of the following:

- **ExportSource: Country Reports.** Reports on economic and business conditions in the countries around the world and links to sites specializing in specific countries.
- **U.S. Importers Database.** Over one million names of U.S. buyers and products. Includes company name and address, type of product, weight, volume, date of arrival, and country of origin.

Domestic

- **Canadian Company Capabilities.** Enables you to find out what others are doing by searching an online database with over 40 000 Canadian companies and 200 000 products and services.
- **Federal Corporations Data Online.** Access information on hundreds of thousands of federally incorporated companies in Canada by searching this database.
- **Canadian Industry Statistics.** Provides information on various aspects of Canadian economic activity. Areas of special emphasis include economics, employment, international trade, investment, public equity financing, and growth indices.
- **Trade Data Online!** Offers import and export statistics by commodity (product), industry and geographic location for a 10-year period. This yields detailed and aggregate Canadian and U.S. information concerning trade trends and market shares.
- **Canadian Importer's Database.** Allows you to obtain a list of major importers by product/commodity or by city. The final report—generated using the latest year's data collected by the Canada Customs and Revenue Agency—will give you names and postal codes of the top 80 percent import companies in your specified sector.

Source: Retrieved from Industry Canada, Strategis website (http://strategis.ic.gc.ca/sc_x/engdoc/researching_markets.html).

In focusing on your industry, break down your search into categories such as life cycles, speed of change, history, competition, recent industry breakthroughs, costs of positioning yourself, target customers, and so on. Later, after you have gathered the data, you can use these categories as idea filters for sifting information through the power marketing funnel.

For example, using the life-cycle concept discussed in Chapter 2 will sharpen a first look at any industry. When you're reading a newspaper and you see a headline that says "CBC tries to shed stodgy image in prime time—but can it be hip?," you make three fast-reflex judgments. First, the industry is entertainment. Second, the segment is network television. Third, the shows are in the mature phase, on their way to decline.

And when you're driving down the street and you see a shopping mall being renovated, you know that the face lift is an attempt to move the mall back from a mature or decline phase into a growth phase. The point of all this is to find an industry segment where there is room for growth.

A second helpful category is competition, which we'll be analyzing in detail in Chapter 5. Competition, which varies with each stage of the life cycle, is an idea filter that can save you years of grief.

A third helpful category is the concept of industry breakthrough or hot button. What really hums in your industry or segment? Remember, the first computers filled large rooms and ran on punch cards. The first industry breakthrough was the printed circuit. The second was the microchip. And the third was computer networks. Could the fourth be the network computer—a personal computer with no hard drive?

Let's return to Anne and Steve. They had a firm idea of their favourite industry. They had done a lot of primary and secondary research and had decided to focus on the information industry. All the numbers told them the information industry was still a growth market. On a personal level, Steve loved the technical world and Anne knew there was a real need for marketers in the technology sector, and she liked working with techies. They had chosen a growth industry, which meshed with their personal visions and goals.

Now it is your turn. Research your favourite industry. Is it in a growth phase? What breakthroughs are occurring? Does your business capitalize on the latest advances in technology and imagination? Put this kind of thinking into Action Step 17.

ACTION STEP 17

Collect secondary data on your favourite industry segment.

What industry segment really attracts you? What's out there that has a magnetic pull you cannot resist? To help you get started, recall what you discovered in Action Steps 9–15.

Start with a wide-angle view by looking at two or three segments that interest you. After you've decided on "your" segment, research in depth. It might help to organize your research into categories such as life cycle, speed of change, history, competition, recent industry breakthroughs, costs of positioning yourself, customer base, and so on.

If you're working alone, it will help to write your industry overview. If you're working with a team, you'll save yourself some confusion if each team member writes an overview, and later shares his or her perspective with the others.

This is a never-ending Action Step. Once you are in business, you will have to be as diligent in keeping up with the industry segment as you were in your initial research.

STEPS 3 AND 4: IDENTIFY PROMISING INDUSTRY SEGMENTS AND PROBLEMS THAT NEED SOLUTIONS

When you write your business plan, you'll need to explain why you have chosen a particular **market gap** and what you believe the resulting business opportunity is. If you have selected a promising opportunity and have communicated your excitement about it, you'll have developed a "hook" for the banker or investor who will read your plan. One example of an industry where market gaps will abound is e-commerce (see Table 3.1). Beverly MacIntyre of BKM Research & Development Inc. found her market gap in the online education and training segment, while Ted Wolff von Selzam of Kinnikinnick Foods found his in the e-retailing of alternative food products.

MARKET GAP

an area of the market where needs are not being met

Anne and Steve had done a lot of primary and secondary research. They knew that computers and the Internet were explosive market segments (see Figure 3.3). They also learned that there was a growth market for computer networks—especially for the small businesses (Table 3.2 on page 52). From their research they had isolated four breakthrough segments: the home computer market, the Internet, Intranet, and computer networks. It would be hard to argue that any of these are not growth segments. The numbers are quite clear—at least for the next couple of years. Wisely, Anne and Steve also listed some of the major problems in the industry: product and service distrust, speed change, information overload, security, cost, and so on.

The secret to focusing on market gaps is to find a target customer—a person or business that needs a particular product or service that you could provide. You then profile your target customer (we do this in detail in the next chapter), and that profile becomes one of your idea filters. Now it's your turn to focus on the segments within your industry and spot some that look promising. Complete Action Step 18. Action Step 19 will help you spot opportunities in your industry

ACTION STEP 18

Identify three or four market gaps that look promising.

Now that you're hip-deep in your industry, scrutinize segments where you think you could survive and prosper. It's time to begin to profile your target customer.

Prepare a combination demographic-psychographic checklist to help you explore target markets. Include items for evaluating:

- Demographic data—age, sex, income, family size, education, socioeconomic status, place of residence, religion, political affiliation, and so on.
- Psychographic data—occupation, lifestyle, buying habits, dreams, interest and leisure activities, ambitions, and so on.

Or, if you're going after a commercial/industrial market, use company size, type of industry, number of employees, location, departments of large companies, and so on.

Tailor your checklist so that it provides a thorough profile of your target customer.

Table 3.1 Internet Commerce—10 Key Metrics

1. Canadians accessing the Internet	1998	37%
	1999	49%
	2000	57%
2. Canadian Internet users that have made a purchase via the Internet	1998	17%
	1999	25%
	2000	31%
3. Global Internet commerce	1999	$195 billion
4. Canadian e-commerce	1999	$4.4 billion
	• Business-to-business 87%	
	• Business-to-consumer 13%	
	2004 $151 billion (estimated)	
5. Canadian SMEs connected to the Internet (SMEs = 500 employees)	1997	31%
	1998	43%
	1999	61%
6. Canadian business (private sector) with websites	1999	22%
7. Businesses that use e-mail by size of firm (no. of employees), 2000	0–4	55%
	5–19	65%
	20–49	77%
8. Businesses that have websites by size of firm (no. of employees), 2000	0–4	18%
	5–19	28%
	20–49	39%
9. Businesses that sell online by size of firm (no. of employees), 2000	0–4	8%
	5–19	11%
	20–49	16%
10. Businesses that buy online by size of firm (no. of employees), 2000	0–4	14%
	5–19	17%
	20–49	21%

Source: Industry Canada, Canadian Internet Commerce Statistics Summary Sheet, retrieved from http://e-com.ic.gc.ca/english/research/rep/e-comstats.pdf

segment. If this exercise draws a blank, go back and do some more brainstorming. Remember, the process of idea generating is not linear. You may have to bounce around for a while.

STEP 5: BRAINSTORM FOR SOLUTIONS

Brainstorming is a process used by many groups—think tanks, middle managers, major corporations, and especially small businesses—to generate fresh ideas (see Box 3.5 on page 53). What follows is a short recap of the brainstorm held by Anne and Steve—with their best friends, Carol and Rick—as they started to transform problems into business opportunities.

> "Anne and I have invited you over for a pizza and to get some ideas on business opportunities," Steve began.
>
> "As you all know," said Anne, "we are thinking about starting our own business. We have done all kinds of research and have decided to focus on

Figure 3.3 Generating Ideas through Segmentation

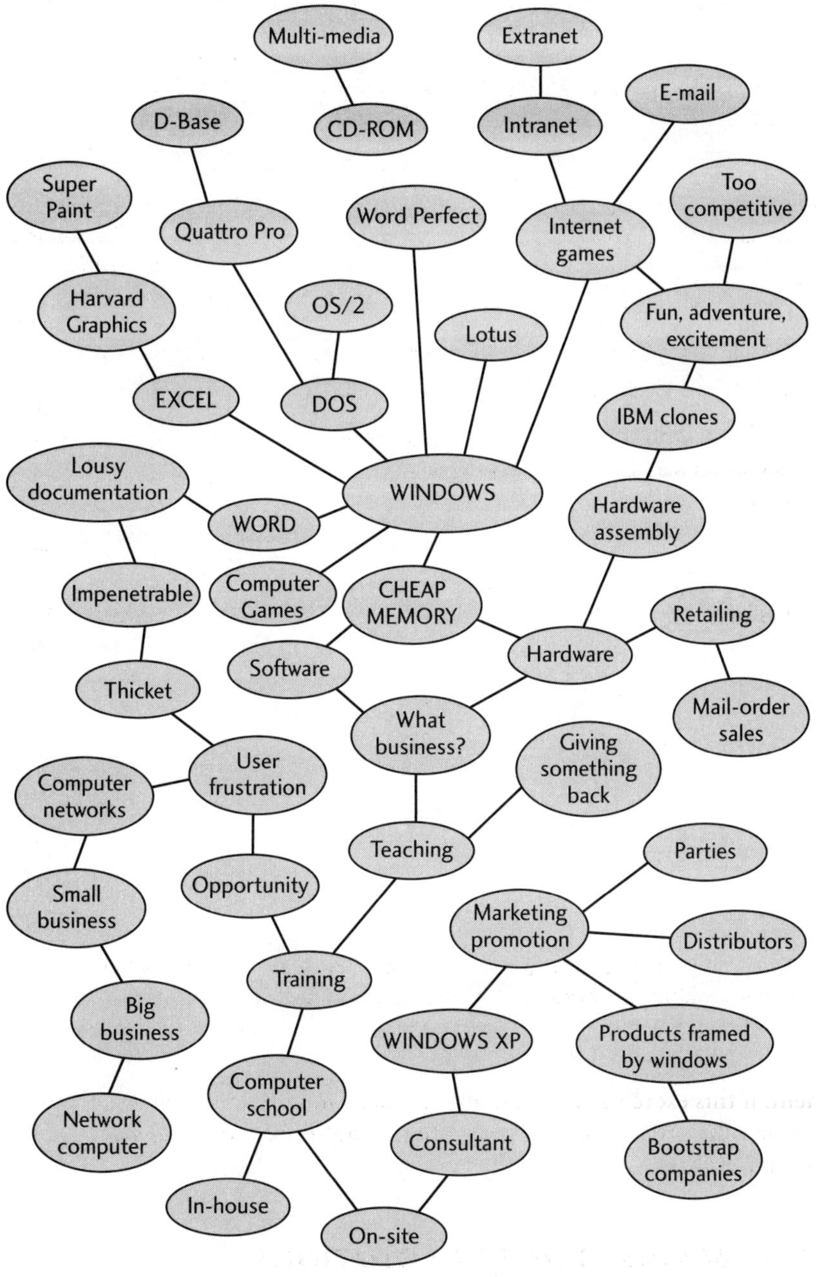

By segmenting the information industry, Anne and Steve were able to identify gaps with growth potential.

ACTION STEP 19

List problems that need solutions.

When you surveyed your friends in Action Step 12, you were approaching the list of problems you need to develop now. The difference is that the problems you are seeking now are those that are unique to the industry you've been exploring.

Get together with people who know something about your industry. Ask them for input and write down everything. Use this input to develop your list.

Each problem you identify multiplies your opportunities to prosper in your segment.

the information industry. We have even identified a few hot segments. We want to brainstorm for more ideas and some solutions to industry problems."

The four spent the first hour throwing out ideas. Some of these did not appear at first to be going anywhere. Rick, for example, thought the company should design computer games and go head-to-head with Sega and Sony. Ideas kept coming out—virtual training, leveraged buyouts,

Table 3.2 Small Business Gets Wired

According to Statistics Canada, the larger you get, the more technology you use.

Use of Technology	Small Firms (6–50 employees) %	Medium-sized Firms (51–250 employees) %	Large Firms (251+ employees) %
Network computer systems	44	75	95
Stand-alone computers	78	84	92
Packaged software	72	94	100
Use custom-developed software daily	41	73	89
Embedded computer systems	10	12	42

Source: Statistics Canada, "Small Business Gets Wired," adapted from *The Daily*, Cat. No. 11-001. Reprinted by permission.

virtual games, software manufacture, hardware assembly, retailing, web design, and on and on. Anne kept writing them down on a flip chart. Finally she said, "I'm exhausted. Time for a break."

When they came back, it was Steve's turn to keep track of the ideas. He flipped to a clean sheet on the chart. Over the next hour, the four friends created a mind map loaded with ideas for a business (see, for example, Figure 3.3).

As the brainstorm session wound down, they had identified two areas to explore. The first area was the installation of and training for network computing systems. Their target market would be small business. Steve had just finished reading about a Statistics Canada survey that said computer networks (especially LANs) were now being installed in small businesses at a record pace. Their second option was Intranet design and installation for small and medium-sized businesses.

"Well, this about wraps it up for tonight. Anne and I have a lot of ideas to mull over," concluded Steve. "We're going have to think about these two options."

"Wait a minute. How will you decide?" asked Carol.

"We'll have to do more research, then use a matrix grid. We learned about the matrix grid in class last week," Anne responded.

It's helpful—and in most cases necessary—to summarize after a brainstorming session so that you can identify the useful ideas. Let's summarize what happened in this session:

1. Using brainstorming, the team identified problems and possible solutions.
2. Most ideas were good ideas.
3. The two ideas that looked best involved computer networks and Intranet systems.
4. It did not seem that Anne and Steve could pursue both ideas at once. They had two different target customers. So, one might have to go on the back burner. (This is not a bad thing. It is always helpful to have budding ideas in your pocket, since every product or service has a life cycle.)

Box 3.5 Brainstorming—The Rules

Brainstorming requires an environment and attitude in which innovative thinking can occur. In a brainstorming session, everyone is encouraged to contribute ideas. Stimulation is provided by the ideas of others. The goal is to come up with lots of ideas, some of which may seem far-fetched or even erroneous, and then, as momentum grows, to see where concepts develop. A key to brainstorming is to reserve judgment initially so that creativity is not stifled. Lastly, brainstorming must be conducted in an environment in which "anything goes." People must not be made to think that their ideas are silly or stupid. Negative statements or actions, reservations, or criticisms are not allowed.

Now that you understand what brainstorming is and what it can accomplish for a business, give it a try with your own business. Assemble your partners or friends and go for it. Action Step 20 gives you some directions.

ACTION STEP 20

Brainstorm for solutions.

Now you need to get really creative. Dig out the list of problems in your industry that you made in Action Step 19. Every problem can be turned into an opportunity.

You'll generate better ideas in the long run if you just let your imagination roll. Don't be concerned with a lot of logic and reason—not at this stage. You might begin with a quick overview of what you know so far and then slide into possible (and impossible?) solutions. A cassette recorder can be useful.

Have fun.

STEP 6: MESH POSSIBLE SOLUTIONS WITH OPPORTUNITIES IN THE MARKETPLACE

While some people like to use lists or mind maps for arriving at opportunities, others prefer a more systematic method. A **matrix grid** can provide the desired structure for decision making. After you have brainstormed some possible solutions, you need to improve your focus on them and evaluate them. The matrix grid in Figure 3.4 helped Steve and Anne do this. The next day, after their brainstorm with Carol and Rick, they reviewed the various criteria on the list. Then they

MATRIX GRID
a screen through which ideas are passed in order to find solutions

Figure 3.4 Goals and Solutions

	Installing computers from home	Service home computers	Network computing	Internet fix-it services	Intranet training	Computer networks for small business	Web page design for small business	Advertising on the net	Specialized "packaged" software	Internet training	Electronic school for small business
Psychic rewards											
Teamwork											
Money											
Safety											
Growth industry											
Time											
Key people											
Fun, adventure, excitement											
Totals											

Use a matrix grid to mesh goals with solutions.

ACTION STEP 21

Mesh possible solutions with your goals and objectives, using a matrix grid.

A matrix analysis will help you focus, especially if you're working with a group and you have diverse objectives to satisfy. If you prepare a large grid and put it on the wall, all members of the team can participate.

Down the left side, list the goals you brainstormed in Action Step 16. Along the top, list the possible solutions you came up with in Action Step 20. Select a rating system to use for evaluating the match of each possible solution with each of your goals. It could be a 10-point scale or a plus-zero-minus system:

Plus (+) = 3
Zero (0) = 2
Minus (–) = 1

When you've rated all of the combinations, find the total for each column. The totals will indicate your best prospects. The rest is up to you.

ranked the top three in order of greatest importance and the bottom three in order of least importance. The top three were then assigned a value of three, while the bottom three were given a value of one. This way, each criterion did not receive the same value.

The group voted on several of the possible solutions they brainstormed. When the numbers were tallied, they decided the network computer business was the preferred option. They liked the idea of working with small businesses. This segment was really starting to heat up. They would provide advice and consulting in computer networks. Their target market would be smaller, independent business that wanted growth. If they succeeded, the Intranet would be the next focus.

Now prepare a matrix grid and weigh your criteria to help you focus on the best course of action. Action Step 21 tells you how to do it.

STEP 7: TAKE STOCK AND FOCUS

What have you learned about the opportunity selection process? Before you answer this, take some time to rethink what you want to achieve in your small business. If you feel a little uneasy about how fast you've run the last couple of laps, perhaps it's because you haven't yet identified your industry. It's time to take stock.

What is your industry?

____

What is your market gap?

____

What are some opportunities for you?

____

____

Now, before you lose the feel for the process, try sketching a rough picture of your journey through your favourite industry. If it doesn't feel like home, you should sense it now. Action Step 22 will help you do this. Now it's time to get started on writing a mission statement for your business.

Mission Statement

Now that you have identified your market opportunity—one that reflects your values—you need to think about a business mission.

MISSION STATEMENT
a statement of your company's purpose and aims

Your personal vision and values give you guidance and direction in the conduct of your life. In much the same way, a business mission—the **mission statement**—is a statement of your company's purpose and aims. Mission statements are normally connected to the values and vision of the business owner. In small business, a mission statement is concise (about 25 words or fewer), briefly describing the product or service, who the target customer is, and what niche or segment is the focus.

YOUR MISSION

Your mission is your road map. First, it states what you believe in—the difference that the organization makes. Second, it becomes a way of measuring your success as you evaluate your results over time against what you stated you wanted to do.

Third, it becomes your promotional message, as you incorporate it as part of your printed material.

A mission statement focuses on the here and now: it identifies the customer(s) and the critical process(es), and it states the level of performance.[5] Peter Drucker, in his book *The Practice of Management*, notes that we should think about a number of factors in developing a mission statement:[6]

1. *Customers.* Who is your target customer?
2. *Product or service.* What is your business all about—in a sentence or two?
3. *Geographic market.* Are you serving your local city, the province, Canada, or—if you are exporting—maybe even world markets?
4. *Concern for financial contribution and growth.* What returns do you expect on your investment and what growth pattern do you expect to achieve (e.g., growth of 5 percent per year)?
5. *Core values and beliefs.* Look back at the list of values you created earlier in this chapter. Are these values consistent with what you want to do?
6. *Self-concept.* Because of knowledge and expertise, you may bring to the business a special skill that will give you a unique niche.
7. *Concern for public image and stakeholders.* Are you an environmentally friendly business, or will you be contributing a percentage of all sales to charity, or are you actively involved in your community?
8. *Concern for employees.* Are you planning to run your business on a team basis? Or will you alone be it?
9. *Technology and systems.* Does your business offer a value-added benefit by using technology or a particular system?

Your mission statement is unique. Some people capture their thoughts in a few words, some take pages. Some people express them in poems, some in music, and some in art. Some experts advise that an empowering mission statement:[7]

- represents the deepest and best within you,
- fulfills the contribution your business will make, and
- deals with your vision and principle-based values.

For example, Anne and Steve's mission statement for their business might read like this:

> *To help growing small businesses improve their profitability, effectiveness, and long-term growth through the implementation of, and training in, computer networks.*

Here are a few other examples of mission statements:

> *To own a flower and gift shop that specializes in highly stylized floral arrangements for "special occasions," and that services the local community.*

> *To be a proud and profitable home-based business providing responsive and efficient word-processing services and laser-quality correspondence to local small businesses.*

> *To sell environmentally friendly cleaning products to convenience stores in our city in order to reduce our growing dependence on chemicals.*

In some cases, the mission statement is embedded or followed up with a set of guiding principles or personal beliefs of the company/owner. For example, Vivienne Jones operates a by-appointment jewellery studio out of her Victorian home in downtown Toronto.[8] Her mission—to create a very personal form of expression through her jewellery—is rooted in her statement of personal beliefs about the way she does business:

> Jewellery to me is much more than "decoration." I see it as a very personal form of expression, both for the maker and for the wearer. I make jewellery for personal creative expression, and my work is an expressive and versatile

ACTION STEP 22

Action Steps

Narrow the gaps and see your target customer emerge.

All right: you've found your segment and you've tested parts of it. Now you need to stay with this segment until you know whether or not it will work for you.

One way to keep concentrating is to make a simple sketch or list that sums up what you've learned so far. Figure 3.3 may help guide you. Use a large sheet of paper, because you need to consider all the important things you've learned here. Begin with your personal vision, values, and business goals and move on through a review of what has happened. After you've done your sketch, identify the gap in your industry that looks most promising for you.

> medium into which I can put my thoughts and ideas and esthetics. Intrinsic to the way I work is my imagining that the pieces I make will be worn and valued and hopefully will become a meaningful object in someone's life. It is perhaps because of the very personal attributes of jewellery that, when asked, I will enjoy working with a client to create a piece for them.

Vivienne Jones's beliefs help her stay true to herself, and to her vision of providing individualized jewellery that is both wearable and meaningful.

If you have been able to isolate an opportunity gap in your industry, it is now time to draft your mission statement. Complete Action Step 23.

Your Strategy

A **strategy** is a broad program for achieving an organization's objectives and thus implementing its vision. It creates a unified direction for the organization in terms of its many objectives. It also guides those choices that determine the nature and direction of an organization.

Before you start developing the strategy for your business, it is helpful to have a context in which competitive strategy is formulated. Figure 3.5 presents a model developed by Professor Michael E. Porter of Harvard Business School. As you review the model, you'll see that the left side refers to "Factors Internal to the

Figure 3.5 Context in Which Competitive Strategy Is Formulated

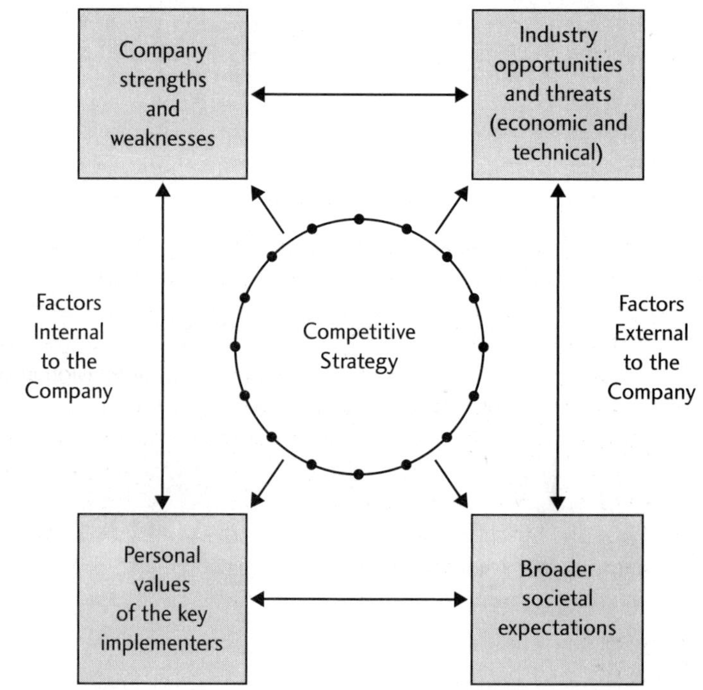

Use this model, developed by Michael E. Porter, to understand the context in which your business strategy will be formulated.

Source: Adapted with the permission of the Free Press, a Division of Simon & Schuster, from *Competitive Advantage: Creating and Sustaining Superior Performance* by Michael E. Porter. Copyright © 1985 by Michael E. Porter.

ACTION STEP 23

Draft your mission statement.

In a short paragraph, describe the purpose or main goal of your business.

- What is your product or service?
- Who is your target customer?
- What is the niche or market segment you aim to exploit?

You may also want to expand your statement by including your core set of values and beliefs, concern for stakeholders and the environment, or your concern for employee well-being.

Now go back and revisit your personal vision. Does your personal vision connect with your business mission? It should. If you are having trouble, here is one example:

Beatrice had a personal vision: "To live a life in which others would remember her with dignity and respect." Her business mission was "to be a respected flower and gift shop owner specializing in highly stylized floral arrangements for 'special occasions' and catering to her local community needs."

As her business mission, Beatrice wanted to be remembered with respect and dignity through her gift of flowers.

STRATEGY

the broad program for achieving an organization's objectives and implementing its vision

Company." You are required, as an entrepreneur, to look at your own strengths and weaknesses—after all, you are the company! Figure 3.5 helps you do that.

Your "Personal Values" will be contained in your value analysis and also in your mission statement. Don't take this section lightly, as it will be your internal guide to your overall business plan.

The right side of the competitive strategic model outlines the two major components to the "Factors External to the Company." "The Industry Opportunities and Threats" are critical to success and survival as a small business. As well, it is important to understand the "Broader Societal Expectations"—the trends discussed in Chapter 2 that your business will face.

Now is a good time to test your business idea. Do the E-Exercise in Box 3.6.

Box 3.6 E-Exercise

Test Your Business Idea

- **Atlantic Canada Opportunities Agency (ACOA)**
  www.acoa.ca/e/business/entrepreneurship/ideas/appendixa.shtml

Visit the "From Ideas to Business Opportunities" page on the ACOA website. Test your business idea by exploring these four themes.

1. *Personal considerations.* Does your business idea satisfy your personal goals and objectives?
2. *Marketing considerations.* Is there a market need for your product or service?
3. *Production considerations.* Will you be able to produce the required volume and quality of products and services?
4. *Financial considerations.* Can your operation satisfy the required financial goals?

In a Nutshell

In the first few chapters, we encouraged you to come to grips with your personal vision and goals and to look at the industry trends with new eyes. In this third chapter, we want you to begin to match your personal vision, values, and goals with market needs. Here we provide you with a seven-step opportunity selection process, and encourage you to brainstorm and complete a matrix grid to help you get your personal vision in sync with your business mission. To illustrate how this process works, we followed the progress of Steve and Anne, who ended up deciding to start their business in the field of network computers. Next, we wanted you to begin thinking about your mission statement. In the final analysis, we hope that we have helped you connect your personal vision to a mission statement for a new business opportunity, and that you are on the way to establishing your strategy for achieving your vision.

Key Terms

market gap
matrix grid
mission statement
strategy
values

Think Points for Success

- ✓ Your business must reflect your personal values. They provide you with guidance and direction in the conduct of your business and life.
- ✓ Select an opportunity by using the seven-step opportunity selection process as a guide.
- ✓ Align your mission statement with your personal values. The statement must state the purpose and aim of your firm.
- ✓ Establish a strategy that attains your vision.

Business Plan Building Block

CURRENT POSITION AND FUTURE OUTLOOK (REFER TO EARLIER WORK IN CHAPTER 2)

You will need to explain your current position and future outlook for this business projected out three to five years. If you are planning for an existing business, you must perform a critical analysis of your current situation and how you will grow the business over the next few years.

Focus on how you are unique and how to build on your strengths. If this is a start-up venture, base your forecast on research and your plans to exploit your market niche.

You began this process in Chapter 2. Now it's time to build, correct, and polish your first attempt.

My business is:

____

____

____

____

____

UNIQUENESS AND DIFFERENTIATION

It is important that you demonstrate that you are addressing an unfilled need. You are different and unique, and you understand the meaning of pricing and value from your potential customers' perspective.

YOUR BUSINESS IS UNIQUE BECAUSE ...

Your product is smaller, faster, neater, more flexible, lighter, more attractive, stronger, and so on. Or your service is quicker, more reliable, mobile. Your people are better trained, your location more convenient. Your prices are competitive and your business has many advantages over existing competition.

Nobody wants to hear about a "me too" business. Stress your differentiation, your position—and translate features into market-hungry benefits. It is important to show how you have an edge over the competition. Try to think in terms of a "personal niche monopoly."

MARKET OPPORTUNITIES

Based on your research, arrange the most promising opportunities in the marketplace according to the following categories:

1. New or emerging markets—gaps and niches
2. Neglected customer needs
3. Failing competitors
4. Complementary product mix
5. Expanded use of existing facilities
6. New geographical and international opportunities
7. Potential for profits

Rank by priority order those that are most attractive now and up to five years forward.

Checklist Questions and Actions to Develop Your Business Plan

POSITIONING YOURSELF AS AN ENTREPRENEUR FOR MARKET OPPORTUNITIES

- ❑ How is your product or service addressing the needs of the target market and offering benefits?
- ❑ What are your business and personal values?
- ❑ Define your market niche.
- ❑ Define the idea filters you used to establish the business viability for your product or service.
- ❑ Complete your mission statement.
- ❑ Revisit and update your business goals and objectives under Checklist Questions and Actions on page 39 (Chapter 2).
- ❑ Identify market segments that have market potential.
- ❑ List industry problems that your business may face, and describe how you would address them.

NOTES

1. Adapted from "Clear Visions: The Top 40 Under 40," The Financial Post Magazine, April 3, 1997, p. 22. Reprinted by permission of The Financial Post Magazine; BKM website (www.bkm.ca); and Industry Canada, Electronic Commerce in Canada, Success Stories, retrieved from http://e-com.ic.gc.ca/english/stories/bkmsucc.html

2. Kinnikinnick Foods website (www.kinnikinnick.ca); and Industry Canada, Electronic Commerce in Canada, Success Stories, retrieved from http://e-com.ic.gc.ca/english/stories/kinnikinnicksucc.html
3. Alex Tilley, March 27, 1995.
4. Personal contact with Art Coren, Kwantlen University College, June 1998.
5. Industry Canada, Steps to Competitiveness, The Quality Journey, retrieved from http://strategis.ic.gc.ca/SSG/sv00041e.html
6. Adapted from Peter F. Drucker, *The Practice of Management* (New York: Harper and Row, 1954).
7. Stephen R. Covey et al., *First Things First* (New York: Simon & Schuster, 1994).
8. Vivienne Jones website (www.viviennejones.com); and Janice Lindsay, "Jewel in Parkdale," *The Globe and Mail*, July 13, 2002, p. L7.

SUGGESTED READING

Brennar, Charles D. Jr. *Proactive Customer Service*. New York: AMACOM, 1997.

Christensen, Clayton M. *The Innovator's Dilemma: When New Technologies Cause Great Firms to Fail*. Boston: Harvard Business School Press, 2000.

Covey, Stephen R. et al. *First Things First*. New York: Simon & Schuster, 1994.

Crawford, Michael G. "The Seven Deadly Marketing Sins." *PROFIT*, January/March 1997, pp. 32–35.

Farber, Barry G. *State of the Art Selling*. Franklin Lakes, NJ: Career Press, 1995.

Gershman, Michael. *Getting It Right the Second Time*. Reading, MA: Addison-Wesley, 1991.

Gunther McGrath, Rita, and Ian MacMillian. *The Entrepreneurial Mindset*. Boston: Harvard Business School Press, 2000.

Hutchinson, Brian. "Merchants of Boom." *Canadian Business*, May 1997, pp. 39–48.

Kanbar, Maurice. *Secrets from an Inventor's Notebook*. New York: Penguin, 2002.

Kelley, Tom, with Jonathan Littman. *The Art of Innovation: Lessons in Creativity from IDEO*. New York: Doubleday, 2001.

Newell, Frederick. *Learn More About Customers and Use What You Learn*. New York: McGraw-Hill, 1997.

Wacker, Watts, Jim Taylor, and Howard B. Means. *The Visionary Handbook: Nine Paradoxes That Will Shape the Future of Your Business*. New York: HarperCollins, 2000.

chapter 4

Profiling Your Target Customer

BUSINESS PLAN BUILDING BLOCK

This chapter will help you collect information you will need to understand, develop a profile of, and connect with your target customer.

LEARNING OPPORTUNITIES

After reading this chapter, you should be able to:

- Understand that your key to survival in small business is the target customer.
- Use your intuition to forecast what will happen in your industry.
- Use primary and secondary research to profile your target customer.
- Simplify the messages you communicate through your business.
- Discover how popular magazines aim at the target customer.
- Match your target customer with what he or she reads, watches, and listens to.
- Become more aware of, and start being on the lookout for, potential partnerships, alliances, and associations.
- Recognize the market and the target customers who are about to surface.
- Gather critical market input from target customers through surveying field interviews.

ACTION STEP PREVIEW

24. Develop your own psychographic profile.
25. Research specific magazines in your business area.
26. Profile three firms using the Canadian Company Capabilities database.
27. Interview or survey prospective target customers.

During the 1990s, traditional bricks-and-mortar small business retailers in Canada had a rough ride. Retailing was not a growth market—just as Canadian giants like Eaton's, Consumers Distributing, and K-Mart found out. Growth, if any, was mostly in the "big box" format imported from the United States with the likes of Home Depot, Price Club/Costco, and Wal-Mart. Other bright spots included selected e-retailers (see Boxes 4.1 and 4.2).

One small Canadian retailer who bucked the retail trend and seemed to thrive over the late 1990s was Just Kid'n Children's Wear Ltd. of Langley, British Columbia. Owned by the brother-and-sister team of Kelly Cahill and Colleen Hazelwood, Just Kid'n was another PROFIT 100 success story.

According to the owners, the major reasons for their success were threefold. First, they latched on to a growth niche in the mature retail market. Their target was the so-called echo boom, the junior baby boom of the mid-1980s during which baby boomers finally decided to have kids of their own.

Chapter 4 will help you prepare part B of your business plan, "The Market and the Target Customer."

Second, they knew who their target customer (TC) was and what the TC wanted. Of their customers, 90 percent were women: 70 percent parents and 30 percent grandparents, relatives, and friends. They ranged in age from 25 to 45, and they tended to have mid to high incomes. According to Hazelwood, their customers were well-off boomers who were prepared to spend more for high-quality, hard-wearing, designer clothes for their kids.

Third, everyone at Just Kid'n constantly kept in touch with the TC. Simply knowing who the customer was and what she or he wanted was not enough. The heart of the Just Kid'n strategy is a customer list with over 100 000 target customer names, addresses, and phone numbers. This database enabled store managers to send a handwritten letter of thanks to the top customers for their business and offer them discount coupons. They even sent birthday cards to their customers' kids, offering a chance to win a free birthday party. Said Cahill: "With this database we can develop a relationship with our customer, who would have a good feeling about us and wanted to come back and shop again and again." The result was pure gold—80 percent of the company's business was repeat.[1]

When Mercedes-Benz, Procter & Gamble, Nike, and Philips Electronics decided they wanted to establish a compelling presence on the Internet, they turned to website developer Critical Mass, a Canadian business-to-business company that has earned a reputation for innovative web personalization.

Critical Mass, a Canadian success story with a host of international awards, began business in 1996. Cofounder Ted Hellard offered to develop the Mercedes-Benz website in three months—no money up front, no strings attached. "If you like it, then you can pay us for it," he told the luxury car manufacturer. "If you don't like it, you've risked nothing." They liked it. Critical Mass is now 240 employees strong, with offices in Toronto, Chicago, and New York.

According to Dan Evans, senior vice-president of Critical Mass, "People expect to go on the net and be treated as individuals. The concept of mass marketing has kind of disappeared. What the Internet has allowed marketers to do is to actually deliver on the promises of one-to-one relationship marketing." Reflect.com, a small U.S. company owned by Procter & Gamble, is his favourite example. The Reflect.com website offers beauty products that are available only online. Selling its own brand of makeup, shampoo, and other beauty products, Reflect.com lets customers tailor their own products by suggesting beauty ingredients they love most. "Critical Mass was involved right from the beginning," says Evans. "We helped develop the whole brand positioning for Reflect.com—the whole concept of profiling and creating a regimen—and then had to tie it all into the back end. Which is, how do you actually get a customized product produced and delivered to somebody within 24 hours?" The product, the container, even the wrapping are all formulated by the registered user through an online interactive process. Says Reflect.com CEO Ginger Kent:

"It's an incredibly powerful idea—like a throwback to the 1800s and how the apothecaries mixed formulas for people." [2]

The major focus of the last chapter was the product or service. Your prime concerns there were the following: "Do I have a product or service that is in a growth segment or a growth market?" and "Are my business goals consistent with my own personal values, goals, and long-term vision?" By now, we hope you have some pretty solid ideas as to what products or services are right for you. In the old way of thinking, entrepreneurs would have next focused their attention on the basic features of the product, such as size, colour, or price. We call this old view a "product-push" mentality, and it goes like this: "I think that there's a market there somewhere, and all I have to do is to produce what I think to be a quality product at a competitive price, and the market will respond with a sale."

Most marketers tell us that a product-push strategy does not work well in today's marketplace. More promising is an important trend called **relationship marketing**—the development of long-term, mutually beneficial, and cost-effective relationships with your customers. Relationship marketing emphasizes a **market-pull approach**. You determine what the customer wants through a customer profile and then adapt or create a product or service to satisfy this want or need. In other words, you design your business around what the customer wants rather than try to make the customer purchase what you want to produce. The market-pull approach explained, to a large degree, the success of Just Kid'n and Critical Mass in the opening vignettes. These thriving companies knew who their target customers were and what they wanted.

RELATIONSHIP MARKETING

the development of long-term, mutually beneficial, and cost-effective relationships with your customers

MARKET-PULL APPROACH

determining what the customer wants through a customer profile and then adapting or creating a product or service to satisfy this want or need

In this chapter, we want you to start thinking about how you can develop a market-pull strategy. This means you will have to begin with a customer profile. We'll also show you how to use key secondary and primary research and resources to your advantage.

The Power of Profiling

Your **target customer (TC)** is the person, type of person, or business that has the highest probability of buying your product or service. An understanding of the needs of the TC is your key to survival in small business. For that reason, you will have to do a profile of your customer. **Profiling** is about describing the needs and behaviour of your TC. In this chapter, we'll focus on specific profiling techniques and sources to help you understand that elusive customer. But first, let's take a look at the different kinds of target customers. Entrepreneurs that we have known tell us you should be watching for at least three target customer groups:

TARGET CUSTOMER (TC)

a person, type of person, or business that has the highest probability of buying your product or service

PROFILING

describing the needs and behaviour of your target customer

1. *Primary.* This TC is perfect for your business and could be a heavy user.
2. *Secondary.* This one almost slips away before you can focus the camera. Sometimes your secondary TC will lead you to the third customer, who is invisible at first.
3. *Invisible.* This customer appears after you open the doors, after you have the courage to go ahead and start your business.

Your primary and secondary target customers are the only customers that you can see right now. However, once you open your business, a new customer may arrive on the scene, and you must always be ready to change so that you can take advantage of new market opportunities. In this chapter, we focus on your primary and secondary customers, but we encourage you to always remember that there are elusive "invisible" customers—the ones that seem to come out of the woodwork once you start your business.

Box 4.1 Bookmark This

Canadian Retailing Trends

Here are two sites that can help you understand the changes that are taking place in Canadian retailing.

- **retailinteractive.ca**
  http://retailinteractive.ca/SSG/ri00006e.html
  Retailinteractive.ca. is a partnership between the Retail Council of Canada and Industry Canada. This site provides independent and small chain retailers with current and historical retail information. For example, the "Canadian Consumer Demographics" page (http://retailinteractive.ca/SSG/ri00140e.html) provides consumer demographics that will help you profile your target market. The "Industry Background" page (http://retailinteractive.ca/SSG/ri00100e.html) will help you as you begin to refine your customer strategy and broaden your market reach. The "Internet Use in Canada" page (http://retailinteractive.ca/SSG/ri00120e.html) tracks how the Internet is changing the way Canadians shop and communicate.
- **Canadian Internet Retailing Report**
  http://strategis.ic.gc.ca/SSG/ir01589e.html
  This page provides an overview of how consumers, technology enablers, and retailers are using the Internet.

There are two basic types of customer profiles:

1. Consumer (or end user)
2. Business-to-business (or supply chain)

We will begin with a consumer profile.

CONSUMER OR END-USER PROFILE

In some businesses the target customer or TC may well be the end user or consumer. This was the situation for Just Kid'n in one of the opening vignettes. Just Kid'n sold its products directly to the customer through its retail outlets. It was a **business-to-consumer (B2C) company** because its "heavy" TC was the consumer or end user. If you're planning to start a B2C company, your customer profile will require **demographics**—the segmenting and statistical analysis of your TC by age, sex, income, education, location, and the like. Recall, for example, that in the case of Just Kid'n, the primary TCs were parents, mainly women between the ages of 25 and 45. You'll also need a new tool called **psychographics**—the first-hand intuitive insight into lifestyle, buying habits, patterns of consumption, and attitudes. Just Kid'n's psychographic target was the high-income boomers who were prepared to pay more for quality, hard-wearing, designer clothes. Although demographics is an important profiling tool, marketers today are beginning to place more emphasis on psychographics. Let's step back for a moment and understand the rationale for this recent marketing trend.

BUSINESS-TO-CONSUMER (B2C) COMPANY
a firm whose "heavy" TC is the consumer or end user

DEMOGRAPHICS
key characteristics of a group of people, such as age, sex, income, and where they live

PSYCHOGRAPHICS
segmenting of the population by lifestyle behaviour, buying habits, patterns of consumption, and attitudes

We've talked about the importance of demographics and how the boomers, in particular, have and will continue to affect market trends. In a strange way, this "bulging" phenomenon (social change), combined with our knowledge-based/change economy (economic change), has forced marketers to ask why

Box 4.2 E-Exercise

- **E-Retailer Profiles**
  http://retailinteractive.ca/SSG/ri00400e.html

Here you will find profiles and assessments of a number of Canadian e-retailers. Learn from their successes, and their mistakes. Click on one of the profiled e-retailer links.
- What were the lessons learned?
- What were the successes and challenges?

people purchase products or services, not simply who is buying. Although the demographics of the population are still predictable, the lifestyle and buying habits are no longer tied to demographics. Today, we have to know *why* people are buying. For example, two adults with a combined income of $75 000, but with no children (**D**ouble-**I**ncome-**N**o-**K**ids) have different spending patterns than two adults earning $75 000 to $125 000, but with four children. Why? Because these two groups have completely different wants and values. People now buy products and services that reflect the needs of their lifestyles, not necessarily their sex, age, or income. The whys and wants of consumer purchases are what psychographics is all about. It is a process of segmenting the population by lifestyles and values, recognizing that people in each segment or slice have different reasons for making a purchase.

There are a number of "propriety" psychographic models in use in North America. Two of the most prominent are the VALS (value and lifestyle model) from SRI International in the United States and the Goldfarb model, which is Canadian but has also been adapted in the United States. We'll focus here on the Goldfarb model, which classifies the Canadian population into nine psychographic segments: disinterested outsiders, tie-dyed greys, protective providers, up and comers, les "petite vie," mavericks, contented traditionalists, joiner activists II, and passive malcontents. Some key characteristics of each of these categories are shown in Figure 4.1 and Box 4.3.

Several Canadian companies can provide you with a psychographic or lifestyle profile for a specific area. For example, Compusearch can provide lifestyles data by postal code. These kinds of data can be obtained in published form for large areas, but when it comes to a specific neighbourhood, you have to pay for the data on that. The cost can range from hundreds of dollars to hundreds of thousands of dollars, depending on the detail you might need. When it's all said and done, you will probably have to do a lot of your own research to get a psychographic handle on your target customer—mainly because of cost factors. This is your opportunity to practise your new-eyes research and learn why people buy things. At worst, you will have fun playing marketing detective.

Now, if you just can't afford the cost of contracting out a psychographic analysis, don't fret. This may be your opportunity to piggyback all of the information gathered for use by media sources. Check out Box 4.4 on page 69 to see how one entrepreneurial firm, D-Code, profiles its target customer—the Nexus generation. Then use Action Step 24 to develop your own psychographic profile.

ACTION STEP 24

Develop your own psychographic profile.

Eventually, you're going to have to do a profile of your target customer. To get some practice and have a little fun in the process, profile yourself as a target customer. You can find out what your own needs and attitudes are by taking the psychographic text on the Goldfarb Consultants website. Visit www.goldfarbconsultants.com, click on Who Are You, and follow the test instructions.

You may even want to invite a few friends to a "psychographic" party. Ask questions. What are their motivators? Why does one brand appeal more than another? This informal primary research will help you understand why people buy specific products and services.

Figure 4.2 Goldfarb Psychographic Segments as a Percentage of the Canadian Population

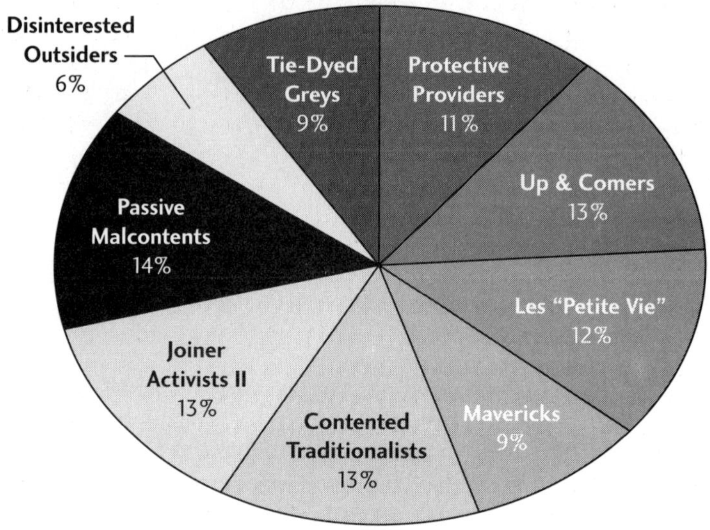

Source: Goldfarb Consultants, retrieved from http://www.goldfarbconsultants.com/psycho/index.html

Box 4.3 Key Characteristics of the Nine Goldfarb Psychographic Segments

Disinterested Outsiders are much less involved and connected with the society around them than their peers. They display a casual indifference to the problems facing society and have little empathy for others or interest in anything outside their immediate lives. They are not ambitious and view work mainly as a way to pay the bills rather than as part of a greater career plan.

Other personality and lifestyle characteristics include:

- Willing to bend rules, ignore ethics when they want something
- Not intellectually curious
- Tend to give up easily when challenged
- Less comfortable with computers, technology than others
- Watch a lot of television (sports, talk shows)
- Not health-conscious
- Somewhat materialistic

Tie-Dyed Greys have very progressive attitudes toward drugs, civil liberties, and the role of women in society, attitudes that are in many ways a carryover from those seen in the "flower children" of the late 1960s. Tie-Dyed Greys are less interested than others in material possessions and place much less emphasis on marriage and children than most Canadians. They enjoy solitude and quiet activities but remain social, although they are less likely than others to enjoy going to parties.

Other personality and lifestyle characteristics include:

- Open-minded on most moral issues (abortion, homosexuality, prostitution)
- Interested in politics and international issues
- Suspicious of big business ethics
- Environmentally conscious

- Enjoy non-fiction programs (news, documentaries) on television
- Enjoy attending cultural events such as theatre, the symphony
- See themselves as more independent than their peers

Protective Providers are hard-working people who value personal initiative and have a very strong commitment to their family responsibilities. They are likely to feel some financial pressures, and as a result place great importance on money issues and are concerned about their ability to keep pace with any increases in the cost of living. They are not likely to get involved in politics or with groups seeking social change and less likely to do volunteer work than others.

Other personality and lifestyle characteristics include:

- Distrustful of governments, politicians
- Price-conscious shoppers
- Concerned about crime, supportive of tougher penalties for criminals
- Proud of their achievements and sensitive to criticism
- Enjoy outdoor activities such as golfing, fishing, hunting, and gardening
- Read less than most other people

Up and Comers are outgoing individuals who do not enjoy spending time alone on solitary pursuits. They are materialistic and looking for instant gratification, as they like to buy the latest gadgets and own expensive things. Up and Comers tend to be conformists who do not enjoy standing out from friends or the rest of society. Maintaining a religious or spiritual side is likely to be of some importance to these individuals.

Other personality and lifestyle characteristics include:

- Optimistic about personal future
- Ambitious, seeking wealth and power
- Somewhat self-centred
- Traditional moral values—uncomfortable with homosexuality, common-law relationships, and new technologies such as in-vitro fertilization and cloning
- Unlikely to volunteer or give much to charity
- Enjoy watching comedies and game shows on TV
- Do not tend to "watch what they eat" or use vitamins or supplements

Les "Petite Vie" individuals are uncomfortable with the hectic pace of modern life and prefer to do things in a relaxed, deliberate manner. Friends and family are of paramount importance to these people, who are very active socially in a small, confined circle of those they know well. They do not view themselves as independent and are less likely than others to see themselves as leaders. They tend to have a high degree of confidence and respect for business leaders and are more likely than most to support government involvement in the economy.

Other personality and lifestyle characteristics include:

- Not likely to try new brands
- Very concerned about crime and violence in society
- Worried about social issues (AIDS, family violence, poverty) but give little to charity and do not volunteer their time
- Open-minded about sexual matters
- Neat and tidy individuals
- Suspicious of strangers, newcomers
- Watch a lot of television

Mavericks are very strong believers in the rights of individuals and are hostile to government intervention in the lives of citizens. They are very confident and self-reliant, and prefer to work out problems on their own rather than ask for or accept help from others. They are unpretentious people who give little thought to the impression they make on others and are not concerned about their appearance. They are more likely than others to engage in risky activities for the fun of it and enjoy seeking out new adventures.

Other personality and lifestyle characteristics include:

- Willing to spend money if it will save them time
- Natural leaders, comfortable with giving direction

- Enjoy challenges, work well under pressure
- Seeking wealth, power more than many others
- Slightly dissatisfied with their current work and home life
- Computer-savvy
- Conservative moral views on homosexuality and working women, but open-minded about modern concerns such as animal organ transplants, cloning
- Interested in politics

Contented Traditionalists are well-adjusted, happy individuals who believe they have achieved a balance in life that would be the envy of others. They place great importance on the family (and in particular children) and consider the well-being of their family ahead of their own personal goals. Loyalty to friends is a very important value for them, and they are trusting of others. They are likely to be involved in their community, both in terms of volunteering and in giving to charitable causes.

Other personality and lifestyle characteristics include:

- Strong religious/spiritual focus
- Conservative values (particularly sexual issues)
- Very ethical and "play-by-the-rules"
- Strong belief in work ethic
- Respectful of authority figures
- Highly organized
- Do not see themselves as materialistic
- Not mechanically inclined

Joiner Activists II are intellectually curious people who highly value education and personal growth. They are engaged in their jobs and are among the most satisfied with their work and with the amount of challenge in their life. They have liberal social attitudes on issues such as homosexuality, abortion, and immigration, and do not support tougher criminal laws or increased police powers. They are politically active and involved in their community, and are willing to take action to right perceived wrongs.

Other personality and lifestyle characteristics include:

- Optimistic about the future (and likely to be doing well financially now)
- Supportive of working women, women's rights
- Secular, non-religious approach to life
- Sympathetic to plight of others
- Have faith in governments and public servants
- Environmentalists, participate in recycling, composting
- Prefer news, documentaries, and educational programs on television
- Health-conscious
- Enjoy cultural activities (theatre, art galleries)

Passive Malcontents are generally unhappy with their daily life at present and are less satisfied with their work, family situation, and social life than others. They place high importance on law and order and are more supportive of tougher sentences for criminals and increased police powers than most other groups. They are less likely than most to make plans for the future and are probably not making a concerted effort to change their life and reach their goals.

Other personality and lifestyle characteristics include:

- Patriotic
- Lack self-confidence
- Enjoy quiet, solitary activities rather than parties and social gatherings
- Tend to trust others and the government to "do the right thing"
- Probably watch more television than they care to admit
- Less likely than others to exercise, are not very health-conscious

Source: Goldfarb Consultants, retrieved from www.goldfarbconsultants.com

Box 4.4 Target Market—The Nexus Generation

Businesses, governments, or other organizations trying to reach Generation X soon come up against a major roadblock: no one knows *exactly* who or what Generation X is!

According to some, Generation X is all about the year you were born: 1963, 1969, or (depending on who's talking), 1976. On the one hand, Generation Xers have been described as wanderers, slackers, and couch potatoes interested only in watching *Simpsons* reruns. On the other hand, they have been portrayed as the most conservative, hard-working generation since those born during the Great Depression. Similarly, some experts say Xers are serious about marriage, while others see the X-generation as a group reluctant to make commitments.

Robert Barnard feels the term Generation X, as a label, is widely overused, ambiguous, and a cliché. "It means too many things to too many different people," says Barnard, a thirtysomething Xer from Toronto. Barnard founded D-Code Inc., a small consulting firm that helps companies and government departments better understand what makes 18- to 34-year-olds tick. In place of the term "Generation-X," D-Code uses the phrase "Nexus generation" to characterize this target group. Nexus means a bridge or connection; in this case, the connection is between the industrial age and the birth of the information age.

D-Code helps its private- and public-sector clients decipher the aspirations, preferences, and unique features of the age group born at this critical nexus. It works with them to design marketing, human resource, or public policy strategies that connect with the Nexus generation, consumers, employees, and citizens. In the process, D-Code strives to build bridges across generations.

The Nexus group is a powerful demographic making up about one-third of the Canadian population. According to D-Code, there are a number of key psychographic likes and dislikes of the Nexus generation:

- For Nexus, financial compensation is not as important as it is to the preceding generations. Nexus ranks quality of life (e.g., longer vacations) and opportunities for on-the-job training ahead of a whopping paycheque.
- Nexus is more skeptical and has less confidence in traditional institutions such as the church, the university, the nuclear family, the state, and the corporation.
- Nexus is more media-savvy, techno-literate, educated, and worldly than any previous generation.
- Nexus is composed of "experience seekers" who put off marriage, kids, and house payments longer than those in previous generations.
- Nexus is more comfortable—and less anxious—about change.
- Nexus uses the Internet more than do other demographic groups.
- For Nexus, mall business ownership is the most desirable occupation.

Sources: Based on personal correspondence with D-Code Inc.; D-Code's website at http://www.d-code.com; and Gayle MacDonald, "The Eyes and Ears of a Generation," *The Globe and Mail*, February 4, 1997, B11.

WHAT WE CAN LEARN FROM MEDIA SOURCES

Mina Cohen was an archaeologist and teacher by training. She had worked on numerous excavations and had been a pedagogic adviser of External Affairs and a teacher at a local high school. Despite her talents and extensive training, it seemed that she was always worried about her next job. The market just wasn't there for her talents. She even had to take a few secretarial jobs to supplement her income.

One day in late summer, she decided to take control of her life and entered a small business program at a local college. At first the course seemed incomprehensible. Techniques such as brainstorming and mind mapping were foreign to her; up to this point, she had been taught, in a "right-brained" manner, to be logical. In the end, however, she decided to persist and stay in the course. Finally, after a few group brainstorming sessions and extensive primary and secondary research, she had an idea: Why not offer archaeological excursions? She would be in the "holidays-with-a-purpose" business. But who were her target customers?

One fall evening, she was curled up, browsing her favourite magazine, *Equinox*. It suddenly occurred to her that these readers might just be her target market. After all, this was *her* favourite magazine. That's when it hit her. Why not send away for the publisher's secondary data on its target readership? In less than a week, the information arrived.

After a quick study of the *Equinox* secondary data, she began to realize that her idea had a real chance to make it. Her primary target market would be well-off couples who wanted to travel and learn. The publisher's data confirmed her intuition and ideas based on her ad-count analysis. Now she was sure that she had a growing market for her services. Her target customers were affluent (they could pay for her services), influential (they would tell and influence others about them), active (they liked travelling and learning), and increasing in number (a large segment would be boomers aged 25 to 49). It didn't take her long to summarize the demographic and psychographic information from the publisher, which would become an important part of the marketing section of her business plan.

As we learned from Mina Cohen, an easy way to understand the power of profiling is to analyze media sources that are aimed at different target markets.

Most, if not all, of the major media sources have conducted extensive research on the demographic and psychographic profiles of their target customer. In many cases, these profiles are available through media kits from the advertising departments of the media sources. For example, if your target customer were travel-oriented, you could ask a travel-related magazine for its readership profile. The key here is, if you know which media sources your target customer reads, listens to, or watches, you can get in-depth profiles from these media companies because they need to know this information for their advertising.

In this section, we focus on magazines (while still recognizing the Internet as an important media source). However, you can take advantage of almost any of the media—especially commercial ones—because of the useful information contained in ads. We could just as easily expand our discussion to include TV programs and radio stations and, to a lesser extent, books and movies.

What can you learn about target markets, consumption patterns, and buying power from the advertisements in a magazine? Put yourself in an analytical frame of mind. Begin by counting the ads. Then notice the types of products that dominate the ads; these ads are probably aimed at the heavy users of those products. Next, study the models; they are fantasy images with which the target customer is expected to identify, connect, remember. The activities pictured in the ads enlarge the fantasy, and the words link it to real life. A good ad becomes a slice of life, a picture that beckons the customer inside, toward the product.

In addition to magazines, customer profiles are also available from newspapers and radio and TV stations. The point is, media advertisers spend lots of money on trying to get the attention of their prospective target customers. We can benefit from this big business advertising. Now it's time to focus your attention on some specific media sources. Use Action Step 25 to conduct research on your target customer at little or no cost to you.

BUSINESS-TO-BUSINESS PROFILE

Many small businesses do not deal directly with the final consumer. Instead, they are a subcontractor and part of the so-called supply chain. Suppose, for a moment, that you decide to start your own editing business. Your target customer may be a publisher, whose customers may be university and college faculty and teaching staff, whose customers are the consumer—the student. As an editor, you have become part of the supply chain in the production of a book. Your target customer will not be the consumer or end user (the student); it will be another business or supplier (in this case, a publisher). As a subcontractor, you will need to profile other businesses—target customers—that could use your services.

Critical Mass, the website developer profiled in one of the opening vignettes, is one example of a **business-to-business (B2B) company** whose target market is other businesses that, in turn, deal with the end user. B2B niche players like Critical Mass are, to a large extent, a byproduct of the **outsourcing** trend of the 1990s—a trend that has given birth to thousands of companies or individuals whose sole purpose is providing services or products, on a contract basis, to other businesses. Factors you should consider when developing your B2B profile are listed in Box 4.5.

As a member of the B2B supply chain, your ultimate goal is to create partnerships, joint ventures, alliances, or associations with your target customer. Rick Spence, in his analysis of Canada's fastest-growing PROFIT 100 companies, con-

Box 4.5 Profiling Other Businesses

Your B2B profile should include the following information:

Company Profile

- Size of business (sales revenue, number of employees, etc.)
- Type of business (e.g., consumer or industrial products)
- Type of ownership (e.g., public, federal, private, provincial, cooperative, non-profit)
- Account size
- Number of years in business
- Location
- Credit risk

End-User Profile

- End-use application
- Ability to reach decision-maker
- Purchase decision (group or individual)

Industry Profile

- Economic and technological trends affecting various industries
- Competing firms
- International vs. Canadian sales
- Barriers to entry

ACTION STEP 25

Research specific magazines in your business area.

Choose at least two magazines that you think your target customer would read. Begin by conducting some new-eyes research, following the example of our analysis of *Equinox*. What strikes your eye? Are the ads aimed at men? At women? At teens or seniors? What appears to be the age range of the target customer? What's the income range? What Goldfarb psychographic group are they targeting? What message are they trying to convey?

Next, turn your attention to primary research. Interview magazine buyers. Ask them why they buy the magazine. Use what they say to add to your reader profile. Without being too obvious, collect as much demographic and psychographic data as you can on these shoppers. Could any of them be your target customer?

Now we want you to do some secondary research. Using your business letterhead, write to the magazines' display advertising departments. Ask for media kits and reader profiles. (If you don't have stationery yet, or if you are in a hurry, see if you can contact them over the Internet or give them a call.)

When the profiles arrive, check them out. How close were your new-eyes and primary research profiles? Are you starting to get a clearer picture of who your target customer is and what she or he wants?

BUSINESS-TO-BUSINESS (B2B) COMPANY

a firm whose target market is other businesses

OUTSOURCING

farming out one or more company operations to specialists

cluded that these types of associations were a key offence weapon of fast-growth companies, helping them to:[3]

- develop better products
- stretch their marketing dollars
- reach more customers
- obtain more feedback on their products or services
- provide better customer service
- extend their operations around the block or around the world

Ten tips for developing and nurturing a successful alliance are shown in Box 4.6. You'll want to keep these in mind, but first you should start a list of possible TCs. You'll need to conduct business profiles of potential partners or business associates. There are all kinds of secondary information you can draw on. In the next few chapters, you'll learn about a number of "hard copy" sources, such as *Fraser's Canadian Trade Directory*. For now, to get you started, we want to introduce you to what we think is the key source of business information, Canadian Company Capabilities, which can be found on the Industry Canada, Strategis website

Box 4.6 Ten Tips for Joint Ventures and Strategic Alliances

Small Business Tips

Successful business alliances are like standing on one foot: easier to start than to maintain. Here are 10 tips on developing and nurturing the most productive joint ventures and strategic alliances possible.

1. *Have a common purpose.* Articulate shared interests and objectives early in the process.
2. *Conduct research.* Assess your organization's strengths and weaknesses. Know where you want to go, and then identify the areas where you need help. Research the market to learn who can help you reach your goals.
3. *Consider mutual benefits.* Before you propose an alliance or joint project to another organization, ask yourself, "What's in it for them?"
4. *Provide a structure.* Having some kind of structure (e.g., which partner does what, and when) in place at the outset can be a useful safeguard against problems.
5. *Consider potential disadvantages.* Identify and address any factors that may undermine the project.
6. *Invest in human resources.* Put the best available person(s) on the project. Your associates and partners deserve quick access to the relevant decision-makers.
7. *Put it in writing.* Spell out your mutual expectations and responsibilities in a contract. Determine allocation of costs. Both sides should obtain legal advice.
8. *Stay in touch.* Keep open lines of communication with your partners. They can be formal (regular reports) or informal ("let's meet for coffee").
9. *Keep tabs.* Use regular feedback sessions to review the project's progress. Is it meeting the goals of both parties? If not, how can you fix things?
10. *Exit stage left.* Before forming an alliance, determine how either side can get out.

Sources: Rick Spence, *Secrets of Success from Canada's Fastest-Growing Companies* (Toronto: John Wiley & Sons Canada, 1997), pp. 117–118; Industry Canada, Strategis, Strategic Alliances: The Concept and Rationale, retrieved from http://strategis.ic.gc.ca/SSG/1/ca00388e.html; and Industry Canada, Strategis, Shared Success, retrieved from http://strategis.ic.gc.ca/SSG/sv00024e.html

(http://strategis.ic.gc.ca). Connecting to Canadian Company Capabilities will help you:

- Locate a list of your potential target customers
- Promote your new business venture
- Provide market research
- Locate Canadian suppliers
- Discover potential partnerships and associations
- Research your competition
- Uncover export opportunities

Canadian Company Capabilities is a database that contains over 40 000 company profiles and over 200 000 products, services, and technologies. As of 2002, this free Industry Canada online service allows you to search for and profile your potential TC by product, geography, or activity. When you are ready to start your business, you will want to register your company in the Canadian Company Capabilities database and promote your products or services worldwide. For now, we want you to learn about this amazing website, get some practice in profiling potential target companies, and begin learning about the power of the Internet. You will even need this source when it comes time to research your competition. Complete Action Step 26.

ACTION STEP 26

Profile three firms using the Canadian Company Capabilities database.
Canadian Company Capabilities
http://strategis.ic.gc.ca/sc_coinf/ccc/engdoc/homepage.html

The Canadian Company Capabilities database on the Strategis website (http://strategis.ic.gc.ca) helps businesses find competitors or organizations that can supply them with products or services they need. The database offers two types of searches: a quick search and a refined search that allows you to search by product, city sales, etc.

Go to the Canadian Company Capabilities database. Select three firms that could be your target customer and carry out a "complete profile" of each of these firms. Just follow the instructions on the site.

If your target customer (TC) is not another business, or you're still not sure exactly who your TC is, we suggest you use this Action Step to practise your profiling skills. It is a great source to learn about potential suppliers or your potential competition. Select any three companies to profile and begin learning about the power of the Internet.

If you don't find what you need, you may want to click on Other Canadian Company Databases. There you will find links to sites that will help you expand your B2B profile.

Primary Research Can Help Too

Secondary sources of demographic, psychographic, or business profiling information may be enough to target customers. Chances are, though, that you'll need to test your profile against reality. Field interviewing and surveying are two important primary research tools that can help you get a more accurate profile of your target customer.

FIELD INTERVIEWING TARGET CUSTOMERS

A lot of people go into small business because they don't have much choice. Many of them have to learn new skills and learn them fast. Fortunately, entrepreneurs tend to be bright, creative, and hard-working. Julia Gonzales is a good example.

> "It's no secret that I was distressed when my husband was transferred. I didn't blame him wanting the transfer; I would have wanted it, too. But I had a terrific job as manager of a full-line baby furniture and bedding store, and to keep both job and husband I'd have had to commute over 160 kilometres daily, five days a week. So, I quit my job.
>
> "But I missed the store, and it was hard living on one salary when we'd gotten used to two. When I started to look for work, I found that my reputation had preceded me. Store owners knew of the place where I'd worked, and they were pretty sure that all I wanted was to work for them to get a feel for the area so that I could open a store of my own and compete with them.
>
> "This gave me an idea. I hadn't *considered* doing that. So when I couldn't find work, I decided to go for it, to go ahead and compete with them. Their fear gave me confidence!
>
> "One thing I learned on my way up from stock clerk to store manager was that it pays to know your customer. So, in the mornings I'd get the

kids off to school, do a few chores, and drive to a baby store. I'd park my car a block away and when customers came out of the store, I'd strike up conversations with them.

"'Hi!' I'd say. 'My name's Julia Gonzales, and I'm doing market research for a major manufacturer who's interested in this area. I'm wondering if you might have a minute to answer a few questions about babies.'

"My enthusiasm must have helped. I like people and babies, and I guess it shows. Being a mother helps me understand other mothers, too. I always dressed up a little bit and carried a clipboard. I'd ask the obvious questions like:

- What do you like about this store?
- What things did you buy?
- Were the people helpful and courteous?

"Sometimes I parked in the alley to research the delivery trucks. At the beach and the shopping malls, I would stop every pregnant woman I saw. I developed a separate list of questions for pregnant women:

- Have you had a baby shower?
- Which gifts did you like best?
- Which gifts seemed most useful?
- What things are you buying before your baby comes?
- What things are you waiting to buy?
- How are you going to decorate the baby's room?
- What do you really need the most?

"The research was time-consuming, but after 30 interviews I had enough information to make some very sound decisions. I also knew the weaknesses of my competition."

One way to get primary data is to interview or conduct focus group discussions among potential target customers, and in some cases this may be the way to go. You could also interview other businesses if your target customer is the consumer or end user.

We saw how Julia Gonzales used interviewing to help her locate her new store. In the next chapter, we'll come back to interviewing again when we're researching our competition. In the meantime, we'll move on and use another skill: surveying to get a more refined picture of our target customer.

SURVEYING TARGET CUSTOMERS

Let's see how Elizabeth Wood used the survey technique to get her started on her own business.

Elizabeth was a supervisor at a local textile plant. Over the last few years, things had been tough. It seemed that she was always hearing about someone being laid off. She wondered when it would be her turn. But as time rolled on, she was becoming less and less concerned. She loved to be creative with food, and she had set her goal: opening a small neighbourhood restaurant.

For some time now, she had been developing her skills in business. She had taken several courses in restaurant and bar management. Next, she took a small business course at a local university. In an attempt to get a handle on her target customer, she read many studies on the eating-out habits of Canadians. She knew that there was a trend to eating outside the home, but what did this mean for her local market? This secondary research was very revealing, but she just couldn't risk her future on someone else's research. She decided to do her own survey. She studied survey design and got plenty of advice from her professor, who had lots of experience in surveying. Crazy's Roadhouse was one of the most popular eating spots in town. Often, Elizabeth would have a bite to eat there, and she got to know Crazy's owner, Max, quite well. She told Max about her dream to open a small restaurant some day, and about how much she was learning in her small business course. They got to talking, and at last Max agreed to let Elizabeth do her survey of his customers. After all, the price was right. She would do the survey free of charge and would give Max her results—a classic win-win proposition.

Elizabeth spent the next few weeks designing her survey. How many customers should she survey? When should she survey? How should she conduct herself? There was so much to do. Fortunately, with the help of her small business teacher, Max, and the team she had been working with in school, she launched a week-long survey of Max's customers. To Max's surprise, customers wanted to fill out the questionnaire. To Elizabeth's surprise, she heard Max explaining to someone that he thought it was about time he learned a little bit more about what the customer wanted.

Stay tuned. We'll hear more about the results of Elizabeth's survey later on. But for now here are three of the major findings related to Max's target customer:

1. The lunch trade (Monday to Friday) customers were older than expected: almost 40 percent were 35–44. In contrast, the weekend customers were younger: 52 percent were 25–44. As for the "after five" crowd, the average customer was even younger—almost 33 percent were under 25.
2. Regarding income, Elizabeth found that the major customer base was the affluent (those with $48 900+ in total family income). As a matter of fact, almost 50 percent of the customers had a professional as the head of the family, and 87 percent had two or more wage earners in the family unit.
3. From a psychographic perspective, Elizabeth found that, at lunch, Max was getting the business crowd who were eating salads and sipping Perrier. Over 60 percent ate at a restaurant at least once a week. In the evening, Max's restaurant attracted the bar crowd.

Elizabeth tried to answer a number of questions regarding the customer base: Why did the customer come to Max's? Where did his customer live and work? Who did the customer think the competition was? When her work was completed and she handed Max her results, Elizabeth got a pleasant surprise. She received a cheque from Max. "Small token of my appreciation," Max said. "It's not a lot, but I really did learn something. I thought I knew my customer before you came along."

Elizabeth didn't earn enough to quit her real job, but it was nice to get paid for developing a customer profile, one she could use to help her start her own restaurant. In the next chapter, we'll come back to Elizabeth and find out what her survey said about Max's competition.

When Julia Gonzales and Elizabeth Wood discovered that they would have to work for themselves, they quickly began to research their target customers. The method they chose was interviewing and surveying. You can do the same thing for your business. Action Step 27 tells you how to do it.

ACTION STEP 27

Interview or survey prospective target customers.

Now that you've profiled several target customers, it's time for you to take a big step. It's time to move from the tidy world inside your head to the arena of the marketplace. It's time to rub elbows with the people who'll be buying your product or service.

You know your TC's habits, income, sex, personality, and buying patterns, and can guess at his or her dreams and aspirations. You've identified the heavy users of your product or service. Now you're going to check out these things by interviewing these potential customers.

Make up some questions in advance. Some of them should be open-ended—that is, calling for more than just a simple yes or no. Here are some questions to help get you started:

- Do you like to shop at this store? Why?
- Why do you shop at this location?
- What need is this store satisfying?
- What products did you buy today?
- Are the salespeople helpful and courteous?
- How did you learn about this store?
- Is this your first visit? If not, how often do you shop here?
- What are you looking for that you didn't find in the store today?
- Where do you live?
- What do you read?

Make Customer Profiling a Reflex

We've tried to help you make customer profiling a reflex. If you keep at it, it will help you adjust your focus continually on the all-important marketplace.

Predicting the needs of every customer is almost impossible to accomplish with 100 percent accuracy. The invisible customer will emerge with needs that have not been anticipated. These customers were previously invisible. An alert entrepreneur will listen carefully to unexpected requests and be quick to respond to these opportunities. The following case provides a typical example.

INVISIBLE CUSTOMERS

Some people go into business for themselves because they can't work for someone else. Some are mavericks who don't like to take orders. Others are dreamers who love their own ideas. Still others, like Fred Bowers, have some handicap that keeps them from getting a job with a large firm.

Fred's experience illustrates that customers sometimes "come out of the woodwork."

> Fred Bowers had planned to have a career in the military until he was injured in a fall from a training helicopter. He could still walk, painfully, but his military career was over. With a medical discharge in his pocket, Fred looked around for work.
>
> "I'd always loved soccer," Fred said, "I'd been a pretty fair player, and my coaching experience had given me a good understanding of kids. I thought there might be a place for a soccer specialty shop in our community, but before I went for financing I spent a year checking it out."
>
> Fred found 18 sporting good shops in the area he was interested in. None of them carried a full line of soccer products. When he began profiling his target customers, Fred came up with two identifiable targets:
>
> - Primary target: boys, ages 6–17
> - Secondary target: girls, ages 6–12
> - Household income (both target): $28 000–$32 000
> - Socioeconomic level: middle, upper middle
> - Interest: sports
>
> Then Fred segmented the youngsters into two groups: members of school teams and members of Canadian Soccer Association teams.
>
> His description of his target customers was so good that when he showed his 52-page business plan to a couple of investors, they put up all the money he needed to start up Soccer City. Because of Fred's knowledge of the game, his store prospered. Schools counted on him for an honest deal, and parents of players counted on him for advice on equipment.

"I had thought I'd just be selling," Fred said. "What I was really doing was providing a service."

After he'd been in business a year, a third market began to emerge. The customers in this third group were adults, mostly foreign-born, from places such as Great Britain, Germany, Mexico, and South America. They had grown up playing soccer and they loved the game. To them, it was a fiercely fought national sport, and they still liked to play. These previously invisible customers would drive 80–120 kilometres to Fred's shop for equipment they couldn't find anywhere else.

"They didn't show up in my research," Fred said. "If I hadn't opened up, I wouldn't have known about them. Now they make up at least 30 percent of my business. One day they weren't there; the next day, they were. I like that. I like it a *lot*. It makes this whole adventure more interesting."

In a Nutshell

Your target customer is the key to your survival in small business. Constructing a customer profile is like drawing a circle around that customer in order to turn the circle into a target at which you can aim your product or service. Before you open your doors, you should profile your target customer at least five times. After your doors are open, it's a good idea to gather data through surveys, interviews, and so on, and to refine the profile monthly.

An "end-user" profile combines demographic data (age, sex, income, education, residence, cultural roots) with psychographic insight (observation of lifestyle, buying habits, consumption patterns, attitudes). The magazines read by your target customer will reveal a well-drawn profile, because the chasers of this very expensive advertising have already researched the customer thoroughly. The Internet is another useful secondary profiling tool, especially if your target customers are other businesses. Surveying and field interviewing are primary research tools that will also help you find your target customers.

Profiling your target customer is important because it shows you:

1. how to communicate your message with a minimum of confusion,
2. what additional service your target customer wants, such as delivery, credit, gift wrapping, installation, post-sale service, and so on,
3. how much the target customer can pay,
4. what quality the target customer wants,
5. where large groups of target customers are located, and
6. who else is after your target customer.

Key Terms

business-to-business (B2B) company
business-to-consumer (B2C) company
demographics
market-pull approach
outsourcing
profiling
psychographics
relationship marketing
target customer (TC)

Think Points for Success

- ✓ *Psychographics* is derived from *psyche* and *graphos*, Greek words for "life" or "soul" and for "written," respectively. Thus, psychographics is the charting of your customer's life, mind, soul, or spirit.
- ✓ Profiling draws a "magic" circle around your target customer. Placing the customer in the centre of that circle transforms the whole arena into a bull's-eye.
- ✓ Segmenting is like slicing pie; it allows you to help yourself to a piece of the pie.
- ✓ You can save a lot of steps by using market research that has been done by others.
- ✓ Contact magazines and newspapers. They employ market researchers.
- ✓ Be sure to use the Internet.

Business Plan Building Block

CUSTOMER PROFILE

Describe your potential customers and why they will want to do business with you. If your TCs are end users or consumers, segment them by demographics (age, sex, income, etc.) or psychographics (lifestyles and buying behaviour). If your TCs are businesses, profile them using the categories provided in our business-to-business profile subsection.

You are demonstrating that you know your market and your research shows that there are enough customers to support your business idea.

Go back and review the material you have developed in the first three chapters of this textbook. You are now ready to explain your customer profile.

It's your turn:

Explain your customer profile: you will need 1–3 pages to elaborate.

BUILDING ASSOCIATIONS/PARTNERSHIPS

Creating associations or partnerships is a key marketing strategy. Try to list some businesses or associations you can create an alliance with. For example, if you want to retail second-hand books, can you associate with a business that is in the coffee business? You could complement each other. While your customers are browsing, for example, they could have a cup of coffee. Make a list of some of the businesses or firms with whom you could strike up an association. Don't forget the non-profit sector. What associations could you create with the Boy Scouts or Cancer Society?

It's your turn:

List potential associations or partnerships, then rank them by priority: this will take at least a page.

Checklist Questions and Actions to Develop Your Business Plan

PROFILING YOUR TARGET CUSTOMER

- ❑ Profile your target market in terms of primary, secondary, and invisible customers.
- ❑ What do the results of your primary research questionnaire tell you about your target market?
- ❑ What information have you developed about your target customer from your secondary research?

- ❑ What characteristics are unique or clearly definable about your target customer?
- ❑ What is the best way to reach your target market?

NOTES

1. Adapted from Rick Spence, *Secrets of Success from Canada's Fastest-Growing Companies* (Toronto: John Wiley & Sons Canada, 1997), pp. 88–89.
2. Critical Mass website (www.criticalmass.com); Silicon Valley Business Inc., "Reflect.com Shines Despite Slowdown," retrieved from www.svbizink.com/headlines/article.asp?aid=1563; and Industry Canada, Electronic Commerce in Canada, Success Stories, retrieved from http://e-com.ic.gc.ca/english/stories/criticalmasssucc.html
3. Spence, *Secrets of Success*, p. 103.

SUGGESTED READING

Bhide, Amar V. *The Origin and Evolution of New Businesses.* New York: Oxford University Press, 2000.

Deluca, Fred, with John Phillip. *Start Small, Finish Big: Fifteen Key Lessons to Start and Run Your Own Successful Business.* New York: Warner Books, 2001.

Foot, David, with Daniel Stoffman. *Boom Bust & Echo.* Toronto: Macfarlane Walter & Ross, 1996.

Ries, Al. *Focus: The Future of Your Company Depends on It.* New York: HarperCollins, 1996.

Ries, Al, and Jack Trout. *Positioning: The Battle for Your Mind.* New York: McGraw-Hill, 2001.

Spence, Rick, *Secrets of Success from Canada's Fastest-Growing Companies.* Toronto: John Wiley & Sons Canada, 1997.

Weiss, Michael J. *The Clustered World: How We Live, What We Buy, and What It All Means About Who We Are.* New York: Little Brown & Company, 2000.

Whiteley, Richard C., and Diane Hesson. *Customer-Centred Growth.* Reading, MA: Addison-Wesley, 1996.

chapter 5

Learning from the Competition

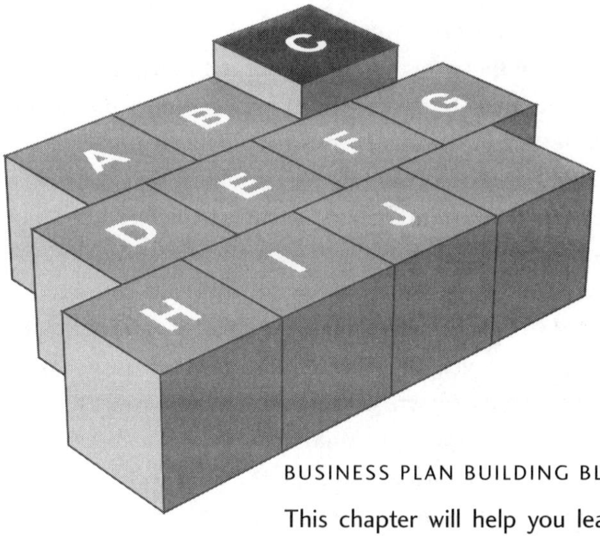

BUSINESS PLAN BUILDING BLOCK

This chapter will help you learn from and define the competition. It will help you build distinctive value for your product or service and further define your specific niche. It will also help you establish what drives your strategy. At the completion of this chapter, you will be able to write a brief competitive overview.

LEARNING OPPORTUNITIES

After reading this chapter, you should be able to:

- Discover how to create and grow your market with the help of your customer and competition.
- Define your real competition through touchpoint analysis.
- Find your position on the competitive ladder through primary and secondary research.
- Develop a competitor review sheet.
- Evaluate your potential competitors using a competitive test matrix.
- Define the unique benefits offered by your product or service.
- Use the four-phase life cycle to change the arena and establish your competitive positioning strategy.
- Discover ways to create uniqueness through service and product change.
- Benefit from partnerships and associations with your potential competitors.

ACTION STEP PREVIEW

28. Do a touchpoint analysis.
29. Create a competitor review sheet.
30. Construct a competitive test matrix.
31. Develop your competitive positioning strategy.

MPact Immedia Corp. is a PROFIT 100 company based in Montreal. It helps firms convert paper-based transactional documents such as invoices, cheques, and bills into a much more efficient electronic system. Competition in the world of electronic commerce is fierce. The lack of industry standardization means that the market is always ripe for new players with new ideas. Among MPact's most feared competitors are the chartered banks. The banks could potentially dominate the market through their financial infrastructure, sheer size, expertise, and massive customer base.

Brian Edwards was president of MPact from 1995 to 1997. When he got wind that the Royal Bank of Canada was eyeing his market, he moved swiftly with a pre-emptive strike. He managed to persuade the Royal Bank to join forces with MPact. Together they formed a joint venture that established Can-Act, a system that allows the

Chapter 5 will help you prepare part C of your business plan, "The Competition."

bank's customers to make recurring business payments to governments, utilities, or trading associates electronically. It was a win-win association. The Royal Bank was able to quickly provide its customers with a distinctive, value-added service. In turn, MPact gained a new customer base along with the marketing clout of a new partner.[1]

Ron Taylor's family had been in the business of building new homes until the early 1990s when there was a recession in the housing market. When the market fell out of new-home construction, the family business closed up and Ron was left with the opportunity to find another career. It wasn't easy. It took healing time and a lot of soul-searching.

In time, his new-eyes research led him into the business of renovating basements. People could not afford high-priced new homes or high interest rates, so they renovated. Secondary research from Statistics Canada and CMHC (Canada Mortgage and Housing Corporation) told him that this was a growth segment. His psychographic research led him to the conclusion that his primary target customers would be those who could not afford to build new homes but who wanted to build a sanctuary for their teenage offspring. He would be in the business of cocooning for teens.

It then came time for him to research his potential competitors. At first, he thought this was obvious. His major competitors were other contractors and builders—after all, if you could build a house, certainly doing a basement renovation would be no problem. But he soon realized that this was the same type of logic that got his family into trouble in the early 1990s. His new business couldn't survive with a market sharing/price-cutting mentality. He could no longer afford to share a market. So, using primary research—interviewing, focus group discussions, and just plain listening—and a new technique called touchpoint analysis he began to build a list of the benefits that his TCs were looking for, and a list of who, in the eyes of the customer, were the best companies or individuals to satisfy their wants. His first list included benefits such as:

- electrical outlets—lots of them for teen toys;
- soundproofing;
- an area equipped for dancing; and
- a bathroom with a full-length mirror.

One night, after a long session with his mentor and some close friends, Ron realized that his competition wasn't other contractors at all. His competition was anyone who could provide the same benefits. In a strange way, he began to realize that even his customer could be a major competitor.

Only a few years ago, the subject of competition conjured up warlike terms such as "beat the competition," "disarm your competitor," "take a piece of their market," and so on. This market-sharing mentality assumed that when you went into business you would take a piece of the action away from someone else. In a steady-state environment in which industries changed at a slow and predictable pace, the focus was on attacking the competition. Since there was little change going on, this strategy seemed to be the only way to drum up new business.

The knowledge-based economy and the new informed customer have changed the way business has to view competition. As we learned from MPact's partnering strategy, the new economy is about learning from and forming alliances and strategic arrangements with the competition. It's about creating your own market niche and continually changing and improving your product or service as the customer dictates. Today, competition is healthy, and it's there to help you change and respond to the market.

In the last few chapters, we learned about the power of marketing and profiling the customer. We've tried to get you to orient your business toward the growth industry segments and customer needs. In this chapter, we explain how your perceived competition can help you further define your specific niche.

Who Is Your Competition?

Recall in Chapter 2 that we talked about defining your business, not in terms of a product or service, but in terms of the benefits your product or service provides to the potential customer. Well, in the same vein, your competition is not necessarily other businesses that provide a similar product. For example, in the opening vignette, MPact's real competitors were almost invisible. Its most dangerous competitors were the major banks, not other firms that had developed comparable technology. MPact was really in the business of providing efficient electronic transfer of business documents. Major banks were MPact's competitors because they could potentially provide this same service and benefits.

In today's economy, your real competition is anyone who provides similar products, services, or benefits to your customer. But you must also be aware of what's called the **invisible competition**—that is, any business that has the capacity and desire to provide similar products, services, or benefits to your customer. For example, imagine you are in the fast-food business in a small town that doesn't have a McDonald's. Then Wal-Mart comes to town. Your invisible competition has just arrived with a McDonald's within its store.

INVISIBLE COMPETITION

people or businesses that have the capacity or desire to provide the same products, services, or benefits that you do

As we learned from Ron Taylor in the opening vignette, your competition is not necessarily who you think it is (although your views are important). Your customers define the competition in terms of who can best satisfy their needs. Taylor used the primary research technique of interviewing his customers to learn about his competition. Strangely enough, he learned that his real competition could very likely be his customers. Let's return to Elizabeth Wood (from Chapter 4) and see how she uncovered the real competitor for Max, the owner of Crazy's Roadhouse, by using another primary research technique: the survey questionnaire.

> Max, the owner of Crazy's Roadhouse, didn't think he needed to know what the customer thought. He knew who the competition was. It was that other roadhouse down the street. Fortunately, Elizabeth knew better. In her restaurant questionnaire, she asked the customers themselves who the competition was: "If you did not eat here today, what restaurant would you have chosen?"
>
> The results gave Max a new perspective on his business. He learned that his competition depended on the dining-out time. At noon, his competition was any restaurant within a two-kilometre radius that could serve the customer fast. The noon-hour trade was more concerned with "getting in and out" than with the quality of the food.
>
> Weekdays from 6 to 9 p.m. and weekends his competition was any restaurant within an 18-kilometre radius of his roadhouse that provided

great food and a fun atmosphere. During this period, Crazy's was perceived as a "destination" restaurant. In contrast to the noon-hour trade, these customers did not value quick service as much as quality food and dining atmosphere.

The crowd after 9 p.m. on both weekdays and weekends had a different need: fun time. Max's competition was not the great eateries, but establishments that catered to the entertainment side of the business. Customers were prepared to drive as much as 50 kilometres to enjoy a good evening out.

Max was taken aback by the survey results. He didn't have a specific competitor at all. He had a number of potential competitors, depending on the dining-out period. With Elizabeth's help, not only did Max get a much clearer picture of his somewhat elusive competitors, but he also began to get some new ideas about how he could promote and grow his business.

TOUCHPOINT ANALYSIS

TOUCHPOINT ANALYSIS

analyzing customers' perceptions of the competition in order to find out what benefits are important to them

People do not just purchase products or services—they also buy what the products and service do for them. The customer wants to know, "What's in it for me? How does it make my life better, easier, more effective and fun?" **Touchpoint analysis** is a way to begin learning about your competition. It involves analyzing customers' perceptions of the competition in order to find out what benefits are important to them.

A touchpoint is any contact that your customer has with any aspect of your competition—advertising, product, packaging, public relations, receptionists, salespeople, and so on. To conduct touchpoint analysis, you gather a small group of potential target customers for a "group think" on your potential competitors. The object is to identify and assess key touchpoints. Here are some touchpoints you may want to consider:

- *Receives advertising in the mail.* What is the quality of the advertisement? Is it mailed first class? Is it addressed to the right person? How many mailings does the customer receive before he or she responds?
- *Responds to advertisement.* How quickly is the phone answered? Is the receptionist pleasant? How long is the customer put on hold before being directed to a salesperson? Is the salesperson knowledgeable, articulate, and able to answer the customer's questions?
- *Places order.* Is the order form easy to fill out and understand? Is the pricing clear? Are alternatives clearly spelled out? Is ordering online straightforward and quick?
- *Receives order.* Does the customer receive the right order at the right time and at the right place? Is there any follow up?
- *Calls to complain or change an order.* Are the customer's complaints or requests to change an order addressed in a timely and considerate fashion? Are follow-up calls made to ensure that the customer's problem has been solved?

DISTINCTIVE COMPETENCY

unique features and benefits that attract customers and encourage customer loyalty

Once you've completed your target analysis, you should be able to answer these questions: What benefits are most important to the customer? What corporate image is your competition projecting? Where do openings exist? Making a list of all the touchpoints allows you to identify your competitors' strengths and weaknesses. A touchpoint analysis will also enable you to develop a **distinctive competency**—

unique features and benefits that attract customers and encourage customer loyalty. Do your own touchpoints analysis by completing Action Step 28. Then take a look at Boxes 5.1 and 5.2 to help you identify your competitors.

Box 5.1 A Quick Guide to Identifying Your Competitors

To identify your competitors, you need the following:

1. an understanding of your current competition,
2. an understanding of your future competition, and
3. an understanding of your customer.

Current Competition

Some ways to better understand your competition may involve:

a. **Trade shows.** Visit industry trade shows and conferences to examine competitors' products, meet their sales representatives, and learn their product line. Look for product substitutes (domestic and foreign) that can add value to your product and customers.

b. **Reverse engineering.** Purchase a competitor's product and dissect it to determine costs of production, methods of manufacture, and possible suppliers.

c. **Competitors' literature.** Request, as a potential customer, product brochures and price lists from existing competitors. They will give insight into the product concepts, promotion, and corporate image.

d. **Industry association journals.** Read industry journals and learn about the publicity competitors are receiving on new products and services.

e. **Site visits.** Walk through competitors' place of business and observe their corporate image, product displays, level of service, and corporate ambiance.

Future Competition

Some likely sources of future competition include:

a. **Product expansion.** A competitor may decide to take advantage of its technology, marketing, or brand name by expanding an existing line.

b. **Market expansion.** A firm outside your geographic area may expand into your territory.

c. **Backward integration.** One of your suppliers who provides many of your components may decide to put them all together, resulting in a competing product.

d. **Forward integration.** One of your customers might decide that he or she can do what you do, but better or cheaper.

Your Customer

Here are some things you should ask your customers in order to determine their product selection process and why they may likely choose a competitor's product over yours:

a. What product names came to mind when you first decided to shop for the product?

b. Why did you think of these names?

c. For what applications or on what occasions are you likely to use the product?

d. What other kinds of products would be just as satisfying in the same situation?

e. Was it price, quality, or something else that determined the purchase of the product?

Source: Contributed by Laurence Hewick, Wilfrid Laurier University, 1998.

ACTION STEP 28

Do a touchpoint analysis.

As you look for a niche in the marketplace, you must continually identify and assess your competitors' strengths and weaknesses. To start your touchpoint analysis, assemble a group of your potential customers. Get them to detail the experience of purchasing your competitors' products or services. Make a list of each contact, or touchpoint, between the target customers and any facet of the competition's business. Then ask the target customers to select and rank the five most important touchpoints. Keep your list of touchpoints on hand because you will revisit it in Chapter 6.

ACTION STEP 29

Create a competitor review sheet.

Using secondary sources of information, compile a list of your competitors. Boxes 5.1 and 5.2 will help you get started. You may also want to consult the telephone book, Fraser's Canadian Trade Directory (www.frasers.com), Scott's Canadian Business Directory and Database (www.scottsinfo.com), or magazines that would appeal to your target market. Don't worry if your list of competitors gets too long. The more competitors you detect, the more you can learn.

Using your list of touchpoints and past research, create a competitor review sheet for each competitor. It should answer such questions as: What is unique about this firm? Who are its target customers? What are its strengths and weaknesses? Evaluate each variable. Keep this Action Step on hand because you will need it to complete Action Step 30.

POSITIONING

the process of establishing in the mind of the consumer a unique image or perception of a company, product, or service

Box 5.2 Bookmark This

The Internet is a great source of competitive information.

Strategis (http://strategis.ic.gc.ca) should be your starting point. In the last chapter, we encouraged you to use the Canadian Company Capabilities database, which contains information on over 40 000 businesses.

Now we want you to investigate other Strategis resources. To get started, we suggest you visit the site's "Company Directories" page (http://strategis.ic.gc.ca/scdt/businessmap/engdoc/1.html). Here you will find links to all sorts of detailed Internet sites that provide competitive information. For example, we found a link to the Canada Yellow Pages (www.yellowpages.ca), in which you can search for businesses by type, name, and location across the nation. We also found a link to the Canadian Trade Index (www.ctidirectory.com/index.htm), which offers a comprehensive directory of over 29 000 Canadian companies, featuring over 94 000 product listings under 25 000 headings.

Competition and Positioning

Basically, competition is a mind game played out in the customers' minds, since that is where buying decisions are made. Inside customers' minds are many "ladders"—for products, for services, for sports figures, for TV programs, for banks, wines, rental cars, and so forth. To compete for a position at the top of the ladder, a business must first get a foothold and then wrestle with other businesses to improve its position. Looking at competition from this perspective helps you focus on the mind of the target customer.

Competition is always changing. You are therefore faced with a constant process of **positioning** your product or service to meet the changing needs of the customer. Action Step 29 will help you define your position on the competitive ladder, using your primary, secondary, and new-eyes research skills.

DISTINGUISHING YOUR PRODUCT OR SERVICE

Once you understand a competitor's strategy, the next step is to understand the key component that gives that competitor a competitive edge. This key component is what Michael Robert has called the company's driving force.[2] All decisions, including those about which products to develop, customers to target, and markets to enter, are based on the driving force. Taking the Porter model of competitive strategy (Figure 3.5 in Chapter 3) a step further, you can select a driving force for your business. You may have more than one of the following components but only one should drive your strategy. The full list appears in Box 5.3.

- *Product-driven strategy.* A product-driven company ties its business to a single product. Future products will resemble current and past products in look and function.
- *User/customer class-driven strategy.* A user/customer class-driven company builds its business around specific customers or users. Johnson & Johnson, for example, makes health-related products for doctors, nurses, and patients.
- *Production/capacity/capability-driven strategy.* A production capacity/capability-driven company focuses its strategy on its production facilities. Specialty printers, for example, exploit the special capabilities of their production facilities.

Box 5.3 What Drives Your Strategy?

Most companies have at least one key component that gives them a competitive edge. Identify your small business strategy from the following:

a. product-driven strategy (e.g., Cow Brand Baking Soda)
b. user/customer class-driven strategy (e.g., Johnson & Johnson)
c. market type/category-driven strategy (e.g., John Deere)
d. product capacity/capability-driven strategy
e. technology/know-how-driven strategy (e.g., Nortel)
f. sales/marketing method-driven strategy (e.g., Avon)
g. distribution method-driven strategy (e.g., Rogers Cable)
h. natural resources-driven strategy (e.g., oil companies)
i. size growth-driven strategy (e.g., Coke, Pepsi)
j. return/profit-driven strategy (e.g., banks)

Source: Michael Robert, *Strategy Pure and Simple II* (New York: The McGraw-Hill Companies Inc., 1998). Reprinted by permission of The McGraw-Hill Companies.

- *Technology/know-how-driven strategy.* Technology/know-how-driven companies get their edge from a distinctive technology.

Which strategy is right for you? No company can excel in all these strategies, so you are going to have to focus on a strategy that distinguishes you from your competitors. The better you understand your competition, the more clearly you will see how you can position yourself for success. Figure 5.1 is a sample **competitive test matrix** that will help you evaluate your potential competitors. Action Step 30 will assist you in developing your own competitive test matrix. Work from your strengths, and remember that strengths are built on knowledge. Knowing your competitors will increase your confidence. Then everyone can win.

Once you've completed Action Step 30, think about your proposed business. What makes your product or service unique? Complete the following statement.

The unique product/service benefits that my target customer values are:

____

____

____

____

____

Up until now, we've talked about positioning your business idea in the mind of the customer. Now we're going to turn our attention to your product or service.

The Competition Life Cycle

Like everything else in life and business, competition has a life cycle that can be grouped into four broad stages: embryo, growth, maturity, and decline. These stages are, for the most part, determined by the product life cycle (see Figure 5.2). Briefly, we can describe the four stages of the competition life cycle as follows:

ACTION STEP 30

Construct a competitive test matrix.

Now that you have a good idea of who your major competitors are, it is time to construct a competitive test matrix as shown in Figure 5.1. List all those competitors or potential competitors and the benefits and features resulting from Action Step 29. Remember, your competitor may not be providing the same products. If you want to sell healthy water, for example, your potential competitors are those who are in the health business. The purpose of this Action Step is to learn from their strengths so you can borrow from their experience and create a better, more unique product or service.

Next, rank each competitor on a scale of 1 to 10 for each benefit category. By the time you're finished, you will have an instant overview of your competition and your opportunities.

What are the strengths of your competitors, and how can you learn from them to improve your idea?

COMPETITIVE TEST MATRIX

a grid used to get a clear picture of the strengths and weaknesses of a competitor

Figure 5.1 Competitive Test Matrix

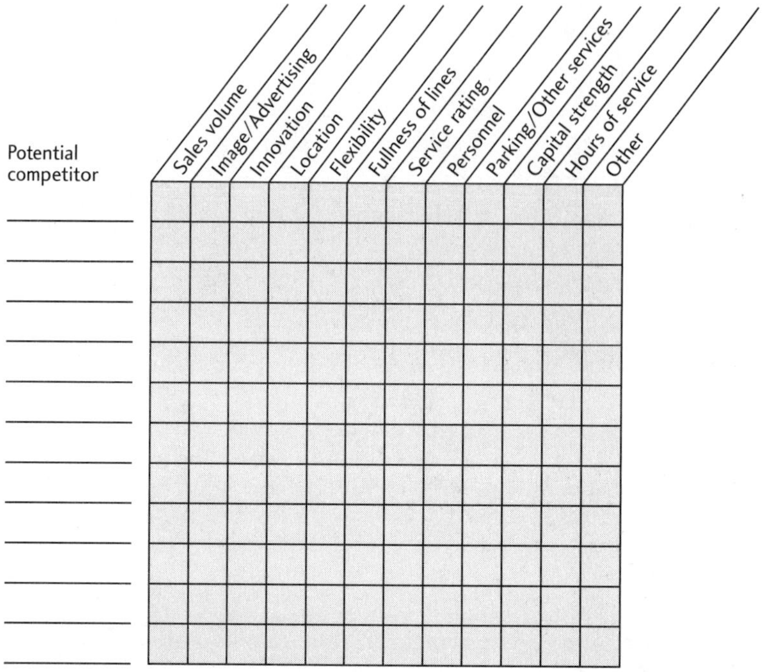

The competitive test matrix can help you evaluate your potential competitors.

1. In the *embryonic* stage, the arena is empty. There's just you and your idea for a product or service and a tiny core market.
2. As your industry *grows*, competitors smell money and attempt to penetrate the arena to take up positions they hope will turn to profit. Curious target customers come from all directions. You have visions of great success.
3. As the industry *matures*, competition gets fierce and you are forced to steal customers to survive. Shelf velocity slows. Production runs get longer. Prices begin to slide.
4. As the industry goes into *decline*, competition becomes desperate. Many businesses fail, and weary competitors leave the arena, which is now silent except for the echoes of battle.

Remember Hugh Hefner and his *Playboy* empire? Well, *Playboy* readers got older (the moving target concept) and the empire became a colony—a very sparse colony. It took Hefner and *Playboy* some 30 years to move through the competition cycle, and that arc was rather smooth and even. Hefner's experience was typical of the way competition used to evolve. Changes occurred slowly. Products, services, and even markets would get stuck in a particular stage. A few years ago, for example, the embryonic stage for a computer software package might have lasted up to two or three years.

No more. The new economy has changed all that. Today, movement from one phase to another can be at lightning speed. It's not unheard of for a product to go through the four cycles in a matter of months. In the high-tech business, for example, a common rule of thumb is six months—that is, you've got six months from the birth of an idea to **product penetration**. After six months, competitors

PRODUCT PENETRATION
a calculated thrust into the market

Figure 5.2 Product Life Cycle and Competition

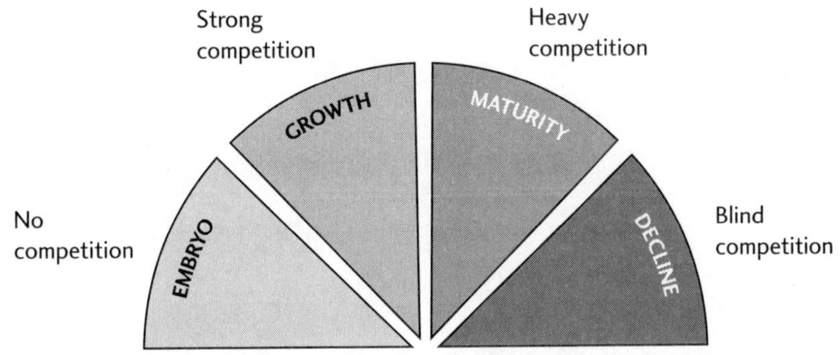

The product life cycle defines four stages in the intensity of competition.

have already entered the market, and the product begins to enter the decline phase. What this means is that, to survive, you must constantly be in touch with the market and compete with the right strategies accordingly. Figure 5.3 and Box 5.4 will help you understand the life-cycle stages more clearly.

Figure 5.3 Product Life Cycle and Strategies

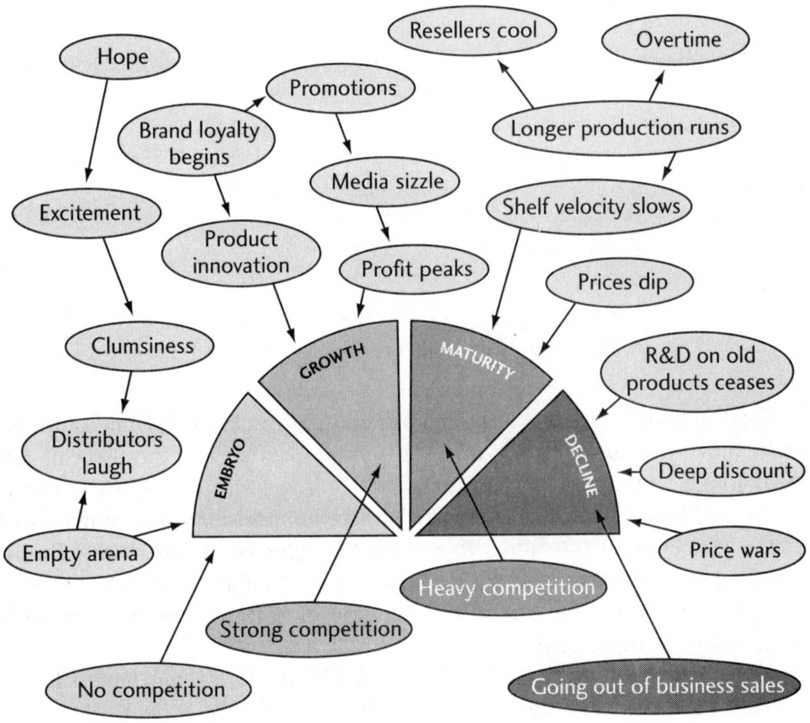

Different competitive strategies are needed at each stage of the product life cycle.

Box 5.4 The Competition Life Cycle

The Embryonic Stage

The embryonic stage is marked by excitement, naïve euphoric thrust, clumsiness, a high failure rate, and much brainstorming. Competition has not yet appeared. Pricing is experimental. Sales volume is low because the market is very small and production and marketing costs are high. It's difficult to find distributors, and resellers demand huge gross margins. Profit is chancy and speculative. Shrewd entrepreneurs, however, can close their eyes and divine the presence of a core market. And persistence can pay off. The authors of the best-selling *Chicken Soup for the Soul* series went to more than 30 publishers before finding the one that launched their multimillion-dollar empire.

The Growth Stage

The growth stage is marked by product innovation, strong product acceptance, the beginnings of brand loyalty, promotion by media sizzle, and ballpark pricing. Product innovation occurs. Distribution becomes all-important. Resellers who laughed during the embryonic stage now clamour to distribute the product. Strong competitors, excited by the smell of money, enter the arena of the marketplace, as do new target customer groups. Profit shows signs of peaking.

The Mature Stage

The mature stage is marked by peak customer numbers and zero product modifications. Design concentrates on product differentiation instead of product improvement. Competitors are going at it blindly now, running on momentum even as shelf velocity slows. Production runs get longer, so firms can take full advantage of capital equipment and experienced management. Resellers, sensing doom, are cool on the product. Advertising investments increase, in step with competition. Prices are on a swift slide down. Any competitor who enters the market now will not survive unless it offers a unique product or service and effectively conveys the benefits of that product/service to the target consumer.

The Decline Stage

The decline stage is marked by extreme depression in the marketplace. Competition becomes desperate. A few firms still hang on. Research and development ceases. Promotion vanishes. Price wars continue. Opportunities emerge for entrepreneurs in service and repair. Diehards fight what remains of the core market. Resellers cannot be found—they've moved on.

Your Competitive Positioning Strategy

In the last few chapters, we've learned that a major objective when starting or owning a business is to position your product or service in a growth segment. If your market is growing at 25 percent a year, you may be able to make a lot of mistakes and still succeed. If, however, you're competing in the mature or decline stage, one mistake can spell disaster. In these stages, you'll be forced to lower prices, take business away from others, or invest lots of advertising money. These are market-sharing conditions, and you don't want to—or shouldn't plan to—share a market.

You really don't want to position yourself in an embryonic competitive stage either. In this initial stage, you will be all alone with virtually no proven market. We know that if you expect to make it, you'll need customers—a receptive market. But this means that you will need some competition, something that is virtually non-existent in the embryonic stage.

In today's changing economy, there is no choice. Your strategy must be a constant "war of movement" (for those of you who still think that your competitive strategy should be warlike) or a constant process of positioning and moving your product or service toward a growth market. The name of the game is change and creating uniqueness as dictated first and foremost by your customers and secondly by your potential competitors. Figure 5.4 depicts this new **competitive positioning** strategy. Yes, you will always have competition, because you need their advice. The secret is to continually learn from your competitors and customers so that you can adjust your product or service to meet the needs and wants of the market. Your competitive strategy is all about changing the arena. By constantly adding benefits to your product or service, you will guide your business into growth segments. Another way to achieve this objective is to strike up partnerships with the competition.

COMPETITIVE POSITIONING

process of positioning and moving your product or service toward a growth market

FORMING STRATEGIC ALLIANCES WITH COMPETITORS

A **strategic alliance** is a partnership between one or more organizations that is formed to create a competitive advantage. Partnerships between competitors is a growing trend. (According to a study conducted by Industry Canada, one in five strategic alliances are formed with competitors.[3]) In the opening vignette, we saw how MPact Immedia Corp. "changed the arena" by forming a mutually beneficial alliance with the Royal Bank of Canada. But MPact did not rest on its laurels. "There are more competitors coming in," said then-president Brian Edwards, "and we're trying to partner with them."[4] Let's see how this technique also worked for Mina Cohen, owner of Archaeological Encounters.

STRATEGIC ALLIANCE

a partnership between one or more organizations that is formed to create a competitive advantage

You'll recall Mina from Chapter 4. She decided she wanted to be in the "travel-with-a-purpose" business. Her product was archaeological excursions. The bad news was that she had created an embryonic product. No one else was offering this kind of service, so she was faced with such questions as: What price do I charge? How can I attract customers without massive advertising? To complicate things

Figure 5.4 Competitive Positioning Strategy

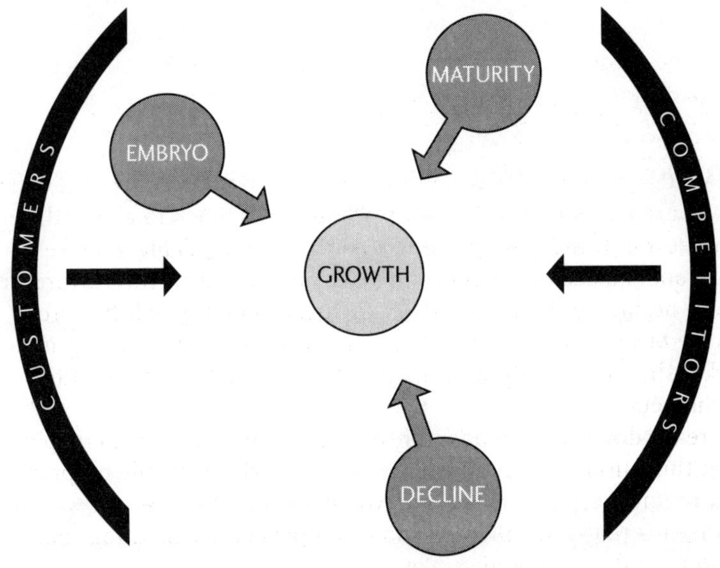

Your customers and competitors are your tools to guide you into a growth market.

even more, her competitive analysis told her that her target customers valued their time and would likely get travel agencies to help them plan their vacation experience. Her competition would be travel agencies that could easily enter her market if they wanted to, and they would have a strong customer base to draw from. Here she was with an embryonic product, trying to position herself and do business in the fiercely competitive travel industry. What a challenge!

As Mina sifted through the ideas she had recorded in her Adventure Notebook, a creative solution gradually took shape. Why not partner with a travel agency interested in the ecotourism market? She would locate the best travel agency in town and offer her excursions as an add-on service. The agents would handle the advertising, pricing, and booking since this was their strength—organizing and planning. Mina could then focus on her strengths—teaching and archaeology—and get paid from the travel package for her knowledge and expertise.

The lesson from Mina's experience is clear. She moved her embryonic product and service into a competitive market by creating an association with her potential competitor. By understanding the needs and strengths of her competitors, Mina was able to create a win-win situation.

CREATING UNIQUENESS THROUGH CHANGE

In today's competitive landscape, "If it ain't broke, don't fix it" has given way to "If it ain't broke, improve or change it, or it *will* be broke." Let's see how James Grenchik, owner of a retail tire company called Tire Pro, used this strategy to revive his flagging business.

It was painfully obvious to James that Tire Pro, a family business serving a large farming community, was in trouble. Every time he turned around, there seemed to be a new competitor setting up shop in his back yard. Canadian Tire, a recent arrival, was starting to cut into his business, and there were rumours that Costco was thinking of moving in. James fought back with price promotions and distress sales, but these traditional strategies just didn't seem to work any more. Profits were eroding.

James realized he had two choices—get out of business or change. Before he made that choice, he needed to evaluate his competitors. In order to get a clear picture of their strengths and weaknesses, he talked to employees and customers, and began to construct a competitive test matrix (see Action Step 30). After months of soul-searching, networking, brainstorming, and reviewing his competitive test matrix, James decided to stay in business. To keep Tire Pro viable, he introduced the following unique benefits:

- *An installment plan for farmers.* This add-on service is a major benefit to Tire Pro's target customers—farmers—who need tires early in the growing season just when they experience cash flow problems.
- *Tires with free rotation and inspection.* Tire Pro's customers now receive a free six-month tire rotation. In addition to the inspection, they get a free report card on potential trouble spots. Every six months, reminder postcards are mailed to customers; this keeps Tire Pro's name and image front and centre in the minds of its customers.

- *A revamped waiting room.* Tire Pro has added some amenities to its shop. While they wait to have their tires serviced, customers can sip free coffee while reading *AgriFamily Business Magazine* or using one of the recently installed computers to search the Internet for the latest commodities report. Another new addition to Tire Pro's waiting room is a bulletin board on which notices (ads for used farm equipment, for example) can be posted.

Tire Pro's competitive strategy is not restricted to add-on services and customer service improvements: James is developing a website that will allow Tire Pro to build an online relationship with its target customers.

YOU CAN DO IT

We have provided you with a number of cases about innovators who worked with and learned from competitors and brought about big changes in the marketplace. It's altogether possible that we may someday be telling such a story about *you*. Yes, you too can do it. You just need to:

- know what business you're in,
- know your target customer,
- know your competition,
- develop a distinctive competency, and
- express your creativity and your entrepreneurial spirit.

Action Step 31 will help you establish your competitive positioning strategy.

ACTION STEP 31

Develop your competitive positioning strategy.

What do you think about joining forces with a potential competitor? Take a look at the competitive test matrix you created in Action Step 30. Who are your potential competitors? What are their strengths and how could you benefit from them? Review Box 4.6 ("Ten Tips for Joint Ventures and Strategic Alliances") on page 72 and reflect on the experience of Mina Cohen. This will help you decide how you can join forces with a competitor and create a win-win situation.

Next, take a good hard look at your product or service. What's unique about it? (review your answer to the statement posed earlier in this chapter, "The unique product/service benefits that my target customer values are ..."). What distinguishes it from the product/service of your potential competitors? Your answers to these questions will help you define your distinctive competency. Now think about what other benefits you can add to your product/service to make it even more unique. (Recall the add-on services James Grenchik introduced at Tire Pro.) Don't be afraid to stretch your imagination.

Now we want you to learn about a benchmarking tool called Performance Plus. Complete the E-Exercise in Box 5.5.

Box 5.5 E-Exercise

Performance Plus

- **What Is Performance Plus?**
  http://strategis.ic.gc.ca/SSG/pm00013e.html

Found on the Strategis website, Performance Plus is an online performance benchmarking tool that helps small businesses determine how they measure up against their competitors by providing detailed financial and employment data on more than 600 business sectors across Canada. This tool uses the Small Business Profiles created from a sample of Revenue Canada tax returns for businesses operating in Canada. To learn more about these profiles, visit the "What Is Performance Plus?" page. Click on Small Business Profiles and discover the answers to these questions:

- What are the Small Business Profiles?
- How are they derived?
- How can you use the profiles?
- How "small" are the businesses represented in the Small Business Profiles?
- What data items are available?

In a Nutshell

Your key source for learning about and defining your competition is your customer. Customers help us determine who our competitors are. Competition is a mind game, because buying decisions are made in the customers' minds. So, we began this chapter by asking you to conduct a touchpoint analysis, and to find your position on the competitive ladder through primary and secondary research. We asked you to evaluate your competition and work to define your distinctive competency by developing a competitor review sheet and a competitive test matrix.

Our attention turned to the four stages of the competitive life cycle—embryo, growth, mature, and decline—and its implications for the enterprising entrepreneur. Your competitive position strategy, we said, should be to create uniqueness by continually adding benefits to your product or service. Listening to customer needs is the best way to guide your business into growth segments.

Case studies in the chapter showed how successful entrepreneurs worked with and learned from the competition. These examples emphasized the key strategies of creating uniqueness through continuous change and establishing special partnerships or associations—even with your competitors.

Key Terms

competitive positioning
competitive test matrix
distinctive competency
invisible competition
positioning
product penetration
strategic alliance
touchpoint analysis

Think Points for Success

- ✓ Customers help you determine who your competitors are.
- ✓ A touchpoint analysis can be conducted by using primary research techniques such as questionnaires, interviewing, and surveying.
- ✓ Learning from the competition will help you position your business.
- ✓ Knowing your driving force or distinctive competency will help you make better decisions.
- ✓ Your competitive positioning creates uniqueness by continually adding benefits to your product or service, and it guides your business into growth segments.
- ✓ Establishing strategic alliances with your competitors also gives you a competitive edge.

Business Plan Building Block

MARKET OPPORTUNITIES

Based on your research, identify the most promising opportunities in the marketplace according to the following categories:

- New or emerging markets—gaps and opportunities
- Neglected customer needs
- Failing competitors
- Complementary product mix
- Expanded use of existing facilities
- New geographical and international opportunities

Now rank those that are most attractive now and up to five years forward.

____

____

COMPETITION

Even though you believe you have little or few competitors, you must make an assessment of whom you are competing with. You should list your major competitors, their dollar volume, market share, marketing methods, financial conditions, prices, service levels, geographic areas served, and weaknesses. Start with a rough draft here and fine-tune it again as you keep developing your plan. Stress unmet needs and niches. Your first draft of this section should use one to three pages.

List major and minor competitors. Estimate their dollar volume by product type and consider their strengths, weaknesses, markets served, and unmet needs. A map of the area is useful—show distances from your site and proximity to market and competition. Back this up with industry data, market surveys, and primary research.

Your turn: this should take 1–2 pages.

MARKET SHARE

Review the total market and estimate your anticipated share penetration from the first through the fifth year.

Your turn:

COMPETITIVE ANALYSIS

Summarize the material you have developed in this chapter to demonstrate that you have not underestimated your competitors. A brief competitive overview could be sufficient for a small firm serving a local geographic area, a specialty distributor, a short-run manufacturer, or a professional service (1–2 pages).

A detailed competitive analysis is needed for larger firms ($2 million to $200 million in projected sales). Write a comprehensive analysis of market share, marketing strategies, pricing, positioning, promotion, distribution, finances, and customers' perceptions (3–10 pages).

Note that the competitive marketplace is imperfect. Sometimes a few kilometres or a few hundred kilometres can make a significant difference in how competitive a business must be. If a mature marketplace is oversaturated, keep exploring other areas. You may find an underserved market that will welcome you instantly with warmth and healthy profit margins.

Checklist Questions and Actions to Develop Your Business Plan

LEARNING FROM THE COMPETITION

- ❑ Define and analyze your primary and secondary competition.
- ❑ Identify your position on the competitive ladder.
- ❑ Construct a competitive test matrix.
- ❑ What is your major competitive positioning strategy?
- ❑ What is unique about your product or service?
- ❑ What do customers think of the competition's product or service?
- ❑ What is the size of the total market, and what share do you expect to achieve in the first, second, and third years, and why?

NOTES

1. Adapted from Rick Spence, *Secrets of Success from Canada's Fastest-Growing Companies* (Toronto: John Wiley & Sons Canada, 1997), p. 114. Reprinted by permission of the author.
2. Michael Robert, *Strategy Pure and Simple*, 2nd ed. (New York: McGraw-Hill Companies, 1998).
3. Sunder Magun, *The Development of Strategic Alliances in Industries: A Micro Analysis* (Ottawa: Industry Canada, 1996), Working Paper No. 13, Cat. No. 21-24/14-1996.
4. Spence, *Secrets of Success*, p. 114.

SUGGESTED READING

Bishop, Bill. *Strategic Marketing for a Digital Age.* Toronto: HarperCollins, 1996.

Hamel, Gary. *Leading the Revolution.* Boston: Harvard Business School Press, 2000.

Hope, Jeremy, and Tony Hope. *Competing in the Third Wave.* Boston, MA: Harvard Business School Press, 1997.

Liautaud, Bernard, and Mark Hammond. *E-Business Intelligence: Turning Information into Knowledge into Profit.* New York: McGraw-Hill Professional Publishing, 2000.

Robert, Michael, *Strategy Pure and Simple,* 2nd ed. New York: McGraw-Hill Companies, 1998.

Spence, Rick. *Secrets of Success from Canada's Fastest-Growing Companies.* Toronto: John Wiley & Sons Canada, Ltd., 1997.

Tapscott, Don, David Ticoll, and Alex Lowy. *Digital Capital: Harnessing the Power of Business Webs.* Boston: Harvard Business School Press, 2000.

Trout, Jack, with Steve Rivkin. *Differentiate or Die: Survival in Our Era of Killer Competition.* New York: John Wiley and Sons, 2000.

Tyson, Kirk W.M. *Competition in the 21st Century.* Delray Beach, FL: St. Lucie Press, 1997.

Wecker, David. *The Maverick Mindset: Finding the Courage to Journey from Fear to Freedom.* New York: Simon & Schuster, 1997.

chapter 6

Marketing Strategies and Promotion: Connecting with the Customer

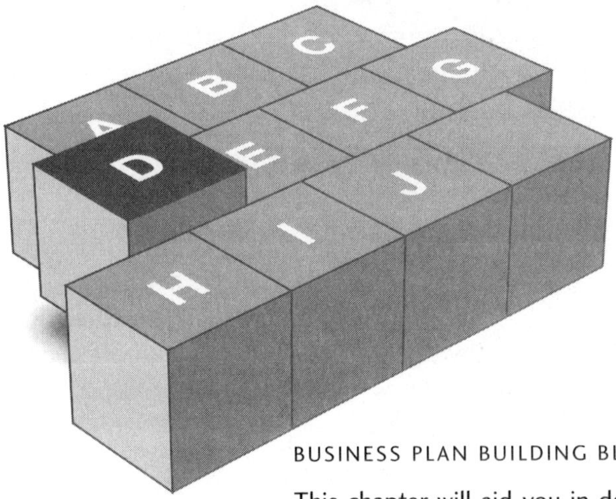

BUSINESS PLAN BUILDING BLOCK

This chapter will aid you in developing the first draft of your marketing strategy, and in shaping your plan to communicate with, service, and provide value-added services or products to your customers.

LEARNING OPPORTUNITIES

After reading this chapter, you should be able to:

- Develop a marketing strategy for your product or service.
- Learn to communicate with target customers, using both conventional and creative promotional methods.
- Use research to determine a marketing strategy.
- Get free publicity.
- Maximize economy in advertising and promotion.
- Understand the value of personal selling.
- Use creative techniques to arrive at the right promotional mix.
- Develop a customer list.
- Promote through networking.
- Build your own network.
- Attach price tags to your promotional strategies.

Back in the mid-1990s, Leon Goren was an accountant working for Deloitte & Touche's Vancouver office. He didn't like the high prices he was paying for his shirts, so he called two of his friends—Keith Beckley (a physicist) and Doug Childerhose (a banker). "I figured there's gotta be a cheaper way to get good dress shirts," Goren recalls. His friends agreed. So they did their research, developed a business plan, invested $25 000, and launched Just White Shirts & Black Socks (JWS). "Our goal was to offer a high-quality product at a reasonable price, with great service," says Goren.

JWS achieved its early success through a grassroots promotion—sending flyers to the offices of friends and colleagues in law offices, accounting firms, and banks—that fostered word of mouth and repeat customers. The partners set up a 1-800 number and a fax line for orders, and established a website (www.justwhiteshirts.com). Today, about 40 percent of the company's annual revenues—in excess of $3 million—come from online sales.

There are some 50 000 names in JWS's North American customer base—time-starved businessmen and other professionals who

ACTION STEP PREVIEW

32. Refine your touchpoints.
33. Brainstorm a winning promotional campaign for your business.
34. Build your network.
35. Attach a price tag to each item of your promotion package.

This chapter will help you prepare part D of your business plan, "Marketing Strategy."

hate to shop. The company has used its keen understanding of its target customers to launch promotional strategies aimed at satisfying their needs. Three times a year, they publish a witty newsletter that's short on sales pitches and long on the kind of information professionals and executives are likely to want (articles dispense advice on such topics as how to dress down and how to find a good dry cleaner). Their website is dynamic and easy to navigate—ordering is simple and delivery is fast. Other promotional strategies include testimonials, gift certificates, and a rewards program similar to that of Canadian Tire. They even used a dash of **impact marketing** in the Spring 1999 issue of their newsletter, which featured the smiling partners pictured three times without pants. "The newsletter, and the picture of us, have become a bit of a trademark," Goren says.[1]

IMPACT MARKETING

a one-off campaign designed to attract the attention of your target market

Chapter 3 discussed the importance of market research, while Chapter 4 focused on your target customers. In Chapter 5, you learned how to analyze your competition. Understanding your market, your target customer, and competition are all part of developing your marketing strategy. Your strategy may be one of differentiating your product from that of the competitor's, segmenting your total market, positioning it in relation to other products, or carving out and defending a certain niche. The marketing strategy in your plan is a "what-to-do" section. In all cases, it is implementing a plan that considers the product or service benefits and values, the primary objectives you want to accomplish, where you are going to locate your business, and finally how you plan to promote your business. Before you reach the point of promotion, you need to be very clear about the focus of your product or service, location, and pricing strategy. Product and price have been discussed in earlier chapters; location is discussed in Chapter 7.

Now that you have profiled your target customer and gained a sense of competition and market niche, it's time to plan a promotional strategy. But each business is unique, and you don't want to throw away money on promotional schemes that don't work.

For example, if your target customer is a college-educated suburban female aged 45–55, who makes over $100 000, owns three cars, rides horseback 10 hours a week, and reads *Practical Horseman* and *Performance Horseman*, your best chance of reaching her is with direct mail.

On the other hand, if your target customers are males and females aged 24–57, with a high-school education and income of $17 000, you'll have to resort to some form of mass-market advertising or, better still, rethink your target market.

PROMOTION

the art or science of moving the image of your business into the prospective customer's mind

Promotion is the art or science of moving the image of your business into the prospective customer's mind. *Promotion* comes from the Latin verb *imovere*, which means "to advance," "to move forward." It's an aggressive word, so learn to say it with a $mile!

As we have learned from the opening vignette, customer service and quality are the cornerstones of any marketing or promotional strategy. This is the point at which we begin our promotion discussion.

Your Promotional Cornerstones: Service and Quality

In Antigonish, Nova Scotia, John Dobson built a five-store giftware retail chain across Atlantic Canada that grew 1264 percent in five years. At South of the Border, he says, "our game plan has been to have the best

> customer service." That means cash refunds, free gift-wrapping year round, and employees who are trained to know their products and empowered to make decisions that favour the consumer. The result is loyal customers who return again and again, and spend $500 to $700 in the stores every year.[2]
>
> IKOR Integrated Facilities Inc., a Toronto office-furniture dealership, is another Canadian success story. IKOR's major promotional strategy is "Wow." Throughout the company's showroom are signs that say "Wow service by IKOR." It's a concept that Igor Korenzvit, founder and president, constantly drums into his staff. According to Korenzvit, "There are three kinds of service you can give to people: less than they expected, which we call 'Yuck'; what they expected, which we call 'Blah'; and more than they expected, which we call 'Wow.' We only deliver Wow."[3]

According to Jim Clemmer, author of *Firing on All Cylinders*, "Customer service and quality are back in vogue." Numerous surveys have consistently shown that improved customer service and quality are key factors contributing to business profit and growth. A Statistics Canada study—*Strategies for Success*—of almost 1500 companies found that customer service and product quality were the most important success factors among growth firms.[4] A 1998 study by Deloitte & Touche Consulting came to the conclusion that customer service was the currency of the digital age: "The most profitable companies ... are adapting to a new customer value paradigm and proactively changing the basis of competition."[5] (Translation: Be more useful to your customer than your competition and you will make a whack of cash.)

Why is delighting the customer with service and quality so important? Here are a few additional market facts:

- You can charge up to 10 percent more if the customer perceives quality service.
- Firms with high service records are 12 percent more profitable than firms without, and their yearly sales growth is 12 percent higher.
- About 68 percent of customers stop doing business with a particular establishment because the employees appear indifferent toward the customer.
- It costs five times more to get a new customer than to keep your present customer satisfied.
- A happy customer will tell five new people, but an unhappy customer will complain to 10 people.

Box 6.1 Small Business Tips

There are seven service secrets that you should keep in mind:

1. Set a new standard for your industry.
2. Don't make clients pay for your mistakes.
3. Measure the service you provide.
4. Provide speedy service.
5. Relieve your customers' stress.
6. Use feedback to stay in touch with the customer needs.
7. Surround your product with customer benefits.

Source: Rick Spence, *Secrets of Success from Canada's Fastest-Growing Companies* (Toronto: John Wiley & Sons Canada, 1997), pp. 143–144. Reprinted by permission.

ACTION STEP 32

Refine your touchpoints.

Retrieve the list of touchpoints you compiled in Action Step 28 ("Do a touchpoint analysis"). Determine how you could make each touchpoint a memorable and exceptional service experience for your target customer. For example:

- If you are sending your customer a package, what could you include to brighten his or her day?
- If you are serving your customer a fast-food meal, what could you do to speed up the service?

As you work to build exceptional customer service, remember that you must do more than just meet your customers' service needs—you must exceed them!

What's worse is that only one customer out of 26 will bother to tell the owner. This means that if only one customer complains, 25 others also have complaints, and each one is telling 10 people.

Remember, the 80–20 rule: 80 percent of the world is influenced by the other 20 percent. Word of mouth by the customer is a major way to get your message out once you are established. A customer who is happy because of quality service is the way to make word of mouth work for you.

Where to begin? If you want to start your own customer service strategy, we suggest the following:

- Recognize that all of us are captive in the midst of a customer service epidemic.
- Think of a customer as "the next person to whom you give your work," at home and in your business.
- Think of service as treating people with genuine care, dignity, and respect.
- Start to practise customer service at home. Serve your family and friends as you would a customer.
- Don't tolerate bad service any more. Make quality service part of your personal and business culture. If we don't do anything about this service disease that has infected Canada, many of us will end up shopping across the border where someone else takes service a little more seriously.
- Find out what leading businesses in your area of interest have done to achieve superior customer service and try to implement similar service strategies in your own business.

Now is a good time to revisit the touchpoint analysis you did in the last chapter. Complete Action Step 32.

Promotional Strategies

THE PROMOTIONAL MIX

Once you have your service and quality in line, the key to connecting with customers is to consider a variety of promotional strategies and then pick the right one. There are four main elements to a promotional strategy:

- Paid advertising
- Personal selling
- Sales promotion
- Publicity or unpaid promotion

PROMOTIONAL MIX

all the elements that you blend to maximize communication with your target customer

Within the four categories is a wide range of other elements, the **promotional mix**, which include:

- Paid media advertising
- Point-of-purchase displays
- Catalogues
- Direct mail
- Money-back guarantees
- Free ink and free air
- Freebies
- Personal selling
- Trade shows
- Industry literature
- Work visibility
- Discount coupons
- Branding
- Promotion in cyberspace

Box 6.2 E-Exercise

- **Sales and Marketing Quiz**
  www.profitguide.com/quizzes/sales.asp

Test your promotional savvy against the experts with this interactive test.

All these elements together make for an overall promotional strategy. You may use some at one time or with one product, and others at another time or with a different product. The E-Exercise in Box 6.2 will help you assess your promotional know-how.

POTENTIAL STRATEGIES

Before you select a promotional strategy, you should have a clear understanding of your promotional objectives. Are you trying to establish a presence in the marketplace? Increase sales? Carve out a niche for your business? Expand your market? Identifying your promotional goals will enable you to spend your marketing dollars wisely as you work to connect with your target customer.

Paid Media Advertising

A sure-fire way to reach out is through advertisements on radio, television, display boards (written or electronic), newspapers, magazines, and trade journals. Advertising tickles the target customer's mind. With a good ad, you can reach right into your TC and create the desire to buy from you.

Advertising has some obvious drawbacks: (1) it can be expensive to create; (2) if you don't spend even more money, your ad won't get exposure; and (3) major advertisers get preferred placements (i.e., the best locations within a publication, store, or business area; or the best time slots on TV or radio).

Advice:

- Make sure that a large percentage of the listeners, viewers, or readers are in one of your TC groups. Otherwise your message is wasted.
- Your best ad is often yourself. Stay visible and remember the importance of personal selling.
- Check with vendors. Ask for tear sheets, copy, and cooperative advertising money, and help on advertising design and layout.
- Check with marketing departments of newspapers. Ask for help, advice, and information.
- Newspapers sometimes offer advertising in special supplements, such as a small business section, at reduced cost. The offer includes free editorial copy.
- Explore creative co-op advertising, in which suppliers share a portion of the cost.
- Don't be afraid to piggyback. Let Madison Avenue build the market. Then use your promotional mix to tell the TC to buy at your place.
- Start small, and test and analyze the results of each promotional campaign.

Point-of-Purchase Displays

These displays, situated usually at or near the checkout counter or front desk, encourage impulse purchases of last-minute items like paperbacks, pantyhose, candy, magazines, and gum. A sharp P-O-P (point-of-purchase) display can improve your image, and it serves as a tireless, silent salesperson, always on duty. A good P-O-P can be used for customer education. If it is hard to understand how to use your product or the benefits aren't clear to the TC, your silent salespeople can deliver the message.

There are, at the same time, a few problems with these displays: (1) you can't sell large items because they crowd customers at the cash register; and (2) the display must sell itself as well as the product. (A tacky P-O-P will turn prospective customers *off* instead of *on*.)

Advice:

- Do weekly evaluations of all P-O-Ps. Make certain your silent salespeople are doing their work.

Catalogues

This sales tool is just right for isolated shoppers and shoppers in a hurry. Because we are becoming so "time poor," even general items are now being purchased via catalogues. Customers can shop at their convenience and not have to worry about store hours, parking, or traffic. Catalogue houses such as Lillian Vernon or Lands' End don't usually manufacture anything, so they are always looking for good products. Use catalogues as another kind of silent salesperson to reach customers if your TC tends to be a catalogue shopper.

If you try printing your own catalogues, you'll run into at least three problems: (1) cost (they are expensive to print and to mail); (2) size limitations (it's tough to sell anything by catalogue that's big, bulky, or inconvenient to ship); and (3) the challenge of establishing and maintaining a reliable mailing list.

Advice:

- Be prepared to take advantage of online catalogues. They are growing in number, especially in business-to-business transactions.
- Let major catalogue houses do your promotion, but make sure you can deliver if your product takes off.
- Before you get in too deep, approach a few major houses with a product description plus photographs. If they don't like your product, they may help you locate a catalogue house that will. The feedback will be invaluable.

Direct Mail

DIRECT MAIL

advertisements or sales pitch that is mailed directly to target customers

This promotional tool lets you aim your brochures and flyers where they will do the most good. **Direct mail** is very important for small business because it can go to the heart of your target market.

The success of direct mail depends on your ability to define the target market. A key to the success of Just White Shirts & Black Socks in the opening vignette was its customer list of over 50 000 target customer names, addresses, phone numbers, and e-mail addresses. This list allows the company to direct mail and develop a special relationship with its target customers. Remember, you have to know exactly who your TC is. If the market is too fragmented for you to do this, direct mail is not for you.

Advice:

- Develop customer lists.

Money-Back Guarantees

You may not have thought of a guarantee as a form of promotion, but it is. You can reach security-minded customers by emphasizing the no-risk features of your product.

The problem is that you must back up your guarantee with time and money. Therefore, if you have a guarantee, don't overlook the cost implications in your income and expense statements.

Advice:

- Figure 5 percent into your pricing to cover returned goods. If the product is fragile or easily misused—and people have been known to misuse just about everything—build in a higher figure.

Free Ink and Free Air

Free publicity through reviews, features, interview shows, press releases, and newspaper columns costs you nothing and can be effective. Free ink and free air are excellent ways to promote because they establish your company in a believable way. The target customer is likely to attach more credence to words that are not paid advertising. The obstacle here is getting media people to think your business is unique and noteworthy.

Advice:

- *Every* business is newsworthy in some way. Dig until you find a different twist. Know the media people. Aim your release at *their* target readers, viewers, or listeners.
- Make your press kit visually appealing, include your story, and send accompanying photos of your principals, your facility, and your product being used or your service being performed.

Freebies

You can use a giveaway, or "freebie," to attract your target customer's attention, stimulate interest in a new product, or gather market research. Box 6.4 shows some examples of effective—and inexpensive—giveaways.

Personal Selling

It doesn't matter if you've never sold before; no one is a better salesperson than you are if you believe in your product or service. You are the business. If you listen

Box 6.3 Bookmark This

More and more, retailers are going online to sell their products. Here are a few examples:

- **Canada Shopping Links**
  www.canadashoppinglinks.com
  —a directory of Canadian retailers offering online shopping
- **TownNet.com**
  www.townnet.com/shopping/olmalls.html
  —a collection of links to online malls
- **Downtown Anywhere**
  www.awa.com
  —links to and descriptions of online retailers
- **CyberSuperStore**
  www.cybersuperstore.com
  —lower end of the online shopping experience

Box 6.4 How Street Smart Are Your Freebies?

Every business has a "freebie" that will help grab the mind of its target customer. This book is full of examples: the toy store retailer who gave away a large jar of pennies in exchange for a start on a customer mailing list; the inventor who gave away one computer lock box in exchange for a mailing list of 1400 names. Here are some more examples of effective, street-smart freebies.

Orange juice. A manufacturer of a new juice squeezer served freshly squeezed orange juice at a trade show.

Hot dogs. A retailer obtained hot dogs and buns from a local hot dog maker, then advertised with promotions that read "Bring your buns to our August Sale at noon." At noon, the line of hot dog lovers stretched around the block. Curious customers, lured by free food and the carnival atmosphere, walked into the store to check out the sale. The cost of this promotion was $66.

Health drink. The distributor of an expensive food blender gave away cups of a health drink and a booklet of recipes at a trade show. Salespeople were on hand to take orders for the blender.

Advice. A men's clothing store employed a woman fashion consultant during the month of December to give advice to women who came in to shop for presents for men.

A flower shop passed out "Green Thumb" information leaflets on plant care.

A hardware store expanded into the parking lot for a "home improvement weekend." Professionals were on hand to give tips and instruction on laying tile, repairing garden hoses, fixing leaky faucets, and installing deadbolt locks.

Often, suppliers will have promotional giveaways.

Source: Adapted in part from Toni Delacorte, Judy Kimsey, and Susan Halas, *How to Get Free Press* (San Francisco: Harbor Publishing, 1981), pp. 120–121, 125, 131–132.

carefully, your TCs will *tell* you how to sell them your product or service. That's why a good salesperson is a creative listener, not a fast talker. Most customers like to talk with the owner of the business. Use that to your advantage. (See Box 6.5.)

PERSONAL SELLING
the selling and taking of orders by an individual salesperson

Unfortunately **personal selling** is expensive, especially if you have to pay others to do it, and it will boost your overhead unless you pay your salesperson only by earned commission. And if you try to do it all yourself, you won't have the time and energy for other things that only you can do. But for small businesses, the best form of promotion is personal selling.

Advice:

- Make everyone in your business a salesperson: delivery people, warehouse people, computer programmers, bookkeepers, clerical people, switchboard operators. If nothing sells, they're out of a job. Remind everyone who works for you that your TC needs a lot of TLC (tender loving care).
- Consider developing a network of sales reps who will work on a percentage of sales. Keep cheerleading. Reps need encouragement, too.
- Increase your personal visibility. Join a business or service club and trade associations. Write a newspaper column. Be bold.
- Stay in touch with your customers and listen to them. If you don't, you may lose your business.

Trade Shows

These shows display your product or service in a high-intensity way. Trade shows focus on customers who have a keen interest in your business area. Your appear-

Box 6.5 Direct Sales Is Alive and Thriving

The Direct Sellers Association of Canada defines **direct selling** as "the sale of a consumer product or service by an independent sales contractor in a face-to-face manner away from a fixed retail location." Direct sales is still alive and thriving, but few firms make house calls like the Fuller Brush salesman or Avon lady of the 1950s and '60s. Direct selling mainstays like Avon Canada Inc. and Amway of Canada Ltd., or Canadian upstarts like Weekenders, have adjusted to the "ding dong" tactics of the past. House parties, offices, and technology are their new stomping grounds—and in many cases, their roads are electronic and their doors were on computer screens. Here are some facts:

Direct Selling: Industry Facts

Estimated 2000 Canadian Retail Sales: $1.6 Billion

Percent of Sales by Major Product Groups

• Home/Family Care Products (cleaning products, cookware, cutlery)	30.5
• Personal Care Products (cosmetics, jewellery, skin care, etc.)	39.3
• Services/Miscellaneous/Other	5.5
• Nutritional/Vitamins	19.4
• Leisure/Educational Products (books, encyclopedias, toys/games, etc.)	5.4

Location of Sales (as a % of sales dollars)

• In the home	71.8
• In a workplace	15.2
• Over the phone	8.4
• At a temporary location	1.7
• Other locations	2.9

Estimated 2000 Independent Sales Contractors: 1,000,000+

Source: The Direct Sellers Association of Canada, retrieved from www.dsa.ca/english.html

DIRECT SELLING

the sale of a consumer product or service by an independent sales contractor in a face-to-face manner away from a fixed retail location

ance at a trade show asserts your position in your industry. The local library should have a copy of the publication *Canadian Industry Shows and Exhibitions*. This will help you learn where to display your products. You may also want to check the CARD (*Canadian Advertising Rates and Data*), which lists many publications under various occupational and industrial classifications. Another option is to visit the Trade Show News Network (www2.tsnn.com).

However, if the show is not in your area, you'll have transportation costs, as well as booths and rental space. Furthermore, unless you're careful and make a study of the layout, you may rent a space that is thin on traffic. See, for example, Figure 6.1.

Advice:

- Share a booth with another small business owner.
- Get your suppliers to help out. Or share a booth with your supplier.
- Combine functions by doing some market research while you're promoting.
- Try to obtain space in a high-traffic area.

Industry Literature

Become a source of information in your industry by producing brochures, newsletters, handbooks, product documentation, annual reports, newspaper columns for the layperson, or even the "bible" for your industry (how would you

Figure 6.1 Map of the Layout at a Trade Show

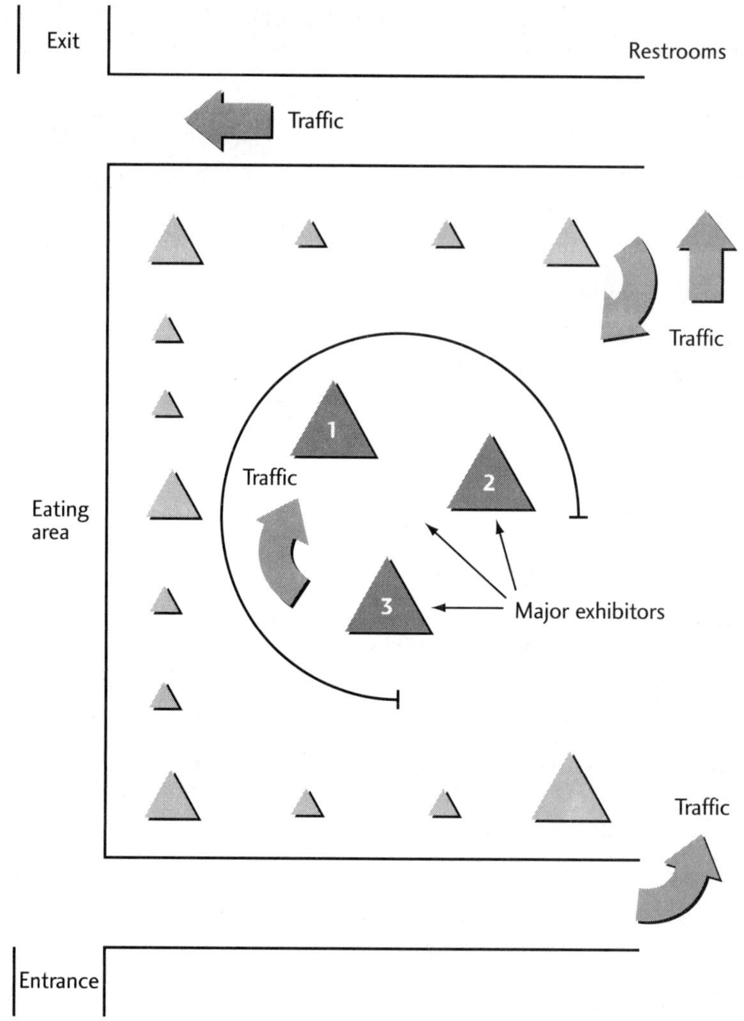

If you can preview the layout of trade show for where the heaviest traffic flows will be, you can position your booth to take advantage of it.

like to be recognized as an expert in your field?). We think this is one of the best promotional devices around if your business lends itself to trade literature promotion.

Remember that expertise is admired and sought out by others. As you grow in expertise, you'll also grow in confidence.

Advice:

- If you're not a good writer, encourage a friend to help.
- Talk is cheap. If you get your thoughts down on paper, you're two steps ahead of the talkers.
- Sometimes joint advertising with a manufacturer in a trade magazine is possible.
- Use your website to inform and help your customers.

Box 6.6 They Said It

"You can't cancel the Web. It's sort of like a child—it requires constant investment."

"To be successful in e-commerce you have to remember one thing above everything else: know your customers, then build the site with them in mind."

"[I]f your market is young people, you probably want a site where there's lots going on—a lot of flash. On the other hand, the majority of our customers aren't into that—they want a quality web experience that doesn't take forever to load and that gets them what they want easily and quickly."

Michael Sachter, Vice-President,
Marketing, justwhiteshirts.com

Source: Industry Canada, Electronic Commerce in Canada, Success Stories, retrieved from http://e-com.ic.gc.ca/english/stories/jwssucc.html

Working Visibility

Most service firms display their presence as they work—they put signs on everything: their business, their trucks, and their work sites. Wherever they're busy, they let people know it. They make themselves visible. One pool cleaning business experienced a dramatic increase in sales after it introduced a policy requiring its cleaners to wear spotless white uniforms.

The drawback here is similar to one of the drawbacks with point-of-purchase display. If the presence you maintain doesn't sell itself—if it is unattractive or if it calls attention to an unappealing part of your business—you will lose potential customers rather than gain them.

Advice:

- Exploit your public activities with signs that tell people who you are.
- Be unique and professional in your image and message.
- Make sure the message is working.

Discount Coupons

Discount coupons are a special form of freebie because they give you positive feedback on your promotion. They should have an expiration date and multiple-use disclaimers (as, for example, a disclaimer that the coupon cannot be used in conjunction with other promotions or discounts). They should also be coded to identify the source so that you can find out where your advertising is paying off, and tested in small quantities before major use.

Everyone seems to like coupons. Even if your product or service is upscale, consider trying coupons as an introduction or at your slow times of the year.

Another twist on the coupon is the entitlement card: "Buy five cups of coffee and get the sixth cup free." There are numerous variations on this theme.

Advice:

- Consider giving away freebies that will catch your customer's attention. Box 6.7 shows some examples of low-cost promotional strategies.

Branding

The coffee mug you carry often has its own identity—maybe telling everyone, for example, that you are a Tim Hortons customer. And maybe it's the same with the baseball cap you wear: the "swoosh" on it tells everyone who's got you branded. A

Box 6.7 More Street-Smart Ideas

Barbara Lambesis, founder of Phoenix-based Marketing Methods, and Margaret Swaine, founder of Toronto-based Pierce Communications, formed a cross-border partnership to help small businesses develop affordable promotional strategies. Lambesis and Swaine, the authors of *101 Big Ideas for Promoting a Business on a Small Budget*, invite their readers to send them their promotional ideas and pay $10 for each idea they decide to print in their book.

Here are a few of Lambesis and Swaine's "big ideas":

- **Walking signs.** Hire a student to model or walk near your store with a sandwich board sign advertising your business.
- **Yellow Pages.** The Yellow Pages are popular because they have a reputation for producing results.
- **Guarantees.** Tom Stoyan, author of *Sell More ... 101 Ideas to Increase Sales Now!*, has a guarantee: "The exercises in this book are guaranteed to work for you. If they do not, I will gladly refund your full purchase price if you provide me with evidence you have worked the ideas for 30 days, along with your sales receipt." As Tom Stoyan will attest, guarantees work.
- **Special sales.** Don't just have a sale—have a happening. Try to be unique. In their book, *101 Big Ideas for Promoting a Business on a Small Budget*, Lambesis and Swaine talk about one store that had a "crack of dawn" sale. At this event, people who purchased at least $25 worth of goods received a free breakfast.
- **Referral incentives.** Remember that Lambesis and Swaine will offer you $10 for a good idea they decide to publish.
- **Special events.** A restaurant called Marble Club holds an annual marble-shooting contest, with the proceeds going to a local charity.
- **Greeting cards.** Often, cards at holiday time get lost in the shuffle. Pick a different time to remember your customer—maybe an "unbirthday" card.
- **Free talks and presentations.** In Chapter 7, you will meet Sheila Mather who gives free talks to groups of small business students.
- **Home parties.** Even if you deal mainly with the business community, invite your customers to your home on a Friday at noon for a light lunch and a swim. If you don't have a pool, try a picnic.
- **Statement stuffers.** It doesn't cost much to include a coupon, flyer, or announcement with your invoice.

Source: Adapted from Barbara Lambesis and Margaret Swaine, *101 Big Ideas for Promoting a Business on a Small Budget* (Toronto: Pierce Communications Press, 1990). Reprinted by permission.

BRAND

a name, sign, symbol, design, or combination of these used to identify the products of a firm

brand is a name, sign, symbol, design, or combination of these used to identify the products of one firm and to differentiate them from competitive offerings. A brand is the promise of the value your customer will receive from you. Smart entrepreneurs figure out ways to make themselves—and thus their business—distinctive.[6]

Advice:

Start with answering the following questions:

- What makes you and your business unique?
- How does your customer benefit from your product or service?
- What would your customer say is your greatest strength?
- What is your most noteworthy personal trait? How is this trait tied to your business?
- Why should your customers buy from you instead of from your competitors?

Promotion in Cyberspace

> J. Robillard, owner of Avant-Garde Engineering Inc. in L'Assomption, Quebec, had a gut feeling that his potential customers were looking online for new product information. So, he ordered up a 25-page website with lots of pictures and product descriptions. His site caught the attention of a Texas contractor who eventually placed an order worth $217 000.

According to PROFIT 100, now is the time to be on the web—even if you don't think your target customer is a potential web-surfer. Every business should have a website. It's your electronic telephone number and a valuable key to success.[7]

Today, anyone can have a website. And almost anyone does. But a site with no visitors is of little benefit to you. How do you make your site worth bookmarking? Sites that can help you build your web presence and stay current with the technology are provided in Box 6.8.

Advice:[8]

- Promote your website offline. Offline promotion of a website can account for a major portion of first-time buyers. Include, for example, your website address in your letterhead and business cards. Be innovative; use every opportunity you have to promote your website with your company name.
- Get your website listed with search engines and directories. This will help your customer find you.
- The title of your web page should clearly indicate the contents or purpose of the site.
- Design your message so that it is simple and easy to update.
- The web is good for selective reading. Help your customers quickly select what they want.
- Remember that your customers may not have the most recent Internet technology. If you design a site that requires the latest technology, you are going to lose some customers—how many will depend on your target market.
- Make your web page action-oriented. Provide your customer with the benefits of purchasing from you.

Box 6.8 Bookmark This

Web Marketing

Here is a list of great sites to help you stay current with technology and promote your product or service on the web:

- **ebiz.enable** (Industry Canada)
  http://strategis.ic.gc.ca/SSG/ee00247e.html
- **Electronic Commerce in Canada** (Industry Canada)
  http://ecom.ic.gc.ca/english/index.html
- **Sales & Marketing** (PROFITguide.com)
  www.profitguide.com/sales/issues_article.asp?ID=791
- **Search Engine Watch**
  http://searchenginewatch.com
- **Advertising Age**
  http://adage.com

- In the interactive world, the ad is only there if the person finds it. Therefore, promoting on the Internet must give the customer a compelling reason to search out the site. According to Don Tapscott, one of Canada's premiere cybergurus, your website must be rich in content, entertaining, and integrated with content.

Sales Reps as Connectors

Suppose you have a new product that has immediate sales potential across the country. How can you connect with the whole country? Should you hire your younger brother to take care of it for you, or should you seek out a professional sales representative, who will act like a commissioned sales agent for you?

An army of sales reps awaits your call. Make your selection carefully. Exercise caution, because the reputation of your sales reps will become *your* reputation.

The best way to find good reps is to interview potential buyers of your goods. Ask them to recommend some reps who have impressed them. When the same name surfaces several times, you will know where to start your contacts. Also, look carefully at who calls most frequently on your TC.

Aggressive reps may contact you. Prepare yourself to ask them the right kinds of questions:

- Who are your customers?
- How many salespeople do you have?
- What geographic areas do you cover?
- What lines have you carried?
- What help can you offer in collecting overdue accounts?
- What ideas do you have for trade show presentations?
- Do you have a showroom?
- Could you work with us on a regional analysis while we get ready for national coverage?
- Do you promote over the Internet?
- What percentage commission do you expect?
- Can I participate in your sales meetings?
- Do you handle competitive lines?
- What kind of reports on your sales calls can I expect?
- What kind of performance guarantees do you offer?
- How can the agreement be terminated?
- Can I pay out after I have collected from customers?

Provide all the encouragement and support to your reps that you can, and never stop being a cheerleader. At the same time, insist on sales call reports that will keep you informed on what is going on in the field, and pack your bags and make some calls with your reps. Write monthly sales letters and encourage feedback from both your reps and their customers. You *could* learn the worst—that a new line has taken your place or that the reps have been sleeping. This feedback will help you evaluate your product line and your reps.

Courtesy as Promotion

A dealer in luxury imported autos mailed 5000 postcards to high-income prospects. The postcard message read something like "Come in and test-drive this road warrior and receive a nice gift."

One potential customer travelled 65 kilometres for his test drive. The gift was a good incentive, but he'd been looking at cars for a year and was about to make a decision, so he wanted the test drive. That morning he had transferred funds to his chequing account. "Honey," he said to his wife as he left the house, "I'll be home with a car." His pink slip on his trade-in smouldered in the glove compartment.

Mr. Serious Prospect entered the dealer's showroom wearing old clothes and clutching his postcard. Four dapper salesmen in three-piece suits had seen him coming and had left the showroom quickly.

Without a salesperson in sight, the prospect spent 10 minutes waiting, reading the literature. The demos were locked, so he couldn't even sit behind the wheel for a fantasy drive. At last, a secretary entered the showroom, asked him for his postcard, and gave him the premium gift. About this time, one salesman returned, hands in his pockets and looking bored. The prospect took the opportunity to ask some questions about the car, to which the salesman responded without enthusiasm in monosyllables—and with a yawn.

Mr. Prospect took his business elsewhere that morning. He found the car he wanted and wrote a cheque for $45 000.

The promotion objective was to bring in customers for a test drive, not to give away premiums. Everything worked except the last person in the chain. How many other deals did that dealer lose during the promotion?

Be dramatic. Impress your employees with the fact that you mean business about customer courtesy. Close down your business for a day and have all employees attend a sales retreat that stresses the importance of potential customers to your remaining in business. Follow up the retreat with incentive programs that reward employees for acts of exceptional courtesy to customers.

Planning Ahead

You need to make a lot of intelligent noise before you open your doors for business. When you open, open with a bang. Start-ups are ironic: you often need to spend a large sum of money to overcome buyer inertia, yet you don't have those dollars to spend. What are you to do? Use your head instead of your chequebook.

Plan for your opening now. Few businesses are profitable at first, so yours probably won't be either. Many of the promotional tools we've just discussed cost very little. You will need to use them to lure customers and build confidence that you are in this game to win. And keep your target customers clearly in mind so that you'll be able to tell them how your product or service will benefit them.

DON'T KEEP YOUR BUSINESS A SECRET

When it comes to promotion, if you fail to plan, you're planning to keep your business a secret. One way to avoid keeping your business a secret is to brainstorm an ideal **promotional campaign** with no holds barred and no worries about costs. Action Step 33 makes sure you consider all of your creative ideas before you discard them because you think they are unrealistic. Save the ideas you come up with in this Action Step because we'll use them later. Box 6.9 shows how two entrepreneurs applied ingenious—and cost-effective—solutions to their promotional needs.

ACTION STEP 33

Brainstorm a winning promotional campaign for your business.

Disregard all budgetary restraint. Pretend that money is no object. Close your eyes, sit back, and develop the ideal campaign for connecting with your target customers. It's okay to "get crazy" with this, because excellent workable solutions often develop out of such unleashed mental activity!

- If your product or service needs a multimillion-dollar advertising promotion with endorsements by your favourite movie star, fantasize that it's happening now.
- If you need a customer list created in marketing heaven, specify exactly what you need and it is yours.
- If you are looking for the services of a first-class catalogue house, just whisper the name three times and you are in business.
- If your business at its peak could use a thousand delivery trucks with smiling drivers who make your TC feel terrific, write down "1000 smiling delivery people."
- If your product is small, brainstorm the perfect point-of-purchase device, perhaps one with slot machines whose money-tubes are connected to your private bank vault.
- How would you promote your product or service over the Internet? Design the perfect website. Watch the money roll in.

This chance to ignore cost won't come around again (reality is right around the corner). But for now, have fun.

PROMOTIONAL CAMPAIGN
a sales program designed to sell a specific product or service or to establish an image, benefit, or point

Box 6.9 Creative Promotional Ideas from *Street Fighter*

Don't be afraid of being different. What's hot? What's cool? What's melting in your arms?

Problem: Salespeople at Wisman's Trusted Appliance & TV, Inc., feared they were losing business when customers left the store to comparison-shop. The opportunity? The owner packed a freezer with ice cream. Every customer who looked at a freezer got a half-gallon carton, *free*. Instead of comparison shopping, the customers raced home to their refrigerators. That gimmick kept Wisman's in the mind of the prospect and helped increase sales by 11 percent.

Contest? Fat prize? Insure yourself at Lloyd's

The owner of a small print shop was tapped for $750 by the organizers of a charity golf tournament. Wanting as much mileage as possible for his promotional dollar, he offered a hole-in-one contest prize of $10 000, to be split between the charity and the first golfer to ace the ninth hole. The owner's picture was taken with an oversize cheque, and the media kept cameras trained on the ninth hole. And if the golfer had sunk one? No problem. The shop owner was insured with Lloyd's of London against business loss, with a premium of $450—$300 less than his name on the donors' board would have cost.

Source: Adapted with permission from *Street Fighter Marketing*, a book published by Street Fighter Marketing, Inc. 467 Waterbury Court, Cohanna, OH 43230, USA. Written by Jeff Slutsky. Website: http://streetfighter.com

Promotion and Market Research

As you gain experience in promoting your small business, you'll see for yourself just how much your promotional strategy and the target customer are interlocked. That's why you can't plan your promotional strategy without building on your market research. This helps you develop your **core benefit proposition**. Your TCs are interested in what your product or service will do for them. You are selling benefits, not features. Your research will help you clarify the benefits of your product or service. That's why you can't plan your promotional mix without dipping back into market research. The pros do both at the same time.

CORE BENEFIT PROPOSITION
a statement about the benefits of your product or service to your target market

ASK CUSTOMERS QUESTIONS TO DEVELOP YOUR MARKETING STRATEGY

Review your customer touchpoints from Action Step 32 and your brainstorm from Action Step 33. Then ask your customers how they perceive your business. Ask them questions such as:

- Is there anything you couldn't find?
- Is this your first visit to this store? (or some other greeting instead of "Can I help you?")
- What do you want and do we have it?
- How does our product or service fit your needs?
- How do we compare in price to the competition?
- Is there more value to you in shopping here than elsewhere?
- Where are you from?
- How did you find us?
- How else might our company be of service?

Listen to the answers your customers give you, and value the information for what it is: primary market research data. Write down each customer's exact words in your Adventure Notebook.

Networking

Another source of promotional power is the technique of **networking**. Networking carries the image of your business to a support group of non-competitive helpers. Gena D'Angelo speaks for many when she gives this testimonial for networking.

> When Rob and I decided to go into business for ourselves, we looked around for more than a year. I had some training in graphics and Rob is good with numbers, so what we finally decided on was a franchised mail-box operation. We paid the franchiser a flat fee and agreed to pay a percentage of our gross as well. In turn, we received assistance and a well-developed business plan.
>
> What they didn't tell us about was networking.
>
> When you're in the mail-box business, giving good service is how you forge ahead. We knew we had to promote our image, and we tried everything—brochures, leaflets, flyers, and full-page display ads in the local newspapers. But the business didn't start rolling in until I joined my first network.
>
> It's a sales lead club, and the membership is varied. We have a real-estate broker, an insurance agent, the president of a small bank, the owner of a coffee service, a printer, a sign manufacturer, the owner of a chain of service stations, a sporting goods store owner, a travel agent, two small manufacturers, and a contractor. We meet once a week for breakfast. If you don't bring at least one sales lead for another club member, you have to put a dollar in the kitty. I've gotten more business from that club than from all my other promotional efforts combined.
>
> I then decided to join another club, and I used the contacts I made to build my own network. Business has been good ever since. We opened our second shop last April, put in a computer to keep track of our customers, and added an answering service. That first year, we networked our way to even more business, and we're planning to open a third shop 10 kilometres south of here by this time next year.
>
> Networking gives you confidence, and it allows you to pass on helpful information to people who aren't competing with you—and to receive that kind of information too.

As a small business entrepreneur, you can network your way to a surprising number of new customer connections, which can spell success in big letters. If you don't have a network, use Action Step 34 to build one. Develop your network and build core groups of people within it. Because a network grows naturally from the loose association of people you already know, and because you are at the centre of the net, it has to help you.

Find out what entrepreneurial guru Rein Peterson has to say about networking in Box 6.10. Then go to Box 6.11 to improve your networking skills.

NETWORKING
communicating through person-to-person channels in an attempt to sell or gain information; talking to people with the purpose of doing business

ACTION STEP 34

Build your network.

Visualize yourself as being in the centre of a web of interpersonal contacts and associations. This web connects you with your family, friends, neighbours, acquaintances, business associates—everyone you know—and it is your potential network.

To develop a functioning network for yourself, write down what you know about each person in your web: business, hobbies, residence, children, interests, and whom they might know. Recall where you met the person. Does the meeting place tell you anything helpful? Are you members of the same group or club? What interests do you share? What is the connection between you and the person?

Now, from all these people, build a couple of core groups. Start with two or three people. Are they interested in networking? Are they diverse enough? (You'll need doers, stars, leaders, technicians, an organizer or two—people who will tend to "balance out" your own talents. See Chapter 12 on team building.) Make sure the people you contact are not competing for the same target customers. The members of a core group must *not* be competitors; if they are, the group won't function as it should.

Set up a meeting. If you are working, breakfast usually works best. If the core group catches on, you can share phone duties and arrange further meetings.

Before you know it, you will be networking your way through the channels of your community, business to business.

Box 6.10 Your Entrepreneurial Know-Who

Rein Peterson is one of Canada's entrepreneurial gurus. Here is what he has to say about networking.

Networking is a basic and critical resource for Canadian entrepreneurs. Nurturing and building personal "know-who" entrepreneurial skills is often a prerequisite for success in pursuing opportunities beyond resources currently in place. People make use of other persons to pass on recommendations, solicit jobs, obtain funds, and so on, but this is often denied in public, for it is regarded as wrong to do so. But research continues to show that:

1. Successful entrepreneurs spend more than 50 percent of their time maintaining their personal networks.
2. Personal entrepreneurial networks outlast individual business ventures.
3. Managing a personal entrepreneurial network requires initiative.

As a result, entrepreneurial students (at the Schulich School of Business, York University) are taught the Nine Rules for Developing Your Entrepreneurial Know-Who:

1. First, you must admit that entrepreneurial know *who* is as important as entrepreneurial know *how*. Be diplomatic, but don't be inhibited about developing contacts that will assist you in starting your new venture. Reciprocity is a universal value. If you help someone else, they are likely to respond in kind. If they do you a favour, consider it an invitation to reciprocate.
2. Be systematic, explicit and forthright in creating and managing your network. Successful entrepreneurs use annotated name card files. There is also software available for your computer to record your contacts' addresses, telephone numbers, birthdays and other relevant information.
3. Assess your network in terms of the specific types of ventures that you peruse. For growing ventures, does your network provide access to financial resources you will continually need—bankers, private investors, angels, other entrepreneurs, etc.? What are your links to knowledgeable professionals—lawyers, accountants, venture capitalists, industry experts, etc.? Are you a member of important industry associations, clubs or civic organizations where you will meet others with similar goals? A typical entrepreneurial network includes about 800 members, only 12 percent of whom are professionals. The vast majority are doers and risk-taking peers like yourself.
4. It helps to place your business venture close to your natural contacts and where others in a similar business are located. For example, the importance of networking among like-minded businesses is evident in the following areas: Kitchener-Waterloo, Kanata, North Toronto, parts of Montreal, Calgary and Vancouver.
5. Use your network regularly. Just like physical fitness requires exercise, networks become stronger and more effective through use. The strengths and weaknesses of your network become apparent only when used.
6. Identify and communicate continuously with the "gatekeepers" in your network. The gatekeepers are the select few special people who are truly committed to you. Not only do they provide you with a sounding board, but they also keep in touch with other potentially useful people of whom you may not be aware or unable to keep in touch with. They know whom you can contact to get help. They form a part of your "virtual" business organization.
7. Assess your network in terms of the entrepreneurial functions you are required to perform: opportunity recognition and risk management. Do you have contacts who can help you spot a potential window of opportunity before the rest of the pack? How many of your contacts are strong enough to tell you when you are wrong?

8. Contribute regularly to your personal network. You need to put something into the well to keep drawing. Social banking, whereby people keep informal track of those who contribute and those who don't, is a fact of life.
9. Don't become a slave to developing your network. Effective entrepreneurship requires a balance between know-how and know-who. You can become ineffective by spending too much time managing your network. It is not a social club, but a business resource.

Source: Rein Peterson, "How Is Entrepreneurship Different in Canada?" in *Mastering Enterprise*, Part One (sponsored by Doane Raymond, Compaq, and Bank of Montreal), *Financial Post* and *Financial Times*. Reprinted by permission of Rein Peterson, Professor and Director of Entrepreneurial Studies, Schulich School of Business, York University, Toronto.

Attach Price Tags to Your Promotional Strategies

A giveaway, like any other promotional strategy, costs money. Look at the ideal promotional strategies you came up with in Action Steps 32 and 33. Then determine the price of each. Action Step 35 walks you through the process. Table 6.1 provides a sample pricing strategy for a flower warehouse.

Don't be discouraged if price knocks out part of your ideal promotional mix. Always evaluate if there is a way to achieve the same result, but with less cost. That's why we've filled this chapter with so many inexpensive promotional ideas. Use the powers of your imagination to brainstorm the best possible promotional effort for your business.

When bankers review a business plan they will definitely want to know how and at what cost you are going to reach your target customers. A well-thought-out marketing promotion plan will demonstrate to your reader that you have done your homework and recognized the benefits and costs of promoting your product or service.

Box 6.11 Bookmark This

Improve Your Networking Skills

- **YouthBusiness.com**
  www.youthbusiness.com

So, you find it hard to go out and talk to people. Or you can't get the answers you want. Why not chat in cyberspace? Visit YouthBusiness.com—a website created by the Canadian Youth Business Foundation—and click on Meeting Place. The Meeting Place for Young Entrepreneurs allows you "to share your ideas, experiences and wisdom as well as providing a forum for discussing issues relevant to entrepreneurs at each stage of business."

Next, click on Networking. You will find all kinds of information you can use to improve your networking skills, including links to networking groups, an article archive, and a free service called "Ask Our Experts."

ACTION STEP 35

Attach a price tag to each item of your promotion package.

What will your customer connection cost? Review Action Steps 32 and 33 and list the top five connections you want with your customers. Then find their cost.

Let's imagine that you have chosen this promotional mix:

1. *Magazine ads.* This choice assumes you know what your TC reads. Contact the display ad department of the magazines. Ask for its media kit, a reader profile, and the rates for its mailing lists for the geographic areas you want to reach. Many magazines will sell lists by a code.
2. *Direct mail.* Look up mailing list brokers in the Yellow Pages under Direct Mail. Ask for information, strategy tips, and sample names to check for mailing list accuracy against your TC profiles. Compare the costs of buying the lists from brokers and from magazines.
3. *Press releases.* Visit the marketing department of your local newspaper for information on targeting its readers. Use this information to angle your release. Catch the reader's attention, but keep the message simple. Be sure to wield the five *W*s (who, what, where, when, why) and the noble *H* (how) of journalism.
4. *Personal selling.* If you cannot reach customers this way yourself, you will need to budget for someone who can. If you plan to sell yourself, locate lead clubs in your area and build a network of contacts. Figure your salary and expenses as a promotional cost. (For tips on how to profile your personality and how it can be balanced by others, see Chapter 12.)

Once you know what each item of your promotional package will cost, you can decide which ones you can afford. Your final plan should look something like Table 6.1.

Table 6.1 Sample Promotional Plan—Flower Warehouse

Promotional Method	Frequency	Annual Cost	Comments
Yellow Pages	Daily	$2 400	Monitor results
Window signs	12/year	$ 360	Support promotions
Point of purchase signs	12/year	$ 240	Support promotions
Newspaper ads	2/month	$3 000	Support promotions
Fliers	12/year	$ 800	With sales promotions
Sales promotions	1/month	$4 500	Holidays and specials
Publicity	12/year	$ 200	Publicize promotions
Personal sales calls	1/week	$ 0	Corporate accounts
Sampling and gifts	As needed	$1 000	Door prizes and referrals
Networking	1/week	$ 600	Sales leads
Thank-you letters	As needed	$ 0	Customer referrals

Source: Adapted from Barbara Lambesis and Margaret Swaine, *101 Big Ideas for Promoting a Business on a Small Budget* (Toronto: Pierce Communications Press, 1990), p. 90. Reprinted by permission.

In a Nutshell

The marketing strategy describes what you have to do to reach your goals and objectives. Within that strategy is promotion. Promotion is the art or science of moving the image of your business into the prospect's mind. Anything that will advance that image is a good tactic to consider. The foundation of any promotional strategy is customer service and quality.

In this chapter, we recommended that you survey the whole range of promotional strategies available to you and then choose the promotional mix that will work best for your unique business. Potential strategies include paid media advertising, point-of-purchase displays, catalogues, direct mail, money-back guarantees, free ink and free air, freebies, personal selling, trade shows, industry literature, work visibility, discount coupons, branding, and promotion in cyberspace.

We also recommended that you seek creative solutions to the problem of promoting within a small budget, and we gave examples of how other entrepreneurs have responded to that challenge. Other topics covered included the proper place of freebies, the reasons why an accurate and up-to-date mailing list is a must for survival, and the importance of networking for sales leads and other information.

Throughout the chapter, we stressed the relationship between market research (your strategy for locating target customers and learning their needs) and promotion (letting your customers know your business can serve their needs and make them happy in the process). The overall message of the chapter is to use your head as well as your chequebook in connecting with the customer.

Key Terms

brand
core benefit proposition
direct mail
direct selling
impact marketing
networking
personal selling
promotion
promotional campaign
promotional mix

Think Points for Success

- ✓ Be unique with your promotions. Instead of Christmas cards, send Thanksgiving cards or April Fool's Day cards.
- ✓ Stand in your target customer's shoes. Think like your TC. Find the need. Find the "ladder" in the TC's mind.
- ✓ Maintain a visual presence.
- ✓ A world in transition means opportunities for entrepreneurship. Fast footwork can keep you in the game.
- ✓ To start your own mailing list, give away something for free. In return, potential customers will give you their names.
- ✓ Rent a Santa. Rent a robot. Rent a hot-air balloon. Rent a talking dolphin.
- ✓ Brand yourself. Create some excitement, because excitement sells.
- ✓ When you think you have it made, keep connecting with that customer anyway. You will never be so big that you can afford to disconnect. Remember this and it will make you rich.
- ✓ Remember to promote the benefits and value of your product or service.
- ✓ Use the Internet to promote.

Business Plan Building Block

ADVERTISING AND PROMOTION

Describe your advertising and public relations plan. What are the most cost-effective ways to reach your customers? Use the data you have developed from the text.

Public Relations—Unpaid Advertising

- Sample news releases (attach)
- Research articles or contributions to trade or technical journals
- Participation in or sponsorship of events
- Contributions to local media (air, press, and others)
- Community charities and/or networking activities

Media Advertising and Direct Mail

- Mail list applications
- Advertising-space buys
- Yellow Pages
- Computer bulletin boards and websites
- TV and radio commercials
- Point-of-purchase displays, signs, billboards
- Brochures and selling sheets
- Business cards and ad specials
- Trade shows and informational seminars

Don't be afraid to be different and unique. Your message has to penetrate a lot of clutter.

Your turn: this will take a page or more.

SERVICE AND SUPPLY

Once the sale is consummated, explain delivery of the product. Take out? Will call? UPS? Purolator? FedEx? and so on. Follow with sales support. What will your customer need from you once the product or service has been delivered? Look for techniques to turn your service into additional sales opportunities.

Your turn:

SALES FORECAST

It's time to start firming up your numbers. Forecast the first year by month and the second through fifth years by the quarter. Expect a slow start and adjust for seasonal months that are consistent with your industry. It is helpful to develop a minimum, maximum, or realistic sales forecast.

Support your numbers with data on total market available, your anticipated share, orders already booked, letters of commitment, and anything else that will support your assumptions.

MARKET STRATEGIES

You have already made sales projections. Now demonstrate how you plan to achieve your sales goals.

Outline your activities to identify your target customers' unmet or undeserved needs. How will you communicate with customers to explain how your firm would benefit them?

This is a general statement that demonstrates that your business is customer-driven. Use information in Chapter 4 to develop a one-page marketing strategy philosophy.

SERVICES AFTER THE SALE

Once you have a customer, what will you do to keep him or her? Phone call follow-up? Correcting shipping or product mistakes? and so forth.

Checklist Questions and Actions to Develop Your Business Plan

MARKETING STRATEGIES AND PROMOTION: CONNECTING WITH THE CUSTOMER

- ❑ What is your marketing strategy?
- ❑ What are the promotional mix goals and objectives?
- ❑ What stimulates your target market to buy or use your product or service?
- ❑ What has the primary and secondary market research told you about promoting your business?
- ❑ Develop a promotional strategy for your business.
- ❑ What percentage and what amount of your promotional budget will be spent on each of the components of a promotional mix, and why?
- ❑ Does your business have a unique twist for a possible publicity story?
- ❑ Why did you select the business name you are using?

NOTES

1. JWS website, News Articles, retrieved from www.justwhiteshirts.com/news/index.html
2. Rick Spence, *Secrets of Success from Canada's Fastest-Growing Companies* (Toronto: John Wiley & Sons Canada, 1997), p. 140.
3. Ibid., p. 140.
4. Ibid., p. 142.
5. Geoffrey Rowan, "Customer Service Forms the Currency of the Digital Age," *The Globe and Mail*, March 18, 1998, p. B25.
6. See, for example, Tom Peters, "The Brand Called You," as first published in *Fast Company*, August/September 1997, pp. 83–94; and Strategis, ebiz.enable, "What Is Branding?," retrieved from http://strategis.ic.gc.ca/SSG/ee00173e.html
7. Spence, *Secrets of Success*, pp. 134–135.
8. Thea Partridge, "Building a Site Profile: Print Invitations, Search Opportunities," *Financial Post*, March 8, 1998, p. N4; and Don Tapscott, *Growing Up Digital: The Rise of the Net Generation* (Toronto: McGraw-Hill, 1998), p. 197.

SUGGESTED READING

Bodean, Nat. *Direct Marketing Rules of Thumb*. Whitby, ON: McGraw-Hill Ryerson, 1997.

Dru, Jean-Marie. *Creative Advertising: Breaking with the Past*. New York: John Wiley & Sons, 1996.

Easto, Larry. *Networking Is More Than Doing Lunch*. Toronto: McGraw-Hill, 1998.

Levinson, Jay Conrad. *Mastering Guerilla Marketing: 100 Profit-Producing Insights That You Can Take to the Bank*. New York: Houghton Mifflin, 1999.

Lewis, Herschell Gorden, and Robert D. Lewis. *Selling on the Net*. Lincolnwood, IL: NTC Business Books, 1997.

Novick, Harold. *Selling Through Independent Reps*. New York: AMACOM, 2000.

Qubein, Nido R. *How to Be a Great Communicator*. New York: John Wiley & Sons, 1997.

Reis, Al, and Jack Trout. *The 22 Immutable Laws of Marketing*. New York: HarperCollins, 1993.

Rosen, Emanuel. *The Anatomy of Buzz: How to Create Word of Mouth Advertising*. New York: Doubleday, 2000.

Schmid, Jack. *Creating a Profitable Catalog: Everything You Need to Know to Create a Catalog That Sells*. Chicago: NTC/Contemporary, 2000.

Siskind, Barry. *Making Contact.* Toronto: ITMC Press, 1999.

Siskind, Barry. "100 Reasons to Exhibit at a Trade Show." *Globe and Mail*, September 17, 1997, Ad Feature.

Zemke, Ron, and Thomas K. Connelan. *E-Service: 24 Ways to Keep Your Customer When the Competition Is Just a Click Away*. New York: AMACOM, 2000.

chapter 7

Location

BUSINESS PLAN BUILDING BLOCK

This chapter will help you select the location that is best for your type of business and the options that may be available.

LEARNING OPPORTUNITIES

After reading this chapter, you should be able to:

- Understand the contribution of location to small business success.
- Understand the uniqueness of your business-location needs.
- Focus on customer needs when evaluating a location.
- Develop a checklist for evaluating potential sites for your business.
- Think about if and when you should locate your business out of the home.
- Use both secondary and primary sources of information in locating your business.
- Understand and negotiate a lease contract.

"In Halifax, there's nothing really like us," Moira Lloyd, co-owner of the Ceilidh Connection, says of the Barrington Street bar. "We're a restaurant on one side, with computers on the other. People can sit here and have a beer and plate of fries while they surf [the Net]." The target customer is between the ages of 20 and 35. The online lounge is particularly appealing to tourists and business travellers who can "return home" in cyberspace.

Choosing the right location was a critical decision for Moira and her partner, Fiona Merry. They wanted to be close to the tourist trade and the downtown core, and within walking distance of the two universities, St. Mary's and Dalhousie. It looks like all their research has paid off. The restaurant is busy and the cyber lounge is booming. "Once the computers caught on, the lounge became our main income here," says Moira. Two very different menus—a food menu and a computer menu—are featured on the cyber café's website (www.ceilidhconnect.ns.ca).[1]

ACTION STEP PREVIEW

36. Fantasize your perfect location.
37. Use your new eyes to evaluate business locations.
38. Seek professional help in finding a location.

While attending Concordia University, Terry Batah bought ArtTec, a failing retail art supply business in Montreal. Her purchase included a tiny location and a large debt load that took Terry three years to clear. The company's next challenge was growth. Terry had two

Chapter 7 will help you prepare part E of your business plan, "Location."

choices—invest in advertising or in a better location. She firmly believes that small retailers should choose the latter. "Advertising is expensive. The extra cost of a corner location is a better bet," explains Terry. "Think of it as investing in your business by giving it more visibility. Regardless of the location, Terry says retailers have to make creative use of what they've got. "Anyone in retail will appreciate that the best advertising remains your store's façade, especially creative windows that are constantly changed and updated," says Terry. "That's what catches your customer's eye."[2]

One of the most important decisions the small business entrepreneur makes is where to locate the business. "Location, location, location" have been touted as the three most important reasons for business success. To some extent, and especially in "store-front" operations, this philosophy has a great deal of merit. For example, if you're a business like the Ceilidh Connection or ArtTec and renting a location for a number of years, a good site selection is critical—and most retail leases reflect this importance in their length and complexity, with 30 to 50 pages not being unusual.

This chapter will lead you through the steps involved in finding a good physical location for your business, and the process, should you need it, of negotiating a lease that will serve you well.

And what if you want to operate your business out of your home? First, congratulations! This is a growth market and you may just be on the right track. We have now entered the age of the "gold-collar," or home-based, worker. More and more of us are working at home like Sheila Mather, who is profiled later in the chapter. The gold-collar worker now represents about 20 percent of the Canadian workforce. All kinds of services and products are now provided by home-based businesses. With the growth in services and the knowledge-based industries, chances are you will, one day, be operating some sort of business out of your home.

That said, in planning to set up your business at home, your location analysis is still just as important as if you were to lease. There are a number of critical location questions that you're going to have to think about: Do the municipality bylaws allow me to operate a business at home? How do I balance my family and work life? How do I deal with my target customers from my home? and so on. In this chapter, we'll also encourage you to consider all the pros and cons of locating your business out of the home, to establish your location strategy as part of your overall marketing strategy, and to encourage you to consider a web-based business.

ACTION STEP 36

Fantasize your perfect location.

Sit down where you won't be disturbed and brainstorm the ideal location for your small business. Get a pencil and paper and let yourself dream. Draw a mind map, or use a list format; the idea is to get your thinking on paper.

For example, if you were going to open a candy-cigarette-cigar stand, you might want to locate in the West Edmonton Mall, where people pass by every hour. Or, if you were going to open an extremely upscale boutique, you might visualize a location in Toronto's Yorkville. If you plan to establish a home-based business and meet with customers at that location, consider such factors as the availability of parking in your neighbourhood.

Once you have the general idea of the type of neighbourhood and location you have in mind, write down what else is terrific about this location. Writing everything down will give you a starting point as you move out to explore the world.

The Importance of Location

WHAT IS THE PERFECT LOCATION?

The perfect location is different for every enterprise. If you're in the housecleaning business, you can work out of a van equipped with a cellular telephone. If you're in the mail-order business, you can work out of a "cocoon" or a post office box. Action Step 36 asks you to brainstorm the perfect location for *your* business.

A good location can make everything easier for a new business. A highly visible building that's easy for your customers to reach will save you advertising dollars. Once you've been discovered and your customer base is well established, however, the physical location may become less important. If you are a retailer, your location will depend on the kind of goods you sell—convenience, shopping, or specialty goods.

Work through Action Step 37. It will help you analyze the effect of location on your shopping habits. Use new eyes to examine your own consumer behaviour.

A Location Analysis Checklist

Before you charge out to scout possible locations for your business, you need to decide what you really need. The checklist below will help you zero in on the criteria that are important to your business. Use a scale of 1 to 10 to rate the relative importance of each item in terms of your target customers. When you finish scoring, go back and note the high numbers, say, anything above 5. Then, after you've read the rest of the chapter, come back to this list to see if your priorities have changed.

RATING IMPORTANCE (1–10)

- ✓ *Neighbour mix.* Who's next door? Who's down the street? Who's going to help pull your target customers to the area? Which nearby business pulls the most customers? If you're considering a shopping centre, who's the anchor tenant (the big department store or supermarket that acts as a magnet for the centre)?
- ✓ *Competition.* Do you want competitors kilometres away or right next door? Think about this one. If you're in the restaurant business (a service that customers shop for, at least in their minds), it can help you to be on "restaurant row."
- ✓ *Security, safety.* How safe is the neighbourhood? Is it as safe as a nursery at noon but an urban jungle at midnight? Is there anything you can do to increase the security?
- ✓ *Labour pool.* Who's working for you, and how far will they have to commute? Does your business require more help at certain peak periods of the year? How easy will it be to find that kind of skilled or technical help you need? How far will they travel? Don't overlook the potential of part-timers, teens, seniors, and homemakers. Are there any zoning restrictions?
- ✓ *Services.* Police and fire protection, security, trash pickup, sewage, maintenance: What is included in the rent, and who pays for those services that are not? Is your location near a bus or subway stop?
- ✓ *Costs.* What is the purchase price if you're buying; or what are the rent or lease costs (and what is the type of lease)? Insurance, improvements, association dues, routine maintenance: who pays for what? Can you negotiate a few months' free rent?
- ✓ *Ownership.* If you're still planning to buy the property, who will you get to advise you on real estate? Consider a lease with an option to buy, but have the contract reviewed by a real-estate lawyer.
- ✓ *Past tenants.* What happened to the past tenants? What mistakes did they make, and how can you avoid those mistakes?
- ✓ *Space.* If you need to expand, can you do it there, or will you have to move to a new site?
- ✓ *Accessibility.* Is your business where your target customer might expect to find you?
- ✓ *Parking.* Most people like to park free and close to your door. Is that possible?
- ✓ *History of the property.* How long has the landlord owned this property? Is it likely to be sold while you're a tenant? If the property is sold, what will happen to your business? What will happen to your tax obligations? If the property goes on the market, do you want the first right to make an offer?

ACTION STEP 37

Use your new eyes to evaluate business locations.

Think about how location affects your spending habits. For example, where do you buy gas for your car? Do you buy it on your way to work or school, or on your way home? Why?

Now, with your Adventure Notebook in hand, look through your home. How important was the location of the retailer when you bought the items you see? For example,

- candy, sodas
- prescription drugs
- washing machine
- designer clothes
- paintings
- wristwatch
- wall hangings
- jewellery
- carpeting
- paint
- mail-order items such as books, CDs, magazines, clothing
- power lawn and garden tools
- VCR
- collectibles
- car, motorcycle
- your home itself
- custom-made golf clubs
- eyeglasses

A random look through your chequebook might trigger your memory. Feel free to add to this list.

How far did you travel, for example, for your last dinner out with a friend? For a carton of milk? A magazine? A lounge chair? A videocassette rental? How far would you travel to consult a brain surgeon?

What conclusion can you draw about the importance of location in making a purchase or providing a service?

Remember also that the cheapest location may not always be the best location.

You can expand on this Action Step by interviewing purchasing agents and buyers of commercial and industrial goods. Ask them what impact location has on their choice of vendors or on their recruitment of employees.

- ✓ *Physical visibility*. Does your business need to be seen? If so, is this location easily visible? Can you make alterations to increase its visibility? Can you install the type of sign you want?
- ✓ *Life-cycle stage of the area*. Is the site in an area that's embryonic (vacant lots, open space, emptiness), growing (high-rises, new schools, lots of construction), mature (building conversions, cracked street, sluggish traffic), or declining (vacant building, emptiness)? What will the area be like in five years? What effect would that have on your business? What do the municipal planners have in mind for the area? When will the highway department tear up the street? (See Figure 7.1.)
- ✓ *Image*. Is the location consistent with your firm's image? How will nearby business affect your image? Is this an area where your customers would expect to find a business like yours? (Look for a place that reinforces your customers' perception of your business.)
- ✓ *Local/municipal licensing*. A wide variety of trades and establishments require a licence fee that can range anywhere from $5 to thousands of dollars. In many Canadian municipalities, for example, licences are required if you operate a limousine service, refreshment vehicles, auctioneer service, billiard and pool hall, and skateboarding facilities. You'll also want to find out about local regulations on the installation, alteration, and maintenance of exterior signs and parking.
- ✓ *Hours of operation*. Most municipalities have bylaws regarding the hours of operation. These hours may be different for various areas within a region. If you're planning a retail operation, be sure to look into this detail.
- ✓ *Utilities*. The high cost for water, sewage, gas, or other utilities may bring some unpleasant surprises. You should list all your utility requirements. Are they adequate? What would it require to upgrade them?
- ✓ *Local zoning bylaws*. Check out the present and future zoning. What restrictions may apply to your business?
- ✓ *Taxes*. Property and business taxes can change from street to street. Try to find out if there are any plans for reassessment.
- ✓ *Approval*. Have you considered necessary approvals, such as those required from health officials, the fire marshal, the city planning office, and the liquor licensing board?
- ✓ *Transportation*. How much will your business depend on trucks, rail, buses, airports, or shipping by water? If you're in manufacturing or distribution, you'll need to determine your major transportation channel. It's also a good idea to have a backup system. A good technique here is to make a diagram of the location and all the lines of transportation your business will use in both receiving goods and customers and shipping goods.
- ✓ *Your target customers*. This is the last but most important criterion. Will your customers—lured by your terrific promotions—find you easily but have no place to park? Consider highway access and potential obstacles that could make coming to your place of business inconvenient or unpleasant. What do your customers really want? Ease of parking? Convenience? Atmosphere? Proximity to work? Even the side of the street is important. (For example, a dry cleaner would want to be on the inbound side of the street so customers can easily drop off their cleaning on their way into the city to work.) Your location must satisfy the needs of the customer, not your own personal needs. This is a particularly important consideration if you're planning to operate out of your home. Are you setting up a home-based business because it is convenient to you or your customer? Remember: you work from home, not at home!

Figure 7.1 Life-Cycle Stages of Business Locales

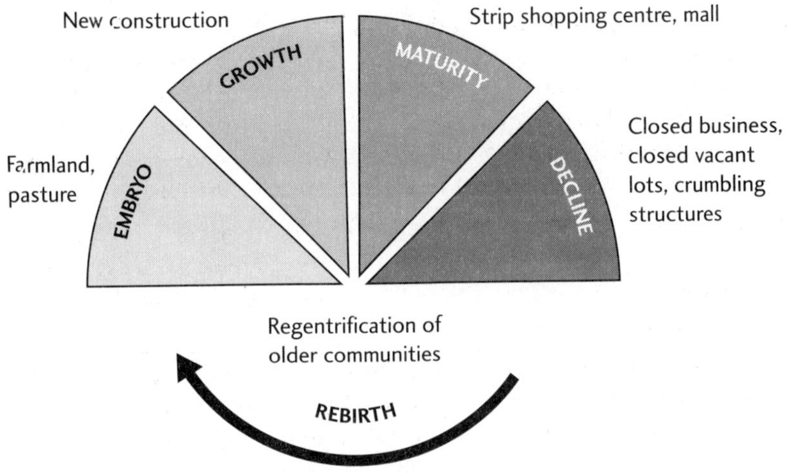

Evaluate the life-cycle stage of each potential location for your business.

The Rise of the Gold-Collar Worker

Exercise + people + fun + work + stress = start a physical fitness program in the workplace. Psychographic thinking and the guidance of visionaries such as Faith Popcorn have been put into practice successfully by Sheila Mather. There she was, on an early Saturday morning, sharing her experience with an audience of soon-to-be businesspeople. She operates her business out of her home, but today this seminar was her location, and she was marketing herself at a local small business seminar called "Look Before You Leap."

Her talk began with a few minutes of low impact aerobics. When everyone was energized, she said, "You don't have to be a rocket scientist. I'm not in the high-tech business per se. But my job is to increase productivity in our growth high-tech sector. I'm in the 'feel good, energy, and people business.' These are the benefits that my customers want. You're also my potential customer, and after exercising, I hope you feel a little better now."

She explained that her home-based location strategy was not about finding a physical site. It was about finding ways to locate herself and her business in front of the customer. "Yesterday, for example, my location was an empty office where I conducted my exercise program for one of my company clients. Today, my location is here at this seminar. In home-based business, your location is fluid, and one thing is for sure: you should plan to be out meeting people, because it is people who will drive your business."

Working at home has become a major trend in the way Canadians do business. About two million Canadian households create jobs, stimulate local economies, and provide a growing commercial market. Most of these home businesses have been in operation for more than one year (44 percent, one to three years; 35 percent, more than three years). Almost half of the home workers are self-employed; 14 percent are substituters (employees who spend part of their day at home); and 39 percent are supplementers (employees who bring work home). According to these statistics, chances are that you will be working out of your home in the future—even if you have another job. In their report on home business, Barbara Orser and Ted James dispel a number of myths about the nature of home-based business (see Box 7.1).

Home business is one of the "golden" industries of the next decade, with the annual growth rate expected to be in the 12 percent range. Major reasons for this trend include:[3]

- *Cocooning.* Many of us are attempting to reduce outside stresses by spending more leisure and work time at home.
- *Computerization.* New high-tech equipment such as fax machines, personal computers, and modems for e-mail and the Internet have made it a lot easier and more convenient to operate out of the home.
- *Two-income families.* It makes it a lot easier to work out of the home when both parents are trying to raise a family and make a living.
- *Growth of the service industry.* A service business generally has lower start-up costs, operational expenses, and equipment costs, making it much more sensible to run your operation out of the home.
- *Higher productivity.* Studies show that productivity increases by 20–60 percent when employees can work during peak times at their own pace. In fact, such

Box 7.1 Dispelling the Myths About Home-Based Businesses (HBBs)

Myth: HBBs are fairly small in number.
Fact: One in four of all Canadian households operates some form of home business.

Myth: HBBs spend all their time at home.
Fact: Less than 40 percent of the workday is spent at the home base; 30 percent is spent on the road and 32 percent at the customer or client's premises.

Myth: HBBs are mostly service providers.
Fact: About 50 percent of HBBs provide service and the remainder are manufacturers and wholesalers.

Myth: HBBs typically occur only in urban areas.
Fact: Nearly half (48 percent) of people primarily running an HBB live in a non-urban area.

Myth: HBBs are motivated by financial reward.
Fact: Intrinsic factors like independence and flexibility are more important motivators for being home-based than financial rewards.

Myth: HBBs create problems for the neighbourhood.
Fact: The number of registered public complaints about HBBs is so small as to be insignificant.

Myth: HBBs deliberately ignore municipal bylaws.
Fact: Forty percent of home-business owners surveyed were not even aware of existing bylaws regulating their business activities.

Source: Barbara Orser and Ted James, *Home Business: A Report Prepared for the Home-Based Project Committee*, Industry, Science and Technology Canada and Employment and Immigration Canada, p. 8. Reproduced with the permission of the Minister of Public Works and Government Services Canada, 1998.

statistics have influenced the new knowledge-based companies to encourage telecommuting.

- *Increased efficiency.* The home worker saves on transportation, rental, furniture and equipment costs.
- *Ergonomics.* The new consumer demands more individual attention. Home-based businesses are well positioned to adapt to changing and individualistic consumer needs.
- *Vigilante consumer.* The new customer is fragile and fickle and craves superior service. This consumer does not tolerate the mediocrity of mass production and sameness.
- *Downsizing.* Today, companies are encouraged to go small and to contract out whenever possible.
- *Mobility.* With the growth in personal care and home care, more and more businesses are going to their customers, which means that a store front is not always necessary.

Starting your business out of the home does not mean that your plan is written on the back of an envelope. It takes just as much care to open and operate a home business as it does to establish a traditional retail business. Before you decide on a location, consider the advantages and disadvantages of operating out of your home. Box 7.2 will help you get started. Weigh the pros and cons carefully. See also Box 7.3 for online resources that could help you run a successful home business.

Getting the Information You Need to Find the Right Location

Businesspeople tend to stay in a location for a while because it is expensive to renovate and move. Thus, selection of your location will be one of your most important start-up decisions. You will want to make sure that you are right in the heart of your target market. So, where do you go for information? We'll begin with secondary sources of location information—that is, published data that have been gathered and compiled by others.

STATISTICS CANADA

Data collected by Statistics Canada could be one of your major sources of secondary information, especially if you are planning to rent, lease, or buy a retail or manufacturing business. But even if you plan to operate your business out of your home, Statistics Canada data can still be useful. For example, you are going to want to know where your target customer lives and works.

Census

The Census of Population is one of the major Statistics Canada sources of information. Census data are gathered every five years (e.g., 1996, 2001, and so on) through a massive survey of the Canadian population (for more details on the Census of Population, see Box 7.4). The data are organized into a number of categories (age, sex, household income, etc.) that are then described and published by Statistics Canada. Census data are produced for a number of standard geographic areas (see Box 7.5 on page 130). Finding the right census information can be time-consuming and sometimes frustrating. To get started, we suggest that you go to the Statistics Canada website (www.statcan.ca) and click on the Census link. Once you have become familiar with census terms and information, we then suggest you visit

Box 7.2 Is Home the Best Place? A Location Checklist

The following checklist may help you determine if you should operate your business out of the home.

- **Target market.** How far will your customers be willing to travel to get to you? Can your business travel or deliver to the customer? How efficient is it for you to serve your customer from your home?
- **Neighbourhood mix.** Do you need other businesses to pull your customer to you?
- **Physical visibility.** Does your business need to be seen?
- **Competitors.** Why would your target customer deal with you out of your home-based business rather than with your competition? What advantages does your home business offer over that of your competitors?
- **Life-cycle stage.** Is your area in an embryonic (e.g., vacant land), growing (e.g., plenty of construction, new schools), mature (e.g., cracked streets, sluggish traffic), or decline (e.g., vacant buildings) stage? Do you want to be doing business in the same location five years from now?
- **Image.** How would your target customers react if they learned that you were operating out of your home? For example, right or wrong, some customers might not take you seriously.
- **Local/municipal.** Do you require a licence, and can you get a licence to operate out of your home?
- **Local zoning bylaws.** Do local bylaws allow you to operate your business out of your home?
- **Space/physical requirements.** Do you have enough space to serve the customer and your business needs effectively? What are your physical requirements? For example, do you need to add a washroom? Do you have a designated area to work? How will the customer enter your location? Do you need a separate entrance?
- **Approvals.** Have you considered the necessary approvals related to health, fire, transportation, environment, and labour?
- **Insurance.** Will your insurance company allow you to operate a business out of your home? How will this affect your insurance premiums?
- **Utilities.** Are there any extra utilities requirements (e.g., extra telephone line)?
- **Work habits/behaviour.** Do you need to "get away in the morning?" Many businesspeople like to completely separate their business and personal lives. Do you have the discipline to work in your home?
- **Lifestyle.** Will your business disrupt your family and personal lifestyles? How will your neighbours feel about you running your business out of your home?

Source: Ron Knowles, *Writing a Small Business Plan: Course Guide* (Toronto: Dryden, an imprint of Harcourt Brace & Company, Canada, 1995), p. 44.

Box 7.3 Bookmark This

Home-Based Business Resources

These websites provide a wide range of resources for people who operate a business out of the home.

- **Business Know-How**
  www.businessknowhow.com
- **BizOffice.com**: Small and Home-Based Business Resources
  http://bizoffice.com/index.html
- **Canadian Home and Micro Business Federation**
  www.homebiz.ca

Box 7.4 Census of Population

What it's about. Provides demographic, social, economic, and cultural information on the Canadian population.

Who is surveyed. All Canadian citizens and landed immigrants aged 15 and over, excluding institutional residents and refugee claimants.

How we collect the data. Household survey; labour market data are collected from a 20 percent sample of the population through self-enumeration, or by canvasser enumeration in remote and northern areas and on Indian reserves.

Frequency. Labour market and income data are collected every 10 years (decennial census), as in the 1991 census, and occasionally collected in the five-year (quinquennial) census, as in 1996.

Response rate. Approximately 95 percent (varies according to questions).

Reference period. The previous calendar year for income and weeks worked; the week worked; the week before Census Day for labour force activity and for class of workers, occupation, and industry of employed persons; the previous 17 months for class of worker, occupation, and industry of persons not employed the week before Census Day.

Geographic detail. Canada, provinces and territories, counties, federal electoral districts, census metropolitan areas, census agglomerations, municipalities, census consolidated subdivisions, enumeration areas, provincial census tracts and block faces (geocoding allows data users to obtain estimates for very specific geographic areas).

Demographic detail. Includes age, sex, education and major field of study, marital status, household relationship, ethnic and cultural origin, mother tongue, language spoken at home, knowledge of official languages, place of birth, citizenship, period or year of immigration, and disability.

Information collected.

- occupational (approximately 500 codes)
- industry (approximately 400 codes)
- class of worker (paid worker, self-employed, unpaid family worker)
- weeks worked in calendar year preceding census
- labour market activities in week preceding census
- wages and salaries
- farm and non-farm self-employment income (net)

Time frame. Wage and salary data since 1901, labour force data since 1951, employment income and total income since 1961.

What makes the data valuable.

- very extensive geographic detail
- extensive number of characteristics available for cross-tabulation
- population coverage includes the Yukon and Northwest Territories
- consistent historical database
- very accurate data

Source: Statistics Canada, "Census of Population," adapted from *Labour Market and Income Data Guide*. April 1992, Cat. No. 75F0010XPB. Reproduced by authority of the Ministry of Industry, 1994.

a main library that carries Statistics Canada information. You should find the information clearly indexed, but don't be afraid to ask the librarian for help.

The major advantages of the census are twofold:

1. *It is comprehensive.* Data can be tabulated by age, sex, employment status, sex, income, and so on.
2. *It is detailed.* Data can be tabulated for small geographic areas, the smallest of which is the enumeration area (about 300 dwellings).

Box 7.5 Bookmark This

2001 Census

To learn more about the 2001 census, visit:

- 2001 Census—Release 2—July 16, 2002
  www12.statcan.ca/english/census01/release/index.cfm

Click on Community Profiles. The 2001 Community Profiles "contain free information for all Canadian communities (cities, towns, villages, Indian reserves and Indian settlements, etc.), counties or their equivalents and for metropolitan areas."

For information on the new standard geographic areas and classification—along with other geography-related changes introduced for the 2001 census—visit www.statcan.ca/english/census2001/dict/geotoc.htm.

The major disadvantage of the census is timeliness. A census is conducted once every five years. By the time the data are published, it could be as many as seven years out of date. However, in many cases, Census data can provide much-needed historical trend information. (See for example, Figure 7.2.)

Other Sources of Statistics Canada Information

The census can be a powerful tool for locating your customer or your business. But it's not the only source, and you should not stop here. A good source of other Statistics Canada information is the Statistics Canada *Market Research Handbook* (Catalogue No. 63-224). Here you will find all kinds of consumer and location information. For example, profiles are provided of key industries in all provinces and 45 major cities. A second important "hard copy" resource document available in most reference centres or libraries is the *Statistics Canada Catalogue* (Catalogue No. 11-204E). This publication has an excellent subject index at the back. Lastly, we encourage you to visit the Statistics Canada website (see Box 7.6 on page 132).

OTHER SOURCES OF SECONDARY INFORMATION

As we know by now, Statistics Canada is not our only source of secondary information. Local municipality and regional governments have all kinds of information, such as traffic counts, so a visit to your local planning office is a must. While you're there, check the zoning bylaws and future plans. For example, you might be awfully disappointed if you decide to locate your home-based business in a municipality that forbids home-operated enterprises. Or locating your business on a road scheduled for sewer work might be your quick ticket to bankruptcy. If you are going into a mall, the mall owners should have a detailed location study. Get their analyses, or don't locate there. Consider potential suppliers. They should know which outlets are doing the greatest business. If you approach them in the right way, they may be pleased to help you. After all, this could mean more future business for them.

Private companies also will, for a price, get you some pretty detailed information. One such firm is MapInfo (www.mapinfo.com), which maintains location databases that are highly targeted and include names of facilities and offices within a specific area.

Commercial real-estate agents can be very helpful, particularly if you're thinking about a retail or manufacturing operation.

Figure 7.2 Census Metropolitan Growth Rates, 1996–2001

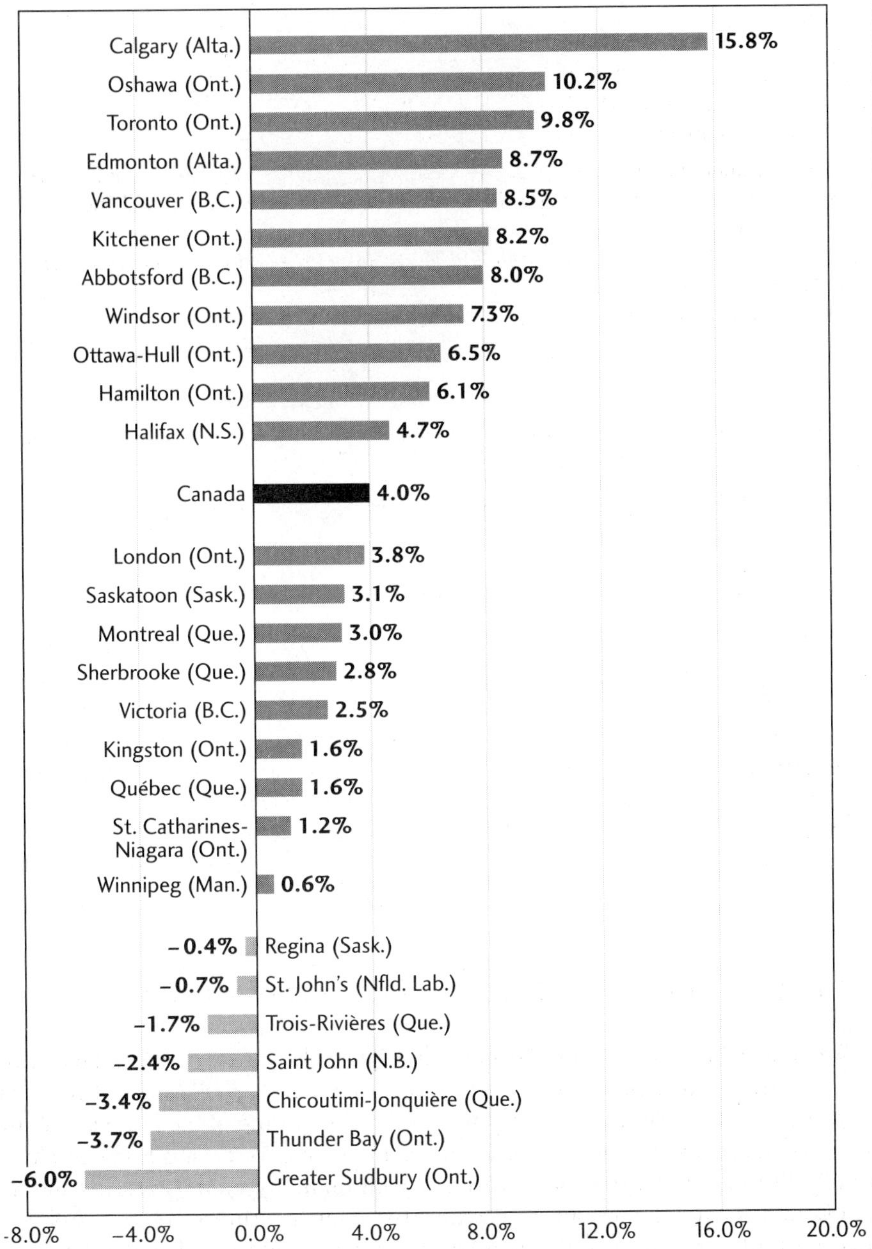

Source: Statistics Canada, Census Metropolitan Growth Rates, retrieved from http://geodepot2.statcan.ca/Diss/Highlights/Page8/Chart1_e.jpg

Finally, we encourage you to get on the Net. Strategis (http://strategis.ic.gc.ca) is probably your best place to start. In Chapter 5, we encouraged you to use Strategis to seek out competitor information. Now we want you to go back to this research and see if you can discover some valuable information for locating your business. Action Step 38 will help you further.

ACTION STEP 38

Seek professional help in finding a location.

Visit a commercial real-estate office to gain information. Commercial real-estate firms have access to planning reports and demographic information that will tell you a lot about growth in the community. Have your plan well in mind and make an appointment beforehand. Dress conservatively.

And leave your chequebook at home!

Box 7.6 www.statcan.ca

Welcome to www.statcan.ca!

From publications to electronic data, census to survey information, **www.statcan.ca** is THE official source for Canadian social and economic statistics and products. Our goal is simple—to provide you with remarkably detailed content on practically every aspect of Canada at a single point of contact. We invite you to browse through our site and discover what the power of information can do for you!

Getting started

Free and priced Canadian statistical information, and plenty of it, is available from the most reliable source.

- Get connected to Canada! Visit Canadian statistics to get free data on many aspects of Canada's economy, land, people and government—all in easy-to-read tables.
- The Daily offers unparalleled access to newly released data, schedules of major releases and announcements of new products and services. Subscribe and receive a free electronic copy delivered to your e-mail every working day.
- Find information about the 2001 Census or check out data from the 1996 Census!
- Look through Community Profiles to get a snapshot of approximately 6,000 communities in Canada, from Newfoundland to the Northwest Territories.
- Purchase online and save time. Whether you're looking for online statistics, downloadable publications or research papers, you'll find them in Our products and services. Rest assured that ordering online is safe and secure. Learn more by reading our online privacy statement.
- Make the grade with our Learning resources, where you'll find a wide variety of statistical products and services, specifically designed for students and teachers.
- Take the Canada Quiz! Explore our site and learn about Canada and Canadians.

Beyond the numbers

Statistics Canada provides much more than just numbers. In addition to the analysis that accompanies each data release, we have a slate of regular analytic periodicals covering a wide range of subjects. Selected articles from these publications, as well as more information about each of them, can be found in In depth. More technical analysis is provided through several series of research papers published by various divisions. These can be found under Our products and services, Research papers (free).

Search here

Get a head start with our comprehensive search engine. You can search the whole site or specify a location. Look through A to Z for an alphabetical listing of topics found on the Statistics Canada site. Browse the online catalogue for a listing of electronic data products, publications, research papers, and custom tabulations.

Source: Statistics Canada, First Visit to Our Site, retrieved from www.statcan.ca/english/about/first.htm

PRIMARY SOURCES OF LOCATION INFORMATION

In the last six chapters, we have talked about your primary research techniques such as brainstorming, interviewing, mind mapping, and so on. As you know by now, we cannot rely strictly on secondary research because it is just that—secondary. For your location analysis, you are also going to have to do some of your own primary research. But the hitch is that there is no formula or set framework

Box 7.7 E-Exercise

Canada Quiz

- www.statcan.ca/english/edu/canquiz/cquiz1.htm

Take Statistics Canada's Canada Quiz and find out what you know about Canada and Canadians. A new set of questions appears about every three months, so you can test your knowledge regularly.

to follow. Nevertheless, this is a real opportunity to practise your new-eyes research. To help, we will provide examples of how some enterprising entrepreneurs did theirs. We then encourage you to find your own creative way.

> Henry wanted to start a dry cleaning business. He knew that the success of his business would depend on the number of cars that passed by a specific point during peak hours. Through experience in the business, he had found a direct relationship between the number of cars and the volume of dry cleaning. What did he do? He did not rely on the traffic counts from his local municipality, although this secondary information was useful in narrowing down possible sites. His answer was to sit in his car for several days and count the number of vehicles that went by his potential sites. After doing this a few times for various locations, he finally found the "perfect" spot.
>
> Today, Henry has 15 outlets and we find him out counting cars, getting ready for his sixteenth store. He tells us that he is in the business of counting cars because, if he can get that right and competition is not a serious factor, then everything else should unfold nicely.

Now let's see how Martha did her primary research by counting people.

> Martha wanted to start a gift store that her favourite grandmother would be proud of. The name of her new business would be Gramma's, so the location had to be right, for she wanted to keep this name for a long time. She also knew from working in gift stores that most of the business would come from the impulse buyer.
>
> A new mall was opening down the street, and the manager, fresh from business school, had loaded her down with site plans, traffic studies, and potential store locations. "You had better hurry," he said. "The good spots are being snapped up awfully fast." Fortunately, her small business teacher was close by and added a little sanity to her life. "It's easy," she said. "Just replicate, and you will know for sure. Find a mall that is under construction and tell me how much business the gift store is doing."
>
> "That's crazy," exclaimed Martha. "You can't possibly know how much a business is doing before the mall is built."
>
> "That's true," said her professor. "Why don't you wait until you know what is going on."
>
> "I'm going to miss this one," protested Martha.

"Yes, you may, but when you find the right location, you will know it, because you will be able to back up the mall research with some of your own primary research."

About six months later, Martha finished doing her pedestrian counts in front of an empty store at a more established mall on the other side of the city. Her own traffic counts and the mall studies convinced her that this was the location for her. Today, Martha's gift store at the more established mall is doing well. She is not making a million, but she is making a good living, and her grandmother is very proud of her.

Here is the lesson she learned: If your business relies on impulse buying, you had better know exactly how many people will go by your door and how many will enter and make a purchase—*before you open your doors.*

By the way, it took over two years to fully lease the new mall that Martha first looked at.

Specific primary research techniques worked for Henry and Martha. The key to their success was knowing who their customers were and what they wanted. Their businesses were driven by the amount of traffic passing by their doors—in one case it was cars and in the other, people. Now let's return to Elizabeth Wood (remember Crazy's Roadhouse in Chapters 4 and 5) and see how she helped Max, the owner, determine whether he had a good location.

"That's a stupid question," quipped Max. "Of course I have a great location—just look at my sales."

"Just a minute," cautioned Elizabeth. "Because you are fortunate enough to have customers, this does not mean you have the perfect location." Elizabeth knew what she was talking about because she was standing in front of Max, a little smugly, with the results of her customer survey. "Let me ask you: where do your customers live?"

"That's easy," said Max. "They live in the neighbourhood. That's why I chose this location." Not wanting to burst Max's balloon, Elizabeth agreed he was partly right. "The fact is, your lunch trade lives at the workplace. That is, 'place of work' is the most important location criterion at lunch. As a matter of fact, the perfect luncheon location would be within walking distance of 'white-collar' industry—one of those new industries that Nuala Beck talks about."

Then Elizabeth explained to Max that most of his lunch customers were forced to drive to his restaurant, and that's why there were always a few empty seats at lunch during the first part of the week. "Now, as for your night and weekend trade," she continued, "most live at least 15 km from your restaurant. Your TCs are 'grazers' who say that their household income is $50 000 plus per year and who come from all over the city. The most important thing to them is that they can get here within 20 minutes and there is adequate parking. Yes, parking is very important to them. You should begin thinking about the potholes in your parking lot before you start losing business."

Now that Elizabeth knew where Max's customers lived and worked, there was a lot more they could talk about. For the next few hours, they brainstormed new ideas and approaches to making the location more accessible to the customer. For example, how could Max speed up the food service at lunch?

Now let's consider the importance of primary research for the home-based business. Remember Mina Cohen from Chapter 4? She was in the travel and learning business. She worked out of her home, but her location was at the dig site. There is no doubt the archaeologists at the site demand that she and her customers "dig" with care. Her location analysis concerns itself with finding prime dig sites for her customers to visit.

For Ron Taylor (Chapter 5) and the business of cocooning (basement recreation rooms) for teens, what is his location? His customer's house, of course. His location strategy is all about finding homes where teens live.

We can't stress it enough. If you operate a service business from home, your location analysis is just as important as if you are renting. After all, your location is at your *customer's* home or place of work. All of these cases point to the need for primary research before you decide your location. If you can support primary analysis with secondary data, so much the better.

Many of you will choose not to operate your business out of the home, although we encourage you to give serious thought to this strategy. For those who plan to rent a location, we'll go now to the complex world of leases.

Some Things You Must Know about Leases

A lease document is drawn up by the property owner's lawyer. Although its language is very specific, the terms spelled out are provisional—that is, the terms are proposed as a starting point for negotiation. Nothing you see in the contract is cast in stone ... unless you agree to it. Obviously, the terms proposed will probably favour the property owner. Consider the proposed lease seriously. Discuss it with your own lawyer and with others who have experience with leases, and determine how best to begin the negotiation. The following pages will guide you through this process.

ENTREPRENEUR, READ YOUR LEASE

Entrepreneur Mick Beatty failed to read the terms of his lease. He thought he had a "gentlemen's agreement" with his landlady, but he was wrong. His story points up the importance of *assuming nothing* when it comes to leases.

> I was on vacation from the East when I discovered the perfect location. It was in the sleepy tourist town of White Rock, on the edge of the world in a fabulous part of British Columbia.
>
> It was late summer, I remember, and I'd just spent a week driving through the mountains from Calgary. When I reached White Rock, I thought I was home.
>
> I discovered Eddie's Pub my first evening in town. It faced the beach, and sitting there sipping a cool one, I could watch the sun reflect off the water. From time to time, people would drift in for a casual drink, and while sitting there, feeling like a million, I must have talked to 20 different folks.
>
> They loved the place, too. And most of them looked upscale.
>
> Vacations don't last forever, and when I got back home, I kept thinking about Eddie's in White Rock. I was working then for one of the

giant megacorporations, making good money in a pressure cooker of a job, and even though I was enough of a culture freak to appreciate Toronto, I wanted more out of life. After one particularly hectic day at the office, I sat and stared out the window, thinking about those three days I'd spent in White Rock, on the beach.

A business trip took me to Vancouver that next spring, and I managed to haggle for an extra day so that I could stay overnight in White Rock and stop in for a drink at Eddie's.

Double surprise.

The sun was shining—and Eddie's Pub was for sale.

I called my banker back East. He said I was crazy. I phoned two buddies, one from college, one from the squash club. They thought it would be fun to be part of a new venture and were ready to invest. I talked to Eddie, the owner, made a deal to pay him so much down and the rest out of profits, and suddenly I owned a small business.

When I phoned my boss in Toronto, he said I was crazy, too. "Living somewhere on a beach is just a dream," he said. But what he said next saved my life. "Tell you what, Mick. Don't pull the plug until you're absolutely sure. We'll give you six months. If you're still out there dreaming, send in your resignation. Meanwhile, have fun. Every man needs a fling before he settles down."

I said okay, and thanks. And that was that.

The location at Eddie's is only 200 square metres. The layout is long and narrow, and we used mirrors from the Gay Nineties to give the place atmosphere. The traffic is mostly walk-in—beach people, stray tourists—and the only promotion I had to do was to put up a sign that said "Happy Hour 4–6:30." I shook hands with my customers, passed out complimentary drinks, served the best espresso in the Vancouver area, and started making money my first day.

Then trouble showed up.

I hadn't been open a week when I got a call from my landlady. She was a crusty-voiced lady I'd barely talked to, and she said over the phone that there had been some complaints about the music.

"Hey," I said. "I'm sorry. Who's complaining?"

"Your neighbours," she said. "They have rights, too, you know."

"Is it too loud?"

"No," she said. "It's not the volume. It's that rock stuff that's causing the trouble. It irritates the other customers."

"Rock?" I said. "It's not rock, it's more like—"

"I don't know what you call it," my landlady said. "But it's got to stop. And right now."

"My customers like it," I argued. "The music is part of my atmosphere."

"Young man," she said, "what your customers like is neither here nor there. I own that property, and I have other tenants to think about. And if you have any questions, I'd advise you to read your lease." She hung up.

Well, I read the lease, carefully. And then I saw a lawyer. He confirmed what I'd read—according to the terms of the lease, my landlady had the power to tell me what kind of music I could play in my own small business.

Incredible, but true.

I tried turning off the music. Right away, my customers missed it. Drink orders fell off. I surveyed my neighbours and made a list of songs they didn't find offensive, but when I played that junk in the bar, my steady customers (who were becoming less steady) asked me to turn it off. As a last resort, I even visited my landlady and tried to **renegotiate the lease.** But she wouldn't budge.

RENEGOTIATE THE LEASE

obtaining a new or modified contract for occupancy

There was only one thing to do. I sold the business. I went back to my job in Toronto. I still owe some money to my partners, and when the tension builds at work, I always think of the sun on the water at White Rock. I'll go back sometime. But right now I'm a little soured on the place. It's too bad. They've got a great beach. And a great little bar where you can sit and watch the sun go down.

My advice? Have a plan, get some experience before you start, and last of all, read the small print in your lease.

ANTICIPATE THE UNEXPECTED

Bette Lindsay has always had a soft spot for books, and when she finally chose a business, it was a bookstore in a shopping centre. She had researched everything—trends, census data, newspapers, reports from real-estate firms, suppliers—but she failed to anticipate an important potential pitfall: dependency on an anchor tenant (a business in a commercial area that attracts customers).

Few small businesses are themselves "destination locations." They must count on anchor tenants to draw traffic. Bette made an assumption that the anchor tenant in her centre would be there forever. This case study shows the importance of having Plan B ready.

My husband and I researched the small business field for almost two years, and my heart kept bringing me back to books. I've read voraciously since I was seven years old, and I love a well-written story. So when a new shopping centre was opening 10 kilometres from our home, I told my husband, "This is it."

Everything looked perfect. They had a great anchor tenant coming in—a supermarket that would draw lots of traffic. The real-estate agent we'd been working with during most of our search showed us the demographics of the area, which documented that we were smack in the middle of a well-educated market. According to statistics put out by the federal government, a bookstore needs a population of 27 000 people to support it. Our area had 62 000 people, and the closest bookstore was more than eight kilometres away.

Everything else looked good, too. We had lots of parking. The neighbours (three hardy pioneers like ourselves) were serious about their business and pleasant to work with.

We wanted to be in for the Christmas season because December is the peak season for bookstores. So we set a target date of mid-October. The contractor was still working when we opened a month later.

We started off with an autograph party and we ran some bestseller specials. And even though construction work from our anchor tenant blocked our access, we had a very good Christmas that year. We started the New Year feeling very optimistic.

One day in mid-January, construction work stopped on our anchor tenant's new building. The next day we read in the paper that the company had gone bankrupt.

Well, the first thing I did was call the landlord. He was out of town, and his answering service referred me to a property management company. They said they knew nothing about what was happening and that all they did was collect the rent. January was slow. So was February, and March. In April, two of our neighbours closed up. The construction debris still blocked customer access. It was a mess.

In May, I finally succeeded in getting in touch with the owner and tried to renegotiate the lease, but his story was sadder than mine.

Fourteen months after we moved in, we finally got our anchor tenant. If I'd suspected it would take anything like that long, I could have built some provision for it into our lease.

Bette and her husband learned the hard way.

HOW TO REWRITE A LEASE

LOCATION ESCAPE HATCH

a way to cancel or modify your lease if the landlord fails to meet the specified terms

You live with a lease (and a landlord) for a long time. If you're successful in a retail business, your landlord may want a percentage of your gross sales receipts. If you're not successful or if problems develop, you're going to want several Plan Bs and a **location escape hatch**—a way to cancel or modify your lease if your landlord fails to meet the specified terms. For example, your lease should protect your interest:

- if the furnace or air conditioning system breaks down
- if the parking lot needs sweeping or resurfacing
- if the anchor tenant goes under
- if the building is sold
- if half of the other tenants move out

The possibility of such grief-producing eventualities needs to be dealt with—with precise words and precise numbers in the lease.

Read the lease slowly and carefully (Boxes 7.8 and 7.9 will help you). When you see something you don't understand or don't like, draw a line through it. Feel free to rewrite the lease if you need to. It's *your* lease, too, you see. If you need help from a lawyer, get it. And make sure that the owner (or the leasing agent) indicates his or her agreement with your changes by initialling each one.

Here's a checklist to start you on your rewrite.

1. *Escape clause.* If the building doesn't shape up or the area goes into eclipse, you will want to get out fast. Be specific. Write something like this into your lease: "If three or more vacancies occur in the centre, tenant may terminate lease."
2. *Option to renew.* Most businesses need at least six months to a year to get going. If your business does well, you will want to stay put. If it does not, you don't want to be saddled with a heavy lease payment every month. Get a lease for one year, with an option to renew for the next two or three.
3. *Right to transfer.* Circumstances might force you to sublet. In the trade, this is called "assigning." Make sure the lease allows you to transfer your lease without a heap of hassle if such circumstances arise.

Box 7.8 The Language of Leases

Before signing on the dotted line, be certain you understand the language of the lease. These terms will get you started:

- **Building gross area.** The total square-foot area of the building when the enclosing walls are measured from outside wall to outside wall.
- **Usable building area.** The square-foot area within the building actually occupied by tenants, measured from centre partition to centre partition.
- **Common area.** The square-foot area of the building servicing all tenants in common, such as lobby, corridors, lavatories, elevators, stairs, and mechanical equipment rooms. The building common area is usually between 10 and 12 percent of the gross building area.
- **Rentable area.** A combination of the tenants' usable building area plus each tenant's pro rata share of the common area.
- **Gross rent.** A rental per square foot, multiplied by the rentable area, to determine the annual rent due on a lease, where the landlord provides all services and utilities, including tenant janitorial services.
- **Net rent.** A rent per square metre (or foot) multiplied by the rentable area to determine the annual rent due under a lease, whereby the tenant also pays, in addition to the rent, its pro rata of all utilities and services and real-estate taxes.
- **Loss factor.** The proportion of usable building area to total rentable area. The usable area is that in which you may put furniture and equipment for actual office use. The rentable area often includes a proportionate share of ancillary building services. The lower the loss factor, the more usable space there is. Loss factors can vary from floor to floor in the same building. Rentable area may be calculated in a different manner for one building than it is for another, and this will affect your comparison of rental proposals.

4. *Cost-of-living cap.* Most leases allow the owner to increase rents along with inflation according to the consumer price index (CPI). To protect yourself, insist on a cost-of-living cap so that your base rate won't increase faster than your landlord's costs. Try for half of the amount of the CPI increase, a standard measure. Thus, if the CPI rises 10 percent, your rate will go up only 5 percent. It's fair, because the owner's costs won't change much. Major tenants in your centre will insist on a cap, so you should be able to negotiate one also. Proceed with confidence.

Box 7.9 Before You Sign ...

Before you sign a lease, ask these questions:

- Does the lease contain an escape clause?
- Does it have an option to renew?
- Can you "assign" the lease if you need to sublet?
- Do you have a ceiling on rent increases?
- Do you have a floating lease scale, according to how much of the centre is occupied?
- Have you tried to negotiate a period of free rent while you are preparing to open the doors?
- Have you negotiated to have the landlord make the needed improvements and charge you for them over the total time of the lease?

5. *Percentage lease.* Percentage leases are common in larger retail centres. They specify that the tenant pays a base rate plus a percentage of the gross sales. An example: $XX per square foot per month plus 5 percent of gross sales over $500 000 per year.
6. *Floating rent scale.* If you're a pioneer tenant of a shopping centre, negotiate a payment scale based on occupancy. For example, you may specify that you'll pay 50 percent of your lease payment when the centre is 50 percent occupied, 70 percent when it's 70 percent occupied, and 100 percent when it's full. You can't build traffic to the centre all by yourself, and motivation is healthy for everyone, including landlords.
7. *Start-up buffer.* There's a good chance you'll be on location fixing up, remodelling, and so on, long before you open your doors and make your first sale. Make your landlord aware of this problem and negotiate a long period of free rent. The argument: if your business is successful, the landlord—who's taking a percentage—will make more money. If your business doesn't do well or if it fails, the landlord will have to find a new tenant. You need breathing space. You've signed on for the long haul. By not squeezing you to death for cash, the landlord allows you to put more money into inventory, equipment, service, atmosphere—the things that make a business go.
8. *Improvement.* Unless you're a super fixer-upper, you don't want to lease a place equipped with nothing but a dirt floor and a capped-off cold water pipe. You need a proper atmosphere for your business, but you don't want to use all your cash to pay for it before you open. Negotiate with the landlord to make the needed improvements and spread the cost of them over the total time of the lease. Otherwise, find a space that doesn't require heavy remodelling.
9. *Restrictive covenants.* If you're running a camera store and part of your income derives from developing film, you don't want a Fotomat booth to move into your centre. If you're selling hearing aids, you don't want a stereo store next door. Build restrictive covenants (things that your landlord cannot do) into your lease to protect yourself.
10. *Maintenance.* When the parking lot needs sweeping, who pays for it? If the air conditioner goes out, who pays? If the sewer stops up, who is responsible for the repairs? Get all of this written down in simple language. Your diligence with words and numbers will pay off.

In a Nutshell

The main purpose of this chapter was to help guide you through the process of finding a location that is right for you, your business, and your customer. We encouraged you to use your new-eyes research as well as secondary sources, and to keep asking the question "What is the best location according to my target customer?"

If you are planning to retail or manufacture your product or service, your choice of location is probably the most important decision you will make. You'll have to live with your selection for a long time. We encouraged you to complete the location filter checklist and begin to understand the language and consequences of leases. Many of you will plan to start your business from your home. This is fine, but don't think that your location analysis is not important. A location checklist for your home-based business was also presented. We wanted you to make sure that your home office will satisfy the needs of your customer and won't destroy your personal life. Lastly, we discussed the need to understand the language and consequences of leases.

Key Terms

location escape hatch
renegotiate a lease

Think Points for Success

- ✓ The irony of the search for a start-up location is that you need the best site when you can least afford it.
- ✓ Take your time selecting a location. If you lose out on a hot site, don't worry; another one will eventually turn up.
- ✓ Even if you start up your business at home, you will need a location analysis.
- ✓ A site analysis for a street-side location should include everything that is unique to a specific building or space. Many successful centres have some dead traffic areas.
- ✓ Who are your business neighbours? Are they attracting your type of customers or clients? What will happen if they move or go out of business?
- ✓ Know the terms and buzzwords—net, gross, triple net, industrial gross, and so on—and be aware that they may mean slightly different things in each contract or lease agreement.
- ✓ Everything is negotiable: free rent, signage, improvement allowances, rates, maintenance. Don't be afraid to ask; a dollar saved in rental expenses can be worth more than $10 in sales.
- ✓ Talk to former tenants; you may be amazed at what you learn.

Business Plan Building Block

This section of your business plan explains why you have selected your location and how it satisfies the needs of your target customers and your business.

Your description should include the following key considerations:

- How close or accessible your location is to the target market.
- The distribution channels you intend to use to reach the target customer if you do not have a store-front location.
- How the location satisfies the exterior and interior requirements for the business (if possible, include a floor plan or photos in an appendix).
- How close the competition is to your location.
- The possibility of expansion.
- Whether the building is leased or owned. Indicate whether the lease has been reviewed by a lawyer (include proof of ownership or a copy of the lease in an appendix)
- Whether the location is in conformity with municipal bylaws and environmental regulations.

Your turn: Using materials from this chapter, describe why you have chosen this site.

Checklist Questions and Actions to Develop Your Business Plan

LOCATION

- ❑ What criteria are important to your location?
- ❑ What secondary research do you need to make a decision about location?
- ❑ If you plan to operate a home-based business, be sure to answer all the questions in Box 7.2
- ❑ Define the importance of location for your target customer.
- ❑ If you are a home-based business, how have you separated work from home?
- ❑ Why have you chosen the site that you have selected?
- ❑ If you have a home-based business, identify any zoning issues you face.

NOTES

1. Adapted from Jeffrey Simpson, "Quite the Little Spot," *The Halifax Herald*, January 24, 1998; and the Ceilidh Connection website (www.ceilidhconnect.ns.ca).
2. Royal Bank, Today's Entrepreneur, "Location, Location, Location," retrieved from www.royalbank.com/sme/te/t_batah.html
3. Gray, Douglas A., and Diana Lynn. *Home Inc.* (Toronto: McGraw-Hill Ryerson, 1989).

SUGGESTED READING

Bredin, Alice. *Set Up a Home Office That Works.* New York: John Wiley & Sons, 1996.

Deschamps, Michelle, Jack Dart, and Graham Links. "Home-Based Entrepreneurship in the Information Age." *Journal of Small Business & Entrepreneurship*, Vol. 14, No. 1, September 1997, pp. 74–97.

Entrepreneur Magazine. *Starting a Home-Based Business.* New York: John Wiley & Sons, 1997.

Gray, Douglas A., and Diana Lynn. *Home Inc.* Toronto: McGraw-Hill Ryerson, 1989.

Keen, Peter G., and Mark McDonald. *The eProcess Edge: Creating Customer Value and Business in the Internet Era.* Toronto: McGraw-Hill, 2000.

Knowles, Ron. *Writing a Small Business Plan: Course Guide.* Toronto: Dryden, 1995.

Pottruck, David S., and Terry Pearce. *Clicks and Mortar.* New York: John Wiley & Sons, 2001.

Raisch, Warren, and William Kane Jr. *The Marketplace and Strategies for Success in B2B Commerce.* Toronto: McGraw-Hill, 2000.

Seybold, Patricia, Ronnie T. Marshak, and Jeffrey Lewis. *Customer Revolution.* New York: Crown, 2001.

Siskind, Barry. *Making Contact.* Toronto: ITMC Press, 1999.

chapter 8

Protecting Your Business from Costly Surprises

BUSINESS PLAN BUILDING BLOCK

You can't include surprises in your business plan, but you can demonstrate to the reader that you have thought of almost everything. This chapter will help you anticipate potential problems and show you how to minimize their effects.

LEARNING OPPORTUNITIES

After reading this chapter, you should be able to:

- Develop a Plan B to minimize the ill effects of unfortunate surprises.
- Determine your insurance needs and costs.
- Understand the importance of shareholders agreements.
- Draft a health and safety policy and action plan.
- Develop a list of precautions that will help minimize the opportunities for employee dishonesty.
- Understand the main characteristics of patents, copyrights, and trademarks.
- Prepare a 12-month start-up checklist.

Patty Fisher really liked kids, so she joined forces with her husband and made plans to open a daycare centre. They secured a bank loan and bought a property in a neighbourhood of young families with an average of 2.5 children. They spent weekends painting and fixing up the place. They worked hard, but it was fun, and it made them feel a part of something warm and cozy.

About three weeks before their opening, they called the light and power people to ask them to turn on the lights. "Sure thing," said sales manager Don Farthington. "Just send us a cheque for $700, and the lights will be on in a jiffy."

"What?" Patty asked. "Did you say $700?" They had around $800 in the kitty, but that was earmarked for emergencies.

"That's right. You're a new commercial customer with a good credit rating. That's the reason the figure's so low."

"You think $700 is low?" Patty asked in disbelief.

ACTION STEP PREVIEW

39. Prepare your Plan B checklist.
40. Calculate your insurance needs and costs.
41. Draft a health and safety policy and action plan.
42. Navigate an online tutorial on patent applications.

Chapter 8 will help you manage risk and prepare parts H, I, and J of your business plan, the financial section.

"For your tonnage," he said, "it's right on the money."

"Tonnage? What tonnage?"

"Your air conditioner," Don said. "You have a five-ton unit on your roof."

"But we're not planning to run it!" Patty said. "The breeze here is terrific. We don't need the air conditioner."

"Sorry, ma'am. Our policy is pretty clear. Sometimes we get three months' deposit, but for your business we'll only require the two. Is there anything else I can help you with today?"

"No," Patty said. "Absolutely nothing." As she hung up, she made a vow to take a good hard look at the daycare budget. They simply could not afford any more surprises like this.

Although a business plan is designed to demonstrate how the business will prosper, there is a need to demonstrate flexibility when things do not go exactly as planned. What can go wrong and what can be done to eliminate downside risk? When you interview successful entrepreneurs and ask them what surprises they had not anticipated when they started, they usually have quite a few. Almost always, you hear that it cost more and took longer than they had planned.

In the opening vignette, aspiring daycare operator Patty Fisher was badly shaken by an unexpected hydro charge. To protect yourself from such unpleasant surprises, you need at least one Plan B; we begin this chapter by showing you how to create one.

ACTION STEP 39

Prepare your Plan B checklist.

Now that you've got your business well in mind, take a few minutes to brainstorm a list of surprises that could cost you money or time, and, if possible, how you can turn these problems into opportunities. Use the checklist in Box 8.1 to help you get started.

Next, conduct some primary research. Talk to businesspeople in your industry. If you are intending a street-side location, ask the neighbours what has happened to them and how they're doing in this location. Talk to vendors, suppliers, customers, and insurance brokers. If you are going to operate out of the home, ask the opinion of other home entrepreneurs.

When you finish your list, put a checkmark beside each item that will cost money.

PLAN B

an alternative strategy for bailing the business out of a tight spot created by some unforeseen or unfortunate situation

Developing a Plan B

Having read the opening vignette, you may wonder how Patty could have overlooked such an important detail. Remember that a budding entrepreneur is confronted with a formidable to-do list. That's why having at least one **Plan B**—an alternative strategy for bailing the business out of a tight spot created by some unforeseen or unfortunate situation—is a must before you open your doors. Box 8.1 presents a Plan B checklist that could help eliminate surprises, while Box 8.2 on page 146 provides some useful online resources.

If you get into the habit of making lists, doing mind maps, and writing everything down in your Adventure Notebook, you'll improve your chances of surviving in small business. Action Step 39 will help you anticipate potential surprises.

Box 8.1 Plan B Checklist

Here's a checklist of some obvious start-up concerns. Add to this list as you think of things.

I. Advisers
- A. Lawyer
- B. Banker
- C. Accountant/bookkeeper
- D. Insurance agent
- E. Commercial real-estate agent
- F. Mentor (advisory board)
- G. Consultants
- H. Suppliers
- I. Chamber of commerce
- J. Professional association
- K. Other organizations

II. Organization
- A. GST registration (if necessary)
- B. PST registration
- C. DBA ("Doing business as" = fictitious business name)

D. Partnership agreement
E. Corporation
F. Other

III. Licences, Permits
A. Business licence
B. Resale permit
C. Department of Health
D. Liquor licence
E. Fire inspection permit
F. Local building inspection
G. Other

IV. Location
A. Lease review (lawyer)
B. First and last months' rent (Rent may have to be paid while making improvements. Estimate time needed to do improvements.)
C. Security deposit
D. Leasehold improvements
E. Insurance
F. Security system
G. Utilities, deposits, estimated monthly costs
1. Electric
2. Gas
3. Water
4. Phone installation
H. Other

V. Auto (Consider new, used, leased)
A. Autos
1. New/used
2. Lease/purchase
B. Trucks
1. New/used
2. Lease/purchase
C. Insurance
D. Maintenance, repairs

VI. Equipment
A. Office
B. Retail space
C. Warehouse
D. Manufacturing area
E. Kitchen
F. Dining area
G. Communication
H. Computer
I. Other

VII. Fixtures
A. Tables
B. Chairs
C. Desks
D. File cabinets
E. Work benches
F. Storage cabinets
G. Display cases
H. Lighting
I. Shelving/storage

VIII. Supplies
Pencils, pens, notepaper, tape, letterheads, dictionary, calendar, appointment book, coffee, tea, soft drinks, bottled water, and so on

IX. Inventory
What are the minimum and maximum average inventory requirements you need on hand to do business on your first day?

X. Advertising/Promotion
A. Signs
B. Business cards
C. Flyers/brochures
D. Displays
E. Ad layouts and graphics
F. Media (newspaper, radio, other) costs
G. Trade show booths
H. Other

XI. Banking
A. Chequing account
1. Cheque charges
2. Interest on account
B. Chequing/bookkeeping system
C. Deposit box
D. Savings/chequing account
E. Credit
1. Credit cards
2. Personal lines of credit or letter of credit
3. Loans and interests
4. Credit from suppliers/vendors

XII. Employees
A. Application/employment forms completed (e.g., employer registration number from Canada Customs and Revenue Agency)
B. Training program

Box 8.2 Bookmark This

- **Checklists for Going into Business**
  www.cbsc.org/english/search/display.cfm?CODE=4005&coll=FE_FEDSBIS_E
  This page on the Canada Business Service Centres website provides questions and worksheets to help you think through what you'll need to know and do.
- **Guide for Canadian Small Business, Canada Customs and Revenue Agency**
  www.ccra-adrc.gc.ca/E/pub/tg/rc4070eq/rc4070eq-01.html
  Start with this page to register your business at the federal level.
- **Meeting Place for Young Entrepreneurs**
  www.youthbusiness.com/services/meeting/level2.cfm?id=0&nav=1.0.0.0.0.0.0.0.0.0
  This virtual meeting place is found on the Canadian Youth Business Foundation's YouthBusiness.com site. Use the discussion boards to get advice from other young entrepreneurs.
- **Talk to Us!, Canada Business Service Centres**
  http://vweb.cbsc.org/english/forms/na/talktous.jsp
  The Talk To Us! software application allows you to connect with a Business Information Officer on the web and by phone. The Information Officer can answer your questions on the phone and at the same time guide your browser to the documents you need through the Internet connection.

Insurance Planning

If you plan on going into business for yourself, you will likely need some sort of insurance. (Types of business insurance are shown in Box 8.3.) If you operate a home-based business, you will probably need insurance as well; in most cases, basic homeowner's insurance will not cover your business needs (see Box 8.4 on page 148). In calculating your insurance needs, you should first consider all the insurable risks faced by your business. In general, the following risks can be covered by insurance if you have followed the law:

- Personal injury to employees and the general public. Some retail stores have become targets for "slip and fall" claims. Certain businesses have higher personal injury claims and you need to protect accordingly.
- Employment practices such as hiring, firing, sexual discrimination, and libel.
- Loss to the business caused by the death or disability of key employees or the owner—an essential coverage needed to protect your business.
- Loss or damage of property—including merchandise, supplies, fixtures, and building. A standard fire insurance policy pays the policyholder only for those losses directly caused by fire. Make sure when dealing with your insurance agent that you understand your policy thoroughly. Keep asking until you do.
- Loss of income resulting from interruption of business caused by damage to the firm's operating assets (storms, natural disasters, electrical blackouts).

Other indirect losses, known as consequential losses, may be even more important to your company's welfare. They include:

- Extra expenses of obtaining temporary quarters.
- Loss of rental income on buildings damaged or destroyed by fire, if you are a landlord.
- Loss of facility use.

Box 8.3 Types of Business Insurance

As an entrepreneur, you can purchase insurance to cover almost any risk. Each of the following types of business insurance protects you from a different type of financial loss.

1. **Fire and general property insurance**—protects against fire loss, vandalism, hail, and wind damage.
2. **Consequential loss insurance**—covers loss of earnings or extra expenses when business is interrupted because of fire or other catastrophe.
3. **Public liability insurance**—covers injury to the public, such as customer or pedestrian injury claims.
4. **Business-interruption insurance**—coverage in case the business is unable to continue as before.
5. **Crime insurance**—protects against losses resulting from burglary, robbery, and so forth. Fidelity bonds provide coverage from employee theft.
6. **Malpractice insurance**—covers against claims from clients who suffer damages as a result of services that you perform.
7. **Errors and omissions insurance**—covers against claims from clients who suffer from injury or loss because of errors you made, things you should have done but failed to do, or warnings you failed to supply.
8. **Employment practices liability insurance (EPLI)**—covers against claims from employees for employment practices: sexual harassment, wrongful discharge, discrimination, breach of contract, libel, and so on.
9. **Key man insurance**—covers the life, death, dismemberment, or physical disability or owner(s) or key employee(s).
10. **Product liability insurance**—covers injury to the public, such as customer use or misuse of products.
11. **Disability insurance**—covers owners and employees against disability and usually allows for payments to be continued during rehabilitation. Disability for an owner is a much greater risk than death, and few owners insure themselves adequately.
12. **Life and supplemental health insurance for employees.**
13. **Extra equipment insurance**—covers specialized equipment not covered in standard policies.
14. **Directors' and officers' liability insurance**—if company stock is held by outside investors, directors and officers should be protected.
15. **Auto insurance**—a business can be liable for injuries and property damage caused by employees operating their own or someone else's vehicle while on company business. The company may have some protection under the employee's liability policy, but the limits are probably inadequate. If employees use their vehicles while on company business, you should purchase non-ownership liability insurance.

- Continuing expenses after a fire—salaries, rents paid in advance, interest obligations, and so on.
- Loss of customer base.

You can protect yourself against consequential losses by obtaining business-interruption insurance (see Box 8.3).

What type or types of insurance should you carry, and how much coverage should you have? To answer these questions, you should consider:

- The size of any potential loss.
- The probability of loss.
- The resources available to meet a loss if one occurs.
- The probability of lawsuits (some industries and areas are heavily targeted).

If a particular loss would force you or your company into bankruptcy or cause serious financial damage, recognize the risk and purchase insurance to help protect your assets. Losses that occur with predictable frequency such as shoplifting and bad debts can usually be absorbed by the business and are often budgeted as part of the normal cost of doing business; the cost of the loss should be incorporated into the price. Where probability of loss is high, a more effective method of controlling the loss is to adopt appropriate precautionary measures and purchase better-than-adequate insurance. The key to purchasing insurance (and all risk management) is: *Do not risk more than you can tolerate losing.*

The insurance planning worksheet in Table 8.1 and Action Step 40 will help you calculate your insurance needs and costs.

In addition to business insurance, you will likely need a business insurance professional who will probably not be the same person who brokered your homeowner's or auto policies. We suggest you network your way to a good business insurance agent—the same way you select a lawyer. You will want someone who understands your business, product liability, errors and omissions, bonding, burglary coverage, and key employee insurance—health, fire, life, and so on.

Insurance companies frequently put together packages for particular types of businesses, such as retail, wholesale, and service. Also explore group rates through your trade association or your local chamber of commerce. Most chambers of commerce offer a small business insurance package. Joining a group insurance program can save you a lot of money.

Remember that insurance is only one of the options to reduce risk—and in some cases, it should be considered the last resort. Insurance can reimburse you only for unintentional, unforeseen, and uncontrollable losses, not for everyday business risks. Other options include eliminating the risk with a Plan B (as we discussed above), reducing it, assuming it, or transferring it to someone else.

ACTION STEP 40

Calculate your insurance needs and costs.

Network your way to a business insurance salesperson. Discuss your business plan with him or her and complete the insurance planning worksheet in Table 8.1. Calculate the cost of insuring your business for the first year (include in your estimate any up-front deposit).

Keep your completed insurance worksheet on hand. It will help you estimate your cash flow in the next chapter.

Box 8.4 Small Business Tips

The majority of home-based businesses lack adequate business insurance. Too often they rely on homeowner's policies, which exclude or limit coverage for commercial activities. Advise your insurance representative about your home-run business.

Make a list of all property that you are using, even in part, for your business. Computers, copiers, and fax machines, in particular, may be used for both personal and business purposes. It may be possible to extend your home policy to cover business exposures. If not, a business policy held with the same insurer may help you avoid problems with claims involving property such as laptops used for both business and pleasure.

Shareholders Agreements with Buy-Sell Option

BUY-SELL OPTION
a statement in a shareholders agreement that spells out what happens if one partner should die, become disabled, or want to sell his or her interest in the business

If you have business partners or associates, it is very important that you draw up a shareholders agreement to spell out the rules and regulations of the partners. The agreement should include a **buy-sell option** that clearly states what happens if one partner should die, become disabled, or want to sell his or her interest in the business. When partners split up, and most eventually do for one reason or another, a

Table 8.1 Insurance Planning Worksheet

Required Insurance Types	Yes	No	Annual Cost($)
1. Personal liability	❑	❑	________
2. General and public liability	❑	❑	________
3. Product liability	❑	❑	________
4. Errors and omissions liability	❑	❑	________
5. Malpractice liability	❑	❑	________
6. Key man insurance	❑	❑	________
7. Directors and officers	❑	❑	________
8. Term life	❑	❑	________
9. Health	❑	❑	________
10. Crime insurance	❑	❑	________
11. Vehicle	❑	❑	________
12. Business interruption	❑	❑	________
13. Extra equipment	❑	❑	________
14. Consequential loss	❑	❑	________
15. EPLI	❑	❑	________
16. Fire and theft	❑	❑	________
17. Business loan	❑	❑	________
18. Bonds (fidelity, surety)	❑	❑	________
19. Other	❑	❑	________
Total Annual Cost			________

shareholders or partnership agreement with a buy-sell formula will very likely save the business and keep you out of court. Think of it as a prenuptial agreement.

Often, these agreements are funded by joint life insurance on the owners, so that if you die, the business or the other owners will collect the life insurance proceeds and use those funds to buy out your interest in the business. Otherwise, your surviving family members may find it very difficult to sell the interest in the business they inherit from you, except at a giveaway price. In many instances, financial institutions will make a "buy-sell" agreement a condition of the loan.

Many small business owners ignore the need for shareholders agreements, or dislike having a will drawn up. They keep putting it off. The few hundred dollars you may spend in legal fees to draw up a partnership agreement is probably one of the best investments you and your associates will ever make. Shareholders agreements are discussed further in Chapter 11.

Workplace Health and Safety

Why worry about safety? Simply because workplace accidents can destroy your business. According to the Canadian Centre for Occupational Health and Safety (CCOHS) and Human Resources Development Canada (HRDC), three people die from a work accident or occupational disease every working day in Canada. On average, a worker is injured on the job every nine seconds—amounting to some

800 000 injuries per year. Every year, about $5 billion is spent to compensate workers injured on the job—about $80 000 for each working minute. When you add to this all the indirect costs—such as replacement workers' wages and training costs, overtime, and so on—the real cost is in the $10-billion range.

Besides the incalculable cost of pain and grief, there are high monetary costs attached to workplace accidents. These costs can include the inability to meet your obligations to customers, wages paid to sick and disabled workers, wages paid to substitute employees, damaged equipment repair costs, insurance claims, workers' compensation, and administrative and recordkeeping costs. Both humanitarian desires and economic good sense have encouraged employers to create and maintain safer and healthier working conditions.

Occupational health and safety (OHS) legislation in Canada outlines the general rights and responsibilities of the employer, the supervisor, and the worker. As a general rule, the legislation applies to all workers performing work for an employer. Exactly who is responsible for what varies by jurisdiction and by workplace. However, the basic guiding principle is that if a worker is injured in the course of performing work for the employer, the employer may be held liable.

There are two basic levels of OHS legislation—federal and provincial. The federal government and each of the 10 provinces and three territories has its own OSH legislation—which makes this issue a complicated and sometimes confusing one. Federal OHS legislation is governed by the Canada Labour Code, Part II. This legislation affects private- and public-sector workers in the federal jurisdiction that includes the following businesses and enterprises:

- The public service
- Crown corporations
- International and interprovincial industries including air, rail, roads, pipelines, banking, broadcasting, shipping and ports, and telecommunications

If you think your business may be governed by federal legislation, we suggest that you visit:

- Occupational Health and Safety, Labour Operations
  http://info.load-otea.hrdc-drhc.gc.ca/~oshweb/homeen.shtml

For the vast majority of small and medium-sized businesses, OHS is governed by provincial law. In each province or territory, there is an OHS Act that normally applies to all workplaces in that region except private homes or farming operations. Usually, a department of labour or ministry is responsible for OHS; in some jurisdictions, however, occupational health and safety is the responsibility of the workers' compensation board or commission. To find out exactly what your responsibilities are, you should consult the relevant legislation and government department/agency. Information on OHS legislative requirements for each province/territory, along with contact sources, is provided on the CCOHS website at www.ccohs.ca (see also Box 8.5). In this section, we will cover four basic elements of OHS legislative responsibilities: government, employee, and employer responsibilities; joint health and safety committees; workplace hazardous materials; and due diligence.

OHS GOVERNMENT, EMPLOYEE, AND EMPLOYER RESPONSIBILITIES

Workplace health and safety is everyone's responsibility. These basic responsibilities, rights, and conditions are well summarized on the following CCOHS web page:

- OHS Legislation in Canada—Basic Responsibilities
  www.ccohs.ca/oshanswers/legisl/responsi.html#_1_2

Here you will find basic answers to the following questions:

- What are the general responsibilities of governments?
- What are the employees' rights and responsibilities?
- What are the supervisor's responsibilities?
- What are the employer's responsibilities?
- What does legislation say about forming health and safety committees?
- What is the role of joint health and safety committees?
- What happens when there is a refusal for unsafe work?

Box 8.5 Bookmark This

Health and Safety Regulations

- **Human Resources Development Canada, Occupational Health and Safety**
  http://info.load-otea.hrdc-drhc.gc.ca/~oshweb/overen.shtml

  Learn about occupational health and safety requirements for businesses that are set forth in Part II of the Canada Labour Code.
- **Canadian Centre for Occupational Health and Safety (CCOHS)**
  www.ccohs.ca

  Learn about provincial/territorial OHS legislative requirements, employer and employee responsibilities, joint health and safety committees, workplace hazardous materials, and due diligence.

JOINT HEALTH AND SAFETY COMMITTEES

A **joint health and safety committee (JHSC)** is a group consisting of labour and management representatives who meet on a regular basis to deal with health and safety issues. In all Canadian jurisdictions, a JHSC is either mandatory or subject to ministerial decision. There are some exceptions, depending on the size of workforce, industry, accident record, or some combination of these factors. In smaller companies, for example, a health and safety representative is all that may be required. In some cases, a representative may not even be needed. The best way to proceed on this issue is to contact your OHS government authority and legislation to make sure you know your legal responsibilities. We also suggest that you visit the following CCOHS web page:

JOINT HEALTH AND SAFETY COMMITTEE (JHSC)
a group consisting of labour and management representatives who meet on a regular basis to deal with health and safety issues

- Health and Safety Committees
  www.ccohs.ca/oshanswers/hsprograms/hscommittees

Here you will find answers to these questions:

- What is a joint health and safety committee?
- Who is responsible for establishing a joint health and safety committee?
- What does a joint health and safety committee do?
- Is a committee or a representative required?
- What are the sources of legislation regarding joint health and safety committees?
- When are health and safety committees required, how many people are on the committee, and who are committee members?

WORKPLACE HAZARDOUS MATERIALS

WORKPLACE HAZARDOUS MATERIALS INFORMATION SYSTEM (WHMIS)
a comprehensive national plan for providing information on the safe use of hazardous materials used in Canadian workplaces

An important part of complying with OHS workplace safety legislation is making sure that you deal appropriately with hazardous materials. The **Workplace Hazardous Materials Information System (WHMIS)** is a comprehensive national plan for providing information on the safe use of hazardous materials used in Canadian workplaces. By law, you must provide information on hazardous material via product labels, material safety data sheets (MSDS), and worker education programs. Information on WHIMS is provided on the following CCOHS web page:

- WHMIS—General
  www.ccohs.ca/oshanswers/legisl/intro_whmis.html

Here you will find answers to these questions:

- What are the main parts of WHMIS?
- Why was WHMIS created?
- How was WHMIS developed?
- Is WHMIS a law?
- What are the duties under WHMIS?
- What are controlled products?
- Who enforces WHMIS?
- How do I get more information?

DUE DILIGENCE

DUE DILIGENCE
the level of care, judgment, and caution that an employer would reasonably be expected to provide in order to prevent injuries or accidents in the workplace

In the context of occupational health and safety, **due diligence** is the level of care, judgment, and caution that an employer would reasonably be expected to provide in order to prevent injuries or accidents in the workplace. As an employer, you may be legally responsible for situations that are not specifically addressed in the OHS legislation. Due diligence requires you to implement a plan to identify possible workplace hazards. Find out more about due diligence by visiting the following CCOHS web page:

- OHS Legislation in Canada—Due Diligence
  www.ccohs.ca/oshanswers/legisl/diligence.html

Here you will find answers to these questions:

- Why does due diligence have special significance?
- How does an employer establish a due diligence program?
- What is an example of a due diligence checklist?

It's time to apply your understanding of workplace health and safety to your own business. Complete Action Step 41.

Theft and Fraud Prevention

One of the nastiest surprises for a budding entrepreneur is employee dishonesty. You might think that because you're small, employees won't steal from you, but that is wrong. Small firms get hit more often than big ones. Here are some examples of employee dishonesty:

- Credit card fraud
- Cheque deception
- Shoplifting

- Cash register vulnerability (e.g., employees shortchanging customers)
- Bookkeeping theft
- Fraudulent refunds
- Counterfeit money
- Fitting room theft
- Burglary
- Robbery
- Theft of items from stockroom, layaway, and displays
- Computer fraud
- Manipulation of time-card data
- Illegal use of company time
- Fraudulent trip expense reports
- "Sweethearting" (discounts for family and friends)

You will not be able to eliminate theft and fraud, but there are a number of things you can do to reduce the risk. You can begin by establishing a code of conduct that clearly communicates the legal—among other—consequences of employee dishonesty; have your employees sign the code of conduct and review it on a regular basis. Next, establish a set of anti-theft/fraud rules and procedures (Box 8.6 will help you get started). If you suspect employee dishonesty, take prompt action.

ACTION STEP 41

Draft a health and safety policy and action plan.

In order to complete this Action Step, you will need answers to these questions:

- How will you encourage a healthy and safe working environment?
- What will be your responsibilities as an owner?
- Who will be responsible for safety?
- What will be the responsibilities of your employees?
- Do you need a safety coordinator?
- What are the rules and regulations for your business regarding workers' compensation?
- Who is your government OHS inspector? What are his or her expectations?

For assistance in developing your occupational health and safety policy and action plan, visit the following CCOHS web page:

- Guide to Writing an OHS Policy Statement www.ccohs.ca/oshanswers/hsprograms/osh_policy.html

Patents, Copyrights, and Trademarks[1]

Patents, copyrights, and trademarks are the three major forms of intellectual property that can be protected through federal legislation. These are important elements of your business. If you fail to protect them, (1) you may lose your business, (2) your ideas may be stolen, or (3) your products may be copied. In Canada, intellectual property is largely the responsibility of the Canadian Intellectual Property Office (CIPO) (see Box 8.7). Because intellectual property laws are complex and subject to change, you should consult with a lawyer who has experience in the area.

Box 8.6 Anti-Theft/Fraud Measures

Here's a list of precautions that will help minimize the opportunities for employee theft and fraud.

- Sign all the cheques yourself.
- Don't let any one employee handle all the aspects of bookkeeping.
- Insist that all bookkeeping be up-to-date and clear.
- Insist that your bookkeeper take scheduled vacations.
- Do regular physical inventories.
- Open all mail containing payments yourself.
- Track all cash transactions and maintain a rolling annual cash flow on a monthly basis.
- Use numbered order forms, and don't tolerate missing slips.
- Insist on **fidelity bonds** for every employee who handles cash.
- Triple-check references on résumés and employment applications.
- If your business is a cash business, be there. Absentee owners, beware!
- Try to eliminate cash by accepting debit, credit, and "smart cards."

FIDELITY BONDING

insurance that protects an employer against employee dishonesty

Box 8.7 Bookmark This

- **Canadian Intellectual Property Office (CIPO)**
  http://strategis.gc.ca/sc_mrksv/cipo/welcome/welcom-e.html

The Canadian Intellectual Property Office (CIPO), a Special Operating Agency associated with Industry Canada, is responsible for the administration and processing of the greater part of intellectual property in Canada. CIPO's areas of activity include patents, copyrights, and trademarks. To learn more about protecting you intellectual property, visit the CIPO website.

TEN THINGS YOU SHOULD KNOW ABOUT PATENTS

1. What is a patent?

PATENT
a federal government grant that gives an inventor exclusive rights to his or her invention

A **patent** is a federal government grant that gives an inventor exclusive rights to his or her invention. Patents cover new inventions (process, machine, manufacture, composition of matter), or any new and useful improvement of an existing invention. Patent protection applies in the country that issues the patent. In Canada, this protection extends for 20 years from the date of filing. Patents are granted for products or processes that are new, workable, and ingenious (novel, useful, and inventive). In this way, patents serve as a reward for ingenuity.

Patenting your invention may take several years. The process usually begins with an initial patent search to compare your invention with current patent and technical literature. Then you assemble a patent application, which includes a detailed description of your invention and the claims that are the basis for your patent protection. In Canada, a patent is given to the inventor who first files an application. It's therefore wise to file as soon as possible after completing your invention because someone else may be on the same track.

2. Why obtain a patent?

Without a patent, you will be able to protect your invention only as a trade secret. Your secret will be out the moment you publish or begin to sell your invention, and anyone will be able to exploit your invention. Even if you can maintain your secret, if someone else independently makes the invention, that person may be able to obtain a patent and prevent you from exploiting the invention.

3. Is a patent application mandatory?

In order to have patent protection, you must apply for and receive a patent. Application fees range from about $350 to $500. Since patent laws are national, you must obtain patent protection in each country in which you want protection.

4. Who can apply for a patent?

The legal owner of an invention can obtain the patent. Typically, the owner is the inventor or inventors. However, if an inventor sells his or her rights, then a second party will own the invention and be able to obtain a patent. If the inventor makes the invention as part of an employment contract, the employer may own the invention and have the right to the patent.

5. How long is a patent effective?

The life of a patent in Canada is 20 years from the date the application was first filed. Payment of maintenance fees throughout the life of the patent is also required to keep it in force.

6. How do I obtain a patent?

You can obtain a patent in Canada by submitting a patent application with the appropriate fee to:

The Commissioner of Patents
The Canadian Intellectual Property Office
Place du Portage Phase I
50 Victoria Street, Hull, Quebec
K1A 0C9

The *Guide to Patents* gives additional information on the requirements for obtaining a patent. You can consult the tutorial on how to write a patent application.

7. Do I need to hire a patent agent?

You can do it yourself, but the Canadian Intellectual Property Office strongly advises that you employ the services of a patent agent. Patent agents are professionals with experience in drafting applications and navigating the patent process. They will be able to help you ensure that you get all of the rights to which you are entitled. A list of registered patent agents is available from the Patent Office.

8. Does a patent in Canada protect my rights in other countries?

No. Patent laws are national, so you must obtain a patent in each country in which you want protection.

9. What are the steps for obtaining a patent?

To get a patent, there are many steps and some complexities along the way. To help you understand the process, the Patent Office has prepared a summary entitled "How Your Patent Application is Processed." A patent application must include: a petition, a description of the invention, an abstract, a claim or claim(s), any drawing referred to in the description, and the filing fee. Consult the *Guide to Patents* to determine what information must be included for each of the above requirements, or go to the tutorial on how to write a patent application.

10. Will the Patent Office ensure that my patent is not infringed?

No. Enforcement of patents is the responsibility of the patentee. Patents can be enforced through the judicial system.

Now is a good time to try your hand at Action Step 42.

> **ACTION STEP 42**
>
> **Navigate an online tutorial on patent applications.**
>
> Suppose that you're an inventor and you want to protect your invention. Visit the following page on the CIPO website:
>
> - Your Patent Application http://strategis.gc.ca/sc_mrksv/cipo/patents/e-filing/menu.htm
>
> This tutorial will help you learn how to prepare a patent application and give you general information about patents and the patent process in Canada. It also explains how you can apply for a patent in another country.

TEN THINGS YOU SHOULD KNOW ABOUT COPYRIGHTS

1. What is a copyright?

Copyright is the exclusive right to copy a creative work or allow someone else to do so. Copyrights provide protection for artistic, dramatic, musical, or literary works (including computer programs), as well as for performance, sound recording, and communication signal. This includes the sole right to publish, to produce or

> **COPYRIGHT**
>
> the exclusive right to copy a creative work or allow someone else to do so

reproduce, to perform in public, to communicate a work to the public by telecommunication, to translate a work, and, in some cases, to rent the work. The copyright of a Canadian author is valid in foreign countries—as long as the country in question belongs to one or more of the international copyright treaties, conventions, or organizations. In a similar fashion, the copyright of a foreign author is valid in Canada.

How long does a copyright last?
Generally, copyright in Canada exists for the life of the author plus 50 years following his or her death. There are some exceptions. Copyright protection always expires December 31 of the last calendar year of protection.

2. To what does copyright apply? Not apply?

Copyright applies to all original literary, dramatic, musical, and artistic works. These include books, other writings, music, sculptures, paintings, photographs, films, plays, television and radio programs, and computer programs. Copyright also applies to sound recordings (such as CDs, cassettes, and tapes), performers' performances, and communication signals. A copyright *does not* apply to themes, ideas, most titles, names, catch phrases, and other short-word combinations of no real substance.

3. Who owns the copyright?

Generally, the owner of the copyright is:

- the creator of the work;
- the employer, if the work was created in the course of employment unless there is an agreement to the contrary;
- the person who commissions a photograph, portrait, engraving, or print for valuable consideration (which has been paid) unless there is an agreement to the contrary; or
- some other party, if the original owner has transferred his or her rights.

4. How do I obtain copyright?

You acquire copyright automatically when you create an original work or other subject matter.

5. Do I have to do anything to be protected?

No. Since you obtain copyright automatically, you are automatically protected by law. However, it is still a good idea to register your copyright and to mark your works with a notice of copyright.

6. What are the benefits of copyright registration?

Registration gives you a certificate stating that you are the copyright owner. You can use this certificate in court to establish ownership. (The onus is on your opponent to prove that you do not own the copyright.)

7. How do I register a copyright?

You must file an application with the Copyright Office and pay a prescribed fee. An application form and instructions can be downloaded from the main page of the Copyright Office (http://strategis.gc.ca/sc_mrksv/cipo/cp/cp_main-e.html). You may file electronically. The registration process normally takes three and a half weeks. The fee covers review of your application ($65), registration ($65), and your official certificate ($35). The registration fee is a one-time expense. Once you have registered, you do not have to pay further fees to maintain your copyright.

8. Do I need to mark my work with a notice of copyright?

This isn't necessary to be protected in Canada; however, you must mark your work with a small "©", the name of the copyright owner, and the year of first publication to be protected in some other countries. Even though it is not always required, marking is useful because it serves as a general reminder to everyone that the work is protected by copyright.

9. What is copyright infringement?

It is the unlawful use of copyright material. Plagiarism—passing off someone else's work as your own—is a form of copyright infringement. The Copyright Office will not prevent others from infringing your rights; the responsibility for policing your copyright rests with you.

10. Can libraries or educational institutions make multiple copies of parts of books or articles for student use?

No. The making of multiple copies requires the consent of the copyright owner. This consent may be obtained through a licensing agreement with a photocopying collective. However, the Copyright Act does allow the copying by individuals of parts of works for private study or research. Such copying should be minimal. This exception falls within the "fair dealing" section of the Act.

TEN THINGS YOU SHOULD KNOW ABOUT TRADEMARKS

1. What is a trademark?

A **trademark** is a word, symbol, or design, or a combination of these, used to distinguish the goods or services of one person or organization from those of others in the marketplace. There are three basic types. *Ordinary marks* are words and/or symbols that distinguish the goods or services of a specific firm. *Certification marks* identify goods or services that meet a standard set by a governing organization. *Distinguishing guise* identifies the unique shape of a product or its package.

TRADEMARK
a word, symbol, or design, or a combination of these, used to distinguish the goods or services of one person or organization from those of others in the marketplace

Will the Trade-marks Office ensure that my trademark is not infringed?
The Trade-marks Office does not act as an enforcement agency. You are responsible for monitoring the marketplace for cases of infringement and taking legal action, if necessary.

Who can register a trademark?
Companies, individuals, partnerships, trade unions, or lawful associations, provided they meet the requirements of the Trade-marks Act.

How long is registration effective?
A registration is valid for 15 years and is renewable every 15 years thereafter upon payment of a fee.

2. What is the difference between a registered and an unregistered trademark?

A registered trademark has been approved and entered on the Trade-mark Register held by the Canadian Trade-marks Office. Registration is proof of ownership. An unregistered trademark may also be recognized through common law as the property of the owner, depending on the circumstances.

3. Why register a trademark?

Registration is direct (prima facie) evidence of exclusive ownership across Canada and helps ward off potential infringers. It enables you to more easily protect your rights should someone challenge them since the onus is on the challenger to prove rights in any dispute. The process of registration, with its thorough checks for conflicting trademarks, will ensure that you are claiming a unique mark, and help you avoid infringement of other parties' rights. A registered trademark is a prerequisite for franchising a business.

Is registration mandatory?
No, but it is advisable.

4. Do I need to hire a trademark agent?

You can do it yourself, but the Canadian Intellectual Property Office strongly advises that you employ the services of a trademark agent. Trademark registration can be a complex process; an experienced agent can save you time and money by avoiding pitfalls such as poorly prepared applications and incomplete research.

5. How do I register a trademark?

You must file an application with the Trade-marks Office in Hull, Quebec. The application undergoes stringent examination to ensure it meets the requirements of the Trade-marks Act.

6. Does registration in Canada protect my rights in other countries?

No. If your products are sold in other countries, you should consider applying for foreign registration. Contact a trademark agent or the embassy of the country in question to find out about procedures.

7. What is the difference between a trademark and a trade name?

A trade name is the name under which you conduct your business. It can be registered as a trademark, but only if it is used as such—that is, used to identify wares or services.

8. May I register my own name as a trademark?

Normally, you may not register a proper name—neither yours, or anyone else's—as a trademark. An exception may be made if you can demonstrate that the name has become identified in the public mind with certain wares or services.

9. What are the steps of trademark registration?

Trademark registration usually involves:

- a preliminary search (done by you or your agent) of existing trademarks;
- an application;
- examination of your application by the Trade-marks Office;
- publishing of the application in the *Trade-marks Journal*;
- time for opposition (challenges) to the application; and
- allowance and registration (if there is no opposition).

10. May I allow other parties to use my registered trademark?

Yes. You may sell, bequeath, or otherwise transfer your rights to a trademark through a process called assignment. You may also license rights to your trademark.

Risks and Off-Setting Actions

When survivors from any field or profession get together, they like to share horror stories. We have collected a few of these in the small business "surprise" area and come up with some preventive actions for them. They're listed in Table 8.2. You can probably think of more for your business.

Getting Advice

Yes, you must be prepared because there's a boatload of surprises awaiting every entrepreneur who enters the marketplace. We've talked about Plan B, formulating your strategy, thoroughly researching your market, and peering into the future to see what lies ahead. But there's another angle to planning: it's called seeking advice.

Think for a moment about where you are right now on your road to the marketplace. You're halfway through this book. You've analyzed your skills and needs. You've probed your past and surveyed your friends. You've discovered what success means to you, and you've plotted trends and found your industry segment. You've profiled your target customer, studied the demographics, and developed a marketing strategy, including your promotion campaign. You've examined the prime and indirect competition. You've used your new eyes to find a dynamite location. Now you need to find a small business guru or establish an advisory board and get some advice.

Where might you find a business guru or someone who should be on your advisory board? Well, what about your banker? Many people come to him or her for money—some of them carrying business plans, others not knowing a spreadsheet from a bedsheet. What about your accountant? What about the real-estate broker who helped you with your search for a location? What about your business insurance specialist or a retired person who is very knowledgeable about your industry? An advisory board should be no more than three to five people. Have you contacted your local Canada Business Service Centre? You can even get advice over the Net.

You can use your network to find other people who may help you. Show them your goals, objectives, and list of potential surprises and ask for their advice. Ask them for their ideas about what other surprises might be in store for you. If one of those persons gives you wonderful advice, consider putting him or her on your advisory board or, if you're incorporated, on your board of directors. Remember, you can make anyone part of your team—your lawyer, accountant, small business professor, even your customer.

Planning Ahead: Twelve-Month Start-up Checklist

Think about the things you need to start action on 12 months before you open your door for business. For example, if you want to place an advertisement in the Yellow Pages, you may need to plan for it 10 months before the business opens or wait until the next edition comes out. Refer to Box 8.8 for an example of a 12-month checklist.

Table 8.2 Preventive Actions to Counter Surprises

Surprise	Opportunities
Your landlord decides to evict you and your business.	Always have a lease reviewed by a lawyer so you know the grounds under which you could be evicted. Get legal help to rewrite the lease so that it favours your business. Keep in contact with the landlord if there are any potential troublesome areas. Make sure you have a renewal clause.
The newspaper does not run the ad for your grand opening.	Make connections with all media. Develop a tickler file. Make sure you see proof sheets. Withhold payment until they do it right.
An hour after you sign your name to guarantee the lease, your best friend and partner gets cold feet and pulls out. You do not have a thing in writing to protect you against partner's remorse.	Have a written shareholders (partnership) agreement up front. Open a special escrow account. Everybody deposits. Everybody signs.
For eight weeks, during your peak season, the city has the sidewalk in front of your store torn up. The noise is deafening.	Network your way into city hall. Make sure you know your council member. Try to rally media sympathy. Use the underdog angle.
Your general contractor goes bankrupt.	Get a completion bond. Ask the bonding agency to expedite.
Your bookkeeper disappears with $100 000, your books, two trade secrets from the company safe, and your spouse.	A fidelity bond would have protected you. Join a singles club.
Your best salesperson is hired away by the competition.	Woo key employees. Keep them involved and informed. Don't take them for granted. Think about giving them a piece of the business. Check the horizon for pirates.
Due to an administrative error, the bank calls in your loan. It is payable in 30 days. If you would like to cash out, they will give you 25 cents on the dollar.	Take a banker to lunch. Take a backup banker to lunch. Try to get a cash flow going in your operation without a line of credit, except for seasonal circumstances. Also be prepared to put extra personal funds into the business.
A new customer pays you by cheque, takes delivery of the goods, and then stops payment on the cheque before you get it to the bank. You were too busy to get a cheque verification/authorization.	No matter how busy you are, take time for important survival tasks. Retain all your invoices and the initial letter of agreement of all goods until they are paid for in full.
Your largest customer declares bankruptcy. The money owed you in receivables is 77 percent of your gross annual sales.	Don't keep all your eggs in one basket.
The bank where you have your chequing account refuses to extend you a $20 000 line of credit to buy a piece of equipment that will double your business.	Keep your banker in your information loop. Make sure you give your banker updates on your business plan, including your planned capital purchases. Get a backup bank. Discuss money long before you need it.

smallbusinessbc.ca/bizstart
- nameReg.php

Box 8.8 Complete Your Own Start-up Appendix for Your Business Plan

1 year before launch

- Research the demand for your product or service from both primary and secondary sources.
- Read an environmental scan that addresses your project.
- Prepare a test market analysis, including an analysis of competition, price, and market share.
- Register your product or service
- Write out your mission and goals and start your business plan.
- Establish your form of ownership.

10 months

- Establish the strength of your equity base and need for venture capital.
- Identify your potential fixed and variable costs.
- Investigate all channels of distribution.
- Identify potential suppliers and establish prices.
- Investigate packaging, design, and potential promotion approach.
- Start search for site location to be established three months before opening.
- Establish a good relationship with a banker and a lawyer.

8 months

- Evaluate the results of the field test and establish prices and promotion strategy.
- Confirm suppliers and prices.
- Start getting confirmed prices on promotion material.
- Prepare an overall capital and operating budget.
- Prepare position descriptions for staff.
- Complete competitive analysis.
- Establish an advisory board.
- Investigate all external funding sources.
- Complete your business name search.

6 months

- Start listing potential locations.
- Meet board of advisers to assess progress and problems.
- Clearly identify target market for your promotion strategy.
- Order any fixed assets that require long delivery time.
- Establish leases where appropriate.
- Gain approval from the appropriate government bodies if producing a product that requires it.
- Place advertisement if necessary in the Yellow Pages (may need to be sooner depending on your start date and the new phone book release).
- Establish bank line of credit.
- If a home business, verify the city/township bylaws.
- Establish your website

5 months

- Finalize location.
- Prepare a design and schedule for leasehold improvements.
- Order signs.
- Order inventory and supplies.
- Contact telephone company for information about home office service options.

4 months

- Contact the leasehold improvements.
- Finalize packaging (including design).
- Finalize your promotional approach.
- Complete details for GST with the Canada Customs and Revenue Agency.

3 months

- Sign for all utilities and hookups.
- Develop job descriptions and place ads for staff.
- Take possession of location.
- Start renovations and install fixed assets.
- Meet with board of advisers.

2 months

- Select staff to start.
- Start marketing approach depending on nature of business, and finalize renovations.
- Start receiving fixed assets.

1 month

- Shelve and price inventory.
- Start staff as required.
- Train new staff.
- Get marketing campaign under way.
- etc., etc., etc.—all you forgot about!

Launch

- Hold grand opening.
- Offer opening specials.

Note that *almost all* the work takes place before the official opening.

In a Nutshell

Start-up needs to go smoothly. What you don't need are expensive surprises that knock you and your business for a loop. Before you open your doors, you need to have anticipated as many potential unpleasant surprises as possible and have a plan of action for each one of them. For example, how would you turn the following unwanted surprises into opportunities?

- Your landlord decides to evict your business.
- Your Yellow Pages ad is terrible.
- The customer that accounts for 75 percent of your business declares bankruptcy.

Expecting and planning for the unexpected can make the difference between life and death in business. As you seek to manage risk by considering your insurance, health and safety, and other needs, just remember two things: no one can anticipate everything, and setting up will probably cost more and take longer than your planning indicates.

Key Terms

buy-sell option
copyright
due diligence
fidelity bonding
joint health and safety committee (JHSC)
patent
Plan B
trademark
Workplace Hazardous Materials Information System (WHMIS)

Think Points for Success

- ✓ Listen to your competition so that you can change and improve.
- ✓ Create partnerships and outsource what you can.
- ✓ Be aware of closing dates for Yellow Pages advertising and other key media.
- ✓ Keep a time log that tells everyone (you, your founders, your key employees) how you are progressing on the plan.
- ✓ Make sure your partners are as committed to the business as you are, and have a shareholders or partnership agreement.
- ✓ Keep an ongoing list of unfortunate surprises that could hurt your business. Write down how you can turn these surprises into opportunities.
- ✓ Always have a Plan B. And a Plan C. And a Plan D.
- ✓ Let some key customers in on your planning; let them see it with their own eyes. Go one step further—create a customer board of directors.

Business Plan Building Block

Develop a list of issues that are unpredictable and difficult to control. List the actions that might be taken to mitigate their impact on this business venture.

Problem **Opportunity**

____

____

____

____

____

____

INSURANCE NEEDS AND COSTS

Make a list of your insurance needs and costs as recorded in your insurance planning worksheet. (See Action Step 40 and Table 8.1.)

____

____

____

____

____

____

____

____

____

____

____

____

Checklist Questions and Actions to Develop Your Business Plan

PROTECTING YOUR BUSINESS FROM COSTLY SURPRISES

- ❑ What operational goals and objectives do you want to achieve?
- ❑ What risks and challenges does your business face, and how will you address each one?
- ❑ Develop a start-up schedule beginning 12 months from the launch, indicating all the activities you must undertake (e.g., place Yellow Pages phone advertisement), along with related costs up to start-up. Note, this could be a two- or three-page schedule.
- ❑ What are the major cash drains in your business?
- ❑ What types of insurance and employee bonding will you have for your business?
- ❑ Do your have a health and safety policy in place?
- ❑ Do you plan to protect your idea, product, or service by obtaining a patent or copyright and/or by registering a trademark?

NOTES

1. Adapted from the Canadian Intellectual Property Office (CIPO) website (http://strategis.gc.ca/sc_mrksv/cipo/welcome/welcom-e.html).

SUGGESTED READING

Bareham, Steve. *Don't Get Caught in Risky Business.* Toronto: McGraw-Hill, 1999.

Canada Customs and Revenue Agency (CCRA). *Guide for Canadian Small Business*: Ottawa: CCRA, 2001.

Holloran, Ed. *Credit and Collection: Letters Ready to Go!* New York: NTC Business Books, 1998.

Industry Canada, Canadian Intellectual Property Office. *A Guide to Copyrights.* Ottawa: Canadian Intellectual Property Office, Publishing Centre, 2000.

Industry Canada, Canadian Intellectual Property Office. *A Guide to Patents.* Ottawa: Canadian Intellectual Property Office, Publishing Centre, 2000.

Industry Canada, Canadian Intellectual Property Office. *A Guide to Trade-Marks.* Ottawa: Canadian Intellectual Property Office, Publishing Centre, 2000.

Jacks, Evelyn. *The Complete Canadian Home Business Guide to Taxes.* Whitby, ON: McGraw-Hill Ryerson, 1998.

Kaplan, Robert S., and David P. Norton. *The Balanced Scorecard.* Whitby, ON: McGraw-Hill Ryerson, 1997.

Scott, Gini Graham, and John J. Harrison. *Collection Techniques for a Small Business.* New York: Oasis Press, 1994.

Smith, Judy, and Michael Shulman. *What to Say When Your Customers Won't Pay.* Toronto: McGraw-Hill, 1998.

chapter 9

The Power of Numbers

BUSINESS PLAN BUILDING BLOCK

Financial management need not be complicated. But you need to pay attention. Cash is the lifeblood of your business. Here is how to build a financial plan and stay in control of the money flow.

LEARNING OPPORTUNITIES

After reading this chapter, you should be able to:

- Formulate a personal financial vision.
- Assemble a team of financial advisers.
- Estimate your start-up costs.
- Create your own balance sheet.
- Project monthly sales and propose a sales forecast.
- Understand that cash is the lifeblood of your business.
- Understand that bills are paid with cash, not profit.
- Create a cash flow projection and a pro forma income statement.
- Use ratios to measure the financial health of your business.

Ray and Joan Stewart were worried about their financial future. It seemed that every time the Canadian economy had a hiccup, large corporations would respond with massive layoff notices. Ever since the dot-com crash in 2000, fortysomething Ray had known that his job with a large technology company was no longer secure. Some of his co-workers had already received their walking papers, and Ray was expecting his own golden handshake any day now. His cash-starved employer would be sorely tempted to replace him and his $75 000 salary with an eager twentysomething content to earn $35 000 a year.

The Stewarts' financial worries did not end there. They were supporting two teenagers, both of whom planned to attend college or university in a few short years. Would they be able to afford the ever-rising tuition fees? As well, a couple of disastrous investments in the stock market had left them wondering if there would be anything besides the Canada Pension Plan to support them in their golden years.

Ray and Joan resolved to take control of their financial future by starting their own business. It was a formidable challenge, and

ACTION STEP PREVIEW

43. Put your personal financial vision in writing.
44. Assemble a team of financial advisers.
45. Estimate your start-up costs.
46. Draft a projected cash flow.
47. Draft a projected income statement—a moving picture of your business.

Chapter 9 will help you prepare parts H, I, and J of your business plan, the financial section.

ACTION STEP 43

Put your personal financial vision in writing.

Sit back, close your eyes, and take a moment to dream. Where, financially speaking, do you want to see your business one year from now? How about five years from now? Ten years from now?

In the space provided below, write down your personal financial vision. Express it in terms of an objective—"to be financially independent," for example.

My personal financial vision is:

Get in the habit of asking yourself every morning, "What am I going to do today that will bring my financial vision one step closer to reality?"

they knew they needed help. Fortunately, Joan had done some networking in her small business class—it led her to Patrick, a small business consultant who specialized in start-ups.

"No more procrastinating," Joan said to Ray one evening. "We'll call Patrick and get our thoughts and fears out in the open. Let's see what he has to say."

They met with Patrick the following week. He listened carefully as they explained their financial situation and voiced their concerns. At the end of the meeting, he said, "If you feel comfortable with me, I will help you. But remember, there'll be a few bumps—especially when it comes to finance. By the way, this first session is free."

In this chapter, we urge you to move beyond your start-up plans and venture out into the uncertain future. It's time to set some numerical goals for your first year of operation and beyond. This chapter will show you how to begin charting your financial future. Our main purpose here is to help you avoid running out of money. We'll also introduce you to some of the basic financial statements a business needs to survive and grow. But before you start working with numbers, you need to have a clear vision of your financial future.

Formulating a Personal Financial Vision

For many budding entrepreneurs, the world of finance is daunting. Ray and Joan Stewart in the opening vignette are typical in that they did not have a clear picture of their financial future. They lacked a personal financial vision.

We can't tell you what your financial vision should be. That's up to you. Some entrepreneurs want to strike it rich. Others, like the Stewarts, seek financial security. Still others set for themselves the goal of earning enough money to support an early retirement. Having a financial vision will not, of course, guarantee the success of your business venture—but it will provide you with some all-important guidance and direction.

Before you begin to formulate your own financial vision, complete the E-Exercise in Box 9.1. It will give an understanding of your financial IQ and your financial fitness. Then move on to Action Step 43 where we ask you to put your financial vision in writing.

Box 9.1 E-Exercise

Test Your Financial IQ and Fitness

- **What's Your Business Finance IQ?** (Royal Bank)
  www.royalbank.com/sme/guides/financing/busfinquiz_intro.html

  If you think you already know or you would like to learn more about the tools and lingo of business finance, try your hand at these 20 questions. They keep track of your score as you go along and give you an assessment of your business finance acumen at the end.
- **How Financially Fit Are You?** (Canadian Bankers Association)
  www.cba.ca/en/content/publications/Man_Mony.pdf

  Do you think you're doing a good job of managing your money? Or do you feel your spending is out of sync with your income? To see what kind of financial shape you're in, take a few minutes to fill out this financial fitness test.

Getting Financial Advice

In the last chapter, we stressed the importance of making a small business guru or an advisory board part of your risk-management strategy. Your business guru, we noted, could be anyone from a banker to a real-estate broker to a knowledgeable retired person. To help you with the financial section of your business plan—and perhaps with the formulation of your personal financial vision as well—you will need to find advisers with expertise in a wide range of financial matters (forecasting, taxes, retirement planning, bookkeeping, etc.). Action Step 44 and Table 9.1 will assist you with the task of assembling a financial team.

ACTION STEP 44

Action Steps

Assemble a team of financial advisers.

Use your networking skills to find people who can assist you in managing your financial affairs. Record the name of each person, along with other relevant information, in a chart like the one shown in Table 9.1.

Consider making one of your chosen financial advisers part of your **advisory board**. In many cases, this person will be your financial mentor. Don't be afraid to ask your mentor, or other financial advisers, to review your personal financial plan. This will help keep you grounded in the financial realities of your business.

Estimating Your Start-up Costs

In small business, you don't just rent a location, throw open the doors, and begin to show a profit. The reality is, it takes time for a start-up to make money. In fact, you're likely to discover that you need a good deal more start-up capital than you ever expected.

To find out how much start-up money you'll need, you will have to complete an **application of funds** table. To begin, we suggest that you divide your application of funds, or start-up expenses, into four categories:

Application of Funds (Start-up)

1. *General start-up costs*—including organizational costs, prepaid expenses, and inventory and office supplies.
2. *Leasehold improvements*—carpeting mirrors, light fixtures, etc.
3. *Equipment*—tables, chairs, computer, etc.
4. *Cash reserve fund*—cash on hand before you start your business (a pool of uncommitted cash).

There is no set formula for estimating the cash reserve you will require for your business. Your cash reserve will depend on your financial needs, and tolerance for risk, among other things. However, one rule of thumb is to estimate your major operating costs for the first month. These would be expenses such as rent, salaries, utility bills, and so on. Then multiply this operational estimate by a multiple of three to yield an estimate of cash reserve required. Another method for calculating a cash reserve fund is shown in Table 9.2.

Table 9.3 on page 170 provides further examples of the types of expenses in the first three categories. Now complete Action Step 45.

ADVISORY BOARD

a group of individuals with expertise in various areas who provide advice but are not normally associated with the day-to-day operations of your business

APPLICATION OF FUNDS

expenses you pay before starting your business

The Opening Balance Sheet

A **balance sheet** is a financial snapshot of the financial health of your business—what it owns and what it owes—at a given point in time. Not only is this key financial statement required by all bankers, but you will need a balance sheet even if you decide to finance your own business. There are two types of balance sheets: the opening balance sheet and the closing balance sheet. We will discuss the closing balance sheet later in the chapter. Here we focus on the opening balance sheet.

An opening balance sheet is a snapshot of the financial position of your business in the period immediately before you open your doors. Table 9.4 on page 171 provides an example of a typical opening balance sheet. The upper section of the balance sheet shows **assets**—the dollar value of what the business owns (equipment or inventory, for example). The lower section shows what the business

BALANCE SHEET

a financial snapshot of the financial health of your business at a given point in time

ASSETS

the dollar value of what the business owns

ACTION STEP 45

Estimate your start-up costs.

Now that you've got your business well in mind, take a few minutes to brainstorm a list of items you'll need to complete Table 9.2—your cash reserve fund. Then move on to Table 9.3 and begin listing and costing all your general start-up items, leasehold improvements, and equipment needs.

Don't rush this Action Step. Getting accurate numbers is critical to the survival of your business. Keep trying to uncover potential surprises and, if necessary, consult with vendors, suppliers, and other entrepreneurs. Write down your estimates in your 24/7 Adventure Notebook.

Table 9.1 List of Financial and Business Advisers

1. Mentor	
Name:	
Company/Firm:	
Address:	
Telephone:	
Fax:	
E-mail:	
2. Banker	
Name:	
Company/Firm:	
Address:	
Telephone:	
Fax:	
E-mail:	
3. Accountant/Bookkeeper	
Name:	
Company/Firm:	
Address:	
Telephone:	
Fax:	
E-mail:	
4. Investment Adviser/Broker	
Name:	
Company/Firm:	
Address:	
Telephone:	
Fax:	
E-mail:	
5. Insurance Agent(s)	
Name:	
Company/Firm:	
Address:	
Telephone:	
Fax:	
E-mail:	

LIABILITIES

the dollar value of what the business owes to parties other than the owner

EQUITY

the dollar value of what the business owes the owner

owes in the form of liabilities and equity. **Liabilities** are the dollar value of what the business owes to parties other than the owner. **Equity** is the dollar value of what the business owes the owner. Sometimes a balance sheet is arranged with assets shown on the left-hand side of the page and liabilities plus equity provided on the right.

Why does a balance sheet balance? The answer is quite simple. By definition:

Table 9.2 Estimating Cash Reserve

Item	Your estimate or monthly expenses based on sales of : $________	Your estimate of how much cash you need to start your business. (see column 3).	What to put in column 2 (these figures are typical for one kind of busi ness. You will have to decide how many months to allow for your business.)
	Column 1 $	Column 2 $	Column 3 $
Salary of owner-manager			2 times column 1
All other salaries and wages			3 times column 1
Rent			3 times column 1
Advertising			3 times column 1
Auto/truck/delivery expenses			3 times column 1
Supplies			3 times column 1
Phone/fax/Internet			3 times column 1
Other utilities (heat/hydro)			3 times column 1
Insurance			2 times column 1
Business taxes			4 times column 1
Bank payments			3 times column 1
Maintenance			3 times column 1
Legal/other professional fees			3 times column 1
Miscellaneous/ unexpected			3 times column 1
Total cash required to cover start-up operations—your cash reserve funds			Add rows 1–14. This amount will be recorded in the current assets of your opening balance sheet (see Table 9.4)

Assets (what the business owns) = **Liabilities** (what the business owes others) + **Equity** (what the business owes the owner)

Now let's examine each of these balance sheet components more closely.

ASSETS—WHAT THE BUSINESS OWNS

Assets are generally divided into three major categories: current assets, fixed assets, and other assets.

Table 9.3 Application of Funds

1. General Start-up Costs	**Subtotal**	**Total**
• Organizational Costs — legal, accounting, government registration, franchise fees, etc.	$________	
• Prepaid Expenses — insurance, licences and permits, first and last months' rent, security deposits, utility deposits, opening advertising and promotion, etc.	$________	
• Opening Inventory/Office Supplies — total inventory and office supplies on hand in order to do business the first day	$________	
Total General Start-up		$________
2. Leasehold Improvements		
— carpeting, mirrors, light fixtures, electrical, plumbing, signage, washrooms, air conditioning, wallpaper and painting, etc.		$________
3. Equipment Costs		
— tables, chairs, desk, filing cabinets, work benches, storage cabinets, cell phone, computer, copier, fax machine, auto, etc.		$________
4. Cash Reserve Fund		
— total cash on hand immediately before the business opens (a minimum of 10 percent contingency). This estimate comes from your calculation in Table 9.2.		$________
Total Application of Funds		$________

Current Assets These are called current because they can be converted into cash or consumed in the production of income in a short period of time. Under accounting rules, the period of time is almost always within one year. Current assets are recorded in order of liquidity. As Table 9.4 shows, they include:

- *Cash.* This is your cash reserve from your application of funds table (Table 9.3). It is the cash the business has available in the business account or on hand immediately before you start your business. This definition of cash could also include marketable securities such as Canada Savings Bonds.
- *Accounts receivable.* This is the total amount of money owed to the business by its customers who have purchased goods and services on credit. On an opening balance sheet, the dollar value of accounts receivable would normally be zero because you have yet to start your business.
- *Inventory/office supplies.* Inventory is recorded as the dollar value of all the physical items you have for sale in the course of doing business; or as the dollar value of the items you use in the course of making your product. Office supplies are items such as paper, pencils, and computer supplies. They are things you will use up over the current (one year) period in the course of selling your products or services. Depending on your type of business, you may want to categorize your inventory and supplies separately. If you have difficulty deciding if an item is a piece of equipment or an inventory/supply item,

Table 9.4 Opening Balance Sheet (date of opening ______)

		$	$	$
ASSETS				
Current Assets				
1	Cash & marketable securities	______		
2	Accounts receivable	______		
3	Inventory/office supplies	______		
4	Prepaid expenses	______		
5	Other current assets	______		
6	**Total Current Assets**		______	
Fixed Assets				
7	Equipment/furniture/fixtures	______		
8	Leasehold improvements	______		
9	Land/buildings	______		
10	Auto/truck	______		
11	Other fixed assets	______		
12	**Total Fixed Assets**		______	
Other Assets				
13	Organizational fees (legal, accounting, etc.)	______		
14	**Total Other Assets**		______	
15	**(6 + 12 + 14) TOTAL ASSETS**			______
LIABILITIES				
Current Liabilities (due within the next 12 months)				
16	Long-term loans (current portion)	______		
17	Short-term loans	______		
18	Accounts payable	______		
19	Other current liabilities	______		
20	**Total Current Liabilities**		______	
Long-Term Liabilities				
21	Long-term loans (minus current portion)	______		
22	Mortgages and liens payable	______		
23	Loans from shareholders (if applicable)	______		
24	Other long-term debt obligations	______		
25	**Total Long-Term Liabilities**		______	
26	**(20 +25) TOTAL LIABILITIES**			______
EQUITY				
27	Cash—owners capital (if a proprietorship or partnership) —shares outstanding (if a corporation)	______		
28	General start-up (organizational costs, etc.)	______		
29	Equipment/material/labour (provide details)	______		
30	**TOTAL EQUITY**			______
31	**(26 + 30) TOTAL LIABILITIES AND EQUITY**			______

think of the former as lasting more than one year (and thus retaining some sort of value) and inventory/office supplies as lasting one year or less (and thus having no appreciable value after that point).

- *Prepaid expenses.* Before you open your business, you'll likely have to prepay your insurance and your first month's rent. Prepaid expenses are classified as current assets because they are considered to be consumed in the production of income. Some banks do not classify prepaid expenses as current assets. Obviously, it would be difficult for them to "cash in" your prepaid insurance if your business were to fail.

- *Other current assets.* This category includes any remaining current assets you might have that can be translated into cash within one year. This might include, for example, a note payable or a security you don't want to cash in just yet).

Fixed Assets Fixed assets are the longer-term (more than one year) holdings of a business that are used to earn revenue or produce products or services. Fixed assets are not for sale in the normal course of doing business. As Table 9.4 shows, fixed assets include such items as:

- Equipment
- Furniture and fixtures
- Leasehold improvements
- Land and buildings
- Autos and trucks

Other Assets These are intangible assets that cannot be assigned a fixed value. Items in this category include franchise fees, organizational fees such as government registrations, consultant fees, franchise fees, and pre-start-up legal and accounting fees.

LIABILITIES—WHAT THE BUSINESS OWES OTHERS

Liabilities are normally divided into two major categories: current liabilities and long-term liabilities. In some cases, the liability section of the balance sheet includes a category called other long-term debt.

Current Liabilities These are outstanding debts or obligations that are expected to come due within one year of the date of the balance sheet. They include the following:

- *Accounts payable*—total money that the business owes to suppliers.
- *Contracts or notes payable*—total money owed within the next year on such items as equipment, leasehold improvements, or a personal loan.
- *Line of credit*—if you have dipped into it.
- *Demand loan*—a loan that is due on demand and thus is recorded as owing within the next 12 months.
- *Long-term loans*—current portion. Let's say that you have negotiated with your bank manager a long-term loan of $35 000. Let's also assume that you have agreed to repay the loan by paying $5000 per year. Part of this yearly payment—let's say $3000 for the purposes of this example—will go to repay the amount you borrowed—that is, the $35 000. This is called the principal portion of a loan. The other part of your loan repayment, in this case $2000, will be used to pay interest charges. The current portion of your long-term debt is the principal payment on your loan for the 12 months following the date of your opening balance sheet. This is the amount due on your long-term debt within the next year. Remember, the current portion *does not* include your interest payments.

Long-Term Liabilities Long-term liabilities, also known as deferred liabilities, are debts that are not due within one year. They include bank loans, loans to shareholders (if you are incorporated), and long-term liens or notes payable. They should not be confused with the current portion of the long-term debt. In the above example of the $35 000 loan, we calculated the current or principal portion (due over the next year) of this long-term loan to be $3000. If we subtract the current portion ($3000) from the total loan ($35,000), we arrive at a long-term portion of $32 000. This is the amount due after the first year.

During negotiations for a long-term loan, a financial institution may ask you to sign a demand note that gives the lender permission to "demand on notice" the full amount of your loan. Technically, a demand note should be recorded as short-term loan (current liability) because your lender can ask you pay the full amount of the loan at any time. Thus, if our $35 000 loan were a demand loan, it would be recorded as a current liability.

Other Long-Term Debt This optional category includes any other long-term obligations such as an equipment loan, a note payable, or a long-term loan to a relative.

EQUITY—WHAT THE BUSINESS OWES THE OWNER

Equity refers to what you, the owner, invests in the business. Equity is not necessarily your cash investment. If, for example, you were to invest your own equipment or inventory, you would record the dollar value of this investment as equity. You might even decide to do the architectural plans, plumbing, or electrical work yourself. This kind of labour or knowledge investment is often called "sweat equity." Some banks and other lending institutions do not consider sweat equity a true equity investment. All we can say is stick to your guns. The value of your work must be considered as equity—otherwise your balance sheet won't balance.

Key Balance Sheet Ratios

In reviewing your balance sheet, your banker will do a few calculations involving some important ratios to determine the financial health of your business. A comprehensive list of ratios is provided in Appendix 9.1 (see page 190). In this section, we focus on two key ratios: liquidity ratios and solvency ratios.

LIQUIDITY RATIOS

Liquidity ratios show the number of dollars of liquid assets available to cover each dollar of current debt (or the ability to pay your short-term obligations). Alternatively, they measure the ability of a company to honour its short-term or current financial commitments. The two basic liquidity indicators are the current (or working capital) ratio and the quick (or acid test) ratio.

Current Ratio The current (or working capital) ratio is calculated by dividing current assets by current liabilities:

$$\text{Current ratio} = \frac{\text{Current assets}}{\text{Current liabilities}}$$

The higher the ratio, the greater the liquidity. As a rule of thumb, the ratio should be greater than two. That is to say, your current assets should be double your current liabilities. This ratio is also a measure of your relative working capital because by definition:

$$\text{Working Capital} = \text{Current Assets} - \text{Current Liabilities}$$

Working capital is not necessarily cash. For example, current assets include inventory and prepaid expenses in addition to cash, while current liabilities include accounts receivable and the current portion of the long-term debt. What this means is that a business could have a relatively strong working capital position (i.e., a working capital ratio of greater than two) but have no cash. For this reason, you should also consider the quick or acid test ratio (discussed below) when evaluating your liquidity position.

Now refer to Table 9.5 for a moment. Start-up Inc.'s current ratio is 20 370 / 33 000 = .62. This ratio tells us that Start-up Inc. has a working capital problem and may in the short term (over the first year) have trouble meeting its debt obligations. A bank is not likely to lend Start-up Inc. money until the company increases its current assets and/or reduces its current debts.

Quick Ratio The quick (or acid test) ratio measures a company's ability to pay current debts by taking into account only the most liquid assets:

$$\text{Quick ratio} = \frac{\text{Most liquid assets}}{\text{Current liablilites}}$$

Most liquid assets are normally defined as cash and marketable securities (e.g., Canada Savings Bonds and treasury bills) and, in some cases, accounts receivable. However, we strongly recommend that you include only cash and marketable securities. There is never any guarantee that you will collect your accounts receivable.

As a rule of thumb, analysts and financial institutions like to see a quick ratio that is greater than one. This means that your opening cash should be able to cover your expected current liabilities over the first year of operation. As Table 9.5 shows, Start-up Inc.'s quick ratio is $8195 / 33 000 = .25. This ratio suggest that the company may not have enough cash to cover short-term financial obligations such as its monthly payments to the bank.

SOLVENCY RATIOS

Solvency ratios measure the ability of a company to meet its long-term debt obligations. The higher the ratio, the higher the risk to the creditor or lender. The two standard solvency ratios are the proprietorship ratio and the debt to equity ratio.

Proprietorship Ratio This ratio is calculated as follows:

$$\text{Proprietorship ratio} = \frac{\text{Owner's investment}}{\text{Total assets}}$$

Banks and other lending institutions like to see a proprietorship ratio that is greater than .50. In other words, if they see that you own at least half the assets, then they know that you, the owner, is committed. Start-up Inc.'s proprietorship ratio is $50 000 / $115 000 = .43. It's a little below the recommended .50, so Start-up Inc. may be asked to increase the owner's investment or reduce its assets.

Debt to Equity Ratio This ratio is calculated as follows:

$$\text{Debt to equity ratio} = \frac{\text{Total liabilities (debt)}}{\text{Owner's equity}}$$

As a rule of thumb, the debt to equity ratio should be less than one. Lenders or creditors like to see that you have sufficient owner's equity to meet all debts. Start-up Inc.'s debt to equity ratio—$65 000 / 50 000 = 1.3—is such that the company would likely be asked by its lenders to reduce its debt or increase its equity.

Table 9.5 Start-up Inc.

Opening Balance Sheet (Date of opening ______)			
ASSETS			
Current Assets	$	$	$
1 Cash & marketable securities	8 195		
2 Accounts receivable	______		
3 Inventory/office supplies	2 600		
4 Prepaid expenses	9 575		
5 Other current assets	______		
6 **Total Current Assets**		20 370	
Fixed Assets			
7 Equipment/furniture/fixtures	53 030		
8 Leasehold improvements	38 800		
9 Land/buildings	______		
10 Auto/truck	______		
11 Other fixed assets	______		
12 **Total Fixed Assets**		91 830	
Other Assets			
13 Organizational fees (legal, accounting etc.)	2 800		
14 **Total Other Assets**		2 800	
15 **(6 + 12 + 14) TOTAL ASSETS**			115 000
LIABILITIES			
Current Liabilities (due within the next 12 months)			
16 Long-term loans (current portion)	3 000		
17 Short-term loans	30 000		
18 Accounts payable	______		
19 Other current liabilities	______		
20 **Total Current Liabilities**		33 000	
Long-Term Liabilities			
21 Long-term loans (minus current portion)	32 000		
22 Mortgages and liens payable	______		
23 Loans from shareholders (if applicable)	______		
24 Other long-term debt obligations	______		
25 **Total Long-Term Liabilities**		32 000	
26 **(20 +25) TOTAL LIABILITIES**			65 000
EQUITY			
27 Cash —owners capital (if a proprietorship or partnership)	40 000		
—shares outstanding (if a corporation)			
28 General start-up (organizational costs etc.)	______		
29 Equipment/material/labour (provide details)	10 000		
30 **TOTAL EQUITY**			50 000
31 **(26 + 30) TOTAL LIABILITIES AND EQUITY**			115 000

Cash Flow and Income Statement: Important Projections

A projected (pro forma) income statement tells you when you're going to make a profit on paper. A cash flow projection tells you whether or not you can pay the bills and when you'll have to visit the banker. Both the income statement and the cash flow projection are necessary for the survival of your business. In this section, we'll begin with cash flow.

CASH FLOW PROJECTION

PROJECTED (PRO FORMA) CASH FLOW

a financial statement that helps you control the money that comes into your business and the money that is spent

A **projected (pro forma) cash flow** is a financial statement that helps you control the money that comes into your business and the money that is spent. The cash flow statement is a tool to help you control this money flow and thus avoid running out of cash. Normally, you should prepare a monthly cash flow for the first year, then a quarterly cash flow for the next two years. The monthly cash flow of a business called DISCovery Bookstore is shown in Table 9.6 (see page 178).

There are three major issues you should consider while you're working out your own cash flow: the sales forecast, collection timeliness, and seasonality.

Forecasting Sales

The most important and often the most difficult step is estimating sales for the first year of a new business. The thirteenth month becomes more manageable because you have a year of experience.

Forecasting sales is as much an art as it is a science. Marketing research is the key to preparing an accurate sales forecast. It involves conducting an industry overview, identifying total sales (internationally, nationally, provincewide, and in your service area), and then determining what part of the market you can reasonably expect to penetrate in the first few years. Trade magazines, census data, suppliers, and major newspapers often have already performed your secondary market research. Don't forget to do your e-research on the Internet.

If you are writing a business plan, attach appropriate printed data to your market research section in the appendix to substantiate your numbers. Fine-tune these numbers by showing your own research and notes from industry experts that support your assumptions about projected sales. A third party's estimate will have more value than yours, so quote as many sources as you can to support your sales forecast. When you list your competitors, don't forget to estimate their market share and the part of their market that you have targeted. The financial community wants to make sure that you have spent a lot of time and thought on your projection because it drives everything else. You want to minimize surprises.

Even "good surprises" can play havoc with a well-considered plan. For example, imagine you receive 10 times the orders you expected and you simply don't yet have the resources to fill them. Unanticipated sales could seriously damage your business if you lack sufficient cash to buy the needed inventory. When forecasting sales, then, you should consider including high, low, and medium sales projections. This will allow you to prepare a Plan B for your cash-in and cash-out estimates.

Forecasting Collections

In your cash flow projection, you're going to have to figure out when you will actually collect your money. For example, if you're in the bed-and-breakfast business, you probably collect your money ahead of time (i.e., when the customer books the accommodation). A retailer normally gets paid when the product is sold. As Table 9.6 shows, DISCovery Bookstore's sales estimate (line 1) is the same as the cash sales estimate (line 5). If you're on the receiving end, it's nice to know there are businesses that collect the dollars up front.

Other businesses must wait to be paid. For example, service trades will bill for their services and often not be paid for 30 or 60 days after the work is completed.

If you're doing consulting work for the government, you may have to wait more than 90 days for payment. If your business falls into this category, you should have a policy in place for dealing with late payments; it will help you avoid a situation in which you are required to pay bills when there is no cash coming in. Box 9.2 shows the typical payment and collection timeless for an electrical service company.

Seasonality

Most businesses experience peaks and valleys. For example, if you're in the ice cream business, sales will "heat" up in the summer and drop off in the fall. The same is true of hardware (especially home-improvement supplies) and auto parts, when everyone is getting the travel bug. If you run a ski shop, you might have to order your skis at a summer trade show, pay for them when they arrive in September, and wait until late February to make the final sale. The owners of DISCovery Bookstore (see Table 9.6) knew from their market research that 50 percent of their sales would be made in the September–December period. Their understanding of the seasonality of their industry helped them determine how much inventory they would need to support sales over the peak period.

Now it's your turn. Action Step 46 leads you through the mechanics of a monthly cash flow projection. We also supply you with a worksheet you can use to prepare your projected cash flow (Table 9.7 on page 180). In addition, all the banks and most major accounting firms can supply you with a disk for preparing your cash flow. Another option is to use an online spreadsheet (see Box 9.3 on page 181). Box 9.4 on page 181 provides you with some important points to consider while you're working out your cash flow.

After you have completed Action Step 46, show the results to an expert. Does the picture look accurate? Does your business have a positive cash balance or a negative one? It's better to know the truth now, while you're working on paper. Paper truth is a lot easier on the pocketbook than real truth.

PRO FORMA INCOME STATEMENT

A **pro forma (or projected) income statement** is an itemized statement of sales (or revenues) and corresponding expenses. Like cash flow, it is an indicator of the financial health of your business. The major difference is that the income statement is not about cash; for example, as we explain below, an income statement

Box 9.2 Electric Works—Payment and Collection Timelines

Payments

- Wages: weekly
- CPP Deductions: monthly
- Income Tax Payments: quarterly
- Raw Materials: 30 days
- Hydro Inspector: 10 days

Collections (even though the terms may be net 30 days)

- 3 or 5 contractors: 45 days
- 1 contractor: 60–90 days
- 1 contractor: 90–120 days

ACTION STEP 46

Draft a projected cash flow.

Begin projecting your cash across the first year of your business. If you don't have an electronic spreadsheet program like Excel, you can download the cash flow budget worksheet from the CCH Business Owner's Toolkit (see Box 9.3). If you don't have access to a computer, use the blank cash flow worksheet provided in Table 9.7.

1. Write down all the cash you'll start the year with. In the case of DISCovery Bookstore, this was $10 000 (see Table 9.6, line 39).
2. For each month, enter the amount of cash you'll receive from sales or accounts receivable.
3. Enter any loans in the month you receive the cash from the lender.
4. Total the above, which will give you the cash available for each month.
5. Now list all disbursements (cash going out). Spread these out, too.
6. Then subtract disbursements from cash available, which gives you a monthly cash flow.
7. Examine your work. Have you explored the quirks of seasonality? Have you discovered the minimum and maximum time lags between when you make a sale and when the business gets paid in cash for the sale? Does the picture look accurate? Have you checked with an expert?
8. Try the "what-if" test:

If your cash flow picture looks good, test your money management skills by dropping in a couple of "what ifs." What surprise expenses could throw a monkey wrench into your new business?

In Chapter 16, Action Step 74, we will ask you to refine these numbers.

Table 9.6 Monthly Cash Flow—DISCovery Bookstore

Step I	Opening Balance	6% July	7% Aug.	9% Sept.	10% Oct.	12% Nov.	19% Dec.	6.5% Jan.	4.5% Feb.	5% March	5% April	8% May	8% June	Total
Step II														
1. SALES		9 000	10 500	13 500	15 000	18 000	28 500	9 750	6 750	7 500	7 500	12 000	12 000	150 000
2. —														
3. TOTAL SALES		9 000	10 500	13 500	15 000	18 000	28 500	9 750	6 750	7 500	7 500	12 000	12 000	150 000
Step III														
Receipts														
4. Cash In														
5. — Cash Sales		9 000	10 500	13 500	15 000	18 000	28 500	9 750	6 750	7 500	7 500	12 000	12 000	150 000
6. — Receivables Collected														
7. — Loan Proceeds														
8. — Personal Investment														
9. — Sales of Assets														
10. — Equity	80 000													80 000
11. — Loans	35 000													35 000
12. —														
13. Total Cash In (lines 5 through 12)	115 000	9 000	10 500	13 500	15 000	18 000	28 500	9 750	6 750	7 500	7 500	12 000	12 000	265 000
Step IV														
Disbursements														
14. Cash Out														
15. — Purchases		5 255	9 880	9 305	8 030	8 720	6 575	5 080	3 760	3 045	6 545	7 440	8 420	82 055
16. — Advertising		200	200	200	200	400	400	100	100	200	100	100	200	2 400
17. — Auto and Truck														
18. — Bank Charges and Interest		300	300	300	300	300	300	300	300	300	300	300	300	3 600
19. — Insurance		450												450

(Continued)

	Opening Balance	6% July	7% Aug.	9% Sept.	10% Oct.	12% Nov.	19% Dec.	6.5% Jan.	4.5% Feb.	5% March	5% April	8% May	8% June	Total
20. — Professional Fees														
21. — Rent		1 200	1 200	1 200	1 200	1 200	1 200	1 200	1 200	1 200	1 200	1 200	1 200	14 400
22. — Business Taxes and Licences														
23. — Telephone		50	50	50	50	50	50	50	50	50	50	50	50	600
24. — Utilities (Heat, Light, Water)		150	150	150	150	150	150	150	150	150	150	150	150	1 800
25. — Wages — Employees														
26. — Principal Draw or Management Salaries		1 600	1 600	1 600	1 600	1 600	1 600	1 600	1 600	1 600	1 600	1 600	1 600	19 200
27. — Term Debt (Principal Portion Only)		250	250	250	250	250	250	250	250	250	250	250	250	3 000
28. — Purchase Fixed Assets	60 790													62 790
29. — Taxes														
30. — Materials and Supplies (1%)		100	100	100	100	100	100	100	100	100	100	100	100	1 200
31. — Miscellaneous (3%)		325	325	325	325	325	325	325	325	325	325	325	325	3 900
32. — Start-up (Application of funds excluding cash reserve)	44 210													44 210
33. —														
34. Total Cash Out (lines 15 through 33)	105 000	9 880	14 055	13 480	12 205	13 095	10 950	9 155	7 835	7 220	10 620	11 515	12 595	237 605
Step V														
Summary														
35. Total Cash In (line 13)	115 000	9 000	10 500	13 500	15 000	18 000	28 500	9 750	6 750	7 500	7 500	12 000	12 000	265 000
36. Plus: Cash Forward (Prev. Mon. — line 39)		10 000	9 120	5 565	15 585	8 380	13 285	30 835	31 430	30 345	30 625	27 505	27 990	
37. Equals: Total Cash Available	115 000	19 000	19 620	19 065	20 585	26 380	41 785	40 585	38 180	37 845	38 125	39 505	39 990	265 000
38. Less: Total Cash Out (line 34)	105 000	9 880	14 055	13 480	12 205	13 095	10 950	9 155	7 835	7 220	10 620	11 515	12 595	237 605
39. Equals: Closing Bank Balance	10 000	9 120	5 565	15 585	8 380	13 285	30 835	31 430	30 345	30 625	27 505	27 990	27 395	27 395

Table 9.7 Projected Cash Flow Statement—Worksheet

STEP I					Month								
Opening Balance	1	2	3	4	5	6	7	8	9	10	11	12	Total
STEP II													
1. Sales													
2.													
3. Total Sales													
STEP III Receipts													
4. Cash In													
5. Cash Sales													
6. Receivables Collected													
7. Loan Proceeds													
8. Personal Investment													
9. Sales of Assets													
10. Equity													
11. Loans													
12.													
13. Total Cash In (line 5 through 12)													
STEP IV Disbursements													
14. Cash Out													
15. Accounts Payable													
16. Advertising/Promotion													
17. Auto and Truck													
18. Bank Charges and Interest													
19. Insurance													
20. Professional Fees													
21. Rent													
22. Taxes and Licences													
23. Telephone													
24. Utilities (Heat/Light/Water)													
25. Wages: Employees													
26. Principal Draw or Management Salaries													
27. Term Debt (Principal Portion Only)													
28. Purchase Fixed Assets													
29. Taxes													
30. Materials and Supplies													
31. Miscellaneous													
32. Start-up Application of Funds (Excluding Cash Reserve)													
33.													
34. Total Cash Out (line 15 through 33)													
STEP V Summary													
35. Total Cash In (line 4)													
36. Plus: Cash Forward (previous month — line 39)													
37. Equals: Total Cash Available													
38. Less: Total Cash Out (line 34)													
39. Equals: Closing Bank Balance													

Box 9.3 Bookmark This

Financial Planning Tools

- **Small Business Tools** (CCH Business Owner's Toolkit)
  www.toolkit.cch.com/tools/tools.asp
  Contains links to a downloadable balance sheet template, a cash flow budget worksheet, and an income statement template. The worksheets are easy to use and can be modified to suit your needs.
- **Performance Plus** (Industry Canada)
  http://strategis.ic.gc.ca/SSG/pm00013e.html
  Use this online performance benchmarking tool to find out where your business stands as compared to a relevant industry average.
- **Attacking Business Decision Problems with Break-Even Analysis**
  www.cbsc.org/english/search/display.cfm?code=4053&coll=FE_FEDSBIS_E&DispMenu=Guides
  This article on the Canada Service Business Centres website illustrates ways in which break-even analysis can be applied to sales, profits, and costs.

records a sale even if you have not yet received the money. Normally an income statement is for a one-year period (sometimes on a quarterly basis). In a business plan, you may have to provide projected income statements for the first five years, depending on the size and complexity of your business.

For those of you who are not familiar with an income statement, we have constructed a typical projected year-end income statement for DISCovery Bookstore (see Table 9.8). Action Step 47 will help you project your own income statement. The major elements of an income statement are discussed below.

Sales On the income statement, all revenue (sales) is recorded even though you may not yet have received the actual cash. For example, in the case of DISCovery Bookstore (Table 9.8), the yearly sales or revenue is $150 000. This figure is the same as the yearly cash sales figure in the cash flow statement (Table 9.6, line 5) for the simple reason that DISCovery is a cash business—when it sells a book, it

ACTION STEP 47

Draft a projected income statement—a moving picture of your business.

You may want to adapt the format shown in Table 9.9 on page 183. Generate the numbers for the projected period as follows:

1. Using data from your cash flow, forecast your sales for the year.
2. Calculate your cost of goods sold, subtract that from sales, and you have gross profit.
3. Add up all expenses and subtract those from gross profit. That gives you the net before taxes.
4. Subtract taxes. (Governments will tax you on paper profit, so you have to build this figure in.)

The figure at the bottom is net profit after taxes for the year.

In Chapter 16, Action Step 75, we will ask you to refine these numbers.

PRO FORMA (OR PROJECTED) INCOME STATEMENT

an itemized statement of sales (or revenues) and corresponding expenses

Box 9.4 Cash Flow—Important Points to Consider

The three most important ingredients in managing and operating a business? CA$H, CA$H, and more CA$H. And yet more than 80 percent of small businesses do not use a Cash Flow Forecast.

- Two factors ensure that you have sufficient cash to operate comfortably:
  1. A 12-month forecast of sales and expenses.
  2. A workable and realistic policy stating when you pay your bills and when you can turn sales into cash.
- Cash flow includes principal, bank payments, and interest—separately.
- Cash flow does not include depreciation, only cash in and cash out.
- Your year-end cash flow provides many of the estimates you'll need for your projected income statement.
- Before offering credit, do a cash flow.

Table 9.8 Pro Forma Income Statement—DISCovery Bookstore

Sales (Revenue)	$150 000
Cost of Goods Sold	
Opening inventory	30 000
(plus) purchases	82 055
Subtotal	112 055
(minus) closing inventory	22 055
(equals) cost of materials	90 000
Total Cost of Goods Sold	90 000
Gross Profit	60 000
Operating Expenses	
Rent	14 400
Utilities	1 800
Salaries—Employees	
Salaries—Principal Draw (Man. Sal.)	19 200
Advertising	2 400
Office supplies	1 200
Insurance	450
Maintenance and cleaning	
Legal and accounting	
Delivery expense	
Licences	
Boxes, paper, etc.	
Telephone	600
Depreciation	4 000
Miscellaneous	3 900
Total Operating Expenses	47 950
Other Expenses	
Interest	3 600
Total: Other Expenses	3 600
Total All Expenses	51 550
Net Profit (Loss) (Pre-tax)	8 450

gets the money right away. However, many businesses operate differently. As we noted in our discussion of cash flow, service trades and government consultants can make a sale and not be paid until 30, 60, or even 90 days later.

Cost of Goods Sold Cost of goods sold is the cost of materials or inventory that you use up over a specified period ($90 000 in the case of DISCovery Bookstore). It is calculated as follows:

- Take the value of your opening inventory/office supplies from your opening balance sheet.
- Add the value of your purchases over the income statement period.
- Subtract the value of your closing inventory/office supplies. This will be the value of the inventory/office supplies from your closing inventory (usually after one year). If you were actually running a business, you would normally get this number by doing a physical inventory.

Gross Profit Gross profit is your total sales minus your cost of goods sold. As Table 9.8 shows, DISCovery's gross profit is $60 000 ($150 000 – $90 000).

Operating Expenses These are the expenses you incur in the day-to-day operation of your business. Many of these items can be taken from the total disbursements column of your cash flow. For example, the yearly rent recorded in DISCovery's income statement (Table 9.8) is $14 400, the same number that appears in the company's cash flow statement (see Table 9.6, line 21).

- *Expenses.* Expenses are recorded in the income statement even though you may not have paid for them yet. For example, If DISCovery had not paid for its rent in the last month, the total rent disbursements in the cash flow would have been reduced by $1200 to $13 200. On the income statement, however, the rent costs would have remained unchanged at $14 400.
- *Principal payments and interest.* Principal payments on a bank loan are not an operating expense and thus are not recorded as an expense in the income statement. Interest payments on a loan are recorded in the income statement as an interest expense ($3600 in the case of DISCovery). please note: interest on a loan is not recorded as an operating expense).
- *Owner's draw.* If you are not incorporated and you pay yourself a wage, you should record this expense as an owner's draw in the closing balance sheet. However, if your business is incorporated and you pay yourself a wage, you should record this expense as a management salary in your income statement.

Table 9.9 Projected Income Statement (period ending ________________)

Sales (Revenue)			________
Cost of Goods Sold			
Opening inventory	________		
(plus) purchases	________		
Subtotal		________	
(minus) closing inventory	________		
(equals) cost of materials	________		________
Total Cost of Goods Sold		________	
Gross Profit			________
Operating Expenses			________
Rent	________		
Utilities	________		
Salaries—Employees	________		
Salaries—Principal Draw (Man. Sal.)	________		
Advertising	________		
Office supplies	________		
Insurance	________		
Maintenance and cleaning	________		
Legal and accounting	________		
Delivery expense	________		
Licences	________		
Boxes, paper, etc.	________		
Telephone	________		
Depreciation	________		
Miscellaneous	________		
Total Operating Expenses			________
Other Expenses	________		
Interest	________		
Total: Other Expenses			________
Total All Expenses			________
Net Profit (Loss) (Pre-tax)			________

- *Depreciation.* Depreciation is a non-cash expense that must be recorded on your income statement. The most common way to calculate depreciation is through a method called "straight line." Add up the equipment and leasehold improvements in your opening balance sheet. Decide how long these will last (5 years, 10 years, etc.). Then divide the total value of your equipment and leasehold improvements by the estimated number of years they will last.

PROFIT IS NOT CASH

A quick glance at DISCovery Bookstore's monthly cash flow (Table 9.6) and income statement (Table 9.8) makes it obvious that profit and cash are not the same thing. DISCovery's profit was $8 450, but its cash increase was $17 395 ($27 395 – $10 000). This increase might have given the bookstore's owners the illusion that they were doing better than they actually were. However, their cash flow did not reflect the fact that they were using up their equipment. It did not take into account depreciation or the fact that DISCovery had a little more cash available because it used up some of its opening inventory and did not replace it. (As the store's income statement shows, the opening inventory was $30 000 and the closing inventory $22 055.) By adjusting for changing inventory in the cost of goods sold entry, the income statement provides a dose of reality.

KEY INCOME STATEMENT RATIOS

Calculating income statement ratios will help you determine how healthy your business is and how it compares to other businesses in your selected industry. A number of ratios that use income statement information are provided in Appendix 9.1.

Gross Profit Margin One of the most common income statement ratios is the *gross profit margin.* It is calculated by dividing the gross profit by total sales. Sometimes this ratio is multiplied by 100 to yield a percentage value. The higher the ratio or percentage is, the higher the profit margin. For example, the DISCovery Bookstore (Table 9.8) has a gross profit margin of $60 000 / $150 000 x 100 = 40%. A gross profit margin of 45 percent would mean that DISCovery would be earning 5 percent more in gross profit for every dollar it sells; its gross profit would be $67 500 and its total profit would increase from $8450 to $15 950.

Profit Margin Another common income statement ratio is the *profit margin,* which equals net profit (before taxes) divided by total sales. In most cases, this ratio is multiplied by 100 to yield a percentage value. Again, the higher the ratio, the better. The DISCovery Bookstore (Table 9.8) has a profit margin of 5.6 percent ($8 450 / $150 000 x 100). DISCovery produces $.0563 in profit for every dollar of sales.

To learn more about your own industry ratio, use the online performance benchmarking tool (Performance Plus) cited in Box 9.3.

Break-Even Analysis

If you know your costs (fixed and variable) and your gross sales, you can calculate your break-even to tell you the level of sales you will need to start making money.

> A small manufacturing company was completing a plan for its second year of operation. Its first-year sales were $177 000. Its fiscal year ended in

December. A sales breakdown for the last three months of the first year looked like this:

October	$24 000
November	$29 000
December	$15 000
Total	$68 000

The owners took a look at the numbers and called in a consultant to help. The consultant gathered information from sales reps, owners, and customers and projected sales for the second year at a whopping $562 000. The owners reacted with disbelief.

"You're crazy," they said. "That's over three times what we did last year."

The consultant smiled. "Didn't you tell me you were going to add three new products?"

"Yes."

"And new reps in March, June, and September?"

"Yes, but—"

"And what about those big promotions you've got planned?"

"Well, sure. We've planned some promotion. But that doesn't get us anywhere near three times last year."

"All right," the accountant said. "Can you do $275 000?"

The owners got into a huddle. Recalling the fourth quarter, they were sure they could stay even, and 4 x $68 000 (fourth-quarter sales) was $272 000. They knew they had to do better than last year.

"Sure. No problem. We can do $272 000."

"All right." said the consultant, rolling out his break-even chart.

"I've just projected $562 000 in sales for the year. To break even, you need only $275 000."

"Hey," the owners said. "We're projecting $90 000 in the first quarter."

"I'm glad you're thinking my way," the consultant said. "Because if you don't believe you can reach a goal, you'll never get there." He paused, then said "By the way, that $90 000 is three times what you did in your first quarter last year!"

"Just tell us what to do," the owners said.

Following a careful cash flow analysis, the consultant determined that the company would need to borrow money. They knew their business—industry trends, product line, competitors, sales, and promotion plans—but there was no way the bankers would believe a tripling of growth. The key to getting the loan was to convince the bankers the company could do better than the break-even, at $275 000. The break-even chart (see Figure 9.1) was built on the $562 000 sales figure. Note on the chart that after $280 000 in sales, the firm has passed its break-even point and is making a profit.

The Closing Balance Sheet

The closing balance sheet will give you a final indicator of the financial health of your business. A typical closing balance sheet is shown in Table 9.10 and its main elements are described below.

Figure 9.1 Break-Even Chart

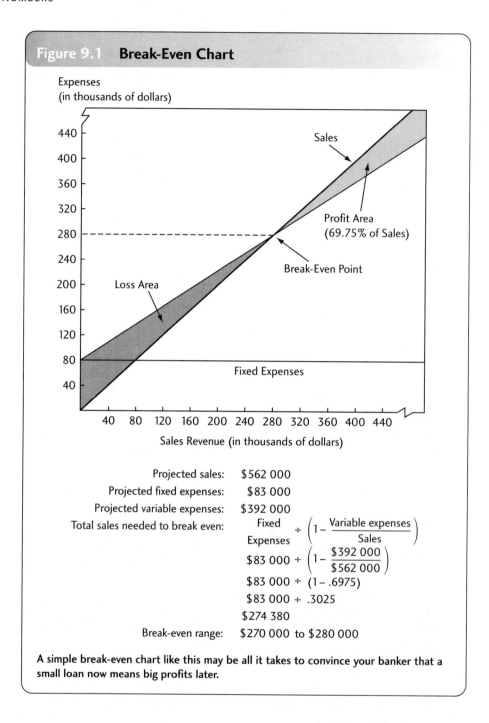

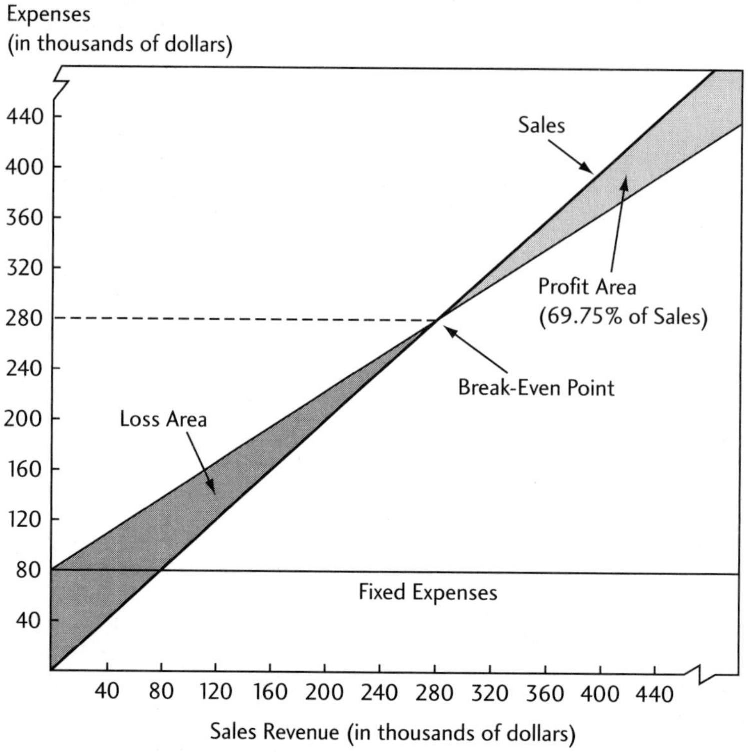

Projected sales:	\$562 000
Projected fixed expenses:	\$83 000
Projected variable expenses:	\$392 000
Total sales needed to break even:	$\text{Fixed Expenses} \div \left(1 - \frac{\text{Variable expenses}}{\text{Sales}}\right)$
	$\$83\,000 \div \left(1 - \frac{\$392\,000}{\$562\,000}\right)$
	$\$83\,000 \div (1 - .6975)$
	$\$83\,000 \div .3025$
	\$274 380
Break-even range:	\$270 000 to \$280 000

A simple break-even chart like this may be all it takes to convince your banker that a small loan now means big profits later.

Assets

- *Cash*—your cash position, the final number in your projected cash flow statement.
- *Accounts receivable*—money owed to your business at the end of the financial period.
- *Inventory/office supplies*—the closing inventory taken from your projected income statement.
- *Equipment*—the equipment estimate taken from your opening balance sheet.
- *Leasehold improvements*—the leasehold improvements estimate taken from your opening balance sheet.

- *Depreciation*—your estimate of depreciation taken from your projected income statement.
- *Other assets*—your estimate of "other assets" taken from your opening balance sheet.

Table 9.10 Closing Balance Sheet (period ending ____________)

ASSETS			
Current Assets			
Cash	______		
Accounts receivable	______		
Inventory/office supplies	______		
Prepaid expenses	______		
Other current assets	______		
Total Current Assets		______	
Fixed Assets			
Equipment, furniture, fixtures	______		
Leasehold improvements	______		
—Depreciation/amortization	______		
Land/buildings	______		
Auto/truck	______		
Other fixed assets	______		
Total Fixed Assets		______	
Other Assets			
Organizational costs	______		
Total Other Assets		______	
Total Assets			______
LIABILITIES AND EQUITY			
Liabilities			
Current Debt (due within the next 12 months)			
Bank loans—current portion	______		
Loans—other	______		
Accounts payable	______		
Other current liabilities	______		
Total Current Liabilities			______
Long-Term Debt			
Long-term (minus current portion)	______		
Mortgage and liens payable	______		
Loans from shareholders	______		
Other long-term debts	______		
Total Long-Term Liabilities		______	
Total Liabilities			______
Owner's Equity			
Equity at start of period	______		
+ Profit over period	______		
– Owner's draw	______		
Total Equity		______	
Total Liabilities and Owner's Equity			______

Liabilities

- *Current debt*—your estimate of the principal due over the next year.
- *Accounts payable*—money for such things as rent and inventory that your business owes to others.
- *Long-term debt or liabilities*—your total principal due for all long-term loans minus the current portion.

Owner's equity

Owner's equity—what the business owes the owner—is calculated as follows:

Equity at start of period (total equity from your opening balance sheet)
+
Profit over the period (net profit from income statement)
–
Owner's draw
=
Total equity at the end of the period

As we noted earlier, owner's draw is recorded in the closing balance sheet only if the business is unincorporated. If you pay yourself a wage and your business is incorporated, you record this expense as a management salary in your income statement.

In a Nutshell

Not surprisingly, many entrepreneurs find it difficult to project numbers for their business. There are several explanations for this:

- They're action people who are in a hurry; they don't think they have time to sit down and *think*.
- They're creative; their strengths are greater in the innovation area than in the justification area.
- They tend to think in visual terms, rather than in numbers or words.

Nonetheless, business is a numbers game and you have to know the rules. In spite of the entrepreneur's feelings about numbers and projections, survival in the marketplace depends on having the right numbers in the right colour of ink. This chapter helps you formulate a financial vision, estimate your start-up costs, create a balance sheet, project your cash flow and pro forma income statement, use ratios to plan your business, and understand the value of break-even analysis.

The idea in projecting numbers is to make them as realistic as possible. That is the key. Your numbers may seem reasonable to you, but you must make them seem reasonable to others as well. You make them believable by keeping them realistic and documenting them properly. You need to relate each projection to your specific business and to industry standards, and then to *document* them (tell where they came from) in your business plan. This chapter will help you make your projections believable to your banker as well as to yourself.

Key Terms

advisory board
application of funds
assets
balance sheet
equity
liabilities
pro forma (or projected) income statement
projected (pro forma) cash flow

Think Points for Success

- ✓ It's cheaper to make mistakes on a spreadsheet before you go into business.
- ✓ When you work out numbers for a business plan, spend time completing your cash flow.
- ✓ When you visit your banker to ask for money, make sure you know how much you're going to need for the long run.
- ✓ Use balance sheet and income statement ratios to test the financial health of your business.
- ✓ Projecting will help you control the variables of your business: numbers, employees, promotion mix, product mix, and the peaks and valleys of seasonality.

Business Plan Building Block

NOW IT'S YOUR TURN

Explain how you developed your sales projections. Use hard data wherever you can. Summarize your research and list people and firms that have influenced your conclusions. Include cost of goods sold, expenses, capital needs, and best- and worst-case scenarios. If you are using computer software to develop your plan, enter the information that you have developed in the text to fill in the cash flow and income statement.

Checklist Questions and Actions to Develop Your Business Plan

THE POWER OF NUMBERS

- ❑ Do you have a financial vision?
- ❑ What are your estimated start-up costs?
- ❑ Validate your sales forecast based on your primary and secondary market research.
- ❑ Identify all your cost and pricing assumptions.
- ❑ Prepare an opening balance sheet.
- ❑ Prepare a monthly cash flow the first year, and a quarterly cash flow for the next two years. Wherever there is a cash shortfall, it will require new equity, debt, or a bank line of credit.
- ❑ What is your fallback position if your sales forecast and cash flow do not reach expectations?
- ❑ Prepare an annual income statement for the first year.
- ❑ Prepare a closing balance sheet.
- ❑ What concerns might the banker have about your pro forma cash flow, income and expense statement, and balance sheet, and what is your response?
- ❑ Is your break-even within range of your minimum sales forecast?
- ❑ How do your financial ratios compare to industry averages obtained from sources such as Performance Plus?

SUGGESTED READING

Canada Customs and Revenue Agency (CCRA). *Guide for Canadian Small Business.* Ottawa: CCRA, 2001.

Canadian Bankers Association. *Small Business Financing; Getting Started in Small Business;* and *Managing Money.* [These publications are free. Write: The Canadian Bankers Association, P.O. 348, Commerce Court Postal Station, Toronto, M5L 1G2 (toll-free 1-800-263-0231).]

Canadian Small Business Financing and Tax-Planning Guide. Toronto: CCH Canadian (updated monthly).

Coopers & Lybrand. *Profit Improvement Opportunities for Retailers 142.* [This clever set of checklists will help you plan and manage your retail business. Other major accounting firms also can be very helpful in providing you with financial information on starting a business. For example, Thorne, Ernst & Whinney distribute free brochures titled *Presenting Your Case for a Loan* and *Starting a Small Business.*]

Costales, S.B., and Geza Szurovy. *The Guide to Understanding Financial Statements.* Toronto: McGraw-Hill Ryerson, 1997.

Fitchett, Gary, with John Alton and Kathleen Aldridge. *Where to Go When the Bank Says No.* Toronto: McGraw-Hill, 1998.

Riding, Allan, and Barbara Orser. *Beyond the Banks: Creative Financing for Canadian Entrepreneurs.* Toronto: John Wiley & Sons Canada, 1997.

Royal Bank of Canada. *Small Business Financing in Canada; Personal Financial Management for Small Business Owners.* [These are free publications. Other major Canadian banks also have free material that could help in starting and financing your business. Visit them and see what they have.]

Sidford, Colleen. "Designing an Effective Cash Flow Forecasting Program." *CMA Magazine,* September 1997, pp. 18–21.

Appendix 9.1

Definitions of the Ratios

Table A9.1 Definitions of the Ratios

Area	Ratio	Formula	Purpose	Conclusion
Profitability	Profit Margin	$\frac{\text{Net Profit}}{\text{Total Sales}} \times 100$	To determine % profit on each sales dollar.	High — Congratulations Low — Think aout increasing sales or decreasing costs (or both)
	Gross Profit Margin	$\frac{\text{Gross Profit}}{\text{Total Sales}} \times 100$	To determine % of gross profit on each sales dollar.	High — Congratulations Low — Think aout increasing sales or decreasing costs (or both)
	Return on Investment	$\frac{\text{Net Profit}}{\text{Total Assets}} \times 100$	To determine effective use of all financial resources.	High — Congratulations Low — Might signal unwise investments — Analyze assets for possible disposal and conversion to cash
	Return on Owner Investment	$\frac{\text{Net Profit}}{\text{Owner's Equity}} \times 100$	To determine adequacy of owner's investment plus effectiveness of use.	High — Congratulations Low — The question must be asked, "Is this the most profitable use of my money?"

Area	Ratio	Formula	Purpose	Conclusion
Cash Flow (Short-Term Position)	Working Capital	Current Assets / Current Liabilities	To measure the ability of a business to meet its current (next 12 months) obligations.	In many businesses 2:1 usually but needs will vary with industry. General: High — Possible excessive investment in inventory or ineffective use of cash. Low — If low or less than 1, the amount and term of money owed by business should be carefully analyzed. Possible debt restructuring or further investment may be necessary.
	Acid Test	Current Assets Less Inventory / Current Liabilities	To determine ability to pay current liabilities using only the highly liquid assets (cash and receivables).	1:1 viewed favourably, but if: High — analyze for ineffective use of cash and/or receivable, possibly indicating adjustments to credit and collection policy. Low — see above, Working Capital
Efficiency	Inventory Turnover	Cost of Goods Sold / Average Inventory Average Inventory = Opening + Closing Inventory / 2	To show number of times inventory is sold and replaced over a given period. Assesses quality of inventory.	Acceptable ratio varies with industry (i.e., perishable goods must turn quickly, while clothes may only turn over on a seasonal basis). Obvious deviations from industry standards may indicate excessive inventory resulting from improper purchases or poor marketing.
	Inventory Supply	365 Days / Inventory Turnover Ratio (see above)	To show average days' supply in inventory (actual number of days to sell and restock inventory)	See comments above. Use as a guide to improve purchases.
	Receivable Turnover	Net Sales / Average Accounts Receivable Average Accounts Receivable = Opening Receivables + Closing Receivables / 2	To measure effectiveness of firm's credit and collection policy.	High — Congratulations. Either an effective credit and collection policy or a basically cash business Low — More attention to control of receivables required
	Average Days Receivable	365 Days / Receivable Turnover Ratio (see above)	To show the average number of days your customers take to pay their accounts.	Low — Congratulations High — Amounts to interest-free loans to your customers. Inform your supplier terms of repayment and if necessary upgrade credit and collection policy to bring Average Days Receivable and Average Days Payable closer together.

Area	Ratio	Formula	Purpose	Conclusion
	Average Days Payable	(Average Payables × 365) / Purchases Average Payables = (Opening Accounts Payable + Closing Accounts Payable) / 2	To show the average number of days you are taking to reimburse your suppliers.	Relate to suppliers' terms of repayment. Over your stated terms, your reputation and future dealings may suffer.
Equity (Long-Term Growth Potential)	Debt Capital Ratio	(Current Liabilities + Long-Term Liabilities) / Total Liabilities	To measure level of creditors' support of your business.	High — Creditors have large claim. Possible warning of excessive debt. Low — Indicates continuing commitment by owner, but refer to profitability area/return on investment ratio for further analysis.
	Owner's Equity Ratio	(Current Liabilities + Long-Term Liabilities) / Owner's Equity	To measure level of owners' commitment to business.	— See above, Debt Capital Ratio — Horizontal analysis will indicate if your investment is increasing or decreasing in value.

Adapted from "Do It Yourself Business Planning Package," from *Analyzing Financial Statements* © Federal Business Development Bank, 1984. Reprinted by permission of the Business Development Bank of Canada.

chapter 10

Shaking the Money Tree

BUSINESS PLAN BUILDING BLOCK

This chapter will help you get your own finances in order and will explain the sources of funds available to you and the usual conditions for repayment. Most businesses underestimate capital needs. Demonstrate in your business plan that you have planned for all contingencies.

LEARNING OPPORTUNITIES

After reading this chapter, you should be able to:

- Understand that you, the owner, will be the major source of start-up capital for your business.
- Determine your credit rating.
- Create a personal financial statement.
- Partner with, and gain the most support possible from, your banker.
- Investigate the lending arena, including government and venture capitalists, for money to fund your new business.
- Identify the pros and cons of debt versus equity financing.
- Determine the types of financing options best suited for your business.

Image Processing Systems Inc., in Scarborough, Ontario, is one of Canada's leading PROFIT 100 companies. It develops and sells machine-vision manufacturing-inspection systems, and is a past master at balancing its financing sources.

Where did it get its start-up money? In nine years, it has looked almost everywhere for sources of funds. It tapped owner's equity, bank funds, friends and relatives, export financing, "angels," venture capitalists, grants from the National Research Council and other government sources, and, finally, a public stock issue. Terry Graham, the firm's president, does not see anything unusual about his firm's financial history. "Any start-up company in Canada finds it difficult to get money," he comments, and then adds a sobering note: "The bank was only supportive in the past year, when we didn't desperately need them anymore."

ACTION STEP PREVIEW

48. Prepare a personal financial statement.
49. Befriend a banker.
50. Prepare to meet your lenders.

Chapter 10 will help you prepare parts H, I, and J of your business plan, the financial section.

In fact, the only resentment he seems to feel is toward the labour-sponsored venture capital funds, which were specifically set up by the federal government, and armed with generous federal and provincial tax incentives, to invest in promising small business. "The labour funds are incredibly conservative," he says. "They are set up as venture-capital funds, but they don't act like it."[1]

Every business, regardless of its size or stage of development, will need some sort of financing. Where do successful entrepreneurs find money to start their business? The answer seems to be "almost everywhere," as we learned from the experience of Image Processing. (Various sources of financing are listed in Box 10.1.) It should come as no surprise, however, that the major source of financing is personal funds from savings, credit cards, personal lines of credit, and so on, injected into the business by the owners themselves. Chances are, you the owner will be the major source of financing. Thus, before you begin to shake the money tree, we encourage you to check out your credit rating, come to grips with your personal financial situation, and think about your risk tolerance.

In this chapter, we'll help you prepare to meet your banker and introduce you to some of the major sources of external capital, including the government. We also want you to be aware of the pros and cons of debt versus equity financing. Throughout the chapter, we encourage you to have faith and persist in your search for money. In Rick Spence's insightful analysis of Canada's PROFIT 100 companies, one of the important lessons he says he learned about successful independent companies was "If your story truly has merit, there is a backer for your business somewhere."[2]

Box 10.1 Sources of Financing

Where Does the Money Come From?

Research shows that 50 percent of small and medium-sized businesses in Canada rely on banks and other financial institutions to provide them with business debt financing (whether for start-up, expansion, or ongoing funding).

Other sources of financing include:

- retained earnings (51%)
- supplier credit (48%)
- personal savings (45%)
- personal lines of credit (37%)
- personal credit cards (36%)
- leasing (28%)
- personal loans (25%)
- business credit cards (22%)
- government lending agencies/grants (13%)
- loans from employees, friends and relatives (13%)
- non-related private loans (5%)
- public equity (2%)
- venture capital (2%)

Source: Thompson Lightstone & Company, Small- and Medium-Sized Businesses in Canada, 1998. Retrieved from the Canadian Bankers Association website (www.cba.ca/eng/Tools/Brochures/tools_small.cfm?pg=8).

Before You Shake the Money Tree

What action should you take when you need money to start a business? Do you ask the bank? Do you ask Aunt Alice or a co-worker? Do you refinance your home?

As we have seen, most new ventures begin with the entrepreneur's own capital. Funds can usually be borrowed if you have other sources of income and collateral, such as sufficient equity in a home. In this section, we'll help you begin the search for start-up financing.

CHECK OUT YOUR PERSONAL CREDIT

If you want to borrow money to buy a car, the loan officer at your bank will need to review your credit history and will probably ask you to provide a credit report. Your credit rating is also an issue when you apply for any type of business loan. How do you find out what your credit rating is? In Canada, there are two consumer credit reporting agencies—Equifax Canada Inc. and Trans Union—that keep track of all your financial moves: payment (or non-payment) of bills, loans, liens, legal judgments, and so on. Under the Consumer Reporting Act, they are required to provide you with a copy of your credit report upon request. Getting this information is no easy task, but Box 10.2 will help you get started.

Few people are aware of how much credit they have. Before you start your business, we want you to consider:

1. Applying for two (additional) credit cards—one Visa and one MasterCard. Set them aside to use only for business expenses when you start.
2. Applying for a personal line of credit with your bank. Usually, depending on the four *Cs* of credit (your cash, character, capacity, and collateral), you can

Box 10.2 How's Your Credit Rating?

To obtain a copy of your personal credit file:
Do not phone, they will not discuss your credit report on the phone. Mail or fax a written request with copies of two pieces of identification to both Equifax and to Trans Union. This service is free. In a couple of weeks, they will mail your report to you. You could also go to their office and ask to see your report.

- Equifax Canada Inc.
  Consumer Relations Department
  Box 190 Jean Talon Station
  Montreal, QC
  H1S 2Z2
  Tel: (514) 493-2314
  1 800 465-7166
  Fax: (514) 355-8502
- Trans Union
  Consumer Relations
  709 Main Street W Suite 3201
  Hamilton, ON L8S 1A2
  Tel: 1 800 663 9980
  Fax: (905) 527-0401

Source: CanLaw, Canadian Lawyer Index, retrieved from www.canlaw.com/credit/credit.htm

obtain anywhere from $5000 to $50 000 of secured or unsecured credit at very attractive rates. If you have a personal line of credit, you are in a much more flexible position with your new business. If you need additional short-term financing, it's available. If not, it can be your security blanket, to be there for you if unexpected expenses should pop up. Other than the cost to establish the line, you only pay when you need to borrow.

3. Applying for a home equity loan or a home equity line of credit.

With regard to these considerations, bankers and credit companies are much more relaxed about extending credit to a "steady citizen": a person with steady employment income. Also, you would be making arrangements for the money when you don't need it. Bankers tend to like lending money to people who don't really need it.

Now it is time to have a little fun. Let's find out how much unsecured credit you have. This will give you a very general picture of how the financial world rates you at this time. On the business side, once you've done this, you can determine whether there are any untapped sources of funds for your start-up, or fallbacks and emergency sources for your business or personal expenses. Use Table 10.1 or a sheet of blank paper. To learn your credit limits on your charge accounts, look at your most recent statements. You may need to call or write to some businesses for this information. When you've filled in the amounts for each account you have, add them up.

Table 10.1 Your Current Financial Sources

Source	Amount/Limit
Department Stores	
Sears	
Bay	
Others	
Oil Companies	
Esso	
Petro Can	
Shell	
Others	
Bank Credit Cards	
Visa	
MasterCard	
American Express	
Diner's Club	
Others	
Personal Lines of Credit	
Bank	
Trust company	
Credit union	
Others	
Any Other Unsecured Credit	
Total Credit Available	

DEVELOP A PERSONAL FINANCIAL STATEMENT

In the last chapter, you estimated your start-up costs. Do you have enough start-up money to be your own banker? You can find out by getting a total for your personal assets (what you own), getting a total for your personal liabilities (what you owe), and then doing the easy arithmetic to determine your **net worth** or personal equity. In other words, you need to prepare a personal **financial statement** to see what you are worth right now. It will look something like the one in Table 10.2.

NET WORTH (PERSONAL EQUITY)

your total personal assets minus your total personal liabilities

FINANCIAL STATEMENT

a list of assets and liabilities that will show your net worth or equity

Table 10.2 Personal Financial Statement

Assets (what you own)	Current Value ($)	Current Value ($)
1. Liquid Assets		
Cash (chequing, savings, etc.)	$________	
Stocks, bonds, etc.	$________	
Cash surrender value of life insurance	$________	
Other liquid assets	$________	
Total Liquid Assets		$________
2. Investment Assets		
Mutual funds, real estate, investments, etc.	$________	
RRSPs/pension fund	$________	
Other investments	$________	
Total Investment Assets		$________
3. Personal (Fixed) Assets		
Furniture	$________	
Residence	$________	
Auto/boat	$________	
Jewellery/art	$________	
Other	$________	
Total Personal (Fixed) Assets		$________
4. Total Assets (1 + 2 + 3)		$________
Liabilities (what you owe)	Current Value ($)	Current Value ($)
5. Short-Term Debt (Liabilities)		
Credit cards owing	$________	
Personal loans (amount outstanding)	$________	
Income tax owed	$________	
Other loans outstanding	$________	
Total Short-Term Debt		$________
6. Long-Term Debt (Liabilities)		
Mortgages (amount owing)	$________	
Loans to purchase investment and other personal assets	$________	
Other long-term debt	$________	
Total Long-Term Debt		$________
7. Total Debt (5 + 6)		$________
8. Personal Equity (4 – 7) (Total Assets - Total Liabilities)		$________

ACTION STEP 48

Prepare a personal financial statement.

Sit down with a pencil and paper and do some figuring. You may want to use Table 10.2 as a template.

1. List everything you own that has cash value and estimate its worth. Include cash, securities, life insurance, accounts receivable, notes receivable, rebates/refunds, autos and other vehicles, real estate, pension, and so on.

   Don't stop now. Go on to list the market values of your home furnishings, household goods, major appliances, sports equipment, collectibles, jewellery, tools, computer, livestock, trusts, patents, memberships, interests, investment clubs, an so on.

   Add up the amounts you've written down. The total represents your assets.
2. List every dime you owe to someone or something: accounts payable, contracts payable, notes payable (such as car loans), taxes, insurance (life, health, car, liability, etc.), mortgage or real-estate loans, and anything else you owe. These are your liabilities.
3. Subtract your liabilities from your assets to find your net worth. It's that simple.

Now you know how much you have. You need these figures to determine your financial needs and also to assess the financial contribution you will be able to make to your business.

Pulling together a personal financial statement is important because it tells you where you are with money now, and it will indicate your borrowing capability. Get some practice by doing Action Step 48.

CHART YOUR PERSONAL MONEY FUTURE

Now it's time to chart your personal money future. Look ahead into the next year. List your expenses, such as those for shelter, food, medical bills, transportation, insurance, phone, school, clothes, and utilities—and then add in 10 percent for a contingency fund. If you need a form with blanks, Table 10.3 will help. If you would prefer to use an electronic spreadsheet, you will find a family monthly budget sheet (along with the article "Making a Family Budget") on the CCH Business Owner's Toolkit website (www.toolkit.cch.com/text/P01_2150.asp).

ASSESS YOUR RISK TOLERANCE

Now we want you to ask yourself, "How much am I willing to risk? $10 000? $20 000? $200 000?" Are you willing to go deeply in debt for your venture? A sushi vendor we once knew worked for more than seven years and spent thousands of dollars before he hit on a successful way to flash freeze his product.

Table 10.3 Personal Financial Cash Budget—Monthly Expenses

Category	Item	Estimated Expenses (Add 10% for contingencies)	Actual Expenses
Housing	Rent/mortgage		
	Heating		
	Electricity		
	Telephone		
	Maintenance		
	Other		
	**Subtotal*		
Food	Weekly groceries and staples		
	Extras during month		
	Restaurant meals/month		
	**Subtotal*		
Transportation	Car, operating, repair		
	Public transit		
	Other (taxis)		
	**Subtotal*		
Personal	Leisure activities		
	Personal care items		
	Hair styling		
	Laundry/dry cleaning		
	Other		
	**Subtotal*		

Category	Item	Estimated Expenses (Add 10% for contingencies)	Actual Expenses
Clothing	Work clothes		
	Family/personal		
	**Subtotal*		
Care-Dependents	Children		
	Adults		
	**Subtotal*		
Debts	Charge accounts/credit cards		
	Loans		
	Other		
	**Subtotal*		
Sundry	Entertainment		
	Newspapers		
	Business search costs/supplies		
	**Subtotal*		
Insurance	Dental/medical		
	Personal/life		
	Car		
	Household		
	Other		
	**Subtotal*		
Medical	Doctor/dentist/optician		
	Prescription drugs		
	Other		
	**Subtotal*		
Taxes	Property		
	Income tax		
	Other		
	**Subtotal*		
Miscellaneous	Education (course fees, books, etc.)		
	Licences (e.g., driver's licence)		
	Church and charity		
	Other		
	**Subtotal*		
Savings	Target your monthly savings		
	**Subtotal*		
Total Monthly Expenses:			

Source: Adapted from Human Resources Development Canada, *Working Solutions: Preparing a Realistic Budget,* Take Charge Self-Help Series, No. 6. Reprinted with the permission of the Minister of Public Works and Government Services, 1998.

Go back to Action Step 48. Do a reality check. Are you willing to give up a successful career with benefits for the unknown? If you lose your house, will you be devastated, or will you pick yourself back up and start again like a true entrepreneur?

You must also consider the risk-tolerance level of the members of your family. Talk with your family about the time and money sacrifices that may be involved in developing your new venture. For many, short-term financial pain is worth long-term gain; for others, it is not worth it! Before leaping into the new venture, decide what you and your family are willing to sacrifice. Above all, try to truly listen to them. Sometimes you can miss the message what with the adrenalin of entrepreneurship.

Now you are a lot closer to finding out how much of your money you can put in the business.

Show Me the Money

BANKS AND FINANCIAL INSTITUTIONS

> Norbert Bolger of Nor-Built Construction, a homebuilder, recalls being initially impressed with his bank. But in five years he watched four bank mangers breeze through his local branch, to the point where he no longer even knew his account manager's name. When Bolger finally went to meet manager number three a year or so ago, he expressed some dissatisfaction with the high interest rate the bank was charging. "It doesn't sound like you want my business," said Bolger, looking for reassurance. Instead, the banker's reply was, "Not really." "Well," said Bolger, "maybe I should go look somewhere else." "Go ahead," said the banker. Bolger recently completed his switch.[3]

You will probably have to deal with a major commercial bank, but don't forget about the other financial institutions such as trust companies, cooperatives, credit unions, and caisses populaires. Although banks are in the business of lending money, they also have a responsibility to their depositors. As such, they have a major aversion to risk-taking and tend to choose the safest deals. Their main objective is to make profit for their shareholders, not to create opportunities for you to make money. They can help businesses to start up and expand, but they have to be picky. Their target for bad debt losses ranges from half to 1 percent. This means that they target to get their money back in 99 out of every 100 loans.

In a start-up case, the odds are that you, the owner, will be the banker and your money will come from personal loans or savings. In the case of an established small business, banks are much more cooperative because the venture is less risky—providing, of course, that the financing is backed up by loads of collateral security. The point is, in a start-up situation, you will most likely deal with a bank or major financial institution because you will need a personal loan, and you are also going to have to set up some sort of business-related account. It is advisable to deal with the bank's small business adviser, although not all bank branches have such a position.

Historically, it has often been said that a banker is a person who lends his umbrella when the sun is shining and wants it back the minute it begins to rain. Like it or not, the small business community is going to have to learn how to keep a banker happy, rain or shine. Here are some possible strategies for dealing with bankers.

Make Your Banker (or any Lender) Part of Your Team Take the time to visit your local banker before you apply for the loan. Find out what he or she wants and be sure to deliver. Bring your banker into the information loop. Make sure your banker understands your product or service before you apply for the loan. In fact, many small business advisers would like to visit you at your location. Make sure your banker knows what you are up to. Try to get him or her excited about your idea. Yes, bankers are people and they can get excited.

Befriend a Banker Build a trusting relationship—even before you ask for the money. Under-promise and over-deliver. Be clear, honest, and thorough.

Don't Surprise a Banker Keep your banker informed. In many cases, keeping a banker informed may be a requirement of your loan. But even if it isn't, savvy entrepreneurs let their banks know about the good and the bad on a regular basis. Bankers are more willing to help if they understand your needs and know that you are trying to anticipate your expected financial needs. If you have a problem, don't procrastinate. Tell the banker right away what you are going to do about it. When you have a line of credit, banks will want to know the status of your accounts payable and receivable. We suggest you plan to send your banker regular updates, even if not requested.

Invite Your Banker to Your Business On your own turf, you won't feel so intimidated and the banker will better understand your business. Communications will flow more easily and your enthusiasm may just become contagious.

Have a Backup Banker Shop around as you would for any major purpose. Make your banker aware—in a non-threatening way—that you do have other options, but don't bluff. Seek out other options even after you get the loan. Bankers respect healthy competition for good clients.

Respect the Banker's Rules Understand the banker's rules to have paperwork completed correctly and on time. Most account managers are overworked. Try to make their job easy.

Have an Up-to-Date Plan You must have a properly prepared financial plan, and you must be able to justify every number.

Get Professional Advice Make sure your banker is aware you are receiving professional advice. Have your loan agreement reviewed by an accountant, lawyer, and, most importantly, an experienced businessperson—your financial mentor.

Be in Sync Make sure you and your banker see eye to eye before you apply for the money. If you foresee a personality conflict, start looking for another banker.

Ask for Enough Show your banker you can forecast and understand your situation. It helps the banker sleep at night, too.

Get Ready for Personal Guarantees Many entrepreneurs say, "I incorporated so I won't have to sign my life away." From a banker's perspective, if you have a new corporation, few assets, and no track record, you'll probably have to personally guarantee your loan. If you do have to sign personally for a loan, make a decision right away to begin finding a way to get rid of personal guarantees. If your business is running smoothly for three to five years, be ready to switch your account to another bank if your bank doesn't want to lift the guarantees.

Negotiate the Best Deal You Can The bank will respect you for being a good negotiator. If you still have a job, negotiate for a line of credit or loan while you are still employed. Personal lines of credit are reviewed each year and chances are you can maintain this line if you keep up a good credit rating.

Understand the Banker's Discretionary Limits Different managers have different maximum amounts they can lend depending on their position and bank policy. Try to find out what the lending limit is for your prospective banker. If it is below the amount you are asking, he or she will need to get approval from a supervisor.

If you are planning to make a loan for your business, remember that banks and financial institutions are in the business to make money for their shareholders. Before you get a loan and "sign on the dotted line," *read the fine print* of your loan agreement. Remember the "buyer beware" rule and be prepared for the following:

Spousal Guarantee In certain provinces, laws governing matrimonial assets might mean that the guarantee of your spouse would be required. Needless to say, you should try to avoid spousal guarantees, but if you do get your spouse to sign on the dotted line, your relationship had better be rock solid.

Premium Rates Be prepared to pay a premium interest rate. Banks consider small business high risk and charge accordingly. For the privilege of controlling your destiny, you can expect to pay as much as the prime rate plus 3 percent on unsecured loans, and usually prime plus 1 percent on secured loans.

Demand Loans Most loans, both operating and term, to small businesses are demand loans. This means that there is a footnote on your financial agreement that says your financial institution can "demand" full payment at any time for virtually any reason. If, for example, your bank manager gets cold feet because of the faltering economy, he or she can call your loan and go after you personally if you have signed a guarantee. Try to avoid this type of demand loan arrangement and, at the very least, try to limit the demand portion of the loan. Always have your own backup plan in place if the bank calls your loan.

Collateral If you have no assets or security, you will not get a loan—period. Banks are not in the business of risking their shareholders' money. All banks will ask for business and personal (if they can get it) security or collateral for your loan. It is common practice to request a collateral amount, which always far exceeds the value of the loan. One Canadian study, for example, estimated that the average bank collateral requested by banks for start-ups was four times the value of the loan. Collateral for established business was at least double the amount of the loan. In effect, banks will ask you to personally guarantee an amount, far in excess of what you are asking for—even if you are an existing business. The more collateral the banks have, the more secure they feel. We reiterate: You should negotiate to limit your collateral, especially if it is personal.

Insurance Most banks and financial intuitions will require you to have the standard personal and business insurance (fire, theft, etc.) to protect them should you have an unexpected problem. In many cases, a bank or financial institution may even require you to sign over your life insurance and disability policies to them. You should make absolutely sure that those close to you are also protected should you die or become incapacitated.

Covenants There are literally dozens of covenants or legal conditions that could be built into your loan agreement to protect the lender. Some of these are likely to include:

- An environmental assessment.
- Maintaining a minimum level of cash.
- Restrictions on certain financial activities, such as the payment of bonuses and dividends without the lender's approval.
- A mandated time period (for example, 90 days after year-end) for providing financial statements to the bank. (If this covenant is in your agreement, try not to agree to providing an audited statement. It could cost you thousands of dollars.)
- A shareholders or partnership agreement.
- A maximum on the size of capital purchases you can make without bank approval.

Fees Banks may require you to pay a range of user and service fees for setting up your line of credit, requesting your loan balance, writing cheques, and using credit card facilities. Some of these fees are negotiable and some are not. Here are the two major user fees that you should try to avoid or at least negotiate.

- *Application fee.* You may be asked to pay a loan application fee (usually ranging from $100 to $200), which is the bank's cost (including the cost associated with preparing a credit application form) for evaluating its opportunity to deal with you.
- *Loan management fees.* You may very well be subjected to additional fees if your bank is required to spend time on activities such as monitoring your accounts receivable or inventory, meeting with clients, and preparing statements.

The point here is that many small business owners don't become aware of these extra charges until after the fact. Find out what your obligations are before you sign anything.

We also encourage you to keep a running list of questions to ask prospective bankers. These will get you started:

- What are your lending limits?
- Who makes the decisions on loans?
- What are your views on my industry?
- What experience do you have in working with businesses like mine?
- Could you recommend a qualified lawyer? Bookkeeper? Accountant? Computer consultant?
- Are you interested in writing equipment leases?
- What kind of terms do you give on accounts receivable financing?
- What is the bank rate on Visa or MasterCard accounts? What credit limit could I expect for my business credit cards?
- What interest can I earn on my business chequing account?
- Do you have a merchants' or commercial window?
- Do you have a night depository?
- If you can't lend me money, can you direct me to people who might be interested in doing it?
- Do you make Canada Small Business Financing (CSBF) loans? (We'll discuss CSBF loans later in the chapter.)
- If I open up a business chequing account here, what else can you do for me?

Action Step 49 will get you started in developing a relationship with a banker.

ACTION STEP 49

Befriend a banker.

Money creates its own world. There are several doorways into that world. Your banker sits at the threshold of one of those doors. (In a sense, your banker is the guardian of the gate.)

Start with a familiar place, the bank where you have your chequing account. Make an appointment to talk to the branch manager. Here are some questions to ask:

1. Do you lend money to new small business?
2. Do you make Canada Small Business Financing (CSBF) loans?
3. What are your criteria for loans?
4. What is your loan approval process?
5. What do you think of my business plan?

If you are happy with your banker's answers, talk over the possibility of opening an account for your business. If you have money tucked away in life insurance or a mutual fund somewhere, ask about the bank's accounts offering premium interest rates.

OTHER SOURCES OF START-UP CAPITAL

> James Brown knows the benefits of looking around. When his doctors told him he would never work again as a fisherman in Nova Scotia, he was able to secure a small loan of $500 from Calmeadow Nova Scotia. He found a loan that was based on his character, "not on collateral." As the business grew, he borrowed a total of $16 000, including supplier credit. He now has two employees and operates year round.[4]

By now, you should have improved your money savvy and developed a firm grasp of your personal finances. And ideally, you've also befriended a banker. Now it's time to zero in, as James Brown did, on some other sources of start-up capital. For more information on sources of financing, see Box 10.3.

Self-Financing Savings and personal loans are the most likely source of financing for small business start-ups. As we have noted previously, personal lines of credit and cash advances from credit cards have also become a major source of financing for small businesses. Use your credit card advances only when absolutely necessary, and not as a source of start-up capital.

Look at the personal financial statement you prepared in Action Step 48 along with your monthly budget (see Table 10.3). Consider your risk tolerance. How much are you willing and able to commit? Can you sell some of your assets? Take a second or third mortgage on your home? How much are you willing to live on each month? Are you prepared to change your lifestyle to accommodate your budget? Consider your risk tolerance and your willingness to make sacrifices before answering these questions.

Family and Friends Some say as much as 50 percent of all start-up money comes from family and friends. Think long and hard before you accept **love money**. At

LOVE MONEY
investment from friends, relatives, and business associates

Box 10.3 Sources of Financing

- **BusinessGateway.ca**
  http://businessgateway.ca/en/hi/finance.cfm
  Search this comprehensive database for financial providers that can meet your specific business needs. Browse a list of banks, credit unions, leasing companies, venture capital companies, and much more.
- **Micro-Credit** (Industry Canada)
  http://strategis.ic.gc.ca/SSG/so03121e.html
  Search through a wide array of micro-credit providers to find financing of less than $25 000 to suit your particular business needs.
- **Government Assistance** (Industry Canada)
  http://strategis.ic.gc.ca/SSG/so01884e.html
  Access a wealth of information about government programs and services relevant to your business situation.
- **Private-Sector Assistance** (Industry Canada)
  http://services.ic.gc.ca/sourcesOfFinancing/instRegistration/Directory?lang=e &stage=1
  Browse a list of banks, credit unions, leasing companies, venture capital companies, and much more.

the moment, you may just be thinking about speeding ahead with your dream, and all you can see is success. The reality is, however, you might lose this money or not be able to pay it back in a timely fashion. Your lender may eventually forgive you, but you may have trouble forgiving yourself.

You might consider asking your lenders to co-sign loans. But remember, that legally obligates them to the debt. So, set a limit on this guarantee. Also, they may be more willing to loan you money if you put up your house, car, or jewellery as collateral.

If you are still willing to borrow from friends and family after reviewing potential issues and problems, here are a few precautions you should take:

- Do not accept more money than your lender can afford to lose. Borrowing Grandma's last $20 000 is not fair to you or Grandma.
- Put everything in writing. Establish a partnership or shareholders agreement (discussed in Chapter 11) detailing the roles of all concerned.
- Make it a business loan, not a personal loan. Have loan papers drawn up. State the time period of the loan, interest rate, payment date, collateral, and late payment penalties.
- Include in the loan a provision for repayment in case of emergencies. This will alleviate a lot of stress and concern for both parties.
- Discuss thoroughly with the lenders the company's goals and any potential problems. Make sure they understand that the loan will be for a certain length of time. If the business starts to be profitable, it may still require their cash infusion. Cash is not profit—as we now know.
- Do not finalize the deal until the lender has discussed it with an independent adviser.

ANGELS

wealthy individuals from the informal venture capital market that are willing to risk their own money in someone else's business

Angels **Angels** refer to wealthy individuals from the informal venture capital market (e.g., retired small-business people) that are willing to risk their own money in someone else's business. In Canada, angels have financed approximately twice as many firms as have institutional venture capitalists. They usually tend to finance the early stages of the business with investments in the order of $100 000.[5] Angels often require an active management or operations role. They are most active in smaller firms where they may even get involved in the "hands-on" day-to-day operations. In larger firms, the role of the angel is more distant and usually takes the form of management advice and counsel through the board of directors.

Angel investors are normally hard to find, but you can start with professional advisers (accountant, lawyer, etc.), your local chamber of commerce and local office of the Business Development Bank of Canada (www.bdc.ca); or visit the "Private-Sector Assistance" page on the Industry Canada website (see Box 10.3).

Suppliers Most suppliers will offer a small business at least 30 days to pay for their product once you are established. Suppliers may also allow you to defer your payments over a longer period of time if you pay some sort of interest charges on the deferred payment. You may even want to negotiate a consignment arrangement with some hungry suppliers. In this case, the supplier owns the goods until you sell them. Box 10.4 describes one strategy that can help you negotiate more favourable terms with your suppliers.

Customers Customers, especially for home-based and service businesses, are a potential source of credit. Don't be shy to ask for a deposit before you provide a service or go out and purchase supplies and materials. For example, if you are in the "fix it" business, get your customers to pay for your materials before you start the job by asking them for a deposit. That way you can be a little more confident you will get full payment and you don't have to tie up your own money.

Box 10.4 The Vendor Statement Form

An often overlooked technique for reducing your capital requirement is to probe your vendors (major suppliers) for the best prices and terms available. Professional buyers and purchasing agents ask their vendors to fill out an information sheet, writing down the terms and conditions of their sales plans. This is a good idea for you as well.

VENDOR STATEMENT

a personally designed form that allows you to negotiate with each vendor from a position of informed strength

A small business owner must buy professionally, and a **vendor statement** will help you do just that. With this form, your vendors' verbal promises become written promises. How well you buy is as important as how well you sell, because every dollar you save by "buying right" drops directly to the bottom line. To compete in your arena, you need the best terms and prices you can get. The statement will help you get the best.

Personalize your form by putting your business name at the top. Then list the information you need, leaving blanks to be written in. Some of the basics include:

- Vendor's name
- Vendor's address, phone number, fax number, e-mail, and website, if applicable
- Sales rep's name
- Business phone (will vendor accept collect calls?)
- Home phone (for emergencies)
- Amount of minimum purchase
- Quantity discounts? How much? What must you do to earn?
- Are dating or extended payments terms available?
- Advertising/promotion allowances
- Policies on returns for defective goods (who pays the freight?)
- Delivery times
- Assistance (technical, sales, and so on)
- Product literature available
- Point-of-purchase material provided
- Support for grand opening (will supplier donate prize or other support?)
- Nearest other dealer handing this particular line
- Special services the sales rep can provide
- Vendor's signature, the date, and some kind of agreement that you will be notified of any changes

Remember, the information the vendor writes on this statement is the starting point for negotiations. You should be able to negotiate more favourable terms with some vendors, because these people want your business. Revise your application form as you learn from experience how vendors can help you.

Leasing About one-third of all small businesses use leasing as a source of debt financing, which amounts to about $3 billion in contracts annually. Commercial banks are now getting more involved in the leasing business.

A leasing company (lessor) will purchase an asset such as equipment, computers, automobiles, or land. The small business (lessee) will then sign a legal agreement to pay the lessor a fixed amount over a specific period of time. There are several types of leasing arrangement, including a "walk away lease or net lease," which entitles the lessee to simply return the asset at the end of the term. A "capital or open end" lease requires the lessee to buy back the asset at the end of the term. Most leases can be tailored to the lessee requirements and the lease type will depend on the situational needs.

The obvious advantage is that a small business does not have to tie up its start-up or operating funds. Unlike loans, leases normally cover the total asset costs, including installation and transportation charges. Lease charges are usually fixed and are likely higher than a bank loan rate. They provide small businesses with a reliable payment schedule. A lease may be one of the few options in hard economic times when loans from financial institutions may not be available. As well, lease payments are a business expense.

Leasing also has its disadvantages. For example, chances are that the lease will cost you more over the long run. Leasing companies are in the business to make money and they have to make their profit margins. Unless you have a specific kind of lease, the small business owner will have no assets to show for after the lease is over. In other words, leases do not improve the asset base of the business. A lease payment commits the owner over a specific period of time, and thus limits the flexibility the owner might otherwise have to sell the equipment for a more efficient factor of production. One other note of caution: lease rates normally carry a high interest.

Employees and Employers If you have a good idea, a current or past employer might well be a possible source of start-up capital. When you hire employees, don't be afraid to offer them a part of the action in return for a small investment.

Micro Lending Programs Several non-government and community-based agencies have initiated innovative start-up programs to aid very small or micro businesses. According to the Department of Finance: "micro-credit refers to small loans made to low-income individuals to sustain self-employment or to start up very small businesses. Although there is no standard definition of micro-credit, in practice such loans are quite small, amounting to a few thousand dollars."[6]

One innovative model of the Canadian Youth Business Foundation is provided in Box 10.5. Another example is the Calmeadow program, used by James Brown to start his business in Nova Scotia (in the case at the beginning of this section). Calmeadow (www.calmeadow.com) also operates in other centres across Canada. There are basically two types of community-based models: the lending circle (also known as peer lending), and very small loans with no group affiliation but which require some sort of security. Since there is no central clearinghouse for these types of micro lending opportunities, you are going to have to start by getting in touch with local economic development departments and chambers of commerce. The Internet is also a good resource (see Box 10.3).

Government Programs There are a number of local, provincial, and federal programs designed to assist small businesses. These plans also change from time to time, so it is important to maintain the most recent information from the respective government. Governments know a growth market when they see one, and they do make an effort to help. In recent years, they have been moving away from

Box 10.5 Canadian Youth Business Foundation: Community-Based Funding Program

Look into the Canadian Youth Business Foundations (CYBF) community-based funding program. This business loan program provides essential start-up credit to youth (ages 18–34) who have good business ideas but not the resources to get up and running.

Loans are available only in locations where CYBF has set up a program in partnership with a local community organization. The pool of funds available in each community is limited. Therefore, loans (up to $15 000) are granted on a merit and need basis, similar to a scholarship, to young people most likely to succeed and where the money will make a critical difference to beginning the enterprise.

At the very least, you're going to need a business plan to qualify. For more information, visit the CYBF website (www.cybf.ca/en_loan.html).

helping finance small business to providing information and advice. However, there still remains a number of financial support programs for small business—the sources of which are far too numerous to detail here. We encourage you to visit a government information office, even before you begin putting the final touches to your plan. A good starting point would be a visit or call to the Canada Business Service Centre nearest you. You can also find a lot of information on government support programs via the Internet (see Box 10.3).

Venture Capitalists With venture capital firms, we enter the world of high rollers and high fliers. Unlike banks, which lend money that is secured usually by real-estate or other "hard" assets, venture capitalists don't lend money. They are equity investors who buy a piece of the business with private or publicly sponsored pools of capital. Venture capitalists gamble on the business's rapid growth, hoping to reap a 300 to 500 percent return on their investment. They often expect at least 35 percent annual return on their investment.

According to the Canadian Venture Capital Association, venture capital people prefer to enter the financial picture at the second stage of a firm's development when the business has proven its potential and needs a large infusion of cash to support growth. In the late 1990s, the hungriest consumers of venture capital were technology companies with high-growth potential. For example, high-tech firms secured about 66 percent of the $2 billion invested from venture capital in 1998.[7] Not surprisingly, the venture capital dried up after the technology bubble burst in early 2000.

ACTION STEP 50

Prepare to meet your lenders.

Know who your potential lenders are and why they should want to help you.

Part A. List potential lenders and investors. Begin with yourself, your family and friends and move on to business acquaintances and colleagues. Don't forget institutional leaders.

Part B. Now quickly list some reasons why lenders should want to invest in your business. What inducements are you offering potential investors? If you're offering them a very small return on investment (ROI), what are you offering that will offset that?

Think about the legal form of your business. Would you attract more investors if you incorporated?

Part C. Test your tactics by talking to a few friends. Tell them: "This is just a test, and I'd like your reactions to my new business venture." Watch their reactions, and make a list of the objections they give you—the reasons why they cannot loan you money.

Using your list of your friends' objections, write down your answers to those objections. Are there any you cannot answer? What does this mean for your business?

Cooperative Partnerships More and more, small businesses are beginning to realize the financial benefits of combining resources in some kind of cooperative arrangements. These types of arrangements go under many names: joint venture, strategic partnering, strategic alliance, corporate partnering, and so on. No matter what business you are in or what business you want to start, you can benefit from establishing strong collaborative alliances. For example, if you are establishing a home office, why not consider entering into an agreement with major customers or clients who need your services? They will supply you with an office and, in return, you provide them with the services they require for a set number of hours per week. If you have a product you want to sell and need the distribution channel, why not enter into a marketing agreement with a larger, more experienced firm? It will market and sell the product that you supply. If you have a new idea and have built a prototype, you don't have to manufacture the product yourself: strike up an arrangement with a manufacturing plant to build the product and you sell it. The number of options available is limited only by your imagination.

Action Step 50 asks you to list potential lenders and investors and to develop your persuasive arguments. Without persuasive inducements to lenders, they have no reason to invest in your business. If you need help in listing your reasons, you might begin by profiling your target customer. You might list industry trends and dovetail them with a scenario of where your product or service fits. Move from there to marketing strategy, selling, the profit picture, and return on investment.

In the final part of Action Step 50, you test your tactics on friends. Ask your friends to respond as though they were potential investors. You want to hear objections so they can be addressed. When you have completed this Action Step, you will be truly prepared to meet your lenders.

Will That Be Debt or Equity?

If you or others invest money in a business and expect, in return, a portion of ownership, this is called an equity or ownership investment. Equity investors, as owners, usually expect a say in the day-to-day operations of the business and how the profit or net income is to be distributed to the owners. When others or even you lend money to a business, this is called **debt financing**—an obligation of a business to repay a lender the full amount of a debt (loan) in addition to interest charges.

DEBT FINANCING

an obligation of a business to repay a lender the full amount of a debt (loan) in addition to interest charges

If a business is financed through debt (a loan), it is obliged to repay the lender the full amount of the debt in addition to interest charges on the debt. A lender does not usually get any ownership rights or say in the operations of the business.

How should you finance your business: debt or equity or some combination of the two? The trick is to find the right balance between debt and equity—one that will satisfy the needs of you the owner, the business, and the market. However, in looking for money to finance your business, remember that any "external" source of capital will always consider the extent of your own financial commitment to the business.

If personal funds (equity) are not sufficient, you must decide on debt or selling a piece of the ownership (also equity) or some combination of the two. Generally, Canadian independent businesses rely far more on debt than on equity, with the banks playing a predominant role as sources of financing.

Listed below are some of the pros and cons of debt versus equity financing.

Advantage of Debt Financing through debt mainly by line of credit is useful in meeting a short-term deficit in the cash flow or in financing lower-risk projects. For example, it would be appropriate where money is needed to fund inventory before it's sold. Some of the advantages of debt are:

- the entrepreneur does not have to give up or share control of the company;
- the term of the debt (loan) is generally limited;
- debt may be acquired from a variety of lenders; and
- the kind of information needed to obtain the loan is generally straightforward and would normally be incorporated into the business plan.

Disadvantages of Debt Taking on debt can become problematic when a project is risky and the return is uncertain. For example, financing new product development makes no guarantee of success in the marketplace. It would be more appropriate to find an investor to share the risk rather than going into debt. Debt can also become a problem if it is not properly managed. The most frequent errors include:

- taking on more debt than the com pany needs to fund expansion;
- adopting too restrictive a policy toward debt and thus not accessing funds that might be readily available;
- misapplying funds in ways that yield inadequate returns and make it difficult for the company to repay its loans; and
- making mistakes in servicing the debt (accepting inappropriate repayment terms, encountering cash flow difficulties, taking on too large a debt-service burden).

Advantages of Equity Many entrepreneurs associate finding an investor with giving up control in their company. An appropriate investor, however, can contribute expertise, contacts, and new business as well as money. If the result is substantial growth in profitability, the original owner's overall wealth will increase, even if his or her share of the company is somewhat smaller. Equity investment is especially appropriate for:

- larger projects with longer time frames or additional skill requirements;
- high-risk ventures where the costs of debt would be prohibitive;
- rapidly growing ventures that may quickly exhaust available bank financing as they expand; and
- situations in which debt financing is not available.

Disadvantages of Equity Finding an investor brings another viewpoint to a company, and there is always the danger of incompatibility and disagreement. Because an equity owner is an integral part of the company, however, it becomes much more difficult to terminate the relationship if disagreements occur. With a partner, it is important to have a shareholders agreement.

There is another point to consider between debt and equity. Canada is a country with significant regional differences, and these may become apparent to entrepreneurs attempting to secure equity financing. In some parts of the country, business may not have the same access to equity capital as do their counterparts established closer to larger financial centres. Access will also be influenced by the availability of government funding through provincial programs and federal regional economic development agencies such as the Atlantic Canada Opportunities Agency and Western Diversification. Regionalism plays less of a role in securing business loans. For example, each of Canada's major chartered banks operates a nationwide system of branches, all of which offer the same access to loans on the same terms in any member branch.

Lastly, equity investment should not normally be used for short-term obligations. For example, it would not make much sense to get a new partner to finance inventory fluctuations. Equity is usually thought of as a long-term financial instrument.

PRIMARY TYPES OF DEBT FINANCING

The major types of debt financing for start-up business are spelled out below. Other, "secondary" types of financing are shown in Table 10.4.

SHAREHOLDERS LOAN

owner investment in the form of a loan

Shareholders Loans Should you decide to incorporate your business—and there are a number of good reasons for doing so, as we will learn in the next chapter—you have the option to invest as a **shareholders loan**. Although many banks will not lend money to a business per se, they will provide a personal loan to the owner who in turn lends the money to the business. There are a number of advantages for an owner to invest in the form of a loan as opposed to equity (through purchasing shares). First, you can deduct the interest payments as a company expense. If you buy shares (equity investment), however, you will receive payment in the form of dividends and these dividend payments are not tax deductible by the company. Second, in most cases it is easier to withdraw your money when it is in the form of a loan. And third, if your loan is properly secured, your investment will be safer in the event of a business failure. The main point here is that there are advantages to lending the company money, but you really should make sure you get sound professional advice.

CANADA SMALL BUSINESS FINANCING (CSBF) LOAN

a loan guaranteed by the federal government under the Canada Small Business Financing Act

Canada Small Business Financing (CSBF) Loans Under the Canada Small Business Financing Act, the federal government guarantees small business loans through Canadian chartered banks and a few other Canadian financial institutions such as caisses populaires, Alberta Treasury branches, and credit unions. The CSBF program has become a major funding source for start-up business. Historically, of the total CSBF loans granted, about one-third have gone to firms less than a year old.

These loans can be used to finance up to 90 percent of the cost of the purchase and improvement of three categories of fixed assets:

- the purchase of land required to operate the business;
- the renovation, improvement, modernization, extension, and/or purchase of premises; and
- the purchase, installation, renovation, improvement, and/or modernization of new or used equipment.

Table 10.4 Secondary Types of Loans and Credit Arrangements

Type of Loan	Explanation
Floor Plan Loan	These loans are mainly provided by manufacturers to stock up goods in the retailers' or distributors' premises. The retailer reimburses the manufacturer for the loan amount when the product is sold.
Bridge Financing	This type of interim financing provides short-term funding to cover the cost of a start-up project until long-term funds become available.
Mezzanine Financing	Mezzanine financing combines long-term lending with an equity position.
Factoring	This form of financing is available from specialized firms (and banks to a limited extent). A business sells its accounts receivable to a factoring company at a discounted rate (as much as 85 percent of a "high" quality account). This will reduce the risk of not receiving a payment and frees up needed cash.
Letter of Credit	Letters of credit are widely used in exporting and importing businesses. One of the most common exporting problems, for example, is collecting the accounts receivable. A popular method—and the most secure one—is a letter of credit issued by the bank of the purchaser. This is the purchaser's guarantee that the money has been set aside and will be paid to the supplier upon satisfactory delivery. Most banks and major financial institutions can provide this letter, given proper security, of course.
Inventory Financing	In some cases, banks and financial institutions will allow small businesses to borrow against a percentage value of their inventory. The business must have inventory that can be readily sold. Depending on the salability of the inventory, the owner could receive financing as high as 70 percent or as little as 30 percent of the market value.
Accounts Receivable	In this type of financing, the money owed by customers of a business (accounts receivable) becomes the collateral for a loan. Banks and financial institutions have been known to provide as much as 75 percent of the value of the accounts receivable that are not more than 60 days old. Again, adequate security is an important consideration in determining the percentage value of the receivables.
Conditional Sale	Some manufacturers will provide financing to small businesses for a particular product on a conditional basis. They will require a substantial down payment and then allow the business to pay for the remaining portion on an installment basis over a period of time. This is termed a conditional sale because the business will own the product only on the condition that all the payments are made.

CSBF loans are available to all businesses operating for profit in Canada—excluding farming, charitable, and religious enterprises—that have annual gross revenues of less than $5 million. Loans cannot be used to acquire shares or provide working capital. The maximum loan may not exceed $250 000. Borrowers must pay the federal government a one-time, up-front loan registration fee of 2 percent of the amount of each loan. This amount may be added to the loan. The maximum rate of interest charged by the lending institution cannot exceed the prime rate plus 3 percent for floating-rate loans and the residential mortgage rate plus 3 percent for fixed-rate loans. This interest rate includes an administration fee of 1.25 percent, which is paid back annually to the government. Personal guarantees may not exceed 25 percent of the amount of the original loan. The maximum period over which a loan may be repaid is 10 years.

It is important to note that some of the terms and conditions and interest rates are negotiable. In the past, at least one major bank has eliminated the requirement for any personal guarantees under the CSBF program. Other banks have reduced the interest rate to prime and added automatic overdraft protection of up to 10 percent of the CSBF loan. Our advice: CSBF loans are a great opportunity, but shop around for the best deal. For more information, visit the "Canada Small Business Financing Program—Loans" page on the Industry Canada, Strategis website (http://strategis.ic.gc.ca/SSG/la01107e.html).

OPERATING LOAN (LINE OF CREDIT)

money loaned to help finance short-term business needs like inventory and accounts receivables

Operating Loans (Line of Credit) An **operating loan** (sometimes called a revolving loan) is used by more than 75 percent of small business borrowers to finance their short-term business needs. Normally, these loans help finance inventory and accounts receivable—that is, customers to whom a product has been sold but the money has yet to be received. Generally, the line of credit is the largest part of the loans outstanding of a small business' debt obligations.

How much can you borrow? In the normal course of business, the amount you can borrow will be determined by whichever is less of the following:

1. Your authorized borrowing limit, which is established by determining your projected maximum (peak) cash needs in any one month of the year. This is one of the main reasons why accurate projected cash flows are so important.
2. Your margin requirements, which means you can borrow only up to a specific percentage of accounts receivable outstanding and inventory on your books in any one month. Although you may have a predetermined operating line of say $50 000, this does not mean that you can go out and use all of it when the need arises. These margins or limits will vary depending on the policies of the bank or financial institution. For example, in the past, banks have been known to finance up to 66 percent (sometimes as high as 75 percent) of accounts receivable that are less than 60 days old. But this margin or percentage will vary depending on the quality of the receivable and the type of industry. As for inventory, the margin or percentage may be as high as 50 percent of market value. This margin is often lower, depending on how easy it is to sell your inventory. The bottom line here is that if you need an extra $50 000 in a given period to finance inventory and receivables, you will only get a portion of this, and the rest will come from your resources.

PRIME RATE

the lowest rate of interest charged by banks on commercial loans to their most preferred customers

What interest rate will you pay? Depending on the financial institution and the business circumstances, you can normally expect to pay 1 to 3 percent above the **prime rate** for an operating loan. The so-called prime rate, set by each financial institution, is the interest rate the institution charges to its most creditworthy clients. Expect to pay higher interest rates for smaller operating loans. For example, you might pay as much as 3 percent above prime for a $25 000 loan and only 1 percent above prime for a $2-million operating loan. The main point is that interest rates for operating loans can differ from financial institution to financial institution, so we encourage you to shop around. You can negotiate a rate closer to prime if you have good security.

What security is required? An operating line of credit will be secured by the accounts receivable or inventory as well as a personal guarantee. Personal guarantees are required because financial institutions will never recover the full value of an asset should your business fail. The amount of your personal guarantee is negotiable. At the very least you should try to limit your personal guarantee to the amount of the unsecured portion of the loan. So, if you have an operating loan of say $25 000 that is secured by inventory for $12 000, then you should try to keep your personal guarantee below $13 000.

Term Loans **Term loans** are used by close to one-half of small businesses and are the major source of medium-term (two to five years) and long-term (greater than five years) financing. In most cases, term loans are used to finance the purchase of fixed assets such as equipment, a truck, or furniture. They may also be used to finance expansion or renovation.

TERM LOAN

loan used for medium- to long-term financing of fixed assets like equipment, furniture, expansion, or renovation

How much can you borrow? Under normal circumstances you will be able to borrow up to 75 percent of the value of buildings or property. In the case of equipment, you should expect to get about 50 percent of the asset value. Normally, you will repay the loan through a fixed schedule of payments, which corresponds to the life of the asset. If you expect a piece of equipment to last five years, then the payments would be spread over five years.

What interest rate will you pay? Term loans can be repaid by either a fixed or floating interest rate. A **fixed rate** is one that remains the same over the period of a loan. A **floating rate** changes in accordance with the fluctuations in the prime rate. Many small businesses prefer a fixed interest rate because they know how much they have to pay and can budget accordingly. However, fixed rates are generally not available for loans of less than $25 000 and banks will normally charge higher interest for a fixed term. The reason is that a term loan usually commits the bank for several years, increasing the risk that a business might deteriorate. It should be noted that when short-term rates are low, financial institutions will be even more inclined to ask for a higher interest premium for a fixed term loan. Why? Because of the increased risk of rising interest rates. As with operating loans, the terms and conditions for term loans differ from bank to bank.

FIXED RATE

interest rate that remains the same over the period of a loan

FLOATING RATE

interest rate that changes with changes in the prime rate

What security is required? Financial institutions will require you to secure a term loan with the asset being purchased and, in most cases, a guarantee backed by personal assets. If you default on the term loan, the institution will be able to liquidate the asset and hold you personally responsible for any outstanding balance. Again, you should always try to limit your personal guarantees to a specific amount.

PRIMARY TYPES OF EQUITY FINANCING

At some point, you are going to have to decide whether or not to incorporate your business. We'll cover the pros and cons of incorporating in Chapter 11. At this point, we want you just to understand that the type or form of equity that your business will require will depend, to some degree, on the legal structure of your business.

If you plan to run your business as a sole proprietorship or partnership, your investment in the business will simply be recorded as an owner's personal investment. You are the owner and your equity is what you personally put into the business. The main point here is that if other partners are involved in your business, a handshake is not enough. You must have some sort of agreement outlining the terms and conditions of each equity investor's contribution. You will need a partnership shareholders agreement that details such issues as: Who is investing what? How will the investment be paid back and under what conditions? What happens if someone dies? What is the procedure for selling out? What happens if the business fails? In the end, a formalized legal agreement should be drawn up and each equity investor must consult his or her own legal and financial adviser. The legal cost of a shareholders agreement is approximately $300 to $500 for a straightforward agreement.

Should you decide to incorporate, we strongly recommend you have a lawyer draw up a shareholders agreement to detail the rights and responsibilities of each equity investor. In the case of incorporation, there are a number of ways that you can structure an equity investment to benefit and protect both you and potential shareholders. For small businesses, the three principal forms of equity financing are common shares, preferred shares, and convertible debentures. Since any formalized equity arrangement can become quite complex, we strongly suggest that you do get some expert advice before you sign on the dotted line.

COMMON SHARES

equity investments that confer part ownership of the company, but not as safe as preferred shares should the company fail

Common Shares **Common shares** confer part ownership of the company and are frequently issued in exchange for a company's initial capital. As the company grows, the shares increase in value and provide dividend income. If the company fails, however, common shareholders risk losing their investment. As an incentive to investors to place capital in small businesses, some provinces have set up development corporations that will repay as much as 25 to 30 percent of a shareholder's investment in such enterprises.

PREFERRED SHARES

equity investments that confer part ownership of the company, earn investors dividends at a fixed rate, and are safer than common shares

Preferred Shares **Preferred shares** may also be offered to investors. Such shares also represent partial ownership of the company. Preferred shares, however, usually earn a dividend at a fixed rate and, in the event of business failure, they are better protected than common shares, although their claim is still junior to that of debt holders. A company derives several advantages from issuing preferred shares. Unlike debts, preferred shares have no maturity date. And dividend payments are not as binding as interest payments on debt.

CONVERTIBLE DEBENTURES

loans that can be exchanged for common shares at a stated price, and are better protected than common and preferred shares

Convertible Debentures **Convertible debentures** are loans that can be exchanged for common shares in a company at a predetermined price. Like other debentures and bonds, they carry a fixed interest rate and a specified date by which they must be paid. As do shareholders, the holders of convertible debentures have the opportunity to benefit if the company grows. They are also better protected than are holders of common or preferred shares in the event of a failure. And because the debenture is a type of loan, interest is tax deductible. As a result, larger companies may find it easier to sell convertible debentures than other types of equity. Issuing convertible debentures is therefore a way to raise equity more cheaply than by selling common shares.

In a Nutshell

Money creates its own world. It has its own customs, rituals, and rules. Before you start asking people for money for your business, spend the needed time researching the world of money. Here are some things you can do to streamline your research:

1. Get your personal finances in order.
2. Take some time, prepare, study the world of finance.
3. Find someone who knows more about money than you do, and keep asking questions.
4. Know that loans are made on the basis of the four Cs: cash, character, capacity (to repay), and collateral.

5. Start to develop the financial section for your business plan. You need to show your plan to bankers, vendors, and lenders. If you feel overwhelmed, start with an outline. (See Chapter 16 for a model plan.)
6. Begin thinking of a banker as your gateway to the world of money.
7. Search out potential lenders.
8. Establish your balance between equity and debt.

Key Terms

angels
Canada Small Business Financing (CSBF) loan
common shares
convertible debentures
debt financing
financial statement
fixed rate
floating rate
love money
net worth (personal equity)
operating loan (line of credit)
preferred shares
prime rate
shareholders loan
term loan
vendor statement

Think Points for Success

- ✓ Your banker can provide a wealth of information. Maintain a good relationship with him or her. If your banker ever turns you down, there is usually a very good reason. Correct it.
- ✓ How well you buy is as important as how well you sell.
- ✓ Partner with your vendors or customers. It's often the best way to get the best deals.
- ✓ In dealing with bankers, vendors, and lenders, use lots of open-ended questions like "What else can you do for me?"

Business Plan Building Block

POTENTIAL SOURCES AND EQUITY AMOUNT

List your potential sources and amount of equity for your start-up business. Complete the table below.

Potential Sources of Equity	**Potential Amount ($) (Market Value*)**
Personal equity	________
Savings	________
Borrow on your life insurance	________
Mortgage your property	________
Obtain a line of unsecured personal credit from your bank, credit union, or other financial institution	________
Sell old stock you have been holding onto, even if it means taking a loss, or get a loan using the securities as collateral	________
Get a part-time job, moonlight your way to more money	________
Invest your own equipment (computer, furniture, tools)	________
Automobile (Will the business own your vehicle?)	________
Inventory (paper, books, software)	________

Leaseholds (fixtures, plugs, paint)	________
Organizational costs (Have you paid for training or have you consulted a lawyer or accountant and paid for this out of your own money?)	________
Sweat equity (the value of the time or labour that you can invest into the start-up of your business)	________
________	________
________	________
________	________
________	________
Total personal equity	________
Other equity sources	________
Friends and family	________
Angels	________
Venture capitalists	________
Government programs	________
Employer and employees	________
________	________
________	________
________	________
________	________
Total other sources	________
Total equity	________

*Note: Market value is the price someone else ("the market") is prepared to pay for this asset.

Potential Lending Sources and Amount

List your potential lending sources and amount. Complete the table below.

Potential Lending Sources	**Potential Amount ($) (Market Value*)**
Banks	
1. ________	________
2. ________	________
3. ________	________
Other financial institutions (trust companies/credit unions, etc.)	
1. ________	________
2. ________	________
3. ________	________
Friends and relatives	________
Cooperative partnerships	________
Suppliers and customers	________
Leasing	________
Employers and employees	________
Government programs	________
Total	________

*Note: Market value is the price someone else ("the market") is prepared to pay for this asset.

Checklist Questions and Actions to Develop Your Business Plan

SHAKING THE MONEY TREE

- ❑ What is the total amount of equity you need to establish and operate your business for the first year? Identify all the sources of funds.
- ❑ Identify your funding shortfall each month from the cash flow, and the funding sources and expected rate of interest.

- ❑ Are there any government, agency, or foundation funding (if you are a non-profit organization) sources for your venture?
- ❑ How much, if anything, do you expect from a venture capitalist, and what ownership are you prepared to forego? Note: If working with a venture capitalist or other partners, what do you expect in a shareholders agreement?
- ❑ Who are your prime vendors? What type of purchase agreement do you have with them?
- ❑ What is your debt to equity ratio, and how does that compare to industry ratios?

NOTES

1. Adapted from Rick Spence, *Secrets of Success from Canada's Fastest-Growing Companies* (Toronto: John Wiley & Sons Canada, 1997), p. 162. Reprinted by permission of the author.
2. Ibid., p. 160.
3. Ibid., p. 166.
4. Adapted from "Growth in the Grassroots," *PROFIT*, October/November 1996, as appearing in Allan Riding and Barbara Orser, *Beyond the Banks: Creative Financing for Canadian Entrepreneurs* (Toronto: John Wiley & Sons Canada, 1997), p. 93.
5. Riding and Orser, *Beyond the Banks*, p. 15.
6. Government of Canada, Department of Finance, retrieved from http://strategis.ic.gc.ca/SSG/so03061e.html
7. Research by Macdonald & Associates Ltd. for Canadian Venture Capital Association, cited in John Heinzl, "Venture Capital Windfall Masks Danger," *The Globe and Mail*, April 3, 1998, p. B23.

SUGGESTED READING

Amis, David, and Howard H. Stevenson. *Winning Angels: The 7 Fundamentals of Early Stage Investing*. Scarborough, ON: Prentice Hall Canada, 2001.

Canadian Bankers Association. *Small Business Financing*; *Getting Started in Small Business*; and *Managing Money.* [These publications are free. Write: The Canadian Bankers Association, P.O. 348, Commerce Court Postal Station, Toronto, ON M5L 1G2 (toll-free 1-800-263-0231)]

Chilton, David. *The Wealthy Barber.* Toronto: Stoddart Publishing, 1989.

Dawson, George. *Borrowing to Build Your Business: Getting Your Banker to Say Yes*. Dearborn, MI: Dearborn Upstart Publishing, 1997.

Fiet, James O. "Fragmentation in the Market for Venture Capital." *Entrepreneurship Theory and Practice*, Vol. 21, No. 2, Winter 1996, pp. 5–20.

"The First Annual Definitive Guide to Small Business Financing in Canada." *PROFIT*, June 1997.

Ginsberg, Larry, and Bruce McDougall. *Small Business, Big Money*. Scarborough, ON: Prentice Hall Canada, 1997.

Industry Canada. *Your Guide to Government of Canada Services and Support for Small Business.* 1996.

Quindlen, Ruthann. *Confessions of a Venture Capitalist: Inside the High Stakes World of Start-up Financing*. New York: Warner, 2001.

Riding, Allan, and Barbara Orser. *Beyond the Banks: Creative Financing for Canadian Entrepreneurs*. Toronto: John Wiley & Sons Canada, 1997.

Robinson, Robert J., and Mark Van Osnabrugge. *Angel Investing: Matching Startup Funds with Startup Companies—A Guide for Entrepreneurs, Individual Investors, and Venture Capitalists.* San Francisco: Jossey-Bass, 2000.

Smith, Richard, and Janet Kiholm Smith. *Entrepreneurial Finance*. New York: Wiley, 2000.

Spence, Rick. *Secrets of Success from Canada's Fastest-Growing Companies*. Toronto: John Wiley & Sons Canada, 1997.

chapter 11

Legal Concerns

BUSINESS PLAN BUILDING BLOCK

In this chapter you will learn about different business forms and how to plan for the one that is right for you.

LEARNING OPPORTUNITIES

After reading this chapter, you should be able to:

- Decide which legal form (sole proprietorship, partnership, or corporation) is best for your business.
- Anticipate potential surprises if you are going into business with someone else.
- Explore the pros and cons of incorporating.
- Conduct secondary research into corporations and incorporating.
- Explore the various municipal, provincial, and federal legal regulations that may affect your business.
- Develop tactics for finding the right lawyer.
- Develop questions for probing the mind of a lawyer.
- Understand the importance of having a will.
- Describe the bankruptcy process.

Henry Bemis was doing really well with his coffee service until one of his on-site coffee dispensers spewed boiling water all over the hands of Jody Dawn, a professional model.

Jody's hands earned her just over $200 000 a year. The day her hands were burned, she was at a branch of a major bank, doing a DeBeers-sponsored commercial for diamond rings and safety-deposit boxes.

Her model's hands were her living and her future. On the advice of her lawyer, Jody sued Henry and his Easy-Cup Coffee Service.

Henry had insurance, and the courts ended up awarding Jody $1 million.

Here's the way the court figured it:

- She made $200 000 a year.
- She could expect an active career of at least five years.
- Five years × $200 000 = $1 000 000

Luckily, Henry had the good sense to incorporate and had a lot of liability insurance. His personal assets were protected and his business insurance paid the bill.

ACTION STEP PREVIEW

51. Do some secondary research on corporations.

52. Take a lawyer to lunch.

Chapter 11 will help you complete parts F and G of your business plan, "Management" and "Personnel."

Although Henry Bemis's story is fictitious, the situation is possible and could happen to you. You may run your small business as a sole proprietorship or in partnership with another entrepreneur, and be confident that it is in the best possible legal form. But are you sure? Or maybe you're in the planning stages of your new business and you don't know what legal form (sole proprietorship, partnership, or corporation) is best. In this chapter, we will look at what kind of corporate structure might be best for you and your business. We'll also prepare you for some of the government red tape, help direct you toward legal advice, encourage you to have a will, and get you to think about bankruptcy.

Legal Forms for Small Business

Generally, your small business can exist in one of three basic legal forms: a sole proprietorship, a partnership, or a corporation. For each of these standard forms of ownership (summarized in Table 11.1), we describe here some of the important business realities—and paperwork—you should be aware of.

The cooperative is a fourth type of legal form to consider. Technically, it's a particular type or variant of the corporate structure. Highlights of this lesser-known form of ownership are presented in the final part of this section.[1] It is also important to note that other business agreements, such as joint ventures, exist.

Table 11.1 Characteristics of the Four Main Legal Forms

	Control	Need for Written Agreements	Raising Money	Taxes	Liability	Continuity
Sole Proprietorship	absolute	may be needed for registration if own name not used	one-person show; save, save, save	profit or loss go with personal income	personally liable for everything	restricted—business ceases to exist when owner gets tired of business or dies
Partnership (Limited)	total control by general partner	overwhelming	lots of laws	profit or loss passed on to ltd. partners	ltd. partners are liable only for $ invested	can be provided for in partnership agreement
Partnership (General)	divided	locate super lawyer	easier if more parties sign	profit or loss passed on to partners	personal liability for debts or misdeeds of partners	depends on buy-sell agreement
Corporation	shared (could be absolute)	locate super lawyer	market your "professional" appeal	some tax advantages to Canadian-controlled private corporations	limited to assets of incorporated entity; shareholders are usually not liable	perpetual existence

SOLE PROPRIETORSHIP

Most small businesses start out as a **sole proprietorship**. If you start a business on your own—without partners—you are a sole proprietor. A sole proprietorship, in the eyes of the law, is not a separate entity from the person: the business and the individual are the same. For example, the assets of the business are owned by the individual, and therefore the revenue and expenses are included in his or her personal income tax return.

SOLE PROPRIETORSHIP

a business that is owned by one person

The primary advantages of the sole proprietorship are:

- It is relatively easy and inexpensive to set up.
- It is directly controlled by the owner/operator.
- It is flexible and little regulated.
- Business losses can be deducted from other income.
- Wages paid for work performed by a spouse are deductible from the income of the business.
- Other investors may be added by written agreement.
- It offers some tax advantages in certain situations. For example, if the business suffers a loss and the owner has income from other sources, that loss can be used to offset the other income. If the business loss exceeds the other income, the unused portion of that loss can be carried forward to offset income in subsequent years. In this way, the business offers its owner a "tax shelter." Losses sustained by a corporation can only be used to offset income earned by the corporation.

The major disadvantages of a sole proprietorship are:

- The owner can be held personally liable for all debts of the business. Personal assets, such as the house and automobile, can be seized for non-payment of bills, provided the necessary legal steps have been taken to do so. To avoid such an unfortunate occurrence, some entrepreneurs register certain personal assets in the name of their spouse. This is allowed as long as it is done at least one year before financial problems are encountered; otherwise, the court may construe the action as a deliberate attempt to outmanoeuvre creditors and will not allow it.
- Opportunity for continuity is restricted. The sole proprietorship ceases to exist when the sole proprietor goes out of business or dies.
- To some extent, the owner's ability to raise capital is limited. Many small businesses encounter financial problems, as their owners are reluctant to share ownership with others who are able to contribute the needed funds.
- The sole proprietor may be required to pay taxes at a higher tax rate in certain situations. Depending on the income level of the owners, tax rates for a sole proprietorship can be higher than those for a corporation. The sole proprietor includes the revenues and expenses from the business on his or her personal tax return, and the income is taxed at whatever his or her personal rate happens to be either in the three previous years and for the following seven years.

Sole proprietorships are regulated by the provincial/territorial governments and legal requirements vary from jurisdiction to jurisdiction; for more information, visit the "Provincial Registrars" web page listed in Box 11.1.

PARTNERSHIP

PARTNERSHIP

an association of two or more individuals carrying on a business to earn income

Many small businesses start as a partnership and it works out well. A **partnership** is an association of two or more individuals carrying on a business to earn income. Legal requirements for forming a partnership vary from province to province, but

Box 11.1 Bookmark This

Legal Forms for Small Business

Sole Proprietorships and Partnerships

- **Provincial Registrars**
  http://strategis.gc.ca/SSG/cs01134e.html
  Click on the province or territory where you want to register.

Corporations

- **Federal Business Incorporation**
  www.cbsc.org/english/search/display.cfm?CODE=1168&Coll=FE_FEDSBIS_E
  Find out how to incorporate federally, and how to complete and file documents online.
- **Federal Not-for-Profit Incorporation**
  www.cbsc.org/english/search/display.cfm?CODE=1170&Coll=FE_FEDSBIS_E
  Visit this page if you are thinking about incorporating a not-for-profit business.
- **Provincial Incorporation**
  Visit the "Provincial Registrars" page cited above.

Cooperatives

- **Incorporating Your Cooperative** (Industry Canada)
  http://strategis.gc.ca/SSG/cs01269e.html
- **The Co-operative Structure** (Canada Business Service Centres)
  www.cbsc.org/english/search/display.cfm?code=4070&Coll=FE_FEDSBIS_E
- **Canadian Co-operative Association**
  www.coopcca.com

GENERAL PARTNERSHIP
a partnership in which each partner has a hand in managing the business and assuming unlimited personal liability for any debts

LIMITED PARTNERSHIP
a partnership composed of at least one or more limited partners and at least one general partner

generally a partnership can come into existence either through a written or oral agreement or, in some cases, even by implication. If you are considering a partnership, you must check out the specific regulations for the province in which you operate your business. (Visit the "Provincial Registrars" web page listed in Box 11.1.)

There are two types of partnerships: general and limited. In a **general partnership**, each partner has a hand in managing the business and assumes unlimited personal liability for any debts. In a **limited partnership**—composed of one or more limited partners and at least one general partner—the general partner assumes both management duties and the downside risk. A limited partner's liability is limited to the amount of his or her original investment as long as he or she has had no role in management decisions.

Note that all partnerships must have at least one general partner.

The advantages to a partnership are:

- It is easy to set up.
- New partners can be added (some claim that this structure is more flexible and has a greater chance of continuity than a sole proprietorship).
- It involves few legal requirements. You can form a partnership with a handshake and dissolve it without one (though this is not a wise endeavour).
- Risk is generally shared equally among partners—except in the case of a limited partnership.
- Partners can provide mutual support and different skills. One of the best things about a partnership is psychological: it offers the moral support and contribution of teammates.
- It offers more potential sources of capital.

- Partners are taxed as individuals, and in some cases (as is with proprietorships) this can be advantageous.

Some of the major disadvantages are:

- Tax and estate-planning options are more limited than for a corporate structure (as discussed below).
- Partners and all their assets—personal and business—are, to some extent, at risk for any losses suffered.
- The reality is that sometimes business and personal liabilities of a particular partner aren't kept entirely separate. This can have potentially disastrous consequences to other partners whose shared business liability could result in unexpected personal losses.
- Decision making may be difficult because each partner may want to have equal rights.
- One partner can make decisions that bind all others.
- Dissolution can be ugly, sometimes resulting in the closing of the business or damaged feelings.

On the surface, partnerships can make a lot of sense. Two or more entrepreneurs face the unknown together and pool their skills. They may be able to raise more capital than one person could alone. But forming a good partnership can be as challenging as forming a good marriage. We strongly suggest that you get everything in writing before you start the business. Write out a partnership agreement with legal advice. Each partner should get his or her own lawyer.

At the very least, your written partnership agreement should include the following:

- rights and responsibilities of the partners,
- capital contributions of each partner,
- role and time that each partner will devote to the business,
- provisions for retirement, death, termination and/or reorganization,
- how net income from business will be divided,
- means for settling disputes, and
- mechanism for dissolving the partnership or winding up the business.

While a partnership agreement may not be legally required, it is highly recommended. Secondly, professional advice is strongly recommended. For example, any partner can enter into a contract on behalf of the partnership. By doing so, a partner can bind all partners in an unfavourable contract, since all partners are jointly and severally liable for the obligations of the partnership.

If you don't think a written agreement and legal advice are all that important, take a moment and see what happened to Phil Johnson when he did not have a partnership agreement.

Your Pal, Steve

I have to admit, the motor-sailor was my idea. I persuaded my partner, Steve Savitch, to buy a boat—actually it was a fancy 14-metre rig called *The Ninja*—for the partnership. We could write off some of the payments as an expense, and it would do our company image a world of good.

Steve and I had been friends for a dozen years and partners in Savitch and Johnson, Business Consultants, for the past three. We'd done quite well and each of us was going to clear over $50 000 this year. I persuaded him we could afford this perk. Besides, my marketing instinct told me it could really help close a few deals.

About two months after we bought the boat—and had a lot of fun—a fellow who sells radar equipment called me. Seems Steve had bought

$2000 worth of radar, and this chap was wondering when he'd get paid. After I hung up the phone, my secretary buzzed me with Mary, Steve's wife, on the line wanting to know where Steve was.

I thought he was on a business trip with a few of our best clients. As it turned out, Steve had disappeared with *The Ninja* and no one knew where. In the end, I got stung for all his business debts, including the payments on *The Ninja*.

The problem was that Steve and I never saw the need for having anything in writing. We were both men of good faith (or so I had thought). We had each pulled our weight in business and we had balanced each other's skills. For the first time in 12 years, I made an appointment to talk to a lawyer. He just shook his head. "You should have come to me a lot sooner, Phil," he said. "A *lot* sooner."

Last week, when I was closing the place down and getting ready to go back to work for my old boss, I got a postcard from Tahiti. "Sorry partner," Steve wrote. "Didn't mean to run out on you, but it was the only way I could handle the home front. These things happen.... Your pal, Steve."

CORPORATION

CORPORATION

a legal entity with the authority to act and have liability separate and apart from its owners

A **corporation** is a legal entity that exists under authority granted by provincial or federal law. It stands legally separate from the owners, and it does business in the name of the corporation. It can sue and be sued.

Because a corporation is an artificial entity, a creation on paper, it needs more paperwork to justify its existence. There are fees required, and meetings of the board of directors. The secretary of the corporation must keep accurate, complete records of what transpires at meetings.

Nonetheless, for many businesses, it's worth forming a corporation because it creates a shield between the creditors and the owner's personal wealth. To keep the shield in place, active owners can become *employees* of the corporation; their business cards have the corporate name and logo and specify their job title. At the same time, owners sign contracts as *officers* of the corporations.

Following are some of the reasons why you should think about incorporating or not incorporating your business. In the end, your decision to do so will depend on two key factors: your tax situation and your desire to limit your liability. However, we do want to emphasize that becoming a corporation won't solve all your problems. In most cases, it won't immunize you against your creditors. The banks, for example, will still want a personal guarantee, which could mean your house. Taxes won't be eliminated either. In fact, in the early years, the bank will treat a newly incorporated business as if it were a sole proprietorship. If you have losses, you are better off as a sole proprietor. Let's start with the major reasons for thinking about incorporating.

Liability A corporation acts like a shield between you and the world. If your business fails, your creditors may not come after your house, your beach condo, your Porsche, your first-born, or your hard-won collections—provided you've done it right.

To keep your corporate shield up, make sure you: (1) hold scheduled meetings; (2) keep up the minute book; and (3) act as if you are an employee of the corporation. Here's an everyday example of the corporate shield at work: One of your employees gets into a fender-bender while driving on company business. If you're a corporation, the injured parties will come after your corporation and not you. (If your employees use *their own* cars on company business, make sure they're insured for a minimum of $1 million.)

See how limited liability helped Henry Bemis in the opening vignette. Again, remember that banks and other creditors will want personal guarantees as well as business guarantees, thus the advantages of the corporation is lost.

You Might Enjoy Some Tax Advantages Taxation laws are complex, and a good accountant can dream up several ways to minimize taxes, regardless of what legal form you choose. However, a concept called "integration" attempts to ensure that income is taxed to the same degree whether it is held by an individual or channelled through a corporation. You won't get rich on your tax savings. Tax laws and rates vary slightly from province to province in Canada. We therefore strongly recommend that you see an accountant to help you determine the best organization form from a tax standpoint. In general, a special small business tax rate applies to income under $200 000 to a cumulative amount of $1 million. Once the $1 million limit is reached, the firm will be taxed at the full corporate rate. Small business tax rates vary from about 15 percent to 23 percent, depending on the province.

However, there are some tax advantages to being incorporated, and the obvious ones are listed below.

1. Only incorporated companies are eligible for manufacturing and processing tax credits.
2. Certain tax-free benefits, such as some insurance premiums, are available only to employees of incorporated companies.
3. In regard to pensions, there are still greater options for tax deferral under the corporate form.
4. Owners of corporations can enjoy potential personal tax savings. For example, once the income of a business reaches a certain level, the total tax paid by the corporation and the owner will be less than that which the owner of a sole proprietorship would pay. The exact level depends on the individual situation. As a ballpark figure, once you start earning $25 000–$30 000 (income after expenses), it would be time to consider incorporating to save you some personal tax.
5. Benefits can be paid to employees in different forms by a corporation, which could yield a tax saving. These forms include salaries, dividends, and profit-sharing plans. In the case of a deferred profit-sharing plan, for example, a corporation can make contributions on behalf of employees. The contributions are allowed as a current business tax deduction, but the employee pays no tax until withdrawals are made. This type of plan is not available to the sole proprietorship. Careful analysis needs to be made in each situation to determine the optimal structuring of an owner/manager's earnings. You should be aware of the different forms of compensation and, if necessary, consult an accountant for advice on those your business should use.

If you want to learn more about the tax benefits of incorporating, a good starting point is the Canada Customs and Revenue Agency website (www.ccra-adrc.gc.ca). Obviously, the whole issue of corporate tax benefits is complicated. You should always seek the advice of a corporate tax accountant in these matters.

You Upgrade Your Image What does the word "corporation" imply to you? IBM? Bell? GM? Heavy hitters, right? Let's look at the word with new eyes.

Corporation comes from the Latin, *corpus*, which means "body." To incorporate means to make or form a shape into a body. Looked at from that angle, incorporating starts to sound creative.

It will sound that way to lots of your TCs, too. As a corporation, you might be perceived to:

- have more longevity and solidity in the world.
- attract better employees.
- enjoy more prestige.

You Have the Opportunity of Channelling Some Heavy Expenses For example, with some legal help, you can write a medical assistance clause into your bylaws. Here's the way it works:

1. Your corporation pays the insurance premium on your health insurance.
2. Your corporation reimburses you for the deductible.
3. Your corporation writes off the money paid to you as a business expense.
4. You aren't liable to pay taxes on the reimbursement.

You Simplify the Division of Multiple Ownership For example, say you're going into the printing and graphic business with two very good friends.

- The business needs $110 000 to get started.
- You can contribute $60 000.
- Friend A delivers $25 000.
- Friend B delivers $15 000.
- You borrow the other $10 000 from your friendly banker.
- The way to handle the ownership is with stock. You get 60 percent. Friend A gets 25 percent. Friend B gets 15 percent.

You Guarantee Continuity If one of your shareholders or founders dies (or departs by motorsailer or other means), the corporation will likely keep chugging along. That's because you've gone through a lot of red tape and planning to set it up that way.

It's one of the few justifications for red tape we know. However, if you are an individual incorporated and you die, the business will likely die with you.

You Can Offer Internal Incentives When you want to reward a special employee, you can offer stock options or a promotion (for example, a vice-presidential title) in addition to (and sometimes in place of) pay raises. Becoming a corporation officer may carry its own special excitement, which gives you flexibility. An ownership position (shares) can also motivate an employee to keep the company's best interest in mind.

You Are in a Good Position for Estate Planning As your company grows, you may want to set up other companies and include members of your family in your organization. At this point, you can engage in complicated share exchange and asset transfers. If you find yourself in this situation, you should consult a knowledgeable corporate estate lawyer.

There are also some potential disadvantages of incorporating. These include:

Potentially Fewer Tax Write-offs at the Beginning Business losses incurred by a corporation can be used for taxation purposes only to offset income of the preceding three years and the seven successive years. If your business suffers losses in its first few years of operation, the losses of the early years could conceivably never be used to reduce tax liability. In the case of a sole proprietorship, however, losses from the business can be used to offset income from other sources in the year in which they are incurred. Thus, if losses are projected in the beginning years of the business and you have income from other sources, it may well be advantageous not to incorporate your business.

Higher Start-up Costs Start-up costs are higher if you choose to incorporate rather than carry on business as a sole proprietorship or partnership. For example, if you choose to incorporate federally, you will have to pay the government $500. Provincial incorporation is usually less expensive. As well, you will be required to do at least one name search, each at a cost of $75. You'll also have to pay additional legal and accounting services which could easily be $2000–$3000. While it is not necessary to obtain legal advice to incorporate, we strongly advise you to do so, particularly if you are considering setting up with a complex share structure. Of course, legal advice means legal fees. These can easily add $200–$1000 to the cost of incorporation.

Increased Paperwork Carrying on business as a corporation may increase the number of tax filings you are required to make. For instance, the Canada Business Corporations Act requires that you file an annual return (Form 22) each year and inform the Corporations Directorate of any changes in your board of directors or the location of your registered head office. You have to file separate income tax returns for yourself, which may lead to an increase in your ongoing professional costs. Your company is also required to maintain certain corporate records. Furthermore, you will likely be asked to register your company in any province or territory where you carry on business. Registration is different from incorporation. While a company may be incorporated only once, it may be registered in any number of jurisdictions to carry on business. You should contact the local corporate law administration office in each province or territory in which you plan to carry on business to determine what filing requirements you will have to fulfill.

Obviously, the issue of incorporation is somewhat complicated. Some of the most frequently asked questions, and their answers, are summarized below.

Who Can Form a Corporation?

Under most circumstances, one or more individuals who are 18 years of age or older can form a corporation. Similarly, one or more companies or "bodies corporate" may incorporate an additional company. These persons or companies are called incorporators. An incorporator may form a corporation whose shareholders, officers, and directors are other persons, or may serve as the sole director, officer, and shareholder of the company. An incorporator is also responsible for organizational procedures, such as filing the articles of incorporation and designating the first directors.

Do I Incorporate Federally or Provincially?

A company can incorporate either federally (under the Canada Business Corporations Act), or provincially under the laws of a province or territory. Whether you incorporate federally or provincially, you will be required to register your business in the province or territory where you carry on business.

A major advantage of incorporating federally is that the head office can be located in any Canadian province, and it can be relocated if circumstances dictate. If you have the intention (either now or sometime in the future) of operating in more than one jurisdiction, you should probably choose to incorporate federally in order to simplify your business relations later. Still, the federal corporation must register in each province in which it is doing business.

Another reason given for choosing federal incorporation is the heightened name protection provided to federal corporations. While every incorporating jurisdiction in Canada screens potential corporations, the level of scrutiny varies. At the federal level, stringent tests are applied before the right to use a particular name is granted.

A final major advantage of federal incorporation is limited liability. A federally incorporated company is considered a legal entity anywhere in Canada. Therefore, its shareholders are protected by limited liability anywhere in the country. In contrast, a provincially incorporated company is a legal entity only in the province or territory in which it is incorporated. Thus, its shareholders are not protected by limited liability if it does business outside of its own jurisdiction.

Despite these advantages, many small businesses still decide against incorporating federally. We can only surmise that this is due mainly to the higher cost of federal incorporation.

What Kinds of Businesses Can Incorporate?

Almost any type of business may incorporate. However, banking, insurance, loan and trust companies, and non-profit corporations are incorporated under different statutes. There are no restrictions such as minimum company size on the businesses.

Do I Need to Hire a Lawyer to Incorporate?

No, though we recommend you do. A lawyer may provide valuable advice, but that is not required for incorporation. If you want to incorporate without a lawyer, get ready for a lot of paperwork.

Do I Need a Board of Directors?

Yes. Your company must have at least one director. In your articles of incorporation, you are required to specify the number of directors. At each annual general meeting, shareholders elect directors (depending on the length or term of office the shareholders choose).

Shareholders may decide that, for various reasons, they want to remove a director they had previously elected. This is a simple procedure. It generally needs the approval of a majority of the votes represented at a meeting of shareholders called for the purpose of removing the director.

Who Can Be a Director?

A director must:

- be at least 18 years old,
- be of sound mind (mentally competent), and
- be an individual (a corporation cannot be a director).

He or she must not be an undischarged bankrupt.

In addition, a majority of the directors of a corporation must be individuals who are ordinarily resident in Canada. You should keep this in mind when electing directors and filling vacancies. There is no requirement for directors to hold shares in the corporation, nor is there any restriction against their holding shares.

What Are the Responsibilities of the Board of Directors?

The company's directors are responsible for the overall supervision of the affairs of the corporation. They approve the company's financial statements; make, amend, and repeal bylaws; authorize the issuance of shares; and call and conduct directors' and shareholders' meetings. The directors, in turn, usually appoint officers, who are responsible for day-to-day operations. In a small, private corporation, one individual may act as sole shareholder, director, and officer.[2]

Must a Company Have Shareholders?

Yes. An active company must have at least one class of shares (ownership) and at least one shareholder (owner). A person or company who owns shares in a corporation is called a shareholder. Generally speaking and unless the articles of incorporation provide otherwise, each share in the corporation entitles the holder to one vote. A person becomes a shareholder by acquiring shares from the company (buying shares from the treasury) or from an existing shareholder. The larger the number of shares held, the larger the number of votes (and, in most cases, control) a shareholder can generally exercise.

Shareholders have limited liability in the corporation, and usually are not liable for the company's debts unless, as noted earlier, the bank requires the owner/shareholders to pledge personal and company assets. On the other hand, shareholders generally do not actively run the corporation. Shareholders also have legal access to certain information about the corporation. For example, shareholders are entitled to inspect (and copy) the corporate records, and are entitled to receive the company's financial statements. Shareholders also elect directors, approve bylaws and bylaw changes, appoint the auditor of the corporation (or waive the audit requirement), and approve certain major or fundamental changes to the corporation. These changes could include matters such as a sale of assets of the business, a change of name, and articles of amendment altering share rights or creating new classes of shares.

Do I Need a Shareholders Agreement?

A shareholders agreement is not necessary, but we strongly advise that you have one, except, of course, if you are a one-person corporation. It is an agreement entered into usually by all shareholders. The written agreement must be signed by the shareholders who are party to it. While shareholders agreements are specific to each company and its shareholders, most of these documents deal with the same basic issues. A typical shareholders agreement includes the following clauses.

Article 1: Definitions
Article 2: Conduct of Affairs of the Corporation
Article 3: Transfers of Shares
Article 4: Real Property
Article 5: Death of a Shareholder
Article 6: Bankruptcy, etc.
Article 7: Powers of Attorney
Article 8: General Sale Provisions
Article 9: Arbitration
Article 10: General Provisions

The relationship among shareholders in a small company tends to be very much like a partnership agreement, with each person having a say in the significant business decisions the company will be making.

Here are some of the major provisions of a shareholders agreement:

- *Who sits on the board of directors.* A very common shareholders agreement provision for a small company gives all the shareholders the right to sit on the board of directors or to nominate a representative for that purpose.
- *How the future obligations of the company will be shared or divided.* The shareholders may agree, for example, that when other means of raising funds are not available, each shareholder will contribute more funds to the company on a pro rata basis.
- *How future shares are purchased.* For example, three equal partners could agree that no shares in the corporation will be issued without the consent of all shareholders/directors. In the absence of such a provision, two shareholders/directors could issue shares by an ordinary or special resolution (because they control two-thirds of the votes) to themselves without including or requiring the permission of the third shareholder/director.
- *The right of first refusal.* This provision states that any shareholder who wants to sell his or her shares must first offer them to the other shareholders of the company before selling them to an outside party.

- *Rules for the transfer of shares.* This provision details how the shares will be transferred in such an event as the death, resignation, dismissal, personal bankruptcy, or divorce of a shareholder. Restrictions can be detailed in plans governing, for instance, when a shareholder can or must sell his or her shares, or what happens to those shares after the individual shareholder has left.
- *Other shareholders agreement provisions.* These may include non-competition clauses, confidentiality agreements, dispute-resolution mechanisms, and details about how the shareholders agreement itself is to be amended or terminated.

Shareholders agreements are voluntary. If you choose to have one—and, as you now know, we recommend you do—it should reflect the particular needs of your company and its shareholders. While undoubtedly the best advice is to keep your agreement as simple as possible, we strongly suggest that you consult your professional advisers before signing any shareholders agreement.

Do I Have to Get a Corporate Seal?

Not necessarily. A corporation under the federal Canada Business Corporations Act, for example, is not required to have a seal. If you wish to have a corporate seal for your corporation, you may purchase one from a legal stationery store or commercial supplier.

If I Decide to Incorporate, What Next?

Our advice: See a lawyer—despite the cost savings of doing it yourself. For example, if proper legal formalities are not followed, the shareholders can actually be liable for the corporation's debts. However, should you want to do it yourself, contact your provincial authority if you want to incorporate locally or the Corporations Directorate of Industry Canada should you decide to incorporate federally. And, if you are going to do it on your own, get ready for lots of paperwork. You may also want to check out the "Federal Business Incorporation" web page listed in Box 11.1.

COOPERATIVE

Although relatively little has been written about cooperatives, you should give some consideration to this form, particularly if you are considering a home-based business that can benefit from a group pooling of talents.

COOPERATIVE
an organization that is operated collectively by its owners

A **cooperative** is a special form of corporate structure, often formed by a number of small producers who want to be more competitive in the marketplace. As such, it can be somewhat complicated. Here are a few distinct features:

Incorporation Generally, at least three people are needed to incorporate a cooperative. You can incorporate provincially (each province has its own legislation) or federally under the Canada Cooperative Associations Act. Each government has its own legal wrinkles, so you are going to need some legal advice or to do a lot of research.

Organization A cooperative is organized and operated for the purpose of providing its members with goods or services. There are various types and structures. Traditional co-ops, such as co-op retail stores, farming co-ops, or housing co-ops, supply service to their members. In worker co-ops, everyone is expected to work in the corporation, and all members are employed in this one business. Worker co-ops can be a useful format for home-based "craft" or "consulting" businesses, where members can pool their talents and benefit from each other's skills. Another format is the marketing co-op where members have their own business (product or service). The purpose of this cooperative organization is to market and sell the different products or services.

Capital Start-up funds for a cooperative are raised by member shares. The return on capital investment to the members is limited by federal or provincial/territorial legislation. For example, the cooperative surplus is normally returned to the members in the form of patronage refunds—sometimes called patronage dividends—and each member receives a share of that surplus proportionate to the business done or work carried out by the member with or through the cooperative.

Voting Each member can have only one vote, regardless of the number of shares he or she possesses.

Liability The cooperative is an entity distinct from its members, who thus benefit from the standard limited liability protection of a standard corporate structure.

Shares Shares cannot be transferred. They must be sold to members of the cooperative.

Priorities Employment security is usually more important than capital, especially in worker co-ops.

Here are a few of the major advantages of a cooperative:

- Given the number of members, there are potentially more sources of capital than in other business forms. In addition, government regulations for raising start-up capital generally favour co-ops.
- Members are owners and are therefore more motivated to produce and be successful.
- Cooperatives offer members plenty of opportunity to network and share ideas and expertise.
- Generally, cooperatives are entitled to receive the standard corporate protection such as limited liability.
- In most cases, it is relatively easy for members to sell their shares to other members.

A few disadvantages of cooperatives are:

- With large member groups it is sometimes difficult to get agreement. Conflict resolution becomes an issue.
- Management is supposed to be a cooperative (shared) responsibility. In some cases, management becomes unwieldy because of differing goals and objectives and, in other cases, a lack of experience.
- Some members find it difficult to work cooperatively or in teams.
- Some major institutions are not familiar or comfortable with how cooperatives work, making financing relatively more difficult to obtain.

Establishing a cooperative is tricky. We strongly advise you to consult with provincial or federal authorities and a lawyer. We also encourage you to network with co-ops in your area to understand how they are managed, and to learn firsthand the advantages and disadvantages of the co-op form of business. You may also want to visit the web pages listed under "Cooperatives" in Box 11.1.

Now it's time to do a little research on your own. Complete Action Step 51.

ACTION STEP 51

Do some secondary research on corporations.

Before you take any action with legal forms, you need a lot of information and professional advice.

We suggest you begin by logging on to the Internet. A good place to start is the web pages listed under "Corporations" in Box 11.1. If you prefer hard copy, go to the library or the resource centre of a college or university. You can also check out the bookstores; handbooks on incorporation through various self-counsel series are helpful.

Once you get familiar with the broad concepts, you may want to do some specific research of companies in your industry. Write to the companies or get on the Net and visit their sites. You may also want to talk to a few small business owners you know. Get their opinion. What kind of structure would they suggest and why?

While you are doing this research, remember to keep looking around with new eyes.

Your Business Name

So you now have a business idea you think will fly. You've spent a lot of time on your business plan and are beginning to think that it just might work. You've come up with a name for your business that you are proud of. Where do you go from here?

We suggest you next think about some legal protection for your name. After all, you don't want someone else to go out and start a business using your name. The process of protecting your business name will depend, in part, on the province where you want to conduct business and your legal form (which is one of the reasons we wanted you to consider your legal framework in the first part of this chapter). What follows is this whole procedure, simplified, but again we advise you to get some professional help.

According to provincial authority, a sole proprietorship or partnership does not necessarily have to register its name. Normally, if your business name is exactly the same as your own name, registration is not needed. For example, Mary Smith could operate a business as Mary Smith without registration. However, she would have to register the name of her business if the business name differed—even slightly—from her name. If she called her business Mary Smith *Consulting*, then she must register that name with the province where she is conducting her business.

Provincial registration does not require the business name to be unique. Thus, in some cases, you can register your business name without a search, but we advise that you do one since you may later find out that there are other businesses with similar names. If your registered name causes confusion with another business, you may be subject to penalties and may even have to change the name of your business. In other words, provincial registration does not necessarily protect your business name.

In searching a name you have two choices: doing a provincial search or doing a federal search. All incorporated businesses must register their corporate name with any province in which they do business. Although provinces will do a name search for you, your best bet is to ask for a federal name search report. If you incorporate federally, and we suggest you do, you will need a NUANS (Newly Upgraded Automated Name Search) report. A NUANS report is a five-page document that includes a list of business names and trademarks that sound similar to the name you are proposing. The list is drawn from the national data bank of existing and reserved business names, as well as trademarks applied for and registered in Canada.

A NUANS will make you aware of any existing businesses that could prevent you from using your business name. It also lets you know whether your proposed trademark is already in use by another business. This saves you from having to change the name of your business later when you find out that you have been infringing on a trademark.

A NUANS report is obtained from private businesses known as Search Houses, which are listed under Incorporating Companies, Incorporation: Name Search, Searchers of Records, or Trademark Agents in the Yellow Pages.

Generally, when you register a name in federal incorporation, you must submit the NUANS report along with your proposed business name. The request for a numbered company is the same with one exception. You may request the federal government to grant your corporation a designating number, followed by the word "Canada" and a legal element, to serve as your corporate name. For this specific case, a NUANS report is not required. Any other kind of proposed name must be supported by a NUANS report. If there is another name that is similar to your name, you will be asked to make a new choice for your incorporated company.[3]

More Red Tape

When you start your business, you will be subjected to all kinds of federal, provincial, and municipal red tape. Box 11.2 provides a checklist of some of the requirements your business may be confronted with. One thing is for certain: you will have to deal with the Canada Customs and Revenue Agency (CCRA). Thus, we focus here on the major CCRA start-up requirements because these will be common for everyone.

THE BUSINESS NUMBER (BN)

Your first step in doing business with the Canada Customs and Revenue Agency is your business number (BN). The BN is the federal government's numbering system that helps to streamline the way it deals with businesses. It is based on the idea of "one business, one number."

Box 11.2 Checklist of Requirements That May Affect Your Business

Have you considered the following?

Municipal

- regulations regarding home-based or home-occupation business
- zoning, rezoning, and obtaining a minor variance
- subdivision approval and consent to severance
- demolition control and permits
- site plan control approval
- construction permit
- licensing of business and trades
- signage regulations
- hours of operation
- food premises inspection
- municipal tax (e.g., realty tax, business tax)
- any more?

Provincial

- health and safety regulations
- workers' compensation
- provincial/territorial employment standards (e.g., hours of work, minimum wage, vacation pay, overtime pay, equal pay for equal work)
- health insurance
- environmental control regulations
- provincial tax (e.g., corporate, retail sales, tobacco, gasoline, land transfer tax)
- any more?

Federal

- Business Number (BN)
- GST/HST
- payroll deductions (e.g., Canada Pension Plan, insurance, income tax)
- food and drug regulations and inspection
- patents, trademarks, copyrights, and industrial designs
- federal corporation tax
- any more?

You will need a BN if you require one of the four CCRA business accounts: corporate income tax, import/export, payroll deductions, or the Goods and Services Tax (GST) or Harmonized Sales Tax (HST). According to government, businesses will eventually be able to use their BN for other CCRA accounts and other government programs. For instance, you will be asked to state the name of the business, its location, and its legal structure. You will also be required to outline what your business's sales will be. Without this type of information, you won't be able to complete the BN registration form.

If you decide you need a BN, you will have to complete Form RC1, Request for a Business Number. For more information, contact your local CCRA office. A good source of information is the CCRA publication *RC2: The Business Number and Your CCRA Accounts* (available at www.ccra-adrc.gc.ca).

GST/HST

The GST is a tax that applies at a rate of 7 percent to the supply of most goods and services in Canada. The HST is a sales tax that applies at a single rate of 15 percent to taxable supplies made in the three participating provinces of Newfoundland, Nova Scotia, and New Brunswick (as of 1997). The HST has the same basic operating rules as the GST. The federal component of HST is 7 percent and the provincial component is 8 percent.

If your taxable revenues do not exceed $30 000, you do not have to register for the GST or HST. However, you can register voluntarily and, in general, we suggest you do.

Although the consumer ultimately pays the GST/HST, businesses are normally responsible for collecting and remitting it to the government. Businesses that must register or that register voluntarily for the GST/HST are called registrants. Registrants can claim a credit, called an input tax credit, to recover the GST/HST they paid or owe on their business purchases. If they pay more than they collect, they can claim a refund. Since there are goods and services that are tax-exempt (most medical and dental services and daycare services provided for less than 24 hours per day, for example), it is important that you check with the Canada Customs and Revenue Agency before you start your business.

To register for the GST or HST, contact your nearest tax services office. You will be asked to fill out Form RC1, Request for a Business Number, as we discussed earlier. You can get more information from the CCRA publication *General Information for GST/HST Registrants* or from the CCRA's website: www.ccra-adrc.gc.ca.

PAYROLL DEDUCTIONS

According to the Canada Customs and Revenue Agency, you are an employer if you: pay salaries, wages, bonuses, vacation pay, or tips to people working for you; or if you provide benefits such as lodging or room and board to the people working for you. If you are an employer, you will be responsible for deducting the following from your employees' paycheques:

- income tax,
- Canada Pension Plan (CPP) contributions, and
- Employment Insurance (EI) premiums.

You may also be required to make payments and be subject to certain regulations under the workers' compensation legislation.

Payroll deductions can be complicated. So before you start your business, we strongly advise you to visit or call your local CCRA office. An adviser may even come to your business and help you get started with all the forms you need. If you have a computer (and you should), the CCRA will give you a disk, *Tables on Diskette* (TOD) (T4143). It contains all the information you need to calculate deductions from your employees' pay for all pay periods. This disk is even available on the Internet on Canada Customs and Revenue Agency's Electronic Distribution System. Another good source of information on payroll deductions is the CCRA publication *Employers' Guide to Payroll Deductions*.

FEDERAL INCOME TAXES

Generally, business income includes any money you earn with the reasonable expectation of making a profit.

If you are a new business entity, your year-end will be December 31 and your tax return will be due at the end of April each year. This business income (or loss) forms part of your overall income for the year. As a sole proprietor, you must file financial statements with your income tax return. It is most likely (if you are not in farming and fishing) that you will be required to submit one of the following two forms along with your T1:

- Form T2124, Statement of Business Activities
- Form T2032, Statement of Professional Activities

A partnership by itself does not file an annual income tax return. Each partner must include a share of the partnership income or loss on a personal, corporate, or trust income tax return. As such, partners must file either financial statements or one of the two proprietorship forms referred to above. Partnership taxes can get a little complicated, so you should get some accounting advice or, at the very least, consult with the Canada Customs and Revenue Agency.

A corporation must file a corporation income tax return (T2) within six months of the end of every taxation year, even if it doesn't owe taxes. Corporations report on an annual basis and are normally free to choose their year-end date. Corporations are also required to attach complete financial statements and the necessary schedules to the T2 return.

Corporate tax is complicated and you definitely should get professional help. But, if you really do want to try it yourself, the best place to start is the "Setting Up Your Business" page on the CCRA website (see Box 11.3).

Box 11.3 Bookmark This

- **Setting Up Your Business** (Canada Customs and Revenue Agency) www.ccra-adrc.gc.ca/E/pub/tg/rc4070/rc4070eq-01.html

"Setting Up Your Business" is the first chapter of the CCRA's *Guide for Canadian Small Businesses*. Topics include:

- How does a sole proprietorship pay taxes?
- How does a partnership pay taxes?
- How does a corporation pay taxes?
- Legal requirements for keeping records
- Retaining and destroying records
- Bringing assets into a business

ACTION STEP 52

Take a lawyer to lunch.

Canvass your business contacts for the names of three to five lawyers with experience in forming small business corporations and partnerships. If possible, concentrate on those who have worked in your industry.

Talk to them by phone first and then take the most promising candidate to lunch. (Lunch is optional, but your inquiries are vital.) Many lawyers offer a free first visit.

The first thing you're looking for is someone you can get along with. Then look for experience in the world of small business. A hot trial lawyer may have a lot of charisma, but you want a nuts-and-bolts small business specialist who can save you time, pain, and money.

Find out about fees and costs. Compare the cost, for example, of having your lawyer write up a complex partnership buyout agreement with the cost of setting up a corporation. Use some questions presented in this chapter to start you off in your discussion.

A good lawyer will offer you perspectives that will be helpful in the formation of your business. You may have to look awhile, and it may cost you some dollars up front, but there's no substitute for good legal help.

Get a Lawyer

The business world has become something of a legal jungle. As an entrepreneur, you can't possibly be expected to know and understand all the laws and their implications. So, take the time to find a lawyer who can help you with your specific needs.

A good small business lawyer can help you create the right business structure for a partnership or a corporation—a structure that gives you the flexibility you'll need. Network your contacts for a lawyer with experience in your industry. You need a lawyer on your team of advisers.

Once you've found one you think might be right for you, make an appointment with him or her.

Be sure to prepare your own agenda for each conversation with the lawyer. If you're organized, you will save money on your fee. Remember, only stay the time allotted or you'll pay extra.

Now you're ready to do Action Step 52.

Get a Will

> The importance of an up-to-date will cannot be overstated. Contrary to what most people believe, if you die without a will, things will not automatically work out as you would have wished. Disaster can result.[4]
>
> —David Chilton, author of *The Wealthy Barber*

If you die without a will, all your assets will be frozen. The courts will then pay off all debts and divide up your business assets according to a set of rigid rules. If you want your property, business, or shares transferred a certain way after your death, you must say so in a will. If you have partners or other owners, make sure they have a will and that you all understand what is going to happen if someone dies. Here are a few rules, drawn from *The Wealthy Barber*:[5]

1. Get a lawyer. Don't do it yourself. There are many issues to consider, both from a business and personal perspective.
2. Make your lawyer aware of your business arrangements.
3. Before you see a lawyer, decide exactly what you want to happen with your business should you die. Make sure that you discuss this with your business partners or other owners. Remember also that you have the right to know what is going to happen to the business if one of your key shareholders or partners dies.
4. Choose an executor. This is a person who will handle your affairs and carry out the will's instruction.
5. Don't procrastinate. Do it now!

Bankruptcy

Entrepreneurs are optimists by nature. As you prepare to open your doors, the last thing you want to think about is the prospect of being forced to close them. But business failures do happen, and it is not too early to learn about some of the legal concerns arising from them.

If nothing else, an understanding of the bankruptcy process should encourage you to be proactive and avoid debt problems in the first place. Box 11.4 will also help you do this.

Box 11.4 Bookmark This

- **Dealing with Debt: A Consumers Guide** (Office of the Superintendent of Bankruptcy)
  http://strategis.ic.gc.ca/SSG/br01035e.html

Many Canadians and Canadian companies will face a financial crisis at some time. Some debt problems are easy to solve, while others need professional assistance. The best way to deal with your financial problems is to get control before they get out of hand.

This booklet may help you decide whether or not you have a serious debt problem. It also gives some suggestions for solving your difficulties and avoiding them in the future.

TEN THINGS YOU SHOULD KNOW ABOUT BANKRUPTCY[6]

1. What is bankruptcy and what are the benefits to the debtor?

Bankruptcy is a legal process, regulated by the Bankruptcy and Insolvency Act, by which you may be discharged from most of your debts. The purpose of the Act is to permit an honest, but unfortunate, debtor to obtain a discharge from his or her debts, subject to reasonable conditions. Once you are legally bankrupt, you are required to perform specific duties as outlined in the Act.

BANKRUPTCY
a legal process, regulated by the Bankruptcy and Insolvency Act, by which you may be discharged from most of your debts

2. How does one become bankrupt?

First, you meet with a trustee in bankruptcy who will assess your financial situation and explain other options available to you. If you decide to become bankrupt, the trustee will help you complete several forms which you will have to sign. You are considered a bankrupt only when the trustee files these forms with the Official Receiver.

3. What happens to my property?

When you declare bankruptcy, your property is given to a trustee in bankruptcy who then sells it and distributes the money among your creditors. Your unsecured creditors will not be able to take legal steps to recover their debts from you (such as seizing property or garnisheeing wages).

You do not have to assign to the trustee exempt property such as basic furniture, tools-of-trade and, under certain circumstances, the goods and services tax credit payments. Exempt property will vary from province to province. Your trustee can tell you what these are.

4. What kind of forms will I have to sign?

You will have to sign at least two forms. One is an "Assignment," and the other is your "Statement of Affairs." In the assignment, you state that you are handing over all of your property to the trustee for the benefit of your creditors. In the statement of affairs, you list your assets, liabilities, income, and expenses. In addition, you will have to answer several questions about your family, employment, and disposition of assets.

5. Does the bankruptcy affect my co-signers?

Your bankruptcy does not cancel the responsibility of anyone who has guaranteed or co-signed a loan on your behalf. For example, if your parent co-signed a loan for you, that parent would be liable to pay the loan in full even if you decide to file for bankruptcy.

6. When is a bankrupt discharged?

There will be an automatic discharge for first-time bankrupts nine months after they became bankrupt unless the trustee recommends a discharge with conditions or it is opposed by either a creditor, the trustee, or the Superintendent of Bankruptcy.

7. What is the effect of a bankruptcy discharge?

The bankrupt is released of most debts. However, some debts are not released, such as an award for damages in respect of an assault, a claim for alimony, spousal or child support, a debt arising out of fraud, any court fine, or debts or obligations for student loans when the bankruptcy occurs while the debtor is still a student or within 10 years after the bankrupt has ceased to be a student.

8. How does bankruptcy affect employment?

For the most part, bankruptcy should not affect your employment. However, there are some special cases. For example, you may have difficulty being bonded. Your trustee will be able to give you more information on other possible restrictions or prohibitions.

9. Is there anything I can do to improve my credit record?

Should you wish to improve your credit record after obtaining your discharge from bankruptcy, you could, for instance, contact your banker and request a meeting. For this meeting, you could bring your paycheque stubs, your budget, and your discharge papers. You could explain that you have obtained your discharge and ask the banker how you can earn your way back to a good credit record.

10. Does it cost anything to go bankrupt?

Yes. There is a filing fee to be paid to the Superintendent of Bankruptcy. In addition, the trustee is entitled to be paid. These fees are prescribed by the *Bankruptcy and Insolvency Rules*.

In a Nutshell

There are three basic legal forms for your small business: sole proprietorship, partnership, and corporation (limited company). You can run a business as a sole proprietorship with a minimum of difficulty. You might need only a city licence, a resale licence, and a business name. If you use a business name other than your own, you will probably need to register the name with your provincial government. Be careful, however—this may not give you exclusive rights to use the name.

The legal paperwork for a partnership is a little more involved. It may be possible to form a partnership with a handshake—but we wouldn't advise it. Get a lawyer and have a partnership agreement drawn up before you start. There are good skill-related reasons for forming a partnership. Let's say you're an inventor; you need a partner who can manage and sell. Let's say you're good at marketing; you need a partner who can run the office and keep the books. You may also form a partnership because you need the financial capital. Remember, however, these are the only two good reasons for forming a partnership—to provide skills and money. At least one of these needs must be met or you're asking for trouble. For example, friendship is not a good enough reason for a partnership arrangement.

Forming a limited company or corporation takes the most paperwork and costs the most money. However, it gives you the most flexibility, as well as a shield in case your business hurts someone.

In this chapter, we also discussed the government red tape that will confront you when you start your business. We recommended that you seek some legal protection for your business name. We also emphasized the importance of using a lawyer to help structure your business and prepare your will. Finally, we asked you to start thinking about some of the legal concerns arising from bankruptcy.

Key Terms

bankruptcy
cooperative
corporation
general partnership
limited partnership
partnership
sole proprietorship

Think Points for Success

- ✓ Know the advantages and disadvantages of the basic legal forms when you establish your business.
- ✓ Get a lawyer and a partnership agreement drawn up before you form a partnership.
- ✓ Incorporation can help limit your liability.
- ✓ Protect your business name and do a NUANS search to make sure you have not infringed on another business's name or trademark.

Business Plan Building Block

LEGAL STRUCTURE

State the type of legal structure—proprietorship, partnership, or a corporation—you intend to institute for your business. List the reasons why you chose this structure.

RED TAPE FILE

Set up a red tape file. Make a list of all the municipal, provincial, and federal regulations you are going to have to comply with. Beside each regulation, write the contact telephone number, address, and other pertinent information.

Checklist Questions and Actions to Develop Your Business Plan

LEGAL CONCERNS

- ❑ Explain why you selected your legal form of ownership.
- ❑ What professionals have you referenced in your business plan, and did you allow for the appropriate cost?
- ❑ What are the major legal risks for your industry, and how will you address them?

NOTES

1. Much of the research for this section was conducted on the Industry Canada, Strategis website (http://strategis.ic.gc).
2. Industry Canada, Corporations Directorate, *Small Business Guide to Federal Incorporation*, retrieved from http://strategis.gc.ca/SSG/cs01146e.html
3. Ibid.
4. David Chilton, *The Wealthy Barber* (Toronto: Stoddart Publishing, 1989), p. 67.
5. Ibid.
6. Adapted from Industry Canada, Office of the Superintendent of Bankruptcy, Dealing with Debt: A Consumer's Guide (http://strategis.ic.gc.ca/SSG/br01035e.html#Introduction).

SUGGESTED READING

Brandt, Steven C. *Stay Out of Court and in Business.* Archipelago Publishing, 1997.

Canada Customs and Revenue Agency. *Employer's Guide to Payroll Deductions.*

Canada Customs and Revenue Agency. *General Information for GST/HST Registrants.*

Canada Customs and Revenue Agency. *RC2: The Business Number and Your Canada Customs and Revenue Agency Accounts.*

Chilton, David, *The Wealthy Barber.* Toronto: Stoddart Publishing, 1989.

Industry Canada. Corporations Directorate. *Name Granting Guidelines.*

Industry Canada. Corporations Directorate. *Small Business Guide to Federal Incorporation.*

Kerr, Margaret, and Joann Kurtz. *Make It Legal: What Every Entrepreneur Needs to Know About the Law.* Toronto: John Wiley and Sons Canada, 1998.

Rurka, Bean P. "Commercial Leases for the Small Business." *Law Now*, October/November 1995, pp. 10–11.

Tillson, Tamsen. "Common Sense Resolution." *Canadian Business*, March 1997, pp. 83–89.

chapter 12

Building and Managing a Winning Team

BUSINESS PLAN BUILDING BLOCK

This chapter will help you manage your business and develop a team that shares your vision and enthusiasm.

LEARNING OPPORTUNITIES

After reading this chapter, you should be able to:

- Understand the basic management functions of leading and organizing.
- Chart your organizational structure.
- Consider the benefits of a virtual or network organization.
- Evaluate the skills that you and the members of your founding team possess.
- Take advantage of your board of directors and external advisers.
- Understand the value of an advisory board.
- Take another look at yourself and identify your strengths, weaknesses, and business needs.
- Use the idea of balance to brainstorm your ideal team and scout potential team members.
- Consider the merits of the just-in-time team, joint ventures, and strategic alliances.
- Realize the need for a mentor.
- Find a winning team of employees.
- Develop an action plan with your new team before you open the doors.
- Take a proactive approach to human resources.

ACTION STEP PREVIEW

53. Understand your personal strengths and weaknesses.
54. Consider a just-in-time team.
55. Find a mentor.
56. Tap your people resources by brainstorming with your team.

MSM Transportation Inc. is a successful PROFIT 100 company, but when Robert Murray and Mike McCarron started out in the late 1980s, they knew they were combining two different types of management expertise, plus two very different personalities. Mike, the company's managing partner and primary marketer, is boisterous and outgoing, passionate, and—as he admits—impulsive. Robert, MSM's president, trained originally as a credit manager, comes across as quiet, thoughtful, and more of a long-term thinker. Oil and water? Of course.

But Robert says the duo's strength lies in the fact that they can disagree, argue feverishly, work it out, and move on. With two partners who share a similar vision for the company, if not the same temperament, debate becomes a positive force that generates new ideas and better decisions. In an industry notorious for its lack of marketing and financial skills, MSM benefits from both personalities because they question each other's assumptions and strategies. Notes Robert, "My partner makes me much more effective and, I believe, much better at what I do."[1]

Chapter 12 will help you prepare parts F and G of your business plan. "Management" and "Personnel."

Your chances of success? Sixty-five percent of new businesses survive their first year; 30 percent survive their first five years; only 15 percent make it for 10 years. The key to your small business survival is how you build and manage your team.

Business success is all about working with people you trust and respect to accomplish your personal and business goals and objectives. Way back in Chapter 1, we explained that success meant different things to different people. Some say, for example, that success is the process of realizing goals that are driven by a compelling vision. We like this kind of definition; however, it makes no mention of the importance of achieving results through people, and today we can no longer make it happen without others. Our new changing economy has created the management need for people to work together to constantly generate new ideas. Today more than ever, business success will depend on how well we manage and work with people, and that is what this chapter is all about: working with people! We will start with the basics of management.

The Basics of Management

LEADING

In the old economy, you were the leader because you were the owner of the business. In the new economy, leadership has to be earned. You don't lead your employees because you own the company. You lead because your employees share your vision and want to follow you. **Leadership** is about creating the work climate that motivates people to do what is expected of them because they believe in what you are doing and share your vision.

LEADERSHIP

act of motivating others to do what is expected of them because they believe in what you are doing and share your vision

Researchers have identified the key ingredients of successful leadership. Studies consistently show that the so-called "transformational style" of leadership brings tremendous payoffs in company performance and innovation. This style has five types of behaviour that inspire exceptional performance:[2]

1. *Visioning.* The leader communicates a compelling vision of the future that is widely shared by the organization's members. The vision describes the ultimate outcome employees need to achieve. Transformational leaders lead by example and act in ways consistent with the vision.
2. *Inspiring.* The leader communicates the vision with passion, energy, and conviction, expresses optimism about the future, and shows enthusiasm about future possibilities. The leader generates excitement in the workplace and heightens others' expectations through symbols and images, which in turn build commitment to the vision.
3. *Stimulating.* The leader arouses interest in new ideas and approaches, and enables employees to think through problems in new ways. The leader who practises intellectual stimulation encourages the rethinking of ideas and the questioning of traditionally accepted ways of doing things. The leader considers "wild" ideas and supports divergent thinking. He or she uses reasoning and analytic thinking to problem-solve and select from the creative ideas generated.
4. *Coaching.* The leader coaches, advises and provides hands-on help for employees to develop their capabilities and improve their performance. He or she listens attentively, understands individual needs, motivations, and aspirations, and expresses encouragement, support, and confidence in individuals' abilities to meet the expectations inherent in the vision. The leader gives constructive feedback, encourages people to take on greater responsibilities, and provides opportunities for development by delegating challenging and interesting tasks.

5. *Team building.* The leader builds effective teams by selecting team members with complementary skills and encouraging them to work together toward common goals. He or she increases team confidence and commitment by giving positive feedback, sharing information, utilizing individuals' skills, and removing obstacles to team performance.

Peter Urs Bender tells us in his classic book, *Leadership from Within*, that this new style of leadership has five key steps:[3]

1. Know yourself: Identify your values, motivations, and personality type.
2. Have vision and passion: See what you love and love what you do.
3. Take risks: Be consistently courageous.
4. Communicate: Bring your vision to others, effectively and with confidence.
5. Check progress and results: Know where you are, so you can get where you want to go.

To learn more about what leadership is all about, see Box 12.1.

Now what is your leadership strategy? How will you empower—or give power to—your business? Be prepared to include a statement about how you are going to motivate your team to achieve the goals and objectives that will make you and them successful. Don't be afraid to show emotion. Emotion is a driving force and, in fact, some experts say that leadership is the emotional part of managing.

Box 12.1 Leadership from Within

Leadership is no longer about being in front of the pack, scoring the most goals, being first in sales, or having the highest position. Peter Urs Bender, "Canada's presentation guru," in his book *Leadership from Within*, helps us understand a new kind of leadership that must "come from within."

According to Bender, leadership is about:

1. **People.** The other things—sales, profit, equipment, numbers, and systems—are important, but they are just tools and measures to help us make progress.
2. **Being the leader of you.** Find a vision, put it into action, and you will automatically become the leader of others.
3. **Internal motivation.** The command-and-control "shape up or get out" behaviour is quickly being replaced with an approach that involves coaching, empowering, and inspiring.
4. **Striving for perfection, while accepting our imperfections.** Being a leader means accepting that we are human.
5. **Change.** It's about making conscious choices to bring about positive change.
6. **Confidence.** You must truly believe that things can be better.
7. **Growth.** Going beyond what we have done before.
8. **Energy.** Energy comes from your belief that something good is about to happen—a belief in a positive future. Energy is contagious.
9. **Creating a positive experience.** Leaders can motivate and make people feel excited and positive about work and life.
10. **Creating results.** True leadership is the ability to turn vision into results.
11. **Reducing fear and increasing hope.** Leaders are able to make changes and increase people's confidence and sense of hope.

Source: Peter Urs Bender, *Leadership from Within* (Toronto: Stoddart Publishing, 1997), pp. 7–11. Reprinted by permission of Stoddart Publishing Co. Limited, Toronto, Ontario.

ORGANIZING

In Chapter 11, we discussed ways in which you might want to organize your business—sole proprietorship, partnership, corporation, or cooperative. But you are also going to have to come to grips with such organizing questions as: What tasks are there to be done? Who does them? How are the tasks to be grouped? Who reports to whom? Where are decisions made? This means you are going to have to think about a structure or organizational framework that will help you accomplish these types of tasks.

The key to developing an organizational structure or framework for your business is to remember that we are deeply entrenched in a business environment that demands innovation, proactivity, and risk-taking. Businesses can no longer form bureaucratic structures that inhibit the transfer of information. Table 12.1 shows the basic differences between the new "organic" structures and the old mechanistic structures. Bureaucracies inhibit the flow of information. In the management section of your plan, you will have to explain how you will organize your activities and structure your business to focus on your target customer and respond to a changing environment.

Traditionally, most small business structures have been organized on the basis of function, geography, or type of customer. Examples of these traditional types of structures are shown in Figure 12.1.

Table 12.1 Organic versus Mechanistic Organizational Structure

Organic	Mechanistic
1. Channels of communication open, with free flow of information throughout the organization	1. Channels of communication highly structured, with restricted information flow
2. Operating styles allowed to vary freely	2. Operating styles must be uniform and restricted
3. Authority for decisions based on expertise of the individual	3. Authority for decisions based on formal line management position
4. Free adaptation by the organization to changing circumstances	4. Reluctant adaptation, with insistence on holding fast to tried and true management principles despite changes in business conditions
5. Emphasis on getting things done unconstrained by formally laid-out procedures	5. Emphasis on formally laid-down procedures, with reliance on tried and true management principles
6. Loose, informal control with emphasis on norm of cooperation	6. Tight control through sophisticated control systems
7. Flexible on-job behaviour permitted to be shaped by the requirements of the situation and personality of the individual doing the job	7. Constrained on-job behaviour required to conform to job descriptions
8. Participation and group consensus used frequently	8. Superiors make decisions, with minimum consultation and involvement of subordinates

Source: Adapted from Dr. Pradip N. Khandwalla, *The Design of Organization* (New York: Harcourt Brace Jovanovich, 1977), p. 411. Reprinted by permission of the author.

Figure 12.1 Charting Your Organizational Structure: Three Traditional Approaches

FUNCTIONAL

The functional approach to an organizational structure is one of the most widely used forms in small business. Teams are formed in accordance with the duties or functions they perform, such as accounting, service, or sales. Shown below is a simple functional organizational chart for a restaurant.

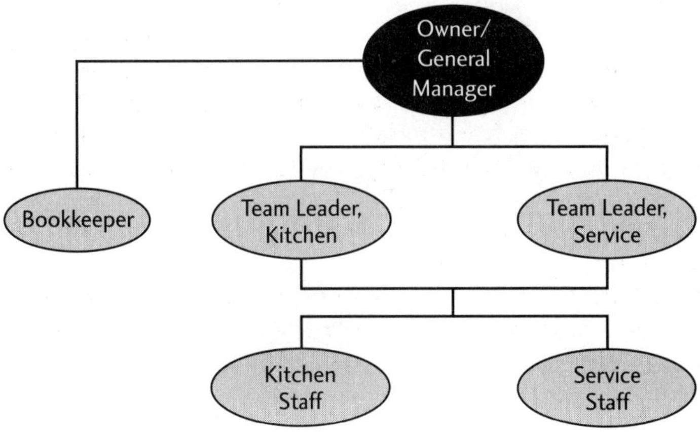

GEOGRAPHIC

Some types of independent businesses may decide to organize on the basis of geography. Provided below is an example of a "flat" service type of organization chart that has a structure based on territory or geography.

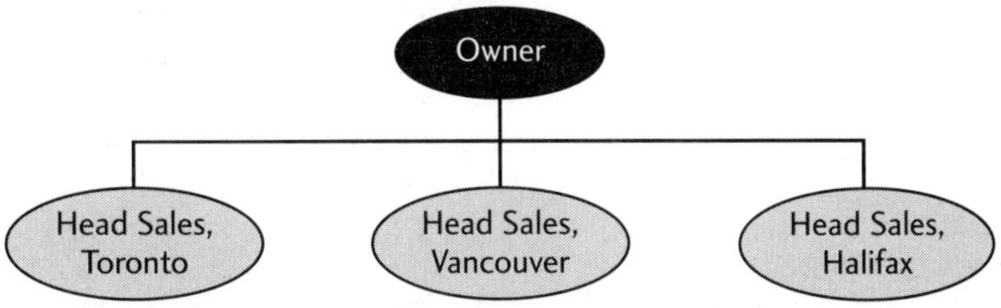

CUSTOMER-DRIVEN

Some independent businesses are starting to organize their company on the basis of type of customer. After all, it is the customer who drives the business. Here is one simple example of a small research and development organization that has a "customer-driven" organizational structure.

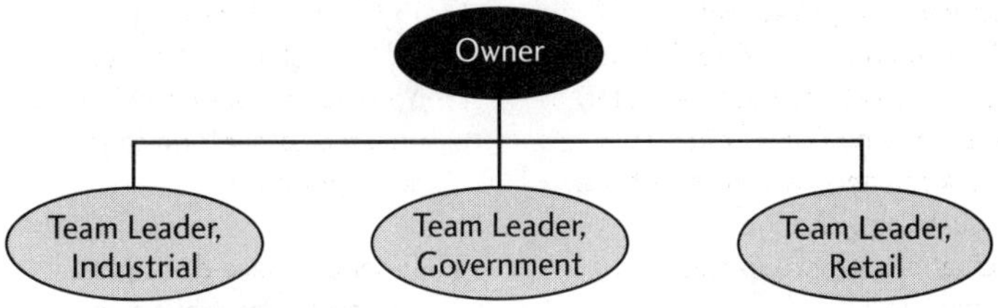

Source: Ron Knowles, *Writing a Small Business Plan: TVO Course Guide* (Toronto: Dryden, an imprint of Harcourt Brace & Company, Canada, 1995), pp. 49, 50. Reprinted by permission.

VIRTUAL ORGANIZATION (OR NETWORK ORGANIZATION)
organizational structure in which the major functions are broken up into strategic business units

STRATEGIC BUSINESS UNITS
independent teams or small businesses that support the functional needs of the main organization

At this point, we want you to consider the benefits of the **virtual** or **network organization.** In this type of organizational structure, the core business functions (such as sales, accounting, retail, and manufacturing) are separated from the main business by small businesses or independent teams, often called **strategic business units**. What this means is that a business no longer has to compete under one roof. Jobs like human resources, advertising, maintenance, and sales can be contracted out to small businesses on an as-needed basis or handled by remote employees.

Here's how the concept might work for an advertising agency. The entire agency might consist of only one person who presents the client with an idea. Once the idea is approved, the single person assembles "associates": graphic designers, copywriters, photographers, models, performers, and media experts to produce the package. The team is virtual—it is not housed in one central location, and might even have a "shamrock" structure as shown in Figure 12.2. This virtual ad agency has little staffing overhead, but can bring together the best talent to provide the client with a high-quality campaign at reasonable cost. Once the project is completed, the team of associates disbands, each member moving on to other projects.

For independent business, the virtual organization can allow the little guy to compete with the larger firm without sacrificing scale, speed, or agility. It is much like forming an all-star team to exploit a market opportunity. Here are some key characteristics of the virtual organization structure:[4]

- *It is customer-driven.* It is created to take advantage of a specific, customer-driven, time-based opportunity.
- *It is flexible.* It is disbanded when the opportunity ceases to exist.
- *It relies on mutual trust and teamwork.*
- *It is based on outsourcing.* Requirements are met with outside resources, not those from inside the organization.

Figure 12.2 The Shamrock Model

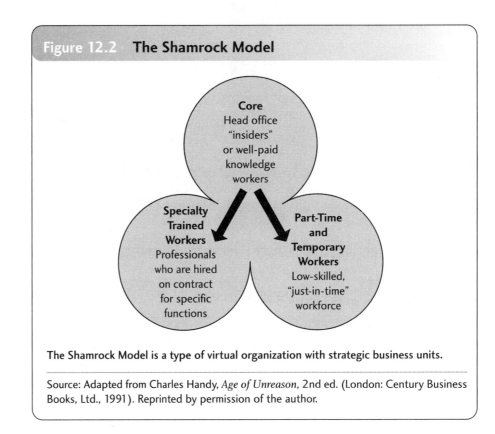

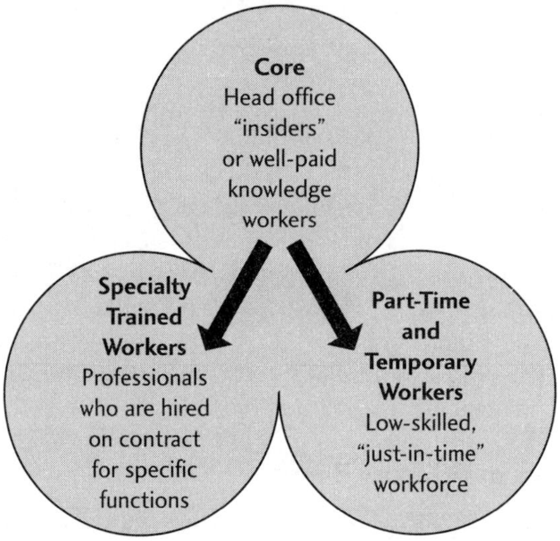

The Shamrock Model is a type of virtual organization with strategic business units.

Source: Adapted from Charles Handy, *Age of Unreason*, 2nd ed. (London: Century Business Books, Ltd., 1991). Reprinted by permission of the author.

- *It promotes supplier competition.*
- *It delegates selling duties to selling agents, not staff.*
- *It offers a web of associates or partners.* The corporate structure is linked by a web of alliances such as partnerships, joint ventures, and associates. This web replaces the traditional core functions such as manufacturing, warehousing, and supply.
- *It relies on outside expertise.* Emphasis is shifted from in-house knowledge to outside expertise.

Teamwork

THE FOUNDING TEAM[5]

A business is only as strong as the people who breathe life into it. Therefore, it is important to think about the skills that you and the members of your founding team possess and how these skills will help bring your product or service to market. Three areas you should focus on are management team profiles and ownership structure, the board of directors or advisory board, and human resources requirements.

Management Team Profiles and Ownership Structure

No matter how large or small your business is, good management is key to its success. It is important to think through and identify all management categories, necessary skill sets and possible job titles. It is not necessary to fill each position with a different person. You should, however, be able to identify the people who are capable of assuming roles when necessary, whether it be yourself or someone else. You should have a current copy of everyone's résumé in addition to profiles of each member of your management team (even if the team is just you) that demonstrates his or her unique skills. You should be able to describe how each person will add to the team's success. And you should be able to answer these questions:

- What are the major categories of business management in your company (marketing, sales, research, administration, etc.)? Explain the functions of yourself and key team members.
- Who are the people who have agreed to work with your business? What are their job descriptions?
- What positions are still unfilled at your company?
- What skills and job experience will the people who fill these positions have?
- What skills do you personally have (including any skills from last job or business). How do these skills correlate with your business?
- What is the compensation package for yourself and the management team (salary, benefits, profit-sharing schemes, etc.)?
- What work contracts, non-competition agreements, and other contractual agreements have you put in place for your management team?
- What is the ownership structure of your business (including percentages controlled by the management team, if applicable)?

Board of Directors or Advisory Board

Paul Obirek discovered the World Wide Web while attending university and it was love at first sight. Two-and-a-half years ago, Paul started a business to design corporate websites, but since that time, the Internet has grown by leaps and bounds. As a result, Paul changed gears and founded Winnipeg-based 21st Strategy Group in 1997. The company's main focus is e-commerce or, as Paul says, "helping business do business on the Internet."

Although Paul has 21 employees, he admits he doesn't have a strong business background. He credits much of his success to following good advice. "My attorney has been my best adviser," says Paul. "He has provided me with invaluable amounts of advice and has become a very strong mentor for me. He's a strong champion for us."

Paul urges other entrepreneurs to avoid the temptation of becoming overconfident. "My one biggest piece of advice, based on the traps I've seen other entrepreneurs fall into, is not to stop listening to your advisers and not to become too overconfident. I'm guilty of that just as much as anybody else. It's very important that you listen quite closely to your advisers."[6]

Creating a board or team of advisers for your company is an excellent way to benefit from the skills and expertise of people you may not yet be able to afford to employ. If you have decided to incorporate, now is the time to give some serious thought to your board of directors. In Chapter 11, you found out that, by law, you must have a board of directors. Many small companies take the easy route and simply elect key shareholders to the board. We want you now to think about forming a board that will provide true guidance and advice to your company. It is your chance to make a lawyer or accountant part of your team. If you need marketing help, elect a marketer. As we learned, your company's board of directors can make some very important decisions in the guidance and direction of your company. You do not want to lose this important opportunity to get outside expertise and advice.

But what happens if you have decided not to incorporate? You can also draw on the power of teamwork and advisers. Forward-looking entrepreneurs have created what is termed an "advisory board." You can include professionals such as bankers, lawyers, and accountants—even your small business professor. (It is important to make sure you look for board members who can supplement skills your business may be lacking; for example, if your business is technology based, try to include people with marketing and finance backgrounds.) Colleagues, associates, and friends can also take on a semi-official responsibility for the company's welfare, and meet with you four or five times a year to review your updated business plan or new objectives, or to discuss difficult problems. Some enterprising entrepreneurs we know have even created a customer board of advisers. Sound a little unusual? Not at all. Since customers drive a business, it only makes sense to set up a formal mechanism like a focus group to listen to their concerns. Even if you are incorporated, an advisory board can be a big advantage. You will need as much help as you can get.

For example, systems integrator Les Systèmes Zenon Inc., another PROFIT 100 company, has an advisory board called "Friends of Zenon." It is a group of advisers who consult on strategy and help head off any problems they see looming. The voluntary, unpaid board includes experts in related technology fields, the company's lawyer, an accountant, and a venture capitalist. "We're very cautious and don't want to lose our focus," Eric Bourbeau explains. "Before we take any potentially risky decisions, we go to those guys and we check everything out. That way we have enough qualified people around us to make sure we rarely do anything stupid."[7]

Human Resources Requirements

Once you have defined your management and advisory team, you need to think about the other employees or independent associates your business may or may not need and what their function(s) will be. In the beginning, it may be just you and a selection of freelance, contract, or part-time help. You will need to think ahead and consider all the options you may be faced with. You will need to understand the labour situation in the area and industry in which you're starting the business and make allowances for the compensation and training of your staff. And you will need to give some thought to the following questions:

- How many people do you require for your business?
- What specific skills do these employees and associates need to possess?
- Are your employees protected by workers' compensation coverage? Is your business registered with your provincial workers' compensation board/commission? Most businesses—by law—need to be.
- Is there sufficient local labour? How will you recruit people if there is not?
- How much does this labour cost now? In the future?
- How will you train your team?
- What is your policy for ongoing training for your team?

BUILDING BALANCE INTO YOUR TEAM

As we learned in the opening vignette, balance, not sameness, is essential in a winning team. For many entrepreneurs who have taken personal ownership of their ideas, finding this new freedom to let go and share their vision can be excruciatingly difficult. Entrepreneurs most in need of help are the stereotypical visionaries who founded a company and set out to do everything themselves. The day of the lone wolf operator is quickly coming to an end. Business today is just too complex. You need to realize that you cannot do everything yourself. You will need a team with different skills and personalities, depending on your strengths and the needs of the business. The key here is not to clone yourself. You need to surround yourself with people who can complement your skills.

> The successful partnership at Tescor Energy Services Inc. provides a good example of this principle. It is a PROFIT 100 company that helps schools, hospitals, and governments reduce energy costs. Gary Johnston, chief administrative officer and minority partner, uses the analogy of the *Starship Enterprise* in *Star Trek: The Next Generation* to describe the ownership team. Tom Tamblyn, the founder and majority shareholder of Tescor, is like Jean-Luc Picard. His strengths are personal integrity and insightful strategic thinking, with a good intuitive sense of what is happening in the market. Tamblyn brought Mario Iusi, chief operating officer, and Johnston on board as minority shareholders to accomplish his business mission. Iusi is described as being like the *Enterprise's* Ricker. A make-it-happen type of person, he combines an understanding of systems with a focused operational bent. Johnston likens himself to the ship's counsellor, Deanna Troi, who always tries to go to the heart of the organization and wants to know how people are feeling. Together, says Johnston, the three partners make a team worthy of the *Starship Enterprise*.[8]

This is a good time for a thorough self-assessment. Begin thinking about your strengths and weaknesses, and the kinds of people you are going to need to create your team. Complete Action Step 53. Then take one or more of the personality tests listed in Box 12.2.

ACTION STEP 53

Understand your personal strengths and weaknesses.

What do you need to be successful? Money, of course, and tremendous energy and leadership. You need a vision, a terrific idea, the ability to focus, a sense of industry and thrift, and the curiosity of Sherlock Holmes. Do you have all these qualities or personality traits? Of course not. That is why you need a team—people to support your effort and to take over tasks that you're weak in or you don't understand.

So we want you to analyze yourself. This will help you know the kind of team you need. Take a few minutes and complete the personality analysis created by Peter Urs Bender in Appendix 12.1 of this chapter. Follow this up by asking yourself: What do I like? What am I good at? What do I hate? What does my business need that I cannot provide myself? Who can fill this need for me?

These simple exercises will help you start building a winning team.

Box 12.2 E-Exercise

Your Personality Profile

- **Know Yourself and Know Others** (KYKO)
  http://kyko-profile.com/kykoonline1.html
  Use this psychological instrument, which is based on the theoretical constructs of Machiavelli and the Needs Theory, to discover yourself and others' personality profiles.
- **The Keirsey Temperament Sorter II** (AdvisorTeam)
  www.advisorteam.com/user/ktsintro.asp
  This online personality inventory, which tells you if you're an Artisan, a Guardian, a Rational, or an Idealist, is used in career development programs at Fortune 500 companies and in counselling centres and career placement centres at major universities.
- **Personality Tests**
  www.davideck.com/cgi-bin/tests/tests.cgi?action=personality
  This page contains links to personality tests ranging from the IPIP-Neo inventory to the P.E.T. Learning Style Assessment.

THE "JUST-IN-TIME" TEAM

You should be on the lookout for people who complement your personality/skills characteristics and compensate for your weaknesses. Because you need to work with people who take ownership of your vision, the "9 to 5" employee mentality may no longer be in the equation. In the traditional team, business owners thought of their members as employees, but your new dream does not have to take the form of an employee/employer relationship. Think outside the box. Think about such relationships as joint ventures or strategic alliances with other companies or formal associations/partnerships with individuals. How about subcontracting, or creating informal partnerships or associations?

JUST-IN-TIME TEAM
a group of individuals who are hired on a contract basis to perform a specific function

Here are a few examples of how **just-in-time teams** can help you:

> A general contractor pulls together a team of subcontractors who can be trusted to build a high-quality building. If the job goes well, there will be other opportunities for this team of specialists, but they only get paid while they are on contract.

> A local printer discovers that her sales ability exceeds her ability to produce. She redefines herself as a "printer's broker" and uses her knowledge to select the most appropriate product from a wide variety of printers. She then sells her own small shop to an employee and increases her income several times over by providing assistance to customers who know little about printing. Her virtual organization now has just-in-time access to hundreds of experienced printers.

With continued corporate downsizing come mushrooming opportunities for alert entrepreneurs to find just-in-time workers. The benefits include:

- Having access to the skills and experience of proven experts in their field.
- Paying only for services rendered.

- Reducing administrative and overhead costs.
- Gaining higher reliability.
- Achieving better quality and consistency.
- Having lower internal development costs.
- Getting a customer who is presold.
- Maintaining flexibility to address new market opportunities instantly.

The just-in time team needs to be customer-driven and opportunity-focused. There must also be agreement and a shared vision among all participants. Partners and opportunities must be selected with care. Performance standards will be critical. Flexibility and adaptability is important. Your just-in-time team might exist for a few weeks or a year or more. Then, when the opportunity has been fully exploited, the team must be prepared to disband quickly and move on to the next opportunity.

Now we want you to take a moment and consider a just-in-time team. Complete Action Step 54.

ACTION STEP 54

Consider a just-in-time team.

Make a list. Better still, create a mind map of the people or firms that might assist your efforts on an "as needed" basis—just-in-time team. Think about a joint venture or strategic alliance with vendors, suppliers, co-workers, and even competitors. Look for those who share your vision. Keep on the lookout and be prepared to expand this list or mind map as new ideas emerge.

PARTNERSHIPS

Consider as partners those firms with special capabilities that will share your risk in bringing a product or service to market. For example, if you have a new product, a team that includes retailers or end users could solve a lot of your marketing problems. Businesses usually form partnerships or associations in two fundamental ways: joint venture and strategic alliance.

Joint Venture

A **joint venture** is usually a goal-oriented cooperation among two or more businesses. It involves the creation of a separate organization owned and controlled jointly by the parties. The joint venture usually has its own management, employees, production systems, and so on. Cooperation is limited to defined areas and, often, a predetermined time frame.

JOINT VENTURE

partnership formed for a specific undertaking; it results in the formation of a new legal entity

Strategic Alliance

A **strategic alliance**, sometimes called a business network, is a goal-oriented cooperation among two or more businesses, based on formal agreements and a business plan. In contrast to a joint venture, however, it usually does not involve the establishment of a separate new organization. The objective is to improve the competitiveness and capabilities of the individual members by using the strengths of the team. Depending on the need, the network may be organized in a variety of forms with regard to function, structure, and organization. If you don't know a lot about strategic alliances, the Canadian Business Network Coalition (CBNC) is a great place to start. Spearheaded by the Canadian Chamber of Commerce and Industry Canada, the CBNC is made up of more than 100 business organizations and educational institutions across Canada. They can work with you to help you form a strategic alliance. Visit the "Business Networks" page on their website (see Box 12.3).

STRATEGIC ALLIANCE

goal-oriented partnership formed between companies to create a competitive advantage

THE INDEPENDENT CONTRACTOR OR ASSOCIATE

Although it is wise to build a web of complementary business associates to assure success of your start-up, the reality is that you may need an employee, or several. Should this be the case, you should first consider the benefits of the "near employee" or the independent contractor.

Box 12. 3 Bookmark This

Visit these web pages to learn more about networking and mentoring.

- **Business Networks** (Canadian Business Network Coalition)
  http://strategis.ic.gc.ca/SSG/mi03272e.html#summary
- **Contact! The Canadian Management Network**
  http://strategis.ic.gc.ca/sc_mangb/contact/engdoc/homepage.html
- **Mentor Programs** (Canadian Youth Business Foundation)
  www.cybf.ca/en_mentor.html
- **Young Entrepreneurs Association**
  www.yea.ca
  This not-for-profit organization provides peer support, social and networking opportunities, and education for entrepreneurs 35 years of age and under.

Many people misunderstand government rules on independent contractors. If you tell the worker when to start and stop work, and if you supply the tools or office equipment, you have an employee. On the other hand, if the work assignment is task- or project-driven, if the worker sets his or her own hours, if you pay by the job and not by the hour, and if most of the work takes place away from your office using the worker's resources, then you may have an independent contractor or associate relationship. Many real-estate agents, for example, that work on straight commission would qualify as independent contractors.

Think about using independent contractors or associates. If you pay by the job, on contract, you can save a lot of administrative costs. To start with, you only pay for work performed. You don't pay for coffee breaks. If the job is not done, you don't pay. Additional employee benefits that you, as an employer, pay take up a big chunk of your payroll. According to a KPMG survey, the wages and salaries that employers pay represent only about 58 percent of payroll costs. The remaining 42 percent are in benefits such as sick leave, employer's contribution to CPP, employment insurance, health insurance, and workers' compensation. What this means is that if you are expecting to pay $100 in wages, the real cost will be $172—$100 for wages and $72 for benefits.[9]

A strong word of caution is in order. You need to be careful about the legal ins and outs of hiring on contract. We strongly recommend you check with both provincial/territorial and federal employment bodies, especially the Canada Customs and Revenue Agency, before you contract work out. Make sure, in writing if you can, that they will accept the conditions you set out for your associates or independent contractors.

GET A MENTOR

James and Brenda found their business mentor when they took a two-day "Look Before You Leap" small business seminar. In time, they were able to bounce ideas back and forth and get valuable feedback from a guest speaker at the seminar who had 25 years of experience in the school of hard knocks. "We couldn't have done it without her," says Brenda. "She gave us strength, direction, and confidence. She agreed to be our mentor on the condition that we become a mentor for a new business owner once we became successful. That made us feel good. For her, it was not a question of if we were going to be successful, it was a question of when. She believed in us—unconditionally."

For independent business, **mentoring** is a mutually beneficial partnership between a more experienced entrepreneur or businessperson, and an entrepreneur who is in the infant or start-up phase of a venture. The experienced partner is one who is reflective about his or her venture and is able to communicate and share his or her understanding and knowledge about what has made the venture grow. The inexperienced entrepreneur or protégé is receptive to the suggestions of the mentor and is also willing to try to implement some of them in the new business.

Mentoring is an ongoing partnership that may last for a number of months before any benefits are realized by either partner. The partners need to commit themselves to regular meetings with a focused agenda. Usually, the mentor has more frequent and in-depth involvement than the advisory board.

Much of what is learned in small business comes from experience, since business, to a large extent, is an art. To be successful, we need to know how successful entrepreneurs think. We need help and direction, and in many cases we will not be able to get what we need from a book. That is why we need a mentor, someone who can give us start-up advice and encouragement.

Essential qualities of an effective small business mentor you should look for include:

- *A desire to help.* Individuals who are interested in, and willing to help, others.
- *Past positive experiences as entrepreneur.* Individuals who have had positive formal or informal experiences with a mentor.
- *A good reputation for developing others.* Individuals who have a good reputation for helping others develop their skill.
- *Time and energy.* Individuals who have the time and mental energy to devote to the relationship.
- *Up-to-date knowledge in the related field.* Individuals who have maintained current, up-to-date technological knowledge or skills.
- *A learning attitude.* Individuals who are still willing and able to learn and who see the potential benefits of a mentoring relationship.
- *Demonstrated effective managerial and mentoring skills.* Individuals who have demonstrated effective coaching, counselling, facilitating, and networking skills.

Although we strongly suggest you get a mentor, mentoring relationships do not always succeed the first time. Four of the most frequent problems with mentoring relationships include:[10]

- *Personality mismatch.* One or both members of the relationship may feel uneasy with the other or they may not be able to achieve the level of friendship necessary for rich communication.
- *Unrealistic expectations.* It is important that expectations are clearly defined from the beginning.
- *Breaches of confidentiality.* In order to develop the type of relationship in which the mentor can be effective, he or she must first be perceived as trustworthy and able to keep confidences, and vice versa.
- *Lack of commitment.* Both parties must do what they say and say what they do.

Table 12.2 provides some guidelines for choosing your mentor. Now it's your turn. Start looking for your mentor. Complete Action Step 55.

MENTORING

a mutually beneficial partnership between a more experienced entrepreneur or businessperson, and an entrepreneur who is in the infant or start-up phase of a venture

ACTION STEP 55

Find a mentor.

First develop a list of attributes you are looking for in a mentor, and areas where you need help. Network with your friends, coworkers, and business associates. Tell them what you're looking for—that is, a successful business owner with a good track record. The perfect mentor would be one with experience in your particular segment. You can also contact your local chamber of commerce or one or more of your local business clubs. See if your local small business centre can help. You can even look for a virtual mentor on the Internet; visit the "Mentor Programs" page on the Canadian Youth Business Foundation website (see Box 12.3).

Once you have located some candidates, develop a set of questions and set up a meeting to pick their brains. Here are some things to consider in selecting a mentor:

- Do you feel comfortable with this person?
- Can you trust him or her?
- Is he or she easy to communicate with?
- Does he or she have experience and contacts that can help your new business?
- Is he or she willing to devote the time to help you?

After you have made your choice and the person has agreed to help you, keep in close contact. See the person at least once a month. Set up regular meetings with an agenda, and use the phone or e-mail to smooth out rough spots.

Table 12.2 Characteristics of Mentors

Mentors Are	Your Mentor Must
winners	have extensive business experience
humble	have at least one admitted failure
caring	truly care about you as a person
believers	truly believe you can move mountains
guides	be able to guide and direct without preaching
encouragers	be able to encourage the answer from within you
honest	have the strength and knowledge to be honest with you
empathizers	be able to empathize, not sympathize
listeners	want to spend time listening to you
excited	be excited about your ideas

Source: Ronald A. Knowles and Debbie White, *Issues in Canadian Small Business* (Toronto: Dryden, an imprint of Harcourt Brace & Company, Canada, 1995), p. 78. Reprinted by permission.

THE FIRST EMPLOYEES

When to hire your first employee is a question often asked. You may require people immediately, but many small firms do well using part-time or temporary workers until the owners have a strong feel for what needs to be done and who is best suited to do the job.

If the first worker needs to provide a high level of technical skill or is a person who can take your organization to the next level, you may need to provide an extra carrot, such as a profit-sharing option. A lot of talented workers prefer the entrepreneurial adventure to big business bureaucracy and will work for less if they share your vision and passion for entrepreneurism.

As you continue to add people, competence is not enough. You are assembling a venture team that wants to see growth and prosperity as much as you do. It is impossible to grow and expand until you have people who are equally capable and motivated to ensure success.

The quest for new employees begins with a written job description. You may not find a perfect fit so don't fence yourself in with too many specifications, yet don't overlook your future needs. Define the duties to be performed and the skills needed to perform them. A small business cannot afford a misfit or an unproductive person. If one person in a four-person organization doesn't work, you have lost 25 percent of your efficiency. Hiring and keeping good people is a critical factor in a firm's success.

If experience is not critical, consider vocational, trade, and professional schools. Local colleges and high schools have placement offices. Often programs are offered through social agencies where the government subsidizes worker training. Always check to see what's being offered. Government often creates programs to encourage employment and help small businesses. The best place to begin your search is the "Employers and Entrepreneurs" page on the Human Resources Development Canada website (see Box 12.4).

Stay out of trouble. In general, you can stay out of trouble if you avoid asking the following questions of a job applicant.

1. Age or birth date
2. Place of birth
3. A woman's maiden name

Box 12.4 Bookmark This

Human Resources Planning and Recruitment

- **Employers and Entrepreneurs** (Human Resources Development Canada) www.hrdc-drhc.gc.ca/common/employr.shtml#addbus
- **Employment Standards Legislation in Canada** (Human Resources Development Canada) http://labour-travail.hrdc-drhc.gc.ca/psait_spila/lmnec_eslc/index.cfm?fuseaction=english

4. Racial or ethnic background
5. Religious affiliation
6. Marital status and sexual orientation
7. Number of children and ages
8. Medical condition or non-job-related physical data
9. Disabilities

Issues related to human rights, employment standards, and hiring are complicated, so the government has created brochures to help explain various regulations. About 90 percent of employee rights legislation comes under provincial jurisdiction, and provincial laws can vary extensively. Failure to follow any legal requirements can result in stiff penalties or even lawsuits from a disgruntled employee. So the best advice we can give you is to be very careful about what you say and check with your provincial labour departments if you have any doubts. You may find it beneficial to use an employment agency to hire your first few employees. For more information on hiring and other human resources planning issues, visit the web pages listed in Box 12.4.

Ask the right questions. The trick is to prepare a list of questions that solicit responses to applicants' skills, experiences, or knowledge needed in the job. Similar questions should be asked of each applicant so that you can evaluate their responses and suitability. You may want to look over a few books that employees use to prepare for job interviews. These could give you ideas on questions to ask. To start, here are some questions that you could use:

1. How did you prepare for this meeting?
2. Why do you want to work for us?
3. How do your skills match the job description?
4. What would you do in the following situation? (Explain a problem they may face on the job.)
5. What type of training will you need to perform this job?
6. What are some of the obstacles you have overcome?
7. What do you expect from a boss?
8. What gives you satisfaction in a job?
9. What do you think you will like most and least about this particular job?
10. What kinds of things disturb you on the job?
11. What have been your most pleasant work experiences?
12. What do you want to be doing in five years?
13. What would your references say about you?
14. What did you like or dislike about your last job?

The growth in part-time employment is exploding. Today, more than one in five workers are part-timers (working less than 30 hours per week). There are a number of advantages for firms in hiring part-time employees. First, since part-time wage rates are typically 60 percent of regular full-time wages, you can reduce your labour costs significantly. Part-time workers usually receive fewer benefits, which reduces yet another company expense. Part-time employment can also be an effective strategy for companies to benefit from the experience of the "retired" workforce, which, as we know, is a growth segment. You need to weigh these benefits against some of the negative long-term implications. For example, overreliance on part-timers may leave your company without any experience or continuity. This could stifle your growth potential, since part-time workers normally have less commitment to you. In addition, the lack of continuity and loyalty becomes an issue if your company contracts out or outsources work. Contractors tend to go where there is money and where long-term contracts are available.

Now, let's see how Charlene Webb built her business using a team of high-energy part-time employees.

After Charlene Webb sold her gourmet cookware shop, she opened a women's specialty store. The shop is small—about 3000 square feet—and is located in a neighbourhood centre in an upscale community of about 10 000 people.

Charlene discovered that her ideal employees were local women who are active in community life and who prefer to work only one day a week. Monday's help is a golfer whose country-club friends come in to visit and buy from her on her day of work. Tuesday the tennis player is on, and her friends have followed her to the store. Wednesday is the yacht club member; Thursday is a leader of hospital volunteers; Friday is a well-known club woman; Saturday is an attorney's wife. All of them are friendly women who know a lot about fashion and have a lot of energy, because they never have a chance to tire from the routine.

Charlene, who writes a society column (as free PR) in the community newspaper, has positioned herself as a social force, and many women have come to view her shop as *the one* to buy from for formal events at the country club and the nearby Ritz Carleton Hotel.

Her part-time helpers are not only an effective marketing tool; they also serve as local fashion consultants. They help Charlene make wise purchasing decisions. They are valuable members of her team, and they are friends as well.

Now it's your turn again. Action Step 56 is to be completed once you have built your team. It's your chance to brainstorm for ways to win. Make the most of all the creative human resources you have just brought on board! Action Step 56 is a great way to end this chapter on team building, and a great way to start your new business.

ACTION STEP 56 (Action Steps)

Tap your people resources by brainstorming with your team.

Before you sign a lease, go into the hole for $50 000 worth of equipment, hire a lot of people, or spend $2000 for a six-line telephone service, get your new team together and brainstorm the organization and objectives of your new business.

A flip chart is a handy tool for keeping track of ideas. One way to begin is to ask all members of your team to write down what they believe would be good objectives to achieve business goals.

You've found some good people, and it's taken some hard work. Make that work pay off by tapping your human resources. Participation leads to commitment. You'll be surprised at how this process can be a good team builder.

If you have trouble narrowing down after the ideas start flowing, go back and review the seven-step procedure in Chapter 3.

In a Nutshell

Leading is a key management function and you'll have to learn how to inspire and empower your team. In addition, you will have to be able to justify and chart your organizational structure. We want you to consider the benefits of a virtual or network organization. We also want you to understand that you won't be able do everything yourself. You will need a founding team with different skills and personalities, depending on your strengths and weaknesses and the needs of the business. We encourage you to think outside the box by considering less traditional team arrangements such as subcontracting, joint ventures, strategic alliances, and mentoring. We also encourage you to take a proactive approach to human resources planning and recruitment.

Key Terms

joint venture
just-in-time team
leadership
mentoring
strategic alliance
strategic business units
virtual organization (or network organization)

Think Points for Success

- ✓ People tend to "hire themselves." How many more like you can the business take?
- ✓ A winning team is lurking in your network.
- ✓ Look to your competitors and vendors for team members.
- ✓ Your company is people.
- ✓ Balance the people on your team.
- ✓ Have each team member write objectives for his or her responsibilities within the business.
- ✓ You can't grow until you have the right people.
- ✓ How much of your team can be built of part-timers and moonlighters?
- ✓ How virtual can you make your business structure?
- ✓ Can you form a joint venture or a strategic alliance?

Business Plan Building Block

GENERAL MANAGEMENT

Who's in charge? Investors or vendors are often more interested in the founders than in the business plan itself. Experience in the same type of business and past business successes are powerful positive components of the plan. Focus on responsibility and authority.

A paragraph or two may be sufficient for each key founder. If retail experience is lacking, list consultants or committed strategic partners who can balance the management team. An organizational chart might be included.

MANAGEMENT AND OWNERSHIP

Name the key players and include their résumés, focusing on their contribution to your business and how they will give you a competitive edge. Save the full-blown résumés of the management team members for the appendix in the back of the plan.

The lender, vendor, or venture capital firm weighs the founding team as one of the most important factors. Present balance and diversity with a history of past achievement. It is here where you would explain your business form (incorporation, partnership, sole proprietorship, or cooperative). If you have more than two people on the team, include an organizational chart.

Your turn again: Who are the players in your business and what role will each play?

List consultants, advisory board members, or strategic partners who can contribute experience or special skills.

HUMAN RESOURCE PLAN

1. Type of workers needed. Include just-in-time, seasonal, or part-time workers

2. Compensation, commissions, bonuses, profit sharing

3. Provincial and federal compliance requirements

4. Performance standards, training, and retraining

5. Workers' compensation and insurance cost

6. Employee handbook (look for professional help)

7. Union contracts

8. Professional certifications

Checklist Questions and Actions to Develop Your Business Plan

BUILDING AND MANAGING A WINNING TEAM

- ❑ What major human resource issues does your business face, and how do you plan to address these issues?
- ❑ Have you included an employment schedule in your appendix and corresponding wage costs for your staff and yourself?
- ❑ Have you allowed for benefits? At a minimum to comply with legal statutory requirements, you need to consider at least 20 percent of your wage and salary costs for benefits.
- ❑ Do you have job descriptions in place and plans to conduct an annual performance appraisal?
- ❑ Do your wage rates fit within the industry norm, and do you pay more than the industry if you are planning to be a "top draw" company?
- ❑ Outline your leadership style, and your strengths and weaknesses as an entrepreneur.
- ❑ How might a "virtual organization" work for you?
- ❑ If you are starting out just with yourself, at what point in sales or other volume indicator will you add a second or a third person?

NOTES

1. Adapted from Rick Spence, *Secrets of Success from Canada's Fastest-Growing Companies* (Toronto: John Wiley & Sons Canada, 1997), pp. 98–99.
2. Excerpted from J. Howell and B. Avolio, "The Leverage of Leadership," *The Globe and Mail*, May 15, 1998, p. C1. © 1998 Ivey Management Services. Used with permission from Ivey Management Services.
3. Peter Urs Bender, *Leadership from Within* (Toronto: Stoddart Publishing, 1997), p. 23. Reprinted by permission of Stoddart Publishing Co. Limited, Toronto, Ontario.

4. Adapted from Steven L. Goldman, Roger N. Nagel, and Kenneth Preiss, *Agile Competitors and Virtual Organizations* (New York: Van Nostrand Reinholdt, 1995).
5. Information for much of this section is excerpted or adapted from Royal Bank, Business Plans, "The Team" (www.royalbank.com/sme/bigidea/team.html).
6. Excerpted from Royal Bank, Today's Entrepreneur, "Listen and Learn" (www.royalbank.com/sme/te/p_obirek.html).
7. Spence, *Secrets of Success*, p. 102.
8. Ibid., pp. 99–100.
9. Cited in Bruce Little, "Statistics Belie Perception of Less Help for the Needy, Part II," *The Globe and Mail*, January 20, 1994, pp. A1, A6.
10. Canadian Youth Business Foundation (www.cybf.ca/en_mentor.html).

SUGGESTED READING

Addresso, Patricia J. *Get to Know Your Employees Before You Manage Them*. New York: AMACOM, 1996.

Bendaly, Leslie. *Games Teams Play*. Whitby, ON: McGraw-Hill Ryerson, 1996.

Bendaly, Leslie. *Organization 2000: The Essential Guide for Companies and Teams in the New Economy*. Toronto: HarperCollins, 1996.

Butteriss, Margaret. *Help Wanted: The Complete Guide to Human Resources for Canadian Entrepreneurs*. Etobicoke, ON: John Wiley & Sons Canada, 1999.

Canadian Business Networks Coalition (CBNC). *How to Network Book: A Practical Guide for Successful Strategic Alliances*. CBNC, 1997.

Drucker, Peter F., and Peter M. Senge. *Leading in a Time of Change: What It Will Take to Lead Tomorrow*. New York: Wiley, 2001.

Fisher, Kimball, and Maureen Duncan Fisher. *The Distance Manager: A Hands-on Guide to Managing Off-Site Employees and Virtual Teams*. New York: McGraw-Hill, 2000.

Kotter, John P. *Leading Change*. Boston, MA: Harvard Business School Press, 1996.

Maxwell, John C. *Developing the Leader Within You Workbook*. Nashville, TN: Thomas Nelson, 2001.

Moss, Kanter Rosabeth. *On the Frontiers of Management*. Boston, MA: Harvard Business School Press, 1997.

Sutton, Walt. *Leap of Strength: A Personal Tour Through the Months Before and Years After You Start Your Own Business*. Los Angeles: Silver Lake Publishing, 2000.

Urs Bender, Peter. *Leadership from Within*. Toronto: Stoddart Publishing, 1997.

Appendix 12.1

The Personality Analysis

Take a few minutes to do the following simple self-assessment. You will learn some fascinating things about yourself in the process. You may also want to compare yourself to others you know—a significant other, your children, or your co-workers.

In the following lists, underline those words (or phrases) that describe you best in a *business* or *work situation*. Total your score for each group of words.

GROUP

A Reserved, uncommunicative, cool, cautious, guarded, seems difficult to get to know, demanding of self, disciplined attitudes, formal speech, rational decision making, strict, impersonal, businesslike, disciplined about time, uses facts, formal dress, measured actions.

Total score: __________

B Take-charge attitude, directive, tends to use power, fast actions, risk-taker, competitive, aggressive, strong opinions, excitable, takes social initiative, makes statements, loud voice, quick pace, expressive voice, firm handshake, clear idea of needs, initiator.

Total score: ________

C Communicative, open, warm, approachable, friendly, fluid attitudes, informal speech, undisciplined about time, easygoing with self, impulsive, informal dress, dramatic opinions, uses opinions, permissive, emotional decision making, seems easy to get to know, personal.

Total score: ________

D Slow pace, flat voice, soft-spoken, helper, unclear about what is needed, moderate opinions, calm, asks questions, tends to avoid use of power, indifferent handshake, deliberate actions, lets others take social initiative, risk-avoider, quiet, go-along attitude, supportive, cooperative.

Total score: ________

Write your total scores below:

A = ________ C = ________

B = ________ D = ________

Next, determine which groups are larger and by how much:

A vs. C: Which is larger? ________

By how many points? ________

B vs. D: Which is larger? ________

By how many points? ________

Filling in the Personality Grid

Now mark your results on the grid below:

To determine where you fit on the vertical axis, look at your A vs. C result. For example:

If A was larger than C by 6 points, put a dot (•) at **A-6**.
If C was larger than A by 5 points, put a dot (•) at **C-5**.
If A and C are equal, put a dot (•) at "0," in the centre of the grid.

To find your place on the horizontal axis, use your B vs. D result.

If B was larger than D by 4 points, put a dot (•) at **B-4**.
If D was larger than B by 7 points, put a dot (•) at **D-7**.
If B and D are equal, put a dot (•) at "0," in the centre of the grid.

In the grid on page 262, draw an X where lines extending from your two points meet (as shown in the sample). The quadrant you're in indicates your personality type.*

*These four personality types are adapted from *Personality Styles and Effective Performance*, by David W. Merrill and Roger H. Reid.

This sample grid shows the results for two different people: one is called a driver; the other is amiable.

Sample Grid

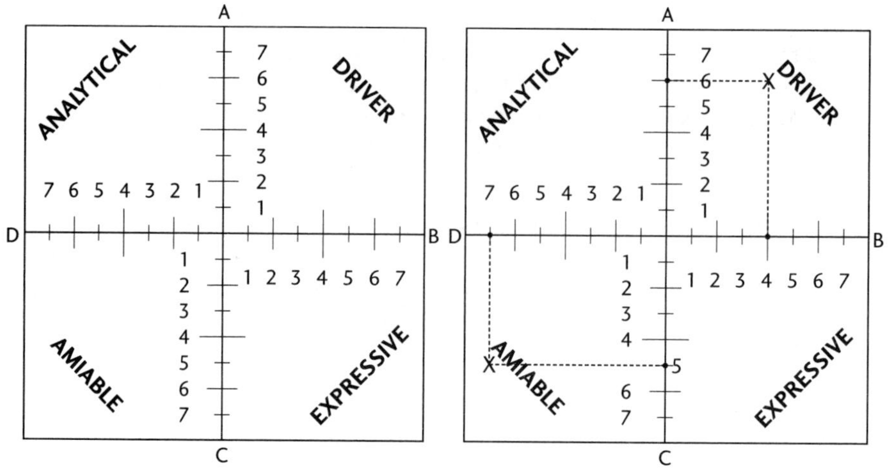

Interpreting Your Results

Now that you know where you fit, let's find out what it means!

The following words describe each of the personality types. Read those that apply to you, and see how these words fit your image of your own personality. Then ask others what they think. It helps to get different perspectives.

After considering your own personality, look at people around you. What personality types do they exhibit?

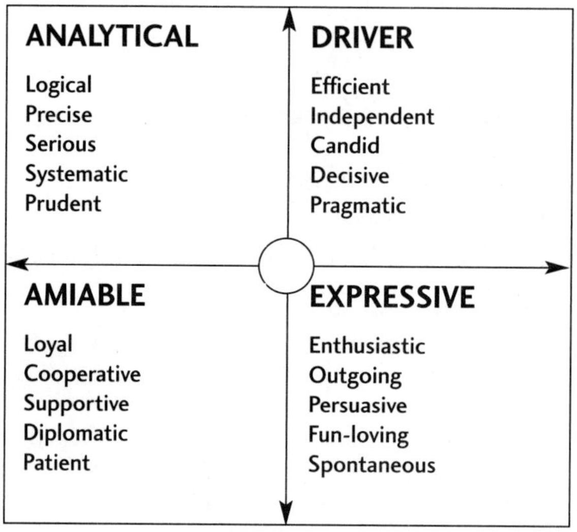

Remember that there is no right or wrong personality type. Different types simply think and act in different ways.

Understanding the Personality Types

Each personality has different needs, values, and motivations. Different levels of assertiveness and responsiveness. Here are some general insights into each type—and some tips to help you get through life a little more easily.

THE ANALYTICAL

Also known as:
Melancholic
Thinker
Thought Person
Processor
Cognitive

The analytical person:

- wants to know "how" things work
- wants to be accurate, and to have accuracy from others
- values numbers, statistics, ideas
- loves details.

Analyticals fear being embarrassed or losing face. They also tend to be introverted and to hide their emotions from others.

THE AMIABLE

Also known as:
Phlegmatic
Feeler
People Person
Helper
Interpersonal

The amiable person:

- wants to know "why?" (e.g., Why am I doing this?)
- wants to build relationships
- loves to give others support and attention
- values suggestions from others.

Amiables fear losing trust or having disagreements with others. While somewhat introverted, they also tend to display their emotions.

THE DRIVER

Also known as:
Choleric
Director
Action Person
Boss
Behavioural

The driver:

- wants to know "what" (What will this do for me/the firm?)
- wants to save time

- values results
- loves being in control, in charge, doing things his or her own way.

Drivers fear giving up control. They tend to be extroverts, but do not like showing their emotions to others.

THE EXPRESSIVE

Also known as:

Sanguine
Intuitive
Front Person
Impulsive
Affective

The expressive person:

- wants to know "who" (Who else is involved; who else have you worked for?)
- values appreciation, applause, a pat on the back
- loves social situations and parties
- likes to inspire others.

Expressives fear being rejected. They are extroverts and usually show their emotions to others.

Source: Peter Urs Bender, *Leadership from Within* (Toronto: Stoddart Publishing, 1997), pp. 60–65. Reprinted by permission of Stoddart Publishing Co. Limited, Toronto, Ontario.

chapter 13

Buying a Business

BUSINESS PLAN BUILDING BLOCK

This chapter will help you investigate the advantages and pitfalls of buying a business.

LEARNING OPPORTUNITIES

After reading this chapter, you should be able to:

- Evaluate objectively businesses that are for sale.
- Understand the pros and cons of purchasing an ongoing business.
- Assess the market value of an ongoing business.
- Recognize when you need professional help.
- Decide whether it is better for you to buy an ongoing business or to begin from scratch.

Ben and Sally Raymundo bought a women's sportswear store in a thriving community about two kilometres from a regional shopping mall. They learned too late that the seller had a more profitable store in another part of the county and that she had used that store's records to misrepresent the store they bought. Here are the particulars:

1. The seller moved the cash registers from the higher-volume store to the store she wanted to sell so that the store's sales were greatly inflated.
2. The price was fixed at inventory plus $10 000 for goodwill. This seemed a bargain for a store whose cash register records showed it was grossing $300 000 per year at a 40 percent average gross margin.
3. Ben and Sally paid full wholesale value ($60 000) for goods that had been shipped there from the other store. The goods were already shopworn and out of date and eventually had to be marked down to less than $20 000.
4. Ben and Sally assumed the remainder of an ironclad lease at $5000 per month, and the landlord made them sign a personal guarantee that pledged their home as security on the lease.

ACTION STEP PREVIEW

57. Prepare a letter of inquiry.
58. Study a business from the outside.
59. Study a business inside out.
60. Probe the depths of ill will.

Chapter 13 investigates the alternative of buying an existing business.

5. The location proved to be a dead foot-traffic location in a marginally successful centre.

Fortunately, Ben had kept his regular job. Sally worked at selling off the unwanted inventory and replaced it with more salable stock. They spent another $50 000 for advertising during the 12 months they stayed in business. It was another year before the landlord found a new tenant and Ben and Sally could get out of the lease.

In this chapter, you'll learn some ways to evaluate businesses that are up for sale. Although we focus on ongoing, independent operations, many of the tactics are the same for evaluating franchise opportunities. We'll discuss franchising more specifically in Chapter 14.

When you buy an ongoing business, you're buying an income stream. You may also be buying inventory, location, goodwill, and an agreement that the sellers will not compete with you. In addition, you may also be buying a training program, a business plan, advertising assistance, lease negotiation assistance, and purchasing advantages.

You should explore businesses for sale whether you're serious about buying or not. By now, you're far enough along on your quest to sense an understanding of the marketplace. Talking to sellers is just one more step in your education in entrepreneurship.

Here are some tips to get you started on your exploration of the pros and cons of buying a business:

1. *Determine which type of entrepreneur you are before taking the plunge.* Some businesspeople are "serial entrepreneurs." They seek out and purchase a business with turnaround potential, work to restore the business to financial health, and sell the revitalized business at a profit. Other entrepreneurs, on the other hand, thrive on the start-up phase of the entrepreneurial journey and are not so interested in the day-to-day operations. A review of the self-assessment Action Steps you completed in Chapter 1 will provide valuable clues as to your own entrepreneurial strengths and weaknesses.
2. *Fall in love with the business, not the deal.* As you conduct your search, make finding the "right opportunity"—as opposed to getting the "right price"—a priority. Ask yourself such questions as: Do I have what it takes to manage this business day in and day out? Will I enjoy interacting with the customers? With the employees? Can I see myself working each day to improve this business? Am I passionate about the business?
3. *Obtain legal representation and financial advice before you sign the contract.* The importance of due diligence cannot be overstated.

Why Purchase an Ongoing Business?

The overwhelming reason for buying an ongoing business is *money*, primarily the income stream, which makes it a good deal. If you do your research and strike a good deal, you can start making money the day you take over an ongoing business. Since most start-ups must plug along for months (even years) before showing a profit, it's smart to consider the business ownership option.

If you find a "hungry seller," you should be able to negotiate good terms. You might get into the business for very little cash up front, and you might also get a good deal on the fixtures and equipment.

HOW TO BUY AND HOW NOT TO BUY

Smart buyers scrutinize everything about a business with a microscope, a Geiger counter, computer analysis, a clipboard, and sage advice from business gurus. They do not plunge into a business for emotional reasons. For example, you may have eaten lunch around the corner at Millie's Cafeteria with your pals for years, and when the place goes up for sale, nostalgia may make you want to write out a cheque for it on the spot. That would be a wrong reason to buy. Don't buy a business that way.

Every business in the country is for sale sometime. Deals are like planes. If you miss one, another will be along soon.

Good buys are always available to the informed and careful buyer, but they may be difficult to discover. Seeking the right business to buy is much like an employment search: the best deals are seldom advertised. In contrast, the worst business opportunities are advertised widely, usually in the classified sections of newspapers. When you see several ads for a particular type of business, you know where the unhappy businesspeople are.

Running your own ad can be a good idea, however. A man ran this ad in the business section (not the classifieds) of a large-circulation Toronto newspaper:

> Sold out at 30. Now I'm tired of retirement and ready to start again. Want to buy a business with over $1 million in annual sales. Write me at Box XXXX. H.G.

H.G. received more than 100 replies, and he says that reading the proposals was one of the most educational and entertaining experiences he's ever had. Five of them looked like good deals, but only one fit his talents and interests. After three months of investigation, he decided he would rather start his next venture from scratch. (The firm he almost bought was a beer distributorship whose supplier went out of business the following year. Perhaps the seller knew something.)

ACTION STEP 57

Prepare a letter of inquiry.

Write a form letter of inquiry and send it to three to five firms that you may be interested in buying. Keep it open-ended; let them make the disclosures.

It's best to learn about businesses for sale by networking, but you can find some of the most eager sellers by their advertising in the newspaper classified section.

Leave your chequebook right where it is for now. This Action Step will cost you practically nothing. The goal is to learn what's out there and how sellers talk about their businesses.

GETTING THE WORD OUT

Once you're ready to look for a business to buy, you'll need to learn what's for sale. These tips will help you do that:

1. Spread the word that you are a potential buyer.
2. Contact everyone you can in your chosen industry—manufacturers, resellers, agents, dealers, trade associations, and so on: Let them know you are looking.
3. Ask your network of bankers, lawyers, CAs, CMAs, and community leaders to help you in your search.
4. Advertise your needs in trade journals.
5. Check out the Internet. The Canadian Company Capabilities database would be a good place to start (see Box 13.1).
6. Send letters of inquiry to potential sellers (see Action Step 57).
7. Knock on doors.
8. Check with business-opportunities brokers.
9. Talk with firms that deal in mergers and acquisitions.
10. Don't allow yourself to be rushed; time is your ally, and the deals will get better.

Action Step 57 will help you get the word out. It should be quite interesting to read the letters you receive in response to your form letter.

Box 13.1 Bookmark This

Buying a Business

- **Canadian Business Exchange**
  www.canadianbusinessexchange.com
  The Canadian Business Exchange is a Canada-wide database for buying and selling of Canadian businesses and discovering investment opportunities. Use it to find a business for sale in your area.
- **Buying an Existing Business** (Canada Customs and Revenue Agency)
  www.ccra-adrc.gc.ca/E/pub/tg/rc4070eq/rc4070eq-03.html - P327_23921
  Learn about the basic tax implications of buying an existing business.
- **Canadian Company Capabilities** (Industry Canada)
  http://strategis.ic.gc.ca/sc_coinf/ccc/engdoc/homepage.html
  This database of over 40 000 company profiles will help you connect with buyers and sellers across Canada.

Investigate the Business from the Outside

Once you've found a business that looks promising, check it out in every detail. After analyzing it from the outside, you'll be ready to move inside, to evaluate the financial records and talk to the owner and attempt to learn the real reasons he or she is selling. But the first step is to get your telescope and your telephoto camera and gather as much information as you can from the exterior. In the opening vignette of this chapter, Ben and Sally Raymundo didn't do this, and they learned about fraud the hard way.

LEARN FROM OTHERS' MISTAKES

What could Ben and Sally have done to avoid their mistake? Many things. They could have asked the mall merchants how well the shopping centre was doing. They could have spent some time observing the store and the shopping mall before they committed. They could have insisted that Sally be allowed to work in the store prior to or during the escrow period, with a clause that would have allowed them to bail out.

Ben and Sally were honest, hard-working people who took the seller at face value. This was a huge error. A talk with suppliers might have uncovered the seller's fraud. They are now suing, and the lawyer they have hired could have helped them before they purchased the business. It's only going to get more expensive for them, and their chance of recovery is slim.

Some sellers don't count the value of their own time as a cost of doing business. This makes the firm show an inflated return on investment (ROI). Let's say such a firm earns $60 000 per year and has an inventory of $100 000. This could be a bad buy if the seller, her spouse, and their two children work a total of 200 hours per week and if a $100 000 investment could earn 8 percent or more per year in high-yield bonds.

Look at each deal from the viewpoint of what it would cost to hire a competent manager and staff at market wage rates. In this case, let's suppose you had to pay $40 000 a year for a manager, $30 000 a year for an assistant, and $30 000 a year for two hourly employees. You would have spent $80 000 and lost the opportunity to earn another $8000 on your investment. Yes, this would be a "no-brainer," but a lot of businesses are bought with even less going for them.

It's time now to go out and investigate a business on your own. Remember what you've learned from Ben and Sally's bad experience, and take along your new eyes and your camera. You'll be surprised how much there is to see. Action Step 58 tells you how to do it.

KNOW WHEN YOU NEED OUTSIDE HELP

We've already discussed the need for a team of small business gurus to help you realize your dream of small business ownership. When you evaluate small business for purchase, however, you may need a special kind of outside help. If you have any lingering doubts about the business you are researching, you may need the perspective of someone who is more objective than one of your team players. If you're not the Sherlock Holmes type yourself, hire someone who is. Your dream may be shattered by this kind of investigation, but you'll save money in the long run.

Here's Georgia's story, worth taking a lesson from.

> My husband, Fred, and I wanted to have a business of our own. We both loved sports, so we decided to look around for a sporting goods store.
>
> We found the perfect store, The Sports Factory, by networking with our sports-minded friends. It was located a block from a complex of tennis courts, three blocks from a new racquetball club, and half a kilometre from a park where volleyball tournaments are held every other month.
>
> An accountant friend checked over the books and said they looked perfect. "Great P and L," he said, "and excellent accounting ratios. If you get the right terms, you could clear 30 Gs every quarter, and that's only the beginning. This buy doesn't even advertise."
>
> We learned that the owner wanted to sell the store because he was tired of it—the long hours, being tied down, and so on. He'd been doing that for a dozen years.
>
> But I wasn't so sure. I sensed we needed help—some sort of Sam Spade of the business world—but Fred was in a hurry to close the deal. I knew Fred was unhappy in his job, but half the money we were going to invest was mine, and I felt something was not quite right. Frankly, the owner of The Sports Factory didn't look all that tired to me.
>
> So I asked around—networking again—and I located a community college professor who knew a lot about small business and had written a book about going into small business. I called him, and he listened very patiently when I told him our story. He said he'd be glad to check things out for us for a small fee. I told him to go ahead, but I didn't tell Fred about it.
>
> Two days later, Harry, my marketplace detective, called and said he had some news.
>
> "Oh?" I said. "So soon?"
>
> "Yes. Do you remember seeing a bulldozer working across the street from The Sports Factory?"

ACTION STEP 58

Study a business from the outside.

Studying the business from the outside will tell you whether you should go inside and probe more deeply.

1. Make sure the business fits into the framework of your industry overview. You want a business that's in the sunrise phase, not the sunset phase, of the life cycle.
2. Diagram the area. What's the location and how does the area fit into the city/regional planning for the future? What is the life-cycle stage of the community? Where is the traffic flow? Is there good access? How far will your target customer (TC) have to walk? Is parking adequate? Is the parking lot a drop-off point for car poolers?
3. Take some photographs of the exterior. Analyze them carefully. Is the building in good repair? What are the customers wearing, driving, and buying? What can you deduce about their lifestyle? Take photographs on different days and at different times of day.
4. Ask around. Interview the neighbours and the customers. What do the neighbours know about the business? Will the neighbours help draw TCs to your business?

   Be up-front with the seller's customers, since they may soon be your customers. What do they like about the store? Is the service good? What changes would they recommend? What services or products would they like to see added? Where else do they go for similar products or services?
5. Check out future competition. Do you want to be close to competitors, or do you want to be kilometres away? Could a competitor move in next door the day after you move in?

"No, I don't. What bulldozer?"

"It started grading last week. Right across the street. I talked to the driver on his lunch break. It seems a developer is putting in a seven-store complex, and one of the stores is going to be a discount sporting goods store." Harry paused.

"Oh, no," I said. "Are you sure?"

He explained that the store going in was part of a monster chain. I could see that we would have a hard time competing with them. I asked him if the owner knew, and if maybe that's why he was so "tired."

"Yes," Harry said, "I double-checked at the city planning office where building permits are issued." And he paused again.

I was having trouble catching my breath. "Could I get this in writing," I asked, "so that I can show my husband? He likes everything documented."

Harry chuckled. "No problem," he said. "I'll e-mail it to you tomorrow. Let me know what you decide, okay?"

"Don't worry," I said. "And thank you very much."

This marketplace detective work cost us $475, but it saved us thousands of dollars and years of heartache. Armed with what we learned through that experience, we examined almost a hundred businesses before we found the right one for us. It pays to investigate.

ACTION STEP 59

Study a business inside out.

Looking at a business from the inside enables you to determine its real worth and to see what it would be like to own it. Make an appointment (or have a business-opportunity broker arrange it) to take a serious inside look at the business you think you want to buy. Before you go, review everything we've explained in this section and write down a list of things you hope to learn while you're there. Don't allow anyone to rush you. Leave the chequebook at home; this fun is free.

Georgia and Fred came very close to buying the wrong business. The outsider's perspective helped them avoid making a terrible mistake. Now it's time to get some inside perspectives.

Investigate the Business from the Inside

Once you've learned all you can from the outside, it's time to cross the threshold for a look at the interior. This is an important, time-consuming process, and it's an important milestone in your quest. Action Step 59 will help you.

There are two ways to get inside the business: you can either contact the owner yourself, or you can get assistance from a business-opportunity broker. We recommend that you use a broker because brokers have expertise and detailed knowledge in business opportunities. You can locate them in the Yellow Pages under "Real Estate" or "Business Brokers" and in the newspaper classifieds.

Call a broker to learn whether he or she has any listings in your area of interest. If so, check out the ones that appear interesting. Be prepared for disappointment.

You will probably look at a number of businesses before you find anything close to your requirements. Nevertheless, you will learn a lot from the experience. Make sure you're clear on your business vision before you start. It is all too easy to let your emotions control your decision.

BUSINESS-OPPORTUNITY BROKER

a real-estate broker or consultant who specializes in representing people who want to sell businesses

DEALING WITH BROKERS

Business-opportunity brokers are active in most large cities, and they often play an important role in matching up sellers with buyers. Their level of competency ranges from specialists who know as much about fast-food franchises like

McDonald's as there is to know, to part-timers who know so little about business that they will only waste your time. A good broker can save you time and be very helpful in playing a third-party role in negotiations.

A broker has a responsibility to represent the seller and is not paid unless he or she sells something. Typically, the broker's commission is around 10 percent, but it's less on bigger deals, and everything is open to negotiation.

Some sellers list with brokers because they do not want it generally known (to their customers, employees, and competitors) that they want to sell their business. Most sellers who list with brokers, however, do so out of desperation because they've already tried to sell their business to everyone they know. Probably nine out of ten fall into this category.

Spending time with a skilled broker can be a fascinating educational experience. If you want a particular type of business and are able to examine a half-dozen that are on the market, you will probably end up with a better grasp of the business than the owners. Network your business contacts to locate a competent broker. Ask brokers for referrals from their former clients. And, as we've said so many times before, leave your chequebook at home. Don't let anyone rush you.

HOW TO LOOK AT THE INSIDE OF A BUSINESS

Once you have your foot in the door and have established yourself as a potential buyer, you will be able to study the inner workings of the business. Take full advantage of this opportunity. For general information on the business valuation process, visit the "Valuation of Small Businesses" web page profiled in Box 13.2.

Study the Financial History

What you need to learn from the financial history is where the money comes from and where it goes. Ask to see all financial records (balance sheet, income statement, and bank statement for at least five years back if they're available), and take your time studying them. If you don't understand financial records, hire someone who does. Your aim in buying an ongoing business is to step into an income stream. The financial records give a picture of that stream.

Box 13.2 Bookmark This

How Much Is a Business Worth?

- **Valuation of Small Businesses** (CCH Business Owner's Toolkit)
  www.toolkit.cch.com/text/P11_2200.asp

This page discusses the role of the business appraiser and how, in placing a price tag on your business, you need to consider:

- **Key factors:** What factors are most important to buyers? What are secondary?
- **Adding value:** How can you boost these important factors before the sale?
- **Recasting financial statements:** How might your accountant adjust your financial statements before showing them to potential buyers?
- **Valuation methods:** What are some of the methods and formulas that are commonly used to put a price tag on a business?
- **Partial interests:** If you're selling part of the business, how does that affect the price?

Look at the history of cash flow, profit and loss, and accounts receivable. If the seller has a stack of accounts receivable a foot high, remember that:

- after three months, the value of a current-accounts dollar will have shrunk to 90 cents;
- after six months, it will be worth 50 cents;
- after a year, it will be worth 30 cents.

Like an auditor, review every receipt you can find. If a tavern owner tells you she sells 30–40 kegs of beer per week, ask to see the receipts from the suppliers. If none is offered, ask permission to contact the suppliers for records of shipment. Make her prove to you that she has bought from suppliers. You can then accurately measure sales. If the seller won't cooperate, walk away; she's hiding something.

Evaluate closely any personal expenses that are being charged to the business. (Your accountant could help you determine a course of action that will keep you out of trouble.) This allows you to get a clearer picture of the firm's true profits. Also, compare the financial results to industry standards, such as information prepared by the Robert Morris Annual Financial Statements for your industry.

It's also a good idea to look at cancelled cheques, income tax returns, and the amount of salary the seller has been paying herself. If your seller was stingy with her own salary, decide whether you could live on that amount.

Tip: You can use the seller's accounts receivable as a point for negotiation, but don't take over the job of collecting them.

Compare What Your Money Could Do Elsewhere

How much money would you be putting into the business? How long would it take you to make it back? Have you figured in your time?

Let's say you would need to put $50 000 into this business, and that the business will give you a 33.3 percent return, which is full payback in three years. Are there other investments you could make that would yield the same amount on your $50 000?

If you will be working in the business, you need to add in the cost of your time; say that's $25 000 per year (your present salary) over the three-year period, or $75 000 (assuming no raises). In three years, the business would need to return $125 000 after expenses and taxes in order to cover the risks involved with your $50 000 investment and to compensate you for the loss of $25 000 in annual salary.

Evaluate the Tangible Assets

TANGIBLE ASSETS

things your business owns (lasting more than one year) that you can see and touch, such as real estate, equipment, and inventory

Tangible assets are the things you can see and touch. If the numbers look good, move on to assess the value of everything you can touch, specifically the real estate, the equipment and fixtures, and the inventory.

- *Real estate.* Get an outside, professional appraisal of the building and the land. It may be worth more as vacant land than as a business.
- *Equipment and fixtures.* You can get a good idea of current values by asking equipment dealers and reading the want ads. Scour your area for the best deals, because you don't want to tie up too much capital in equipment that's outmoded or about to come apart. Suppliers have lots of leads on used equipment, so check with them. If you're not an expert in the equipment field, get help from someone who is. Find out the maintenance costs in the last two years.
- *Inventory.* Count the **inventory** yourself, and make sure the boxes are packed with what you think they are. Make certain you specify the exact contents of shelves and cabinets in the purchase agreement. Don't get careless and write in something vague like "All shelves are to be filled." Specify what goes on the shelves. More importantly, find out if the inventory is salable, and if the styles and models of the stock are still valid. Don't accept old stock unless at a very low discount.

INVENTORY

items carried in the normal course of doing business that are intended for sale

Once you've made your count, contact suppliers to learn the current prices.

If you find merchandise that is damaged, out of date, out of style, soiled, worn, or not ready to sell as is, don't pay full price for it. Negotiate. This is sacrifice merchandise and it should have a sacrifice price tag.

Talk to insiders. There's no substitute for inside information. Every detective takes it seriously.

- *Bankers.* It is a must to discuss business with your banker and, ideally, with the current owner's banker. The latter will be limited on what he or she can say, but your banker will be a good help in analyzing the financial statements.
- *Suppliers.* Will suppliers agree to keep supplying you? Are there past difficulties between seller and supplier that you would inherit as the new owner? Remember, you're dependent on your suppliers. How do suppliers evaluate the business?
- *Employees.* Talk to the key employees early. In small business, success can rest on the shoulders of one or two persons, and you don't want them to walk out the day you sign the papers.
- *Competitors.* Identify the major competitors and interview them to learn what goes on from their perspective. You need to understand the industry fully. Expect some bias, but watch for a pattern to develop. (Chapter 5, you'll remember, tells how to identify the competitors.)

Get a Non-Competition Covenant

Once you buy a business, you don't want the seller to set up the same kind of business across the street. Customers are hard to come by, and you don't want to pay for them and have them spirited away by a cagey seller. So get an agreement, in writing, that the seller will not set up in competition with you—or work for a competitor, or help a friend or relative set up a competitive business—for the next five years. You will need a lawyer to prepare such an agreement. Be sure to specify the exact amount you're paying for the non-competition covenant. That way, the Canada Customs and Revenue Agency will allow you to deduct it against income over the life of the covenant.

Analyze the Seller's Motives

People have all kinds of reasons for selling their business. Some of these reasons favour the buyer, while others favour the seller.

Here are some reasons for selling that can favour the buyer:

1. retirement, ill health
2. too busy to manage, seller has other investments
3. divorce, family problems
4. disgruntled partners
5. expanded too fast, out of cash
6. poor management
7. burned out, lost interest

These reasons for selling will favour the seller (Buyer, beware!):

1. local economy in a decline
2. specific industry declining
3. intense competition
4. high insurance costs
5. increasing litigation
6. skyrocketing rents
7. technological obsolescence
8. problems with suppliers

9. high-crime location
10. lease not being renewed
11. location in a decline

Examine the Asking Price

Many sellers view selling their firms as they would view selling their children; that is, they are emotionally attached to the business and they overvalue its worth. Pride also plays a role; they might want to tell their friends that they started from scratch and sold out for a million. If you run into irrational and emotional obstacles, walk away or counter with unreasonable terms—such as $100 down and 10 percent of the net profits for the next four years, up to $1 million.

Some industries have rule-of-thumb benchmarks for pricing. For example, a service firm might be priced at six to twelve months of its total revenue. Such pricing formulas are often unwise. The only formula that makes sense is the return on your investment minus the value of your management time:

Return on Investment (ROI) = (Hours spent × Value of your time per hour)

If you can earn 10 percent without sweating on high-grade bonds, you should earn at least a 30 percent return on a business that will make you sweat.

PRICE/EARNINGS (P/E) RATIO
the market price of a common stock divided by its annual earnings per share for the latest 12-month period

It can be useful to consult the newspaper financial pages to learn the **price/earnings (P/E) ratios** of publicly traded firms. Firms whose P/E ratios are low (the stock price is less than 10 times its earnings) are not regarded as growth opportunities by sophisticated investors. Firms with above-average P/E ratios (price is more than 25 times its earnings) are regarded as having above-average growth potential. Thus, you should be willing to pay a higher price for a firm with above-average growth potential than for one that is declining. In fact, you should not buy a declining business unless you think you can either purchase it very inexpensively and turn it around or dispose of its assets at a profit.

Negotiate the Value of Goodwill

If the firm has a strong customer base with deeply ingrained purchasing habits, this has value. It takes a while for any start-up to build a client base, and the wait for profitability can be costly.

Some firms have built up a great deal of *ill* will—customers who have vowed never to trade with them again. A large proportion of the businesses on the market have this problem. If the amount of ill will is great, the business will have little value; it may be that *any* price would be too high.

GOODWILL
the dollar value obtained when you subtract the total value of the tangible assets from the purchase price

A smart seller will ask you to pay something for **goodwill**. You'll therefore need to play detective and find out how much goodwill there is and where it is. For example, consider the seller who has extended credit loosely. Customers are responding, but there's no cash in the bank. If you were to continue that policy and keep granting easy credit, you could be in the red in a couple of months. Or maybe the seller is one of those very special people who is loved by everyone and will take the goodwill with him—like a halo—when he walks out the door.

So negotiate.

You can determine the value of the goodwill by subtracting the total value of the tangible assets from the purchase price. Let's say the asking price for the business you'd like to buy is $145 000 and that its tangible assets (equipment, inventory, and so on) are worth $95 000. In other words, the seller is trying to charge you $50 000 for goodwill. Before you negotiate, do these things:

1. Compare the goodwill you're being asked to buy to the goodwill of a similar business on the market.

2. Figure out how long it would take you to pay that amount. Remember, goodwill is tangible; you'll be unhappy if it takes you years to pay for it. Even the most cheerful goodwill comes out of profit.
3. Estimate how much you could make if you invested that $50 000 in a high-yield security.
4. How long would it take you to reach the same level of profitability, starting from scratch?

This gives you a context in which to judge the seller's assessment of the value of goodwill, and you can use the hard data you have generated to negotiate a realistic—and more favourable—price.

Learn Whether Bulk Sales Escrow Is Needed

You need to know whether any inventory you would buy is tied up by creditors. If it is, the instrument you'll use to cut those strings is a bulk sales transfer, a process that will transfer the goods from the seller to you through a qualified third party.

If there are no claims by creditors, the transfer of inventory should go smoothly. If there are claims, you'll want to be protected by law. Either consult a lawyer who has experience in making bulk sales transfers, or get an **escrow company** to act as the neutral party in the transfer. Ask your banker or accountant to recommend one. Try to find one that specializes in bulk sales escrow.

BULK SALES ESCROW

an examination process intended to protect buyers from unknown liabilities

ESCROW COMPANY

a neutral third party that holds deposits and deeds until all agreed-upon conditions are met

AN EARNOUT SUCCESS STORY

Sam Wilson had held several key executive positions in large manufacturing firms after receiving his MBA from Western University in the early 1990s. His last position was as vice-president of a medium-sized firm with branch offices throughout North America. Sam got squeezed out when a large conglomerate purchased the firm and moved the headquarters to London.

After doing some freelance management consulting, Sam arranged to purchase an executive search firm that specialized in finding engineering talent in the aerospace industry. Buying the business seemed like a good idea to Sam because the business had been profitable for more than 20 years. The key personnel agreed to stay with the firm. It had loyal customers, a solid reputation, and Sam knew it would take him years to build a similar business from scratch, even though he understood the business.

He purchased the business for no cash down and agreed to pay off the entire purchase price from the earnings over the next five years. (This is called an **earnout**—a contractual arrangement in which the purchase price is stated in terms of a minimum, and the buyer of the business agrees to make future payments to the seller based on the achievement of predefined financial goals after the closing.) The seller was an older man who had known Sam's reputation as a winner. Sam was one of the few prospective buyers who were willing to pay full price for the business and seemed qualified to continue the growth of the firm.

EARNOUT

a contractual arrangement in which the purchase price is stated in terms of a minimum, and the buyer of the business agrees to make future payments to the seller based on the achievement of pre-defined financial goals after the closing

Buying a business on an earnout basis is an option only if the seller has great confidence in the buyer's skills and knowledge of the business. Thus, the burden of persuading the seller to agree to such terms is on the buyer. It's necessary to show the seller that the business will continue to show a profit.

The Decision to Buy

Even if you think you're ready to make your decision, don't do it—not yet. Read the checklist in Box 13.3 first. It reminds you of 33 important details you might have overlooked. Even if you know you've found your dream business, complete this checklist before you sign the papers.

Box 13.3 The Before-You-Buy Checklist

- ❑ How long do you plan to own this business?
- ❑ How old is this business? Can you sketch its history?
- ❑ Is this business in the embryonic stage, the growth stage, the mature stage, or the decline stage?
- ❑ Has your accountant reviewed the books and made a sales projection for you?
- ❑ How long will it take for this business to show a complete recovery on your investment?
- ❑ What reasons does the owner give for selling?
- ❑ Will the owner let you see bank deposit records? (If not, why not?)
- ❑ Have you calculated utility costs for the first three to five years?
- ❑ What does a review of tax records tell you?
- ❑ How complete is the insurance coverage?
- ❑ How old are the receivables? (Remember, age decreases their value.)
- ❑ What is the seller paying himself or herself? Is it low or high?
- ❑ Have you interviewed your prospective landlord?
- ❑ What happens when a new tenant takes over the lease?
- ❑ Has your lawyer checked for any potential problems in the transferral of licences and permits?
- ❑ Have you made checks on the currency of the customer lists?
- ❑ Who are your top 20 customers? Your top 50?
- ❑ Is the seller locked into one to three major customers who control the business?
- ❑ How well is the business using technology, computerized systems, and business management?
- ❑ Are you buying inventory? What is the seller asking?
- ❑ Have you checked the value of the equipment against the price of used equipment from another source?
- ❑ To whom does your seller owe money?
- ❑ Has your lawyer checked for liens on the seller's equipment?
- ❑ Do you have maintenance contracts on the equipment you're buying?
- ❑ Has your lawyer or escrow company gone through bulk sales escrow?
- ❑ Have you made certain that:
  - you're getting all brand names, logos, trademarks, and so on that you need?
  - the seller has signed a non-competition covenant?
  - the key lines of supply will stay intact when you take over?
  - the key employees will stay?
  - the seller isn't leaving because of stiff competition?
  - you are paying for goodwill but taking delivery on ill will?
  - you aren't getting the best terms possible?
  - you're buying an income stream?

PREPARE FOR THE NEGOTIATIONS

Let's say you know you're ready to buy. You've raised the money, and the numbers say you can't lose, so you're ready to start negotiating. (If you're an experienced entrepreneur, you already know how to negotiate. If not, some good books on the fine art of haggling are listed in the references section at the end of this chapter.)

We suggest two things about negotiations. First, when it comes time to talk meaningful numbers, the most important area to concentrate on is *terms,* not asking price. Favourable terms will give you the cash flow you need to survive the first year and then move from survival into success. Unfavourable terms can torpedo your chances for success, even when the total asking price is well below market value.

Second, when the seller brings up the subject of goodwill, be ready for it. Goodwill is a "slippery" commodity; it can make the asking price soar. It's only natural for the seller to attempt to get as much as possible for goodwill. Because you know this ahead of time, you can do your homework and go in primed to deal. Action Step 60 will help you do your homework. When the seller starts talking about goodwill, you can flip the coin over and discuss ill will—which hangs on longer, like a cloud above the business.

ACTION STEP 60

Probe the depths of ill will.

How many products have you vowed never to use again? How many places of business have you vowed never to patronize again? Why?

Make a list of the products and services you won't buy or use again. Next to each item, write the reason. Does it make you sick? Does it offend your sensibilities? Was the service awful?

After you've completed your list, ask your friends what their negative feelings about particular businesses are. Take notes.

Study the two lists you've made. What are the common components of ill will? How long does ill will last? Is there a remedy for it, or is a business plagued by ill will doomed forever?

Now turn your attention to the business you want to buy. Survey your target customers. How do they feel about the business? You need to learn as much as you can about any ill will that exists toward the business.

Have fun with this step, but take it seriously—and think about the nature of ill will when your seller starts asking you to pay for goodwill.

PROTECT YOURSELF

Evaluate each business opportunity by the criteria we present in this chapter. When you find one you think is right for you, start negotiating. Your goal is the lowest possible price with the best possible terms. Start low; you can then negotiate up if necessary.

If you are asked to put down a deposit, handle it this way:

1. Deposit the money in an escrow account.
2. Include a stipulation in your offer that says the offer is *subject to your inspection and approval* of all financial records and all aspects of the business.

Doing this gives you an escape hatch so that you can get your deposit returned—and back out of the deal—if things don't look good. Also, consider working in the business for a few weeks with the option to back out if you have a change of heart.

NEGOTIATING THE PRICE

What is a fair price? Obviously, the values of the seller and of the buyer are arrived at from widely separated viewpoints.

The seller has committed considerable time and money to the business, often for less return than could have been earned elsewhere, and sees the sale as the opportunity to make up for the years of "doing without." The buyer, on the other hand, is concerned only with the present state and future potential of the business and cares little for the time and effort invested by the vendor.

The price of a business is related to the ability of that business to generate revenue. This is determined, in large part, by the assets of the business. If you are purchasing assets, the seller will usually have a spec sheet prepared, listing the assets and offering an estimate of their value. The asset value may be calculated using various formulas, including:

- Fair market value: the price of similar assets on the open market;
- Replacement value: what it would cost to replace the asset (i.e., from the original supplier);

- Liquidation value: what the asset would bring if the business were liquidated (as in a bankruptcy); or
- Book value: based on the company's balance sheet.

In that list of assets, however, goodwill may be included, representing the value of intangibles, such as location, reputation, and established customer base of the business. Goodwill is virtually impossible to value objectively. It depends more on instinct and gut feeling than on a strict accounting formula.

The aggregated value of individual assets, however, tells only part of the story. The real value of the business depends on the income that it generates. This may not be directly related to the value of the assets, especially in service businesses. We therefore encourage you to look at the company's income history over a period of years (at least three is usual) to determine what its gross revenues, costs, and profit were. You are really buying that annual profit and one way of looking at the purchase price is in terms of a return on your investment. Start your own investigation by asking for the most recent three years of financial data. Who prepared this data? Is it part of a formal audit? Even if the statements are audited, remember that auditors depend on the paper they are given. There may be a lot hidden under formal statements certified by an accountant.

You can do your own audit by asking the seller for permission to see the actual records of the enterprise. Deposit books, invoices, repair bills, payroll slips, sales slips, and so on will tell you far more about the condition of a business than will an audited statement. You may have to sign a non-disclosure agreement to get access to this type of information, but it gives you a clear picture of the quality of the records and the controls in place to manage the business. If records are scanty and poorly kept, you may not know how much work will be involved in cleaning up the operation if you actually take it over. Adjust your offer accordingly.[1]

As a basis for opening negotiations with a vendor, you might wish to use the following formula, adapted from advice provided by the Business Development Bank of Canada. It is not intended to be an all-inclusive answer to establishing a final price, but it is a valid mathematical approach, based on available hard data, and can serve as a test of the price being asked for the business.

Since we are suggesting that the formula be used to test the asking price, you will need copies of the financial statements for the business. It is only from these figures that a valid analysis can be made.

Pricing Formula

Step 1 Calculate the tangible net worth of the business.

This is, in its simplest form, the total tangible assets (excluding goodwill, franchise fees, etc.) less total liabilities (both current and long term).

Step 2 Estimate the current earning power of this tangible net worth if this amount was to be invested elsewhere (stocks, bonds, term deposits).

This earning power will vary with economic trends and other factors, but should be based on current interest rates.

Step 3 Determine a reasonable annual salary that could be earned by the owner if similarly employed elsewhere.

Remember to take into consideration benefits paid by the business (automotive, insurance, pensions, etc.) in determining a comparable outside salary.

Step 4 Determine the total earning capacity of the owner that would result from the net worth invested, plus employment sources, by adding the results of steps 2 and 3.

Step 5 Calculate the average annual net profit of the business.

This average will be the total of profit from all financial statements available (before any management salaries or cash withdrawal for partners, proprietors, taxes, etc.), divided by the number of years used in the analysis. We suggest three years minimum, but preferably five years for an accurate result.

Step 6 Calculate the extra earning power of the business by subtracting the result of step 4 from that of step 5.

This figure represents the additional money you can expect to earn if you buy the business, rather than invest an amount equal to the net worth and obtain or retain outside employment.

Step 7 Calculate the value of intangibles by multiplying the extra earning power (step 6) by a figure that we will refer to as the development factor.

This development factor is designed to weigh such things as uniqueness of the intangibles, time needed to establish a similar business from scratch, expenses and risk of a comparable start-up, price of goodwill in similar firms, and so on.

If the business is well established and successful, a suggested factor of 5 or more might be used; a more moderately seasoned firm might rate a factor of 3; and a young but profitable business may rate a factor of only 1.

Step 8 Calculate the final price.

This is arrived at by adding the tangible net worth of the business (step 1) to the value of intangibles (step 7).

Here is one example of how this formula works. Assume you are interested in purchasing the XYZ Company Limited, and the asking price is $200 000. At your request, the owners of XYZ have given you the following financial statement representing the last complete year of operation. (Note that we are using only one year's statement in this example. When using this formula for real, you should attempt to obtain statements for at least three, but preferably five years.)

XYZ Company Limited
Balance Sheet
As at Dec. 31, 20XX

Assets		
Current		
Cash	$ 180	
Accounts Receivable	6 560	
Inventory	13 150	
Total Current	19 890	
Fixed		
Land	5 000	
Buildings	35 000	
Equipment	14 500	
Furniture	1 800	
Vehicles	11 500	
Less: Accumulated Depreciation	8 100	
Total Fixed	59 700	
Total Assets		$79 590

Liabilities		
Current		
Bank	$ 3 000	
Accounts Payable	6 600	
Current Portion—Long-Term	1 100	
Total Current	10 700	
Long-Term		
Long-Term Mortgage Loan	21 500	
Equipment Loan	9 600	
Total Long-Term Liabilities	31 100	
Less: Current Portion	1 100	
Total Long-Term	30 000	
Total Liabilities	40 700	
Shareholders' Equity		
Share Capital	10 000	
Retained Earning	28 890	
Total Shareholders' Equity	38 890	
Total Liabilities and Shareholders' Equity		$79 590

XYZ Company Limited
Operating Statement
For the 12 months
ended Dec. 31, 20XX

Sales (Revenue)		**$250 000**
Cost Of Goods Sold		
Opening Inventory	$ 12 000	
Purchases	151 150	
	163 150	
Closing Inventory	13 150	
Total Cost of Goods Sold		150 000
Gross Profit		100 000
Operating Expenses		
Advertising	1 500	
Automobile	2 400	
Bad Debts	300	
Depreciation	3 700	
Equipment Rental	400	
Insurance	1,200	
Interest and Bank Charges	4 000	
Management Salaries	16 000	
Miscellaneous	400	
Office Supplies	1 100	
Professional Fees	800	
Taxes and Licences (Municipal)	300	
Telephone	800	
Utilities	2 100	
Wages and Benefits	40 000	
Total Operating Expenses		75 000
Operating Profit		25 000
Less: Income Taxes[a]	6 250	
Net Profit		$ 18 750

[a]Arbitrarily set at 25% for demonstration purposes only. Rates can vary not only provincially but within individual businesses.

Formula Calculation (figures have been rounded)

1. Tangible Net Worth	$39 000
2. Earning Power (assume 10%)	3 900
3. Reasonable Salary for Owner	16 000
4. Earning Capacity	19 900
5. Average Annual Net Profit (operating profit before taxes, $25 000 + owner's salary, $16 000)	41 000
6. Extra Earning Power	21 100
7. Value of Intangibles (development factor of three)	63 300
8. Final Price (63 300 + 39 000)	102 300

By applying the formula, you come up with a suggested final price of $102 300. This compares with an asking price of $200 000.

Any price negotiated must, of course, be related to the new financing of the business. The combination of personal investment and borrowed money may be very different from the position of the vendor and as such will produce a very different operating result. Your negotiations will be strongly influenced by what you can afford.

Once you are satisfied that you have given full consideration to all factors affecting the proposed acquisition and you are ready to proceed, your offer should be formalized by a purchase agreement. Be sure to seek professional help and advice in the preparation of this agreement.

THE CONTRACT

Ultimately the sale of a business involves a combination of final price, other terms, and overall risk. You may be prepared to pay a higher price as long as other conditions (such as the seller agrees to take a mortgage on easy terms) are suitable. Or you may opt for a lower price in which you assume more of the risks of the transaction. The precise mix will vary in accordance with the nature of the business and the inclinations of the individuals involved.

Once you have arrived at the terms, the details should be spelled out in a contract that itemizes all aspects of the sale. The following is a summary of some standard items that are usually found in such a contract:[2]

- A definition of what is being transferred, from whom to whom, and at what price. This should include an itemized breakdown of costs so that you have a record of the value of each asset, both those you can claim for depreciation and those you cannot.
- Details of any leases or liabilities that you are assuming in making the purchase.
- The method of payment (in cash, by cheque, in shares in another company, in bonds), on what date, and by what means.
- Any adjustments to the price to cover financial transactions occurring between the moment the offer is signed and the closing date (this could include sale of inventory, equipment purchases, tax payments, etc.).
- Guarantees by the seller of the truthfulness of information supplied and provisions for any penalties in the event that information is not accurate.
- A description of the seller's obligations in operating the business up to closing, implementing the transfer of ownership, and performing any post-sale duties or services.
- How to deal with any losses or damages that might occur to the business between the signing of the agreement and the closing date.
- A clause restricting the ability of the seller to compete with the business once the sale is closed, or limiting the seller's freedom to start up similar ventures.

- Any conditions that should be met prior to closing (such as validation of deeds, liabilities, or agreements entered into by the business).
- Details of closing, including the date, time, place, and individuals effecting the transfer.
- Compensation to be paid by the seller to the buyer as damages or compensation if information is found to be false.
- The amount of the security deposit the buyer put up and held in escrow for a period of time as a guarantee that all terms and conditions have been satisfied.
- Who would decide the case in the event of a dispute.

EXPECT SOME PLEASANT SURPRISES

Well you've come a long way and you've worked hard on your research. You may be wondering if the digging was worth it. Only you can answer that. There are bargains to be found out there—businesses like Woolett's Hardware. For hunter-buyers with vision and persistence, beautiful opportunities are waiting behind ugly façades.

> I heard about Woolett's being up for sale more than a year ago. I'd just opened up my second store at the time—it's also in the hardware line—and it took me just about a year, April to April, to streamline the paperwork. Thanks to a computer and a good manager, my sanity remained intact.
>
> So, when I finally got over there to check things out, Woolett's had been on the market about a year and a half. One look from the street and I could see why.
>
> The store was a mess. The building was pre–World War II and so was the paint. Out front, the sign was sagging. The parking lot needed lots of work; there were potholes 15 centimetres deep. The entryway was littered with scraps of paper.
>
> Inside, things weren't much better. The floor needed a good sweeping. The merchandise was covered with dust. And all around there was this feeling of mildew, age, and disuse. It was dark—like a cave. It was tough finding a salesperson, and when you did, you couldn't get much help. Yet, there were customers all over the place.
>
> After you've been in business a while, you develop a sort of sixth sense about things. And the minute I stepped into the store, I knew there was something special about it, something hidden, something the eye couldn't see right off. I knew I had to dig deeper.
>
> A visit to the listing real-estate broker didn't help much. "Make us an offer," he said. "We just dropped the price yesterday. To $400 000."
>
> "What do the numbers look like?" I asked.
>
> He dug into a slim manila folder. "Last year," he said, "they grossed just under $600 000. The net was around $200 000."
>
> "What about inventory?" I asked. "What about loans and **liens** and accounts receivable? When can I interview the manager? And why is the owner selling?"

LIENS

a legal obligation filed against a piece of property

"Are you just asking that," he said, "or is this for real?"

"This is for my son," I said. "He's new to the business, and we don't want a lot of surprises."

"Like I said, make us an offer."

"Let me check the books," I said. I deposited $500 with an escrow company, making sure I got my usual escape clause—a deposit receipt saying my offer for the business was contingent on my inspection of all assets and my approval of all financial records. Doing this has saved me tons of heartburn medicine over the years.

The minute they got wind of a buyer, the manager and two of the employees up and quit. The back office was a mess, and it took me three days of searching to find something that would tell me I was on the right track. I found a supply of rolled steel. It was on the books at $12 000, but I knew it was worth $150 000. I took that as a buy signal.

The next day, I made an offer: $12 000 down, with the balance to be paid out of profits over the next five years. The owner accepted, and we cleared escrow in 30 days.

The first thing we did was clean the place up. We surfaced the parking lot with asphalt, added a coat of paint, fixed the door, added lighting.

Business picked up right away. My son, newly married, was settling down and learning the business. He seemed to have managerial talents. Buying this business was a pleasant surprise.

In a Nutshell

There are two good reasons to explore businesses for sale: you'll learn a lot by exploring the marketplace, and you might find a gem like Woolett's Hardware—a business that will make money right from the start.

A final note of caution is in order. Buying a business can take time and it certainly involves new risk. In making the purchase, you are assuming new responsibilities to those who helped you finance the deal, to any employees working for the business, to its suppliers, and to its clients. Before you buy, do your homework, complete the checklist provided in Box 13.3, and make sure you have a watertight contract in place.

Key Terms

bulk sales escrow
business-opportunity broker
earnout
escrow company
goodwill
inventory
liens
price/earnings (P/E) ratio
tangible assets

Think Points for Success

✓ Stick to what you know. Don't buy a business you know nothing about.
✓ Don't let a seller or a broker rush you. A business is not a used car.

- ✓ If your seller looks absolutely honest, check him or her out anyway.
- ✓ Worry less about price; work harder on terms.
- ✓ Most good businesses are sold behind the scenes, before they reach the open market.
- ✓ Make sure you're there when the physical inventory takes place. Look in those boxes yourself.
- ✓ Get everything in writing. Be specific.
- ✓ Always go through bulk sales escrow.
- ✓ Buying a corporation is tricky. Have an experienced lawyer and accountant help you.

Checklist Questions and Actions to Develop Your Business Plan

BUYING A BUSINESS

- ❑ Why would you buy a business rather than start from scratch?
- ❑ What are the potential "icebergs" (unknowns or major risks) in buying a business?
- ❑ Establish the value of goodwill. Is the business worth this amount?
- ❑ What would be the cost involved in starting from scratch versus buying a business?

NOTES

1. Industry Canada, Strategis website, retrieved from http://strategis.ic.gc.ca/sc_mangb/contact/engdoc/homepage.html. Reprinted by permission.
2. Ibid.

SUGGESTED READING

Bauman, Robert, and Peter Jackson. *From Promise to Performance.* Boston, MA: Harvard Business School Press, 1997. [Merger leads to a brand new company.]

Burbank, Ted. *In and Out of Business … Happily.* Niantic, CT: Business Book Press, 2001.

Chan, James. *Spare Room Tycoon: The Seventy Lessons of Sane Self-Employment.* London: Nicholas Brealey, 2000.

Collins, James C., and William C. Lazier. *Beyond Entrepreneurship: Turning Your Business into an Enduring Great Company.* Upper Saddle River, NJ: Prentice Hall, 1995.

Joseph, Richard A., Anna M. Nekoranec, and Carl H. Steffens. *How to Buy a Business: Entrepreneurship Through Acquisition.* Chicago, IL: Dearborn Trade, 1993.

Maher, Barry. *Filling the Glass: The Skeptic's Guide to Positive Thinking in Business.* Chicago, IL: Dearborn Trade, 2001.

Nottonson, Ira N. *Secrets to Buying and Selling a Business.* Central Point, OR: Oasis Press, 1999.

Snowden, Richard W. *The Complete Guide to Buying a Business.* New York: AMACOM, 1997.

West, Thomas L. *The 1997 Business Reference Guide.* New York: New York Business Brokerage Press, 1997. [Business valuation and contracts.]

chapter 14

Buying a Franchise

BUSINESS PLAN BUILDING BLOCK

This chapter will introduce you to the world of franchising and help you decide if buying a franchise is right for you.

LEARNING OPPORTUNITIES

After reading this chapter, you should be able to:

- Appreciate the vast world of franchising.
- Understand key franchising terms and conditions in an agreement.
- Understand the relationship between franchisor and franchisee.
- Learn the benefits and liabilities of owning and operating a franchise.
- Decide whether buying a franchise is the right step for you.

"You're only here for a cup of coffee," Orv Lahey, our small business professor, told us that first day of class, a few years ago. How ironic. I had a passion—and still do—for coffee and always wanted to own a coffee shop. So it was an omen that Orv came out with this nugget at our first encounter.

I researched the market and came to the conclusion that I needed a partner, a strong partner who could secure me a good location, provide the right training, and be ready to move with the times. I didn't want to be out there alone. I wanted to be part of a strong organization. I felt I couldn't compete in the coffee business as a mom-and-pop operation. After months of investigation, I chose Second Cup.

I've just completed my first year in business, and I can tell you that I made the right decision. Our team has exceeded sales targets and our costs are in line. I know franchising isn't the option for everyone. You hear a lot of horror stories. But it's worked out for me.

My manager, Aaron Cope, and I went through an intensive three-week training program at Second Cup. The company made sure I had a realistic business plan and that my financials were reasonable. I was well prepared and I knew what I wanted. When I was offered a street-front location, I turned it down—it wasn't what I had

ACTION STEP PREVIEW

61. Conduct secondary research on franchising.
62. Investigate the franchise system by interviewing franchisors and franchisees.

Chapter 14 investigates franchising, an important doorway to small business.

in mind. Through perseverance and a lot of networking, I finally found a triple-A mall location. I bought the business from a Second Cup franchisee. It impressed me that Second Cup was prepared to do what it could to help her sell the business. Most of all, it was supportive and did what it said it would.

On the negative side, I have to follow its system religiously, but I knew going in that that would be the price I would have to pay. However, I still get a chance to vent my entrepreneurial ideas at franchise association meetings.

If you are going to buy a franchise, here's my advice:

- Get a mentor.
- You're more likely to succeed if you stick to what you know best. Make sure you and the franchisor have the same vision.
- Always get advice from a lawyer and an accountant. You don't have to follow it. But at least listen to them.
- Have a business plan.
- Teamwork is everything. If you can't work in a team, you may as well pack it in.
- Find out how the franchisor helps franchisees sell their business. I considered this a litmus test of Second Cup's corporate culture.[1]

Our walk-through of opportunities in small business is almost finished. Decision time approaches. If you've followed the Action Steps, you've spent several months gathering data and talking to people in small business. In Chapter 13, we explored buying a business and talking to sellers. In this chapter, we look at another option: acquiring a franchised business.

The franchising industry is enormous. If you were to buy or rent a car tomorrow morning, put gas in it, buy a coffee and doughnut, purchase some paint, and then go to a fast-food restaurant for lunch, chances are you would support a franchise at every stop. Here are some franchising facts:

- According to Industry Canada, about 40 cents of every retail dollar spent in the retail sector goes to some franchise business.
- There are approximately 1100 different franchises in Canada.
- Some 13 000 Canadians have chosen franchising as their entrepreneurial gateway and franchises employ over 60 000 people.
- There is one franchise outlet for every 1200 Canadians.
- Franchise revenues are estimated to be in the $100-billion range.
- According to the Canadian Franchise Association, the franchising industry's growth rate in the latter half of the 1990s was 7 percent annually.

What is a franchise? Is a franchise for you? When does it make business sense? Are you ready to surrender some of your independence? Is this a good first business, a stepping stone to the future entrepreneurship you seek? We'll try to help you answer these questions in this chapter.

FRANCHISE

authorization granted by a manufacturer or distributor to sell its products or services

FRANCHISOR

the firm that sells the rights to do business under its name and continues to control the business

What Is a Franchise?

BUSINESS FORMAT FRANCHISE

A **franchise** is a special kind of partnership in which one company (the **franchisor**) grants the right to sell its products or services to another company or individual (the

franchisee). It's a distribution system used by businesses to sell or market their products or services.

A variety of franchise business arrangements exist. If you drop by Second Cup for a cup of coffee, buy a dozen doughnuts at Tim Hortons, or get your muffler fixed at Speedy, you have just experienced familiar examples of the so-called **business format franchise** system. This type of franchise is one in which the product, method of distribution, and sales and management procedures—the business format—are highly controlled. The franchisor "blueprints" every aspect of the business and then sells this business format to a franchisee. The main job of the franchisee is to staff and run the operation. This is the most popular type of franchise system—one that encompasses most businesses, from used clothing to lawn care and even tax preparation.

FRANCHISEE

the individual operator who is licensed to operate under the franchisor's rules and directives

BUSINESS FORMAT FRANCHISE

a type of franchise in which the product, method of distribution, and sales and management procedures are highly controlled

DEALERSHIP RELATIONSHIP FRANCHISE

A second type of popular franchise system is the **dealership relationship franchise** (also termed a licensing or associate relationship). Here the dealer or associate (franchisee) buys the right to distribute a franchisor's product or service. These types of licensing arrangements are less restrictive than the business format arrangement, where the key is standardization. Dealership franchisees distribute and sell the product under the franchisor's conditions, but are left relatively free from any other franchisee obligations. Home Hardware and Century 21 are good examples of this kind of arrangement. Another example would be Coca-Cola and Pepsi, which license or franchise out the right to distribute their products to a local bottler, but don't normally tell the licensees how to run their business operations.

This chapter focuses mainly on business format franchising—the most common type of franchising—although much of the discussion also applies to the dealership or licensing format.

DEALERSHIP RELATIONSHIP FRANCHISE

also called licensing or associate relationship, a type of franchise in which the franchisee buys the right to distribute a franchisor's product or service

Why Buy a Franchise?

In theory, a successful franchise system can benefit the customer, the franchisee, and the franchisor—a win-win situation.

WHAT THE CUSTOMER GETS

Imagine that you're on a holiday. You have been driving for hours and it's time for lunch. Do you have lunch at Wendy's or Taco Bell, or do you take a chance and pull in at a flashing "Joe's Diner" sign? If you're like the average Canadian, you'll choose a name that is familiar. Why? Because to some degree, you've been branded. You've become comfortable with a product and gained a certain attachment to it. You know what to expect even if it isn't perfect; you keep returning. It's hard to get out of this comfort zone.

"Customer satisfaction" and brand loyalty are the key reasons for buying a franchise. Each franchise outlet is cloned to offer a consistent standard of service and product. If the franchise system runs as planned, customers will know what to expect and how much they will pay every time. Franchises give customers a sense of security. Should a dispute arise, customers know that they can appeal to a larger organization. Franchises give the appearance that they will be around for the long run. Also, there is a good chance the "owner" will be around, and customers like to know that they can speak to the owner should the need arise.

WHAT THE FRANCHISEE RECEIVES

Let's examine what you may receive when you buy a franchise from a franchisor. In principle, a franchise can provide:

1. *Brand-name recognition.* If you pick the right franchise with a high, positive consumer profile, you will have a recognizable brand.
2. *Support from the corporation.* Corporate services can include help with site selection, employee training, inventory control, vendor supplies and connections, a corporate-produced business plan, lease negotiations, layout assistance, and more.
3. *Training.* The franchisor will teach you the business and provide ongoing training.
4. *Financial support.* Lenders often prefer to lend to new franchises over new start-ups.
5. *Template.* You are buying a proven business plan and strategy that work.
6. *Purchasing power.* You may share in economies of scale in purchasing goods, services, and promotion.
7. *Corporate monitoring and assistance.* You are likely to receive psychological hand-holding and field visits from the franchisor.
8. *Less risk of failure.* The failure rate of franchises is less than half of self start-ups.
9. *National/regional promotion.* You will get pretested promotion and marketing programs
10. *Additional units.* You are likely to get opportunities to buy another franchise in your area.

WHAT THE FRANCHISOR ASKS OF YOU

FRANCHISE FEE

fee paid by a franchisee for the rights to represent the franchisor in a given geographic area for a specified length of time, commonly five to ten years

ROYALTY FEE

ongoing obligation to pay the franchisor a percentage of the gross sales

Franchisors earn money in several ways:

1. They collect a **franchise fee** for the rights to use their name and system. This can range anywhere from $3000 for a small service firm to over $100 000 for a well-established name such as that of a hotel, auto dealership, or major restaurant. The franchise fee is usually paid by the franchisee on the day the franchise agreement is signed.
2. They normally collect a **royalty fee**, which ranges from 2 to 15 percent of the annual gross sales. Some franchisors collect their royalties by charging a percentage on the purchase of supplies rather than on sales.
3. Some may make a profit on the markup of items (such as store fixtures) that they sell directly to franchisees.
4. Some may receive volume rebates or other benefits from suppliers, which are not passed on to the franchisees.
5. They may require franchisees to pay advertising and promotion fees. These generally range from 2 to 5 percent of the franchisee's gross sales. Some of these are directed toward local promotions, but most go into the national advertising fund. In some cases, depending on the age of the franchise, it may be possible to ask for some concessions in the payment of these fees.

In addition, growth and market penetration are key benefits. Franchisors can expand their business quickly with limited capital from the original owners. A number of growth options are available. Some franchisors, for example, provide incentives for their successful franchisees to own multiple units. Other aggressive franchisors have been known to sell geographic territories to master or subfranchisors. The job of master or subfranchisors is to grow the business (i.e., sell franchises within the designated area). In turn, these quasi-franchisors receive a portion of the franchise fees or royalties.

Investigating Franchise Opportunities

According to Mac Voisin, from the highly successful M & M Meat Shops Ltd. in Kitchener, Ontario, a franchise chain of over 150 outlets, "True entrepreneurs will die of frustration in a franchise system because they want to do everything their own way."[2] As Voison points out, many of you may not be comfortable operating by the franchisor's strict rules and regulations. Your entrepreneurial spirit may make it difficult for you to follow detailed rules and policies. But that doesn't mean you shouldn't keep your eyes open. You can learn a lot by examining the way good franchises work. It makes sense to evaluate franchise opportunities (especially those in your industry), because, at the very least, it will give you a better picture of the marketplace. To begin your investigation, complete Action Steps 61 and 62.

THE FRANCHISE AGREEMENT AND SYSTEM

When you purchase a franchise, you will be required to sign a contract that could be as long as 50 pages and with numerous appendices attached. This contract is the franchise agreement, which lays out the system you will be working within, and

Box 14.1 Bookmark This

Franchise Information and Resources

- **YouthBusiness.com**
  www.youthbusiness.com
  Click on Franchise to access an article titled "Why Buy a Franchise?"
- **BusinessGateway.ca.**
  http://businessgateway.ca/en/hi/index.cfm
  Do a search on "franchising" to access government services and information.
- **Siskinds Franchise Law Group**
  http://franchiselaw.ca/book.html
  Download the booklet *Franchising Your Business.*
- **Franchise Comparison Work Sheet** (Entrepreneur.com)
  www.entrepreneur.com/Home/HM_Static/1,4472,formnet_analysis,00.html
  Use this form to help you determine the attractiveness of each prospective franchise you are considering.

Franchise Databases and Directories

Use the following sites to search for franchising opportunities.

- **Canadian Franchise Association**
  www.cfa.ca/investigate.html
- **The Virtual Franchise Expo**
  www.vifexpo.com
- **FranchiseShowroom.com**
  www.franchise-conxions.com
- **CanadianFranchise.com**
  www.canadianfranchise.com/index.asp
- **Franchise Directory**
  www.franchisedirect.com/directory

ACTION STEP 61

Conduct secondary research on franchising.

A great place to start exploring the world of franchising is the Internet. Do a web search on "buying a franchise." To narrow your search, check out the sites listed in Box 14.1. Begin with the information-related sites, then move on to the franchise databases and directories and do some comparison shopping. Which franchises are hot and which ones are on their way out? This is a learning exercise, so record any franchising terms or good ideas you come across in the course of your search.

Next, visit the websites of two or three franchisors and submit an e-mail request for a franchise information packet. (Alternatively, use the information on their sites provided that it is comprehensive enough.) Write a one-page summary identifying the advantages and disadvantages of each of your selected franchises. The Franchise Comparison Work Sheet, which can be downloaded from Entrepreneur.com (see Box 14.1), will help you do a comparative analysis.

ACTION STEP 62

Investigate the franchise system by interviewing franchisors and franchisees.

Franchises are everywhere: Tim Hortons, Boston Pizza, Second Cup, RE MAX, Dale Carnegie, Holiday Inn, Esso, Hertz, and many, many others. To learn more about the system, interview people on both sides of the franchise agreement.

Part A: Franchisors. Leave your chequebook at home and interview at least three franchisors. Here are some questions to start you off:

- What is the business experience of the franchisor's directors and managers?
- How many years has the franchise been operating?
- What are the start-up and ongoing royalty fees and other assessments?
- What level of training and service could I expect before and after I open, and what support is given?
- What is the turnover rate of the franchisees?
- Is the territory well defined?
- What are the minimum volume requirements?
- Is the franchisor a member of the Canadian Franchise Association?
- Is the franchise registered in Alberta or Ontario?
- How can the franchise be bought back or cancelled by the franchisor?

Part B: Franchisees. Now interview at least three franchisees. Ask them the same questions, with emphasis on the type of support they receive from the franchisors.

the rules and policies that you are bound to operate by. It goes without saying that you need to get legal advice before you sign the agreement. The typical clauses in the contract include:

- Definitions
- Grant and Term
- Franchise Royalty Fee and Sales Taxes
- Reports
- General Services of Franchisor
- Compliance with System
- Manual
- Training
- Advertising and Promotions
- Leasing of the Premises
- Improvements to the Premises
- Engagement in Similar Business: Non-Disclosure of Information
- Trademark
- Insurance
- Indemnification
- Events of Default
- Effect of Termination
- Assignment
- General Provisions
- Renovations
- Schedules: Premises; Trademark; Sublease; Payment Schedule

BUYER BEWARE: SOME PITFALLS OF FRANCHISING

An article in *The Globe and Mail* notes that "Franchising has reached a crossroads. It's in danger of becoming disreputable. Franchise lawyers and desperate franchisees tell the same stories, again and again. Investors are told a location makes $10 000 a week when it actually brings in $2000; in some cases, refundable deposits are never returned; and some chains ask for deposits as high as $40 000 before giving the franchisee a contract to review."[3]

More notable pitfalls that plague the franchising industry include:

Encroachment According to some franchise experts, encroachment is the number one issue in the franchise industry. **Encroachment** is a situation in which franchisors compete with franchisees by putting a store nearby or operating through an alternative distribution channel such as mail order or the Internet. For example, H & R Block now offers tax service on the Internet; you can buy a Tim Hortons coffee and doughnut at your local Esso station; and the Body Shop has retail outlets as well as mail-order distribution. What this means is that established franchisees are finding it more and more difficult to protect their territory.

ENCROACHMENT

situation in which franchisors compete with franchisees by putting an outlet nearby or setting up alternative distribution channels such as mail order or the Internet

Ground-Floor Opportunities Beware of the so-called "ground-floor" ("grow with us") franchise opportunities. A franchisor offering such "opportunity" is experimenting with your money. If you buy a franchise, you should be buying a recognized brand name, a proven business plan, excellent field support, and experience that demonstrates the particular franchise will work in your location. Otherwise you are better off to do it yourself. A concept is not normally considered established until it has been in business four to five years.

Minimum Franchise Legislation As of 2002, the federal government had no franchise legislation protecting franchisees. As a result, Canada has often been termed the Wild West of the franchise industry. That's because almost any company can become a franchisor. In most provinces, all you need is a franchise agreement and a naïve franchisee ready to sign. There are very few legal requirements or restrictions stopping you from starting your own franchise. Alberta and Ontario are the only provinces that have put in place any substantive franchise legislation (information on this legislation is available at www.cfa.ca/legal.html). Outside of Alberta and Ontario, franchisors are not legally required to provide you with the following types of information about the company:

- balance sheet and income statement information
- number of franchises
- bankruptcy history
- background of the owners and/or key officers
- revenues and expenses of the franchisor
- turnover rate of franchisees

Signing Personally If you are going into a partnership with a franchisor, we strongly advise you to keep your legal distance. You don't want to get your personal assets mixed up with a franchisor's business. Form a company, and sign the franchise agreement in the company name. If a franchisor wants personal guarantees, be prepared to say no.

Few Facts Are franchisees more successful? American statistics would support this, but there are no Canadian data. Are franchises more profitable? Again, we don't know. Most evidence is anecdotal and relies on information from franchised associations. For example, we told you that franchising grew at about 7 percent per year over the latter half of the 1990s. Here we relied on information from the Canadian Franchise Association. We trusted that its sources were accurate. There are no regular government surveys on franchising in Canada. In fact, no major survey on franchises has been conducted since the early 1990s. Beware of an ambitious franchisor who presents you with an extensive list of franchise benefits and fictitious claims like "only 5 percent or 8 percent of all franchises fail."

The Canadian Franchise Association (CFA) is one of the few sources of franchise information. The organization has about 350 members who are required to disclose certain types of information to prospective franchisees. As of 2002, you could find this disclosure information on the CFA website (www.cfa.ca/disclosure.html). This disclosure requirement, however, is not backed by government legislation. Still, check the website for prospective franchisors and see if they are registered. If they are not members, find out why. If they are, you should be able to find some information. Keep in mind, though, that members are not required to file financial information about their operations. In other words, a franchisor could be close to bankruptcy and you may not know it. Beware that some franchises, like Pizza Pizza, have been asked to leave the organization.

Saturated Markets Competition has become intense among competitive franchisors, which has led to a tendency for franchisors, especially fast-food outlets, quick-printing shops, and specialty retailers, to saturate market areas, thus resulting in many failures.

Poor Training Some training programs are poor or non-existent.

Supplies Stipulation Some franchise agreements stipulate that you must buy your supplies from the franchisor. Problems emerge when franchisees are required to pay non-competitive prices (i.e., they are overcharged) for products supplied by the franchisor.

Insiders First Typically, current franchisees are offered prime locations before outsiders or first-time franchise buyers are. Rarely is a new player offered a sure thing. Invariably, new players are offered franchisees that have already been passed over.

Non-Refundable Deposits Some franchisors ask for a refundable deposit during the time the buyer is negotiating an agreement. This is supposed to show the buyer's good faith. Be careful if you are presented with this request. Seek legal advice and place the money in trust with your lawyer, not the franchisor's. There have been cases where refundable deposits were never returned.

Evaluating a Franchise

Evaluating a franchise opportunity is much like evaluating any other business that's up for sale, but because of the nature of franchisors, you need to ask some additional questions. For example:

- How long has this franchise been in business?
- Who are the officers?
- Has the franchise gone bankrupt or been convicted of any criminal offences?
- How many franchise outlets are operating right now?
- How well does this franchise compete with similar franchises?
- Where is this franchise in its life cycle?
- What will this franchise do for me?

In Chapter 13, we presented a checklist to use in evaluating an ongoing business you are considering buying. The majority of that checklist applies to franchises as well. To supplement it, we're giving you a checklist prepared specifically for evaluating franchise opportunities (see Box 14.2). The questions will help you generate a profile of the franchise and make a wise decision.

CHOOSE YOUR PRODUCT OR SERVICE WITH CARE

As a potential franchisee, you should know everything about the product or service the franchise system delivers. Naturally, an exclusive product or service, or one that is of superior quality and value, is a good business bet. But these aren't the only criteria for judging the competitive strength of the product or service. There are good profits to be made or lost in products that are essentially not different from others in the market—except in how they are marketed. One franchise can be much the same as another, but if its marketing is superior, it can overpower the competition.

So, when you try to assess the competitive strength of the product or service you're interested in, keep your focus wide. Consider everything it takes to deliver that product or service to customers. Then ask yourself how well your prospective franchisor does all of these things.

REASONS FOR NOT BUYING A FRANCHISE

Many entrepreneurs have decided against buying franchises. Here are some of the reasons they have given:

- I know the business as well as they do.
- The franchise name is not all that important.

Box 14.2 Franchise Evaluation Checklist

General

	yes	no
1. Is the product or service:		
a. considered reputable?	______	______
b. part of a growing market?	______	______
c. needed in your area?	______	______
d. of interest to you?	______	______
e. safe,	______	______
protected,	______	______
covered by guarantee?	______	______
2. Is the franchise:		
a. local?	______	______
regional?	______	______
national?	______	______
international?	______	______
b. full-time?	______	______
part-time?	______	______
possible full-time in the future?	______	______

3. Existing franchises
   a. Date the company was founded ______________________
   Date the first franchise was awarded ______________________
   b. Number of franchises currently in operation or under construction
   ____
   c. References
   Franchise 1: owner ______________________
   address ______________________
   telephone ____________ date started ____________
   Franchise 2: owner ______________________
   address ______________________
   telephone ____________ date started ____________
   Franchise 3: owner ______________________
   address ______________________
   telephone ____________ date started ____________
   Franchise 4: owner ______________________
   address ______________________
   telephone ____________ date started ____________
   d. Additional franchises planned for the next 12 months ____________
4. Failed franchises
   a. How many failed? ______ How many in the last two years? ______
   b. Why have they failed?
   Franchisor reasons: ______________________
   ____
   Better Business Bureau reasons: ______________________
   ____
   Franchisee reasons: ______________________
   ____

(Continued)

5. Franchise in local market area
   a. Has a franchise ever been awarded in this area? ______________________
   b. If so, and if it is still in operation:
      owner ______________________
      address ______________________
      telephone ______________________ date started ______________________
   c. If so, and if it is no longer in operation:
      person involved ______________________
      address ______________________
      date started ______________________ date ended ______________________
      reasons for failure ______________________
      ____
   d. How many inquiries have there been for the franchise from the area in the past six months? _____
6. What product or service will be added to the franchise package:
   a. within 12 months? ______________________
      ____
   b. within two years? ______________________
      ____
   c. within two to five years? ______________________
      ____
7. Competition
   a. What is the competition? ______________________
      ____
      ____
8. Are all franchises independently owned?
   a. Of the total outlets, _____ are franchised, and _____ are company owned.
   b. If some outlets are company owned, did they start out this way, _____ or were they purchased from a franchisee? _____
   c. Date of most recent company acquisition ______________________
9. Franchise operations
   a. What facilities are required, and do I lease or build?

	build	*lease*
office	_____	_____
building	_____	_____
manufacturing facility	_____	_____
warehouse	_____	_____
______________________	_____	_____
______________________	_____	_____

   b. Getting started — Who is responsible for:

	franchisor	*franchisee*
feasibility study?	_____	_____
design?	_____	_____
construction?	_____	_____
furnishings and equipment?	_____	_____
financing?	_____	_____
employee training?	_____	_____
lease negotiation?	_____	_____

(Continued)

Franchise Company

1. The company
   a. Name and address of the parent company, if different from the franchise company:
      name ______
      address ______
   b. Is the parent company public ______ or private? ______
   c. If the company is public, where is the stock traded?
      Toronto Stock Exchange ______
      over-the-counter ______
      ______ ______
2. Forecast of income and expenses
   a. Is a forecast of income and expenses provided? ______
   b. Is it:
      based on actual franchisee operations? ______
      based on a franchisor outlet? ______
      purely estimated? ______
   c. Does it:

	yes	*no*
relate to your market area?	______	______
meet your personal goals?	______	______
provide adequate return on investment?	______	______
provide for adequate promotion and personnel?	______	______

3. What is the best legal structure for my company?
   proprietorship ______
   partnership ______
   corporation ______
4. The franchise contract
   a. Is there a written contract? ______ (Get a copy for lawyer and accountant to review.)
   b. Does it specify:

	yes	*no*
franchise fee?	______	______
termination?	______	______
selling and renewal?	______	______
advertising and promotion?	______	______
patent and liability protection?	______	______
home office services?	______	______
commissions and royalties?	______	______
training?	______	______
financing?	______	______
territory?	______	______
exclusivity?	______	______

Source: Adapted from C.R. Stigleman, *Franchise Index/Profile*, Small Business Management Series, No. 35 (Washington, DC: Small Business Administration, 1973), 31–41.

- Why pay a franchise fee?
- Why pay a royalty and advertising fee?
- My individuality would have been stifled.
- I don't want others to tell me how to run my business.
- I didn't want a ground-floor opportunity where I'd be the guinea pig.
- There were restrictions on selling out.
- If I didn't do as I was told, I would lose my franchise.
- The specified business hours did not suit my location.
- The franchisor's promotions and products did not fit my customers' needs or tastes.
- They offered no territory protection.

A Final Word about Franchises

After reading about the list of "buyer beware" cautionary notes, you are probably thinking about closing the book on franchising. We're not trying to discourage you, but we want you to be very careful. A franchise is a partnership and you need to make sure you can work under the controls of its system. You need to look at franchising as an option—the E-Exercise in Box 14.3 will help you evaluate your suitability for becoming a franchisee—and an example to learn from. Remember that there is no reason why *you* cannot be the franchisor. If you can develop a winning formula, then with a little entrepreneurial flair you can become a franchisor yourself. Many entrepreneurs have done this and it's another reason for learning all you can about franchising now. In the opening vignette, we discussed a successful franchise, Second Cup. Boston Pizza International Inc. and Yogen Früz World-Wide Inc. are two other notable examples:

> Boston Pizza started out as one restaurant in Edmonton called the Boston Pizza and Spaghetti House. By 1997, it had been transformed into a franchise organization and one of the *Financial Post*'s "50 best managed private companies" with over $140 million in sales.
>
> Aaron and Michael Serruya started Yogen Früz in Toronto's Promenade Mall in the late 1980s. By 1997, it had become a PROFIT 100 company and

Box 14.3 E-Exercise

Is Franchising Right for You?

You need to consider several personal issues when deciding whether franchising is the best option for you. The self-test and checklists below will help you determine how well you might fit into a franchise operation.

- **Franchising**—An Interactive Self-Test (The Virtual Franchise Expo)
  www.vifexpo.com
  Click on Franchising to access the test.
- **Franchisee Checklists**—Evaluating Yourself (Franchise Direct)
  www.franchisedirect.com/icentre/evaluate.htm#intro
- **Checklists for Franchisees** (Canada Business Service Centers)
  www.cbsc.org/english/search/display.cfm?CODE=4010&Coll=FE_FEDSBIS_E

had grown into about 3000 frozen yogurt outlets worldwide, most of which were franchised.

If you are not ready to be on your own yet, franchising may be the start for you. The Second Cup franchisor in our opening vignette made a go of it. But you need to do your homework and get some experienced advice. Before you sign a franchise agreement, read every paragraph in it and find a lawyer with franchise experience. Make sure you understand every clause. Suppose, for example, that your franchise agreement says you must buy supplies from the franchisor at competitive prices. Does competitive mean "competitive relative to what other franchisees in the system are paying"? Or does it mean "competitive in relation to other outside suppliers"? Furthermore, what happens if the franchisor cannot supply the product? As we now know, franchise law in Canada is virtually nonexistent, so your lawyer must know how the clauses of a franchise agreement have been interpreted and how the courts have settled franchisee–franchisor disputes. Lastly, we emphasize that you have a right to insist and receive full disclosure of all financial information. Exercise this right.

In a Nutshell

There are many good reasons to consider buying a franchise. Notably, if the brand name is respected, you'll already be positioned in the marketplace; and if the franchisor is sharp, you'll inherit a business plan and a strong corporate partner that can work for you. It's important, however, to examine the franchise's appeal with consumers carefully; you want to get a marketing boost from the name. Depending on the franchise, you may also get other services for your money (e.g., help on site selection, help on interior layout, and vendor connections), but the main thing you're buying is brand-name recognition.

Just as if you were investigating an ongoing independent business, study the opportunity thoroughly. Examine the financial history and compare what you'd make if you bought the business to what you'd make if you invested the same money elsewhere. Most of all, before you sign anything, get good legal and financial advice.

Key Terms

business format franchise
dealership relationship franchise
encroachment
franchise
franchisee
franchise fee
franchisor
royalty fee

Think Points for Success

- ✓ Avoid ground-floor opportunities. "Grow with us" might really signal *caveat emptor* ("Let the buyer beware").
- ✓ Talk to franchisees.
- ✓ The franchisor gets a percentage of gross sales for advertising and royalty fees whether the franchisee enjoys a profit or not.
- ✓ Do you really need the security blanket of a franchise?
- ✓ Read the proposed agreements carefully.
- ✓ Would you be comfortable relinquishing your independence?

Checklist Questions and Actions to Develop Your Business Plan

BUYING A FRANCHISE

- ❑ Why have you selected a franchise as your method of start-up?
- ❑ What were your lawyer's comments on the franchise agreement?
- ❑ Do your personal vision, goals, and personality match a franchise form of ownership?

NOTES

1. Prepared by Doug Tam, franchise owner, Second Cup, St. Laurent Mall, Ottawa, ON. Reprinted by permission.
2. Mac Voisin is quoted in John Southerst, "If You're 'Entrepreneurial,' Forget Franchising," *The Globe and Mail*, May 8, 1995, p. B5.
3. John Southerst, "Franchising Stumbles Along Perilous Path," *The Globe and Mail*, May 25, 1998, p. B11.

SUGGESTED READING

Canadian Franchise Association (CFA). The following publications are available from the CFA, 2585 Skymark Avenue, Suite 300, Mississauga, ON L4W 4L5; phone: (905) 625-2896 or (800) 665-4232; fax: (905) 625-9076; website (www.cfa.ca/bookstore.html):

- CFA Information Kit
- *CFA Franchise Canada* (The Official CFA Directory)
- *Franchise Law That Matters* (Franchise Law Group of Osler, Hoskin & Harcourt LLP)
- *Franchising Your Business* (Siskinds Franchise Law Group)
- *Franchising: So You Want to Be on the Leading Edge* (Dennis Epstein and Horwath Orenstein)

Seid, Michael, and Dave Thomas. *Franchising for Dummies*. Etobicoke, ON: John Wiley & Sons Canada, 2000.

2002 Franchise Annual (INFO Franchise News).

chapter 15

Exporting: Another Adventure Beckons

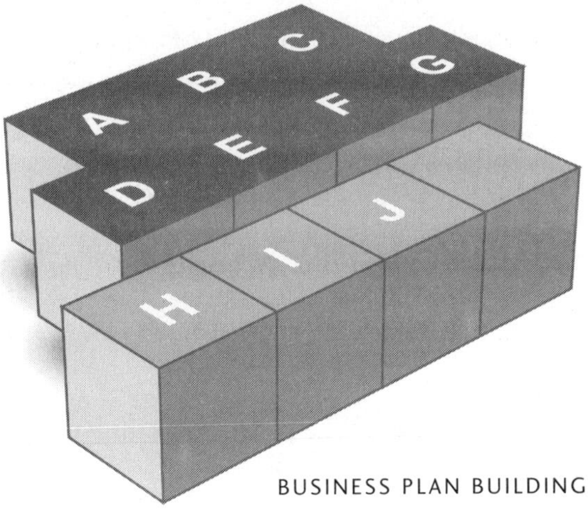

BUSINESS PLAN BUILDING BLOCK

We encourage you to consider exporting your product or service. It's an adventure you will want to investigate before you start your business or once your business is established. If you have chosen exporting to be part of your business, read the chapter carefully and complete the "Export Plan Outline" at the end of the chapter.

LEARNING OPPORTUNITIES

After reading this chapter, you should be able to:

- Become "export ready."
- Do an export SWOT analysis.
- Become aware of the key exporting issues.
- Understand and use key exporting strategies.
- Become aware of export advisers and sources of help.
- Understand the importance of cultural awareness.
- Draft a preliminary export plan.

Acadian Seaplants Ltd., a small company in Dartmouth, Nova Scotia, harvests seaweed and turns it into products that are used by food, botanical, feed, and agro-chemical industries around the world. Acadian is a Canada Export Award winner, exporting 91 percent of its products to more than 35 countries. Its success has proven that East Coast Canadians can compete and win in the global marketplace.

What has made Acadian Seaplants so successful? According to its president, Louis Deveau, the company's prosperity is due to its high-quality product, advanced technology, and aggressive research. Its competitive strategy is to invest heavily in technology, product, and market research. As much as 15 percent of its revenues is plowed back into sustainable harvesting technology, resource and technology management science, and cultivation.[1]

ACTION STEP PREVIEW

63. Do an export SWOT analysis.
64. Map out your export strategy.

Chapter 15 encourages you to consider exporting.

You may already have your plate full with the domestic market. The number of things to do in a day is endless, and you think you simply don't have the time to export. Or do you? Thanks to technology, politics, and the evolving international economy, many markets that were once only accessible to big companies are now within reach of the individual entrepreneur. Almost 30 Canadian enterprises exported commodities in 1999, 26 percent more than did so in 1993. Of these businesses, about 62 percent were smaller firms with annual exports of less than $1 million.

We think exporting is an opportunity that should not be overlooked by most entrepreneurs. For many of Canada's emerging businesses, like Acadian Seaplants in the opening vignette, export markets are absolutely essential. Here's what a few of the numbers say to support exporting:

- Almost 80 percent of the companies in *PROFIT* magazine's survey of Canada's 100 fastest-growing firms exported their product. Thirty percent derived at least three-quarters of their revenue from foreign sources.[2]
- In 2001, exports of goods and services were in the $415 billion range, accounting for about 40 percent of our economic output.[3]
- Our major trading partner is the United States, which in 2001 accounted for almost 85 percent of our exports.[4]
- Some 3 million working Canadians (one out of every three) owe their jobs to Canada's success in the global marketplace. Every $1 billion in exports sustains 11 000 jobs.[5]
- Export firms expand employment 20 percent faster than non-exporting firms, and are 10 percent less likely to fail.

Historically, Canada's small businesses have not taken full advantage of the opportunities in the export market. However, while only about 10 percent of our small businesses export, there are some encouraging indications of change. For example, almost two-thirds of the PROFIT 100 companies became heavily involved in exporting over the latter part of the 1990s. A shining example of this new breed of small business is Oasis Technology Ltd. of North York, Ontario, a software company that develops programs for electronic funds transfer. It was the number one company on the PROFIT 100 list. Over a five-year period, Oasis had a mind-boggling growth rate of 10 114 percent. All its revenue came from exporting. "Our strategy has been to attack markets in Latin America, China, and the Middle East, which have no real banking infrastructure," says Ashraf Dimitri, who founded the company in 1990. Datalog Technology Inc. in Calgary and Hummingbird Communications Ltd. in North York, Ontario, are two other examples of fast-growing PROFIT 100 companies that have relied almost exclusively on exporting.[6]

Today, the new knowledge-based economy has levelled the playing field—especially in the service sector. Small companies can serve the world market with a global telecommunications network connected to the Internet. Short production runs in manufacturing industries aided by computer-assisted programs can meet the needs of niche markets more efficiently than long production runs. Small business will continue to prosper in the new world arena that's taking shape. Yes, there are all kinds of entrepreneurial opportunities in the export market. So let's look at the challenges. Chances are, those export markets aren't as far away as you think.

The Start-up Fundamentals[7]

Many first-time exporters often become involved in exporting in an unplanned way. Ultimately, they become frustrated, disoriented, and discouraged when they learn that export markets are usually much more difficult to penetrate than expected.

We call this situation **export shock**. If you are thinking about exporting, your primary objective right now should be to plan to minimize this export inertia. We suggest you begin by taking a closer look at your export motivations and readiness, and follow this up with a **SWOT analysis**—an honest appraisal of your internal Strengths and Weaknesses and external Opportunities and Threats.

EXPORT SHOCK

the difficulty of opening an export market

SWOT ANALYSIS

honest appraisal of your internal Strengths and Weaknesses and external Opportunities and Threats

MOTIVATIONS FOR EXPORTING

What would be your motivation for entering the export market? Review the following list of reasons and choose the ones that apply to you.

- ❑ Dispose of excess domestic product.
- ❑ Supplement domestic sales with occasional foreign orders.
- ❑ Stabilize seasonal domestic markets.
- ❑ Extend the life cycle of existing products.
- ❑ Use existing capacity more efficiently.
- ❑ Build a base for long-term growth.
- ❑ Diversify the company's markets.
- ❑ Exploit unique technology or know-how.
- ❑ Improve return on investment over the medium to long term.
- ❑ Acquire knowledge and experience to help compete at home.

Of these factors, the first four reasons do not create a compelling case for undertaking a major export effort. By contrast, the other factors provide a more solid basis for making a sustained commitment to develop an export business. It takes time and effort to learn the technical aspects of exporting, understand foreign markets, and build relationships with foreign customers and intermediaries. Success in exporting normally stems from following a business strategy that focuses on achieving long-term goals such as market expansion or diversification, acquiring a better understanding of customer needs and market trends, or leveraging a company's specific knowledge or technology.

Entrepreneurs are busy people. Their attitudes and level of commitment toward an exporting goal play crucial roles in determining whether their company will be successful abroad. Scarcity of managerial time, as well as concern over the risks and barriers that confront the prospective exporter, can deter many small firms from exporting. Now ask yourself the following questions:

- Do you have reservations about entering foreign markets?
- Do you see exporting as a peripheral or sporadic activity for your company?
- Do you believe it is unnecessary to develop a strategic export marketing plan?
- Do you plan to restrict your export effort to selling through Canadian-based "middlemen"?
- Are you willing to devote a significant amount of time to pursuing export business?
- Are you committed to making sufficient funds available to develop foreign markets?
- Are you prepared to trade off profits in the early stages of an export effort for gains in the longer term?
- Do you want to develop long-term international relationships?

A positive answer to the first four questions suggests a relatively weak rationale for developing an export business. A positive answer to the remaining questions indicates a stronger willingness to view exporting as a key strategic goal of your business.

Remember, too, that export success requires both patience and commitment from your team. Everyone involved must understand why the effort is being made, the nature of his or her particular role, and how benefits over time will accrue both to the company and to the individuals who work in it. We therefore suggest you first examine the export motivations of your team members as well as yourself. To determine your export readiness, do the E-Exercise in Box 15.1.

SWOT ANALYSIS

By now you should already have a good perspective on your company because of your planning in the domestic market. What you are trying to do here is to take a strategic look at your business's strengths and weaknesses from an exporting perspective, get some ideas of what you'll need to export successfully, and then use these ideas to focus your market research. Most strategic planning begins with a SWOT analysis—an organizational method of assessing a company's internal Strengths and Weaknesses and external Opportunities and Threats. A SWOT analysis will help you answer a number of key questions. Let's start with your internal strengths and weaknesses.

Internal Strengths and Weaknesses

Here you are trying to define your company's competitive expertise. You'll also want to deal with critical weaknesses and find strategies to improve them. Table 15.1 will help you get started on this process. Before you complete this table, however, be aware of the following:

Product/Service Most successful exporting firms have already established a strong base in their own country. If your sales have been limited to local customers or to just a single Canadian region, you may be better advised to channel your ener-

Box 15.1 E-Exercise

Are You Ready to Export?

- **Export Development Canada** (EDC)
  www.edc.ca/index_e.htm

  Click on Future Exporters and fill in a questionnaire that will help you address four key questions:

  1. Is there an appetite for your product or service?
  2. Is your company ready to take on the export challenge?
  3. Do you have financing in place?
  4. Have you developed a comprehensive business and marketing plan?

- **Tools for Exporters** (Industry Canada)
  http://strategis.gc.ca/SSG/sc01716e.html

  - **Export Readiness Diagnostic**
    The Export Readiness Diagnostic for Service Firms is specifically designed for companies wishing to export their services.
  - **Export Skills Inventory**
    The Export Skills Inventory chart may assist you to take inventory of your current skill levels and determine the best method to fill skill gaps.

Table 15.1 Your Exporting Strengths and Weaknesses

Internal Attributes	Strength	Weakness
Service and Product		
Patented protection	_____	_____
Production process	_____	_____
Quality service/product	_____	_____
Packaging and presentation of service/product	_____	_____
Timely delivery	_____	_____
After-sales servicing of products	_____	_____
Delivery system	_____	_____
Services strategy	_____	_____
Responsiveness to customers	_____	_____
After-sales follow-up	_____	_____
Financial		
Financial resources	_____	_____
Cost advantages	_____	_____
Price advantages	_____	_____
Knowledge/Skills and Track Record		
Ability to speak foreign languages	_____	_____
Familiarity with foreign cultures/business practices	_____	_____
Contacts in a potential foreign target market	_____	_____
Contacts in the Canadian export community	_____	_____
Experience in conducting international negotiations	_____	_____
Experience with the technical aspects of international trade	_____	_____
Direct experience in exporting	_____	_____
Knowledge of where to obtain people with required skill sets	_____	_____
Operating history in domestic market	_____	_____
Others		
______________________	_____	_____
______________________	_____	_____
______________________	_____	_____

gies into penetrating other Canadian regional markets. Exporting is apt to come easier once you have been successful elsewhere in Canada. If you have previously exported on an intermittent basis or have sold your product to a Canadian-based intermediary such as an export trading company, you may have acquired experience that can assist you in making exporting an ongoing part of your business.

Human Resources Exporting is typically more time-consuming than pursuing domestic business. To succeed, you should aim to devote your full-time effort to exporting, at least in the start-up stage. If you have a team, be careful not to add a new set of export-related tasks to the responsibilities of people who already have their plates full. Should that happen, your domestic business will suffer and your export effort will likely not succeed.

Consider hiring (on contract) or assigning someone with prior experience in international business to help you with the mechanics of exporting. Tapping into relevant knowledge and experience from your own team may give your company an edge in evaluating or exploiting possible export opportunities.

Financial Situation A company whose financial position allows it to devote resources to export market development is well placed to make a significant commitment to exploiting international business opportunities.

If immediate profitability, cash, or working capital is a key priority underlying every business decision, export market development may not make sense, since it often requires a willingness to forgo short-term profits for long-term opportunity.

Operating History and Track Record Generally, companies that have been in business for at least a few years will be in a stronger position to try exporting than younger firms. They will have mastered the basics of managing their business, their product or service will have proven itself in the marketplace, and their cash flow will have stabilized.

External Opportunities and Threats

Now that you have taken an inside look at your company's strengths and weaknesses, ask yourself what your company's best external opportunities and possibilities are. Then identify the most important and emergent threats and how these can affect your business.

Your external opportunities and threats will depend on the general physical, economic, political, and cultural factors shaping the economic and institutional environment of your potential target markets. Table 15.2 will help you do an external opportunities and threats analysis. First, be aware of some major external issues:

- If your product depends on timely delivery or is expensive to ship, then the foreign markets that are accessible to you will be limited to those within a certain distance or travel time.
- Sophisticated after-sales service or specialized training required to make use of what you have to offer may restrict sales to markets with a population that has relatively high income and literacy levels.
- Luxury products are marketable primarily in wealthier economies where consumers focus on product features rather than price.
- Products that depend on or vary with climatic conditions must be sold in markets where the weather is suitable.
- Products that must be financed in order to be sold will be difficult to sell in countries where such financing is hard to obtain or unavailable.
- Punitive trade barriers or foreign government controls may make some countries difficult export targets.

Now it's your turn to do a SWOT analysis. Try your hand at Action Step 63.

ACTION STEP 63

Do an export SWOT analysis.

If you have a solid business idea, try a SWOT analysis from an exporting perspective. Make a list of your internal strengths and weaknesses, and your external opportunities and threats. Use Tables 15.1 and 15.2 to guide you.

If you still don't have a business in mind, think internationally. Get out a paper and pen and do some international brainstorming. What export opportunities are out there that you can take advantage of? How can you be part of the export revolution?

Key Points You Need to Know for Start-up

So far, we have directed our attention to your export readiness. We've tried to help you be aware of export opportunities, examine your exporting expectations, and analyze your strengths and weaknesses. Many of you may have already decided that exporting, at this time, is not right for you because you still need to focus your business on the local market. If this is the case, you may want to shuffle quickly through this section. Later, when you're ready to move into the export market, you can return to this part of the book.

For those of you who have decided that exporting may be the way to go for your business, this section is designed to help you do your homework. Before you launch into foreign soil, there are some key points about exporting you should be aware of, and several valuable sources of information to tap.

Table 15.2 Opportunities and Threats Checklist, from an Exporting Perspective

Market Characteristics	Opportunity	Threat
Demographic/Physical		
Population/market size	_____	_____
Population density and distribution	_____	_____
Climatic factors	_____	_____
Shipping distances (especially relevant for perishable and expensive-to-transport products)	_____	_____
Physical distribution and communication networks	_____	_____
Communications infrastructure (phones, faxes, modems) and overall technological sophistication (relevant for service providers)	_____	_____
Economic		
Level of economic development	_____	_____
Growth rates and potential	_____	_____
Industrial structure, per capita income	_____	_____
Income distribution	_____	_____
Consumer spending patterns and trends	_____	_____
Openness of the economy to imports	_____	_____
Import penetration and import sources	_____	_____
Currency and exchange rate factors	_____	_____
Balance of payments of the foreign government	_____	_____
Political/Governmental		
Political stability	_____	_____
Government involvement in the economy and in business	_____	_____
Legal framework for doing business	_____	_____
Provisions for the resolution or redress of grievances	_____	_____
Controls over foreign trade	_____	_____
Major trade policy instruments and tariff barriers	_____	_____
Non-tariff barriers such as standards and regulations	_____	_____
General state of relations with Canada	_____	_____
Sociocultural and Environmental		
Literacy rate	_____	_____
Language and customs	_____	_____
Cultural norms and characteristics	_____	_____
Business practices	_____	_____
Others		
________________________	_____	_____
________________________	_____	_____
________________________	_____	_____

FINDING INFORMATION AND ADVICE ABOUT YOUR TARGET MARKET

If you are export-ready, you'll first have to screen out a number of prospective foreign target markets. Then, you'll need to gather more detailed information on those that seem most promising.

For most small Canadian companies just beginning to export, the United States is the most popular initial foreign market. The reasons are easy to understand. Not only is proximity a factor, but also many Canadian companies benefit from close cross-border business ties, common language and culture, and similar consumer tastes and business practices.

In your research of foreign markets, many sources of information are available to assist you. Some of the most useful are:

Direct Contact Foreign visits and participation in foreign trade shows and fairs provide many opportunities for direct contact.

Periodicals Various Canadian and U.S. trade and business magazines regularly run features on specific foreign markets.

Department of Foreign Affairs and International Trade (DFAIT) Staff at DFAIT regularly compile market profiles of the countries to which they are posted. Information contained in these profiles and other department publications can be obtained from the Internet (see Box 15.2).

Other Federal Government Departments Some of these departments/agencies include: Agriculture Canada, Atlantic Canada Opportunities Agency, Business Development Bank of Canada, Canadian Commercial Corporation, Export Development Corporation, Industry Canada, International Development Agency, Multiculturalism and Citizenship Canada, Standards Council of Canada, and Statistics Canada.

Trade Commissioners About 500 of Canada's trade commissioners live and work "on site" in more than 140 cities around the world. They are the eyes, ears, and voice of Canadian exporters and an invaluable link to foreign markets. Trade commissioners abroad can help you enter your target market by assessing your entry strategy, identifying potential partners, and providing you with on-site visit support. Prepare thoroughly before you approach the trade commissioners overseas. Then ask very specific questions to get the detailed and tailor-made answers you need. For more information on trade commissioners, visit the Canadian Trade Commissioner Service website (www.infoexport.gc.ca/Entry.jsp).

Provincial Governments Provincial governments have trade and/or industry departments that deal with export promotion and assemble foreign market intelligence relevant to Canadian businesses.

Business Associations Canadian trade and industry associations also have information about foreign markets. For example, the Canadian Exporters Alliance, the Canadian Chamber of Commerce, and the Canadian Manufacturers Alliance all offer materials and seminars on foreign markets.

Foreign Embassies You should consider contacting the embassies or trade commissions representing countries that interest you and ask for information on economic conditions, trade patterns, and business conditions and practices in their home countries.

Bilateral Business Councils Numerous bilateral business councils are active in Canada. Examples of country-to-country councils include the Canada–Korea Business Council, the Canada–Poland Chamber of Commerce, and the Canada–India Business Council. Regionally oriented groups include the Pacific Basin Economic Council and the Canada–Arab Business Council.

Intermediaries Businesspeople in Canada with ties to, or ethnic roots in, a target market can be a valuable source of information and assistance. But it should be remembered that they may not be objective sources of information.

Databases Several major commercial databases (such as Dow Jones, Dow Jones Interactive, and Dun & Bradstreet) carry international economic and business information, country/industry profiles, bibliographic references, and recent newspaper and periodical articles. For information about these databases and how to access them, a good starting point is the nearest public or university library or the Internet (see Box 15.2).

Export Advisers/Experts Often, the most useful information comes directly from people who possess firsthand knowledge of the market targeted. Such people include:

- Foreign distributors
- Potential foreign customers
- Editors of specialized trade or business magazines
- Diplomatic personnel
- Other federal or provincial government officials
- Canadian companies that currently sell in the market

Internet This should become one of your main sources of export information. There are numerous websites dealing with exports. The primary government export-related sites are provided in Box 15.2.

CHOOSING AN ENTRY STRATEGY

Generally, there are three ways to enter a foreign market: through an intermediary, by direct selling, and through a partnership.

Intermediaries

If you're new to the exporting game, your best bet for entering a foreign market may be through an intermediary. This is particularly true if some or all of the following conditions apply:

- You are unfamiliar with the target market.
- You plan to make only small or intermittent export sales.
- You are selling a low-cost, mass-produced product.
- The target market has a large number of end users and high sales potential.
- Your product requires extensive on-site training and support.
- Your company is not able to provide after-sales service or customer support.
- The product is normally sold through local distributors in the target market.

Agents/Representatives An **agent** obtains and transmits orders from foreign customers and receives a commission from the exporter in return for the effort. The agent sells at prices the exporter sets and does not normally stock the product. If you use an agent, remember that the risk of loss or non-payment and the responsibility for service and warranty remain with you.

A **manufacturer's representative** is a specialized agent who generally operates within a given geographic territory and who sells related lines of manufactured goods to a specific group of customers. Using a manufacturer's representative is a common way of distributing industrial and commercial products in the United States.

AGENT
intermediary, working on commission, who sells an exporter's products to foreign customers

MANUFACTURER'S REPRESENTATIVE
specialized agent, working on commission, who sells a manufacturer's products to a specific group of customers within a given geographic area

Box 15.2 Government Export Information Sources

- **Department of Foreign Affairs and International Trade** (DFAIT)
  www.dfait-maeci.gc.ca
  DFAIT is the centrepiece of Canadian government information on opportunities and requirements for exporting abroad.
- **Export Development Corporation** (EDC)
  www.edc.ca
  The EDC provides a full range of trade finance services that help exporters and investors do business in up to 200 countries, including higher-risk and emerging markets.
- **Canadian Commercial Corporation** (CCC)
  www.ccc.ca
  As an export facilitator, the CCC provides Canadian companies with access to market opportunities and a wide range of export contracting services.
- **ExportSource.ca**
  http://exportsource.ca/index_e.cfm
  ExportSource.ca is Team Canada Inc.'s online resource for export information. Click on the links—including Step-by-Step Guide to Exporting—under "Preparing to Export" to begin your research.
- **Interactive Export Planner**
  www.prodt.businesscanada.gc.ca/exporter/Eng/app_templates/home_en.cfm
  The Interactive Export Planner will help you prepare an export plan for a new or existing business.
- **Take a World View ... Export Your Services**
  http://strategis.ic.gc.ca/SSG/sc01071e.html
  This information source on exporting is intended to help individuals and/or firms become export-ready quickly and strategically.
- **Step-by-Step Guide to Exporting**
  http://exportsource.gc.ca/heading_e.cfm?HDG_ID=2
  This comprehensive guide helps you assess your export capabilities, and steers you through planning and executing your first exporting venture.
- **Best Practices and Exporting Successes**
  http://strategis.ic.gc.ca/SSG/sc01673e.html
  This collection of best practices and service exporting successes of a number of Canadian companies and organizations is intended to provide readers with an opportunity to learn from the experiences of others. The featured companies are of various sizes, and from diverse business interests and locations across Canada. Some of the firms are new to exporting, while others derive practically all their revenues from the international marketplace.

Both agents and representatives are authorized to enter into contractual sales agreements with foreign customers on behalf of the Canadian exporter. They usually work on a commission basis and are paid only when they sell your product. Depending on the agreement, they may or may not be paid for their expenses. When searching for foreign agents and representatives, look for those who handle complementary products, which are likely to facilitate sales of your product.

FOREIGN DISTRIBUTOR
intermediary who purchases products from an exporter and resells them

Foreign Distributors The role of a **foreign distributor** differs from that of an agent or manufacturer's representative. Unlike agents, distributors actually purchase the exporter's product and then resell it to local customers. Because it assumes risks, a foreign distributor typically insists on longer payment terms and on control over your product once it takes possession of it.

A significant potential advantage for the Canadian exporter is that the distributor is often able to provide after-sales service in the foreign market. The main disadvantages of using a foreign distributor are that your margins are reduced, you have less control over the product and price, and you do not benefit from direct contact with foreign customers.

Trading Houses **Trading houses** (about 500 to 600 in Canada) are domestically based intermediaries that market Canadian goods abroad. A full-service Canadian trading house handles all aspects of exporting, including conducting foreign market research, arranging merchandise transportation, appointing overseas distributors or agents, exhibiting products at trade shows, and advertising and arranging documentation. The trading house can take full responsibility for exporting on behalf of Canadian companies that generally lack direct experience in this area.

TRADING HOUSES
domestically based intermediaries that market exporters' goods abroad

In Canada, organizations formed by the Council of Canadian Trading Houses and the Association des maisons de commerce extérieur du Québec may be able to direct you to a trading house that is appropriate for your needs.

Direct Selling

Advances in telecommunications and process technologies, more efficient transportation linkages, the growth of just-in-time delivery systems, improved inventory management techniques, and a host of other developments mean that **direct selling** by exporters in foreign markets became a more viable option for small Canadian companies over the 1990s.

DIRECT SELLING
selling to foreign markets without an intermediary

In the long term, selling directly to foreign retailers or end users may yield higher margins for the exporter than selling through an agent or distributor. It may also mean lower prices for the foreign customer. Moreover, it allows the seller to benefit from closer direct contact with end users. But direct distribution can also have disadvantages. Since the company will not have the services of a foreign representative or distributor, it must take the time to become familiar with the foreign market and with the export process. Building a direct sales force can entail a significant commitment of time, effort, and up-front costs.

Partnerships

Another option open to small business exporters is to develop some form of partnership abroad. One example is given in Box 15.3. Sometimes known also as strategic alliances (covered in Chapter 12), partnerships can help overcome the many challenges of doing business internationally. They may be useful to product exporters seeking to overcome various kinds of trade barriers and import restrictions. They are also useful to service exporters seeking a local presence and representation.

A well-structured partnership offers concrete benefits to both sides:

- Each company focuses on what it does and knows best.
- The partners share the risk and therefore minimize the consequences of failure.
- Partnering extends each side's capabilities into new areas or ideas.
- Resources can be pooled to help both sides keep pace with change.
- Small firms can use partnering to take advantage of economies of scale and achieve the critical mass needed for success. Through partners, a company can approach several markets simultaneously.
- Partnering can provide a firm with technology, capital, or market access that it might not be able to afford or achieve on its own. Both sides can translate

Box 15.3 Dare to Be Different

In Chapter 4, we highlighted Just Kid'n Children's Wear. After several calls from foreign retailers, President Kelly Cahill finally found a global partner he liked: a $4 billion Singapore mail-order company. Cahill created 10 mix-and-match items and marketed them under a new name, "Dare to be Different." Almost overnight, he entered the Asian export market. Just Kid'n supplied the product and the Singapore company sold and distributed it.

Alliances, like this, with larger international companies are one of the main reasons PROFIT 100 companies have been so successful in the export market. "There's no doubt that most PROFIT 100 companies use bigger international associates to crack the international market," says Cahill.

Source: Adapted from Rick Spence, *Secrets of Success from Canada's Fastest-Growing Companies* (Toronto: John Wiley & Sons Canada, 1997), p. 117. Reprinted by permission of the author.

the synergy gained into a competitive advantage that will help them succeed in the global marketplace.

For all its advantages, partnering also carries a few potential disadvantages:

- You may have to give up some freedom of action.
- You may have to spend considerable energy on just managing the relationship.
- Occasionally, partnerships can lead to dependence on another firm.
- With many forms of partnership, there is always the danger that strategic or proprietary information may be inadvertently shared or leaked outside the alliance.

The different types of international partnering are shown in Table 15.3.

PRICING YOUR PRODUCT OR SERVICE

Even for the experienced exporter, the pricing decision is one of the most challenging aspects of selling in foreign markets. Setting your price is a complex decision, but here are a few basic guidelines.

First, you need to understand that pricing is generally a more complicated issue for product exporters than it is for service exporters. In many professional service contracts, price is determined by the exporter's daily rate plus expenses. The crucial pricing decision revolves around the rate that is competitive in the country and what other companies charge for similar types of expertise.

If you are exporting a product, you have to begin by determining what costs will be added to the price of your product as it makes its way to the market.

Table 15.3 Types of Export Partnerships

Form of Partnering	Description/Considerations
Joint venture	• An independent business formed through the cooperation of two or more parent firms, normally for a specific purpose. • Traditionally used to avoid restrictions on foreign ownership when the business in question is entering a foreign market. • Useful if the project requires commitments that are more complex and comprehensive than what can be spelled out in a simple contract.

Form of Partnering	Description/Considerations
	• Suitable for longer-term arrangements that require joint product development as well as ongoing manufacturing and marketing. • Can also be used as a way of developing a local presence for the service exporter.
Licensing	• Not usually considered to be a form of partnership, but it can lead to partnerships or be an important element in their formation. • A firm sells the interested party the rights to use its products or services, but it still retains some control over the product or service. • Issues subject to negotiation include royalties, patents, sublicensing possibilities, rights to sell and manufacture, duration of the arrangement, geographical limitations of the licence, exclusivity, and issues related to the updating of technology.
Cross-licensing	• Increasingly popular form of strategic alliance between two firms, whereby each licenses products or services to the other. • A relatively straightforward way for companies to share products or expertise without the complications of closer collaboration. • Less likely than other partnerships to achieve much synergy because it involves minimal cooperation.
Cross-manufacturing	• A form of cross-licensing in which companies agree to manufacture each other's products. • May be combined with co-marketing or co-promotion agreements through which companies cooperate to advertise and sell each others' products. • A comprehensive cooperative agreement could involve cross-licensing, a shared promotion campaign, or even the formation of a joint venture to market each others' products. • Most agreements do not involve licences or royalties, but some rights to the product may be worked into the agreement.
Co-marketing	• Firms sell and market complementary products. • Sometimes done on the basis of a fee or percentage of sales. • An effective way to take advantage of existing distribution networks and an ally's knowledge of local markets. • Allows firms with complementary products to fill out a product line while avoiding expensive and time-consuming development.
Co-production	• Represents cooperation in the production of goods. • Enables firms to optimize the use of their own resources, to share complementary resources, and to take advantage of economies of scale. Cooperation may involve the manufacture of components or even entire products. • Many foreign engineering firms have entered joint production agreements with domestic firms that have manufacturing expertise (in the form of an alliance to make components used by all the competitors).
Franchise	• Represents a more specific form of licensing. • The franchisee is given the right to use a set manufacturing process or service delivery process, along with set business systems or trademarks, and the franchisor controls their use by contractual agreement. • The franchisor is remunerated through an initial franchise agreement fee, from royalties on sales and, in some cases, through control of supplies to the franchisee.

Table 15.4 A Typical Export Cost Sheet

1. Unit Cost	$ 650
fixed	300
variable	350
2. Labelling ("Made in Canada" label)	10
3. Tax/Duty Adjustments (subtract)	160
GST rebate	70
duty drawbacks	10
non-applicable fixed costs	80
4. Net Production Cost (1 + 2 – 3)	500
5. Packaging	45
6. Forwarding Agent's Fees	65
7. Promotional Costs	50
8. Other Costs (financing charges, documentation preparation, export credit insurance)	30
9. Export Commissions (10% of selling price to U.S. agent)	140
10. Total (4 + 5 + 6 + 7 + 8 + 9)	830
11. Trucking Costs	130
12. Merchandise Insurance	20
13. Customs and Clearance Fees	45
14. Profit (Export Income)	375
15. Final Price (10 + 11 + 12 + 13 + 14) (truck-delivered selling price, cleared through Customs)	$1400

Table 15.4 provides you with a list of the types of costs you may incur, which often makes it more expensive than in Canada. At this stage, we strongly advise that you double-check your calculations with customs and insurance brokers and government trade officials. You want to make sure that you have included all the correct costs. Once you know your costs, your next step is to determine what price you have to charge to make it worth your while. Exporters generally rely on a handful of methods to calculate their prices on goods or services sold in foreign markets. Here are three common methods:

DOMESTIC COST PLUS MARKUP
simplest pricing approach that adds domestic costs and a markup to include export costs

Domestic Cost Plus Markup **Domestic cost plus markup** is the simplest pricing approach that allows you to maintain your domestic profit margin. It involves taking your domestic costs and markup, and then adding export costs such as packaging, tariffs, freight, and insurance. If you are exporting a service, you would take your basic daily rate and add export-related costs. The main disadvantage of this approach is that it ignores market and demand conditions in the foreign country. For example, you may be able to reduce your domestic cost per unit with a higher volume of sales.

FULL-COST PRICING
pricing approach that includes fixed and variable costs and a profit margin

Full-Cost Pricing **Full-cost pricing** considers fixed as well as relevant variable costs, including those specific to exporting, in establishing prices. It allows you to recover your total costs, to which a profit margin is then added to yield the final price. But again, it overlooks the competitive situation in the target market.

MARGINAL-COST PRICING
pricing approach that includes floor price (unit cost) and marginal (export) cost

Marginal-Cost Pricing **Marginal-cost pricing** is a good strategy for some manufacturers and retailers who have surplus capacity on an ongoing basis. This means that the goods or services for export could be produced without a major increase in the company's fixed costs. To calculate your marginal cost price, you would add the following two elements: floor price plus markup.

- *The floor price* is the unit cost based on out-of-pocket costs of producing and selling the merchandise for export (including costs specific to exporting, such as product modification, packaging, and labelling). Floor price includes only those extra or incremental costs involved to export your product (i.e., your export or marginal costs).
- A markup to the estimated marginal (export) cost to yield export profit margin.

Marginal-cost pricing usually produces a lower export price than domestic cost plus markup or full-cost pricing, because it does not include many of the fixed domestic costs such as rent and administration. It is more complicated, though some argue that it provides a more accurate picture of the cost of getting your product to a foreign market, and helps to isolate the profitability of your export business.

Your ultimate decision on the costing method will depend, to a large degree, on your purpose for exporting. For example, if you are exporting to fill export plant capacity (as is the case for many manufacturers) or to keep your employees busy in the off-season, any price that returns more than the marginal cost of exporting may be enough for you.

Once you have determined an export price that will net you a profit, you will then have to deal with the exchange rate. When you sell your product in a foreign country, a critical question is how much you will get in Canadian dollars. That will depend on the exchange rate. Let's assume that the Canadian dollar is trading at $0.65 U.S. You decide that your export price for your product will be $1 Canadian. This would mean you could sell your product in the United States for $0.65 and you would get, in return, $1 Canadian for each product sold. But what if the exchange rate goes to $0.70 U.S.? You would now have to increase your price to $0.70 in the United States to maintain your export profit margin. How do you predict these kinds of fluctuations in the exchange rate? To prepare yourself, contact government officials, foreign exchange officials, and international banking officers. Use the experts to guide your guesstimate, and keep in mind that you probably will want a little room for safety in your price policy.

Determining your export price is just one of the many details that go into selling your product outside of Canada and, with exports, it is sometimes the details that determine success or failure. So, once you have determined your price, you need to do some networking. Review your strategies and plans with those who are familiar with successful export pricing in your target market. Canadian trade commissioners are a good place to start, but we also suggest you revisit our previous list of exporting sources provided above under "Finding Information and Advice About Your Target Market" (see page 305). You will need to know if your price is in line. Will the market respond? Did you forget anything?

PROMOTIONAL STRATEGIES

Well-planned foreign-based promotional strategies often play a key role in the achievement of success in international markets. Here are some important promotional considerations.

Promoting Services A service provider's offerings usually involve some conventional advertising, but personal selling is the most effective. In many service-oriented sectors, a company's reputation spreads by word of mouth or personal referrals. Many service contracts are issued by government institutions or international development agencies, and the supplier has to keep an eye on what contracts are being put out for tender. In such cases, the major form of promotion tends to be "lobbying" the support of the Canadian government through the embassy, although the services of an agency such as the Canadian Commercial Corporation or the Canadian International Development Agency can also be important.

Packaging Recognize that it will likely be necessary to redesign your Canadian packaging before trying to sell your product abroad. For example, some colours, signs, pictures, and symbols used on products sold at home may be inappropriate or even offensive in certain foreign markets where consumer tastes and values differ from those at home. Foreign sales agents and distributors will be able to provide useful advice on package design and many other matters related to this facet of promotion.

Promotional Options There are several options for advertising your product or service in foreign markets: trade/business magazines, directories, other publications and media, direct promotional materials such as brochures, and trade fairs and exhibitions.

Promotional Materials The materials for your export promotion campaign must be "internationalized." You cannot simply rely on what you use at home. Here are some important points to remember:

- Where necessary, rewrite your sales letters and literature to adapt the materials for foreign markets.
- Pictures are often an effective way of communicating your message and portraying the application of your product or service.
- Consider whether you should translate your materials into the language of your target market.
- In non-English- and non-French-speaking countries, examine the meaning and acceptability of brand names and logos used in Canada. Make sure that no negative or inappropriate connotations are conveyed.
- Make sure that colour and symbols used in promotional material are sensitive to local tastes and consumer preferences. A special distributor kit can be helpful in responding to inquiries from this source. The contents might include product specifications and a catalogue, background information on the product, product samples, annual reports or other concise summary information on your company, a questionnaire to help you learn more about the foreign agent or distributor, and a proposed understanding or representation agreement.

Trade Fairs and Exhibitions Trade fairs can be an effective way of familiarizing yourself with other markets and promoting your product with prospective foreign buyers. The main goal of trade fairs and shows is to encourage business exchanges between buyers and sellers of a particular category of products. Most trade shows and exhibitions focus on specific industries. As an exporter, your objectives in participating in these events are to display your merchandise, make business contacts, investigate the market, learn more about your competitors and their products, and make some sales.

Promoting in the United States Small exporters are advised to approach the United States as a series of distinctive regional markets and to adapt their promotional strategies accordingly. The continental United States can be divided into at least five main regions: the northeast, the midwest, the southeast, the southwest, and the Rocky Mountain/western states. Often it makes sense to break these regions into smaller subunits or even to focus on particular states. American buyers tend to perceive companies based in Canada as being domestic or "North American." They want to make their purchases in the same manner they do when buying from U.S.-based suppliers. As a consequence, many exporters choose to deal directly with any U.S. customs requirements. The priorities of American buyers are generally the same as when they deal with domestic suppliers: a competitive price, good quality, on-time delivery, and superior service.

EXPORT FINANCING

Financing is central to the success of smaller businesses intending to export. In both the product and service areas, exporting brings additional risks in terms of payment delays, disputes, and defaults. The major issues in export financing are: methods of payment, ensuring payment, credit management, and managing exchange rate risk.

Methods of International Payment

There are a variety of ways in which the Canadian exporter can arrange to be paid. Four common short-term financing methods, in order of increasing risk to the exporter, are: cash in advance, letters of credit, documentary collections, and open account transactions.

Cash in Advance **Cash in advance** is the most secure option for an exporter, since it eliminates all risk of non-payment and bolsters working capital. Unfortunately, few foreign buyers are willing to pay full cash in advance. On occasion, a buyer will provide a portion of the contract by way of cash in advance as a down payment when Canadian vendors need financing to manufacture the goods ordered by the buyer. In the case of services, a partial payment may be made upon signing a contract, after which progress payments are matched to deliverables.

CASH IN ADVANCE
short-term financing method in which a foreign buyer pays an exporter cash before goods are delivered

Letters of Credit **Letters of credit** are frequently used in international commerce. The most common form of payment, a commercial letter of credit or documentary credit, is issued by a bank at the request of an importer, in favour of a supplier/exporter, to finance the importation of goods or services. By issuing the documentary credit on behalf of the importer, the bank lends its own name to the transaction. Thus, the bank obligates itself to pay the exporter, provided that the exporter complies strictly with the terms of the credit. In effect, this eliminates the credit risk of the buyer. Both the foreign and the Canadian bank receive fees for providing this service.

LETTER OF CREDIT
sometimes called documentary credit, a document issued by a bank at the request of an importer, in favour of a supplier/exporter, to finance the importation of goods and services

There are several varieties of a letter of credit. An irrevocable letter of credit, for example, cannot be amended or cancelled without the consent of all parties, including the exporter. In contrast, a revocable letter of credit can be cancelled without the exporter's consent and, as such, is not a true guarantee of payment. If you are not prepared to accept the credit risk of the issuing bank, you can also insist on a confirmed letter of credit. A letter of credit issued by a foreign bank can be confirmed by a Canadian bank, constituting a guarantee of payment. This is an undertaking by the Canadian bank to pay if the foreign bank does not. The most secure form of letter of credit is one that is both confirmed and irrevocable.

DOCUMENTARY COLLECTION
an unconditional order from the exporter requiring the buyer to pay on demand or at a determined time a specified amount to a specified person

Documentary Collection There are several types of collection methods. A **documentary collection** is the most common type. It consists of a bill of exchange, which is an unconditional order, signed by the exporter, requiring the importer to pay on demand or at a determined future time a specified amount of money to a specified person. It is accompanied by commercial documents that confer ownership of the goods shipped. A "clean collection" is a bill of exchange not accompanied by shipping documents, as these are sent directly to the buyer. In both forms of payment, there is evidence of a legal obligation on the part of the importer.

Collections provide the exporter with a lower level of security than letters of credit, and the bank charges are less. However, in some cases, especially in dealing with countries where the banking system is less developed and letters of credit may not be available, collections may be the only alternative.

OPEN ACCOUNT TRANSACTION

a form of collection that involves little or no conditions of payment

Open Account Transactions With **open account transactions**, the exporter has sole responsibility for determining the ability and willingness of the purchaser to pay. Banks provide no protection. The exporting party must finance the transaction with its own funds. Selling on open account is arguably the easiest way to make export sales, since this arrangement incurs minimal costs to the exporter and involves little paperwork. However, it may also be risky. Open account transactions are appropriate when you trust your foreign customers and have access to bank credit. The foreign importer should have an established credit record and, preferably, should be located in a country with a stable economy and government.

Ensuring Payment: Types of Security

When selling into a new and unfamiliar market, one precaution is to demand more secure forms of payment. Apart from the payment terms mentioned earlier, there are other forms of security. The most common is export insurance. Both federal government agencies (such as the Export Development Corporation) and private insurance firms will offer policies to protect your export receivables. Insuring receivables offers exporters another advantage. Because they are essentially guaranteed, most banks will accept insured receivables as security if the exporter wants to borrow additional working capital.

A different type of security is provided by the Canadian Commercial Corporation (CCC) (www.ccc.ca). Its role is to facilitate a deal between Canadian suppliers and foreign purchasers by providing assurances to both sides. For foreign buyers, the CCC undertakes to guarantee the performance of the Canadian supplier, ensuring that goods or services will be delivered as specified. For Canadian exporters, the CCC guarantees that payment will be made if the terms of the contract are fulfilled and, in many cases, it can even accelerate payments.

Credit Management

Credit management is a key concern for most businesses when they deal with their domestic customers. The same issue arises when you begin to export. Often, it is necessary to extend credit in order to win and retain foreign customers. But before doing so, always check the buyer's creditworthiness. This is comparatively easy to do in the case of importers located in the United States and many European countries. Also important is to take into account the political/economic stability of the importing country, the availability of credit insurance, and the value of the sale both in absolute terms and in relation to your total sales.

Managing Exchange Rate Risk

International trade can put either the importer or the exporter at a foreign exchange risk. A contract that is to be paid in the exporter's currency (the preferred option for the Canadian exporter) could leave the importer at risk of currency fluctuations. By contrast, the Canadian exporter may be put at risk when the contract specifies payment in the importer's currency.

Such risks can be reduced or avoided by hedging in the foreign exchange market. Hedging involves negotiating the future payment by the importer at the exchange rate prevailing at the time the contract is signed. This eliminates the exporter's exposure to the risk of possible fluctuations in the value of the importer's currency against the Canadian dollar. Banks and other financial institutions can assist you in taking steps to manage your exchange rate risks. Ideally, however, you should try to transfer exchange rate risk to the foreign importer of your product by persuading that company to agree to make payment in Canadian (or perhaps U.S.) dollars. However, as a small business, you will likely lack the expertise or time to become involved in the foreign money market.

GETTING YOUR PRODUCT OR SERVICE TO MARKET

Understanding what is involved in getting your product or service into the foreign target market is an important part of the export process. To a large extent, the challenges you will face in export delivery depend on whether you are exporting a service or a product.

Exporting a Service

The challenges associated with providing services to a foreign market are quite different from those of providing goods. Your ability to deliver services to the customer will depend on factors such as the following:

- The extent and reliability of telecommunications links in the target market.
- The degree to which an infrastructure of computers, Internet, faxes, modems, etc. exists in the target market.
- The frequency and convenience of regularly scheduled transportation links between Canada and the target country.
- The relative technological sophistication, receptivity, and flexibility of customers in the target market.
- The support you may receive from official channels, government departments, and international development agencies.
- Your ability to satisfy legal regulations governing work permits or professional certification.

Exporting a Product

You have four options for getting your goods to your foreign customers: trucking, rail, air, and ocean. No matter what option you choose, the process of international transport is complex. Here are some of the issues you will have to deal with:

Packing of Goods Proper packing and marking is necessary for goods entering international markets. Merchandise shipped internationally, particularly by ocean or regular air freight, is susceptible to damage and loss. In selecting the appropriate packing method, you have to consider such factors as weather conditions, "at port" and handling facilities, risk of damage, and the risk of theft and pilferage.

Marking Marking containers identifies your goods in relation to the consignment or cargoes of other shippers. Marks shown on the shipping containers must conform to those shown on the commercial invoice or bill of lading. Required markings include such items as buyer's name or some other form of agreed identification, point or port of entry into the importing country, and gross and net weights in kilograms and pounds.

Product Labelling Beyond marking the container, you may also have to provide your products with labels suited to the target market. Product labelling is no trivial matter. Your goods may not clear customs or may not be admitted into the country of destination unless your product labels conform to all local requirements. You will have to deal with such issues as use of the local language, name of the country where the product was made or manufactured, name of the producer or shipper, and product details such as weight, ingredients, and so on.

Insurance International carriers assume only limited liability for your goods when they are shipped by air or water. If you are shipping abroad, you will need marine transportation insurance to protect both ocean- and air-bound cargo and to cover connecting land transportation. There are different types of marine insurance, but we strongly suggest you consider "all risk" insurance, which is the most comprehensive type of transportation insurance, protecting against all physical loss or damage from external causes.

Documentation for Overseas Shipping Shipping documents allow your product to pass through customs, be loaded on a carrier, and be transported to the destination. A number of documents are required for overseas shipping. These generally fall into two basic categories: shipping documents and collection documents. Key shipping documents include packing lists, validated export licences (if required by Canadian law), domestic bills of lading, and other export documents. Principal collection documents include commercial invoices (the seller's bill of sale), consular invoices (required by some foreign countries), certificates of origin (attesting to the origin of the exported goods), and import licences.

Freight Forwarders As you can see by now, the transport of goods to a foreign country is complex, and that is why even the most experienced exporters often choose to get expert advice. We strongly recommend that you use the assistance of a freight forwarder for the international transport of goods. Freight forwarders are specialists in handling and shipping goods for sale to foreign countries. Effective use of a forwarder is particularly critical for companies new to exporting. Among the specialized services they offer are:

- Selecting a suitable carrier for your product and target market.
- Negotiating all arrangements with the carrier.
- Coordinating the movement of cargo to the port of embarkation.
- Preparing the necessary documents.
- Providing advice on the packing, labelling, and marking of goods.
- Arranging warehouse storage and cargo insurance.

CULTURE AND COMMUNICATION

SLM is a Toronto-based company that sells software systems for electronic banking. After just four years in business, it had more than quadrupled its revenues. At least 80 percent of its revenues now come from outside Canada. How did this small Canadian company become so successful in penetrating the world market? According to Govin Misir, SLM's Guyana-born president and chief executive officer, "The company has incorporated cultural awareness into the way it does business." As this example shows, if you want to succeed in the international marketplace, you must ensure that your communications are linguistically and culturally appropriate.[8]

Here are a few interesting illustrations:[9]

- You should always use your right hand when you accept or pass food in India.

- When most Canadians "table" a proposal, they intend to delay a decision. In Britain, "tabling" means that immediate action is to be taken.
- For many Arabs, their signature on a contract is much less meaningful than the fact that they have given their word.
- Pepsico marketers created a promotional campaign, in China, based on the theme "Come Alive with Pepsi." Sales were slow. They later found out that the direct Chinese translation of their slogan was "Bring your ancestors back from the dead."

To help us think about our communication styles, anthropologists tend to divide cultures into two basic types: high context and low context (see Figure 15.1). Communications in **high-context cultures** tend to depend not only on the message itself, but on everything that surrounds it. Mexico would be a good example of a high-context culture. Communications in **low-context cultures** tend to rely on explicit verbal and written messages. Examples of countries with low-context cultures include Switzerland, Germany, and Canada. What this means is that if you are the type of Canadian who wants to "shake hands and get down to business," you may hit a cultural roadblock if you are trying to export to Mexico. In Mexico's high-context culture, it's wise to allow lots of time for relaxed meals and relationship building.[10]

HIGH-CONTEXT CULTURE

culture in which communication depends not only on the message itself, but also on everything that surrounds it

LOW-CONTEXT CULTURE

culture in which communication tends to rely on explicit written and verbal messages

Clearly then, before you begin your exporting journey, you are going to have to do your cultural homework. It is not enough to learn how to say a few things in another language or have your mail translated. Communication goes beyond the spoken or written language. It has to do with history, political and social environment, culture, and traditions. This means that you may have to visit your target several times or get professional advice and training. The point is that the way of conducting business differs in every country and sometimes even within regions of a country. You can't expect to be successful until you have mastered the business and social culture.

A FINAL "EXPORT READY" CHECKLIST

Before you launch your product or service onto foreign soil, we want you to review the following checklist of questions. It might also be a good idea to note some of the most common errors made by novice exporters, shown in Box 15.4.

- ❑ Are you ready to commit the resources and time to attempt exporting?
- ❑ Are you comfortable with and knowledgeable about the choice of target market?
- ❑ Are you confident that you have the right product or service for that market?

Figure 15.1 Low- to High-Context Continuum

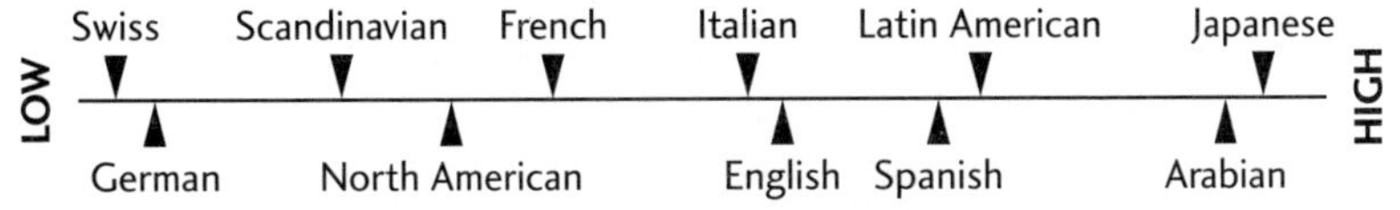

Eleven global regions denote a continuum of low- to high-context cultures.

Source: Gene Boone and David Kurtz, *Contemporary Business Communication*, Second Edition. Copyright © 1994. Reprinted by permission of Prentice-Hall, Inc., Upper Saddle River, NJ.

Box 15.4 Ten Common Exporting Errors

1. The company did not gather all the necessary background information about the target market. It failed to devise a meaningful marketing plan before attempting to export.
2. The company did not have the commitment or the determination to overcome the difficulties associated with exporting, and it lacked the resources to meet the financial obligations incurred during the initial stages of exporting.
3. Not enough attention was paid to choosing a foreign agent or distributor. The one chosen performed poorly and the company became discouraged.
4. In the first flush of enthusiasm, the company spread itself too thin, attempting to enter several different markets, rather than focusing on one and establishing a base of expertise and strength from which further efforts might be undertaken.
5. The company regarded exporting as a safety net, turning to it only when the domestic market experienced a downturn and abandoning it when domestic business recovered. It did not develop a long-term strategy or presence.
6. The company treated its foreign partners, agents, and distributors with less consideration than it treated its partners and associates at home.
7. The company refused to modify its products to respond to regulations or cultural preferences in its target markets.
8. The company attempted to operate exclusively in English and did not bother to provide itself with capabilities in the language of the target market, nor did it seek to produce documents in that language.
9. The firm attempted to do everything by itself instead of engaging specialists such as freight forwarders and customs brokers to handle the technical details of exporting.
10. The company failed to investigate the potential benefits of partnerships, joint ventures, and technology exchanges as a way of enhancing its export efforts.

ACTION STEP 64

Action Steps

Map out your export strategy.

By now you should have completed significant export research and a SWOT analysis. You have isolated a target export market. It's necessary to establish your export strategy, which should deal with:

- selection of service offerings or products
- selection of primary and secondary target countries/regions
- market entry strategy (from intermediaries, all the way to on-site manufacturing)
- pricing strategy
- promotion strategy
- payment/collection policies and procedures
- distribution strategy

Once you have completed your strategy, you are ready to draft your export plan.

- ❑ Have you become familiar with the necessary technical information?
- ❑ Are you confident with your choice of entry or distribution strategy, and do you feel you have the right partners or associates?
- ❑ Are you confident your price is competitive?
- ❑ Do you have a promotional plan?
- ❑ Can you finance the transaction?
- ❑ Have you chosen an appropriate way of delivering the shipment?
- ❑ Do you have an adequate understanding of the culture of your target country?

If you're satisfied with these answers, it's time to map out your exporting strategy. Complete Action Step 64. You will then be ready to piece together an export plan. To help you, use the following "Export Plan Outline" as a guideline for the "export plan" section of your business plan or simply on its own as your export plan. Another export plan template can be found in ExportSource.ca's Step-by-Step Guide to Exporting (see Box 15.2).

Export Plan Outline

Corporate Overview

- Background
- Description of service or product
- Types of target customers

Export Objectives

- Reasons for pursuing international markets
- Statement of Expectations (e.g., market share, revenues/profits)
- Time frame for profitability

Export-Related Strengths

- Analysis of strengths and weaknesses
- Strategies for enhancing competitiveness

Export Opportunities/Threats and Target Markets

- Identify market types
- Evaluate markets through market research
- Select target market

Identification of Resource Requirements

- Human resources
- Financial resources
- Facilities requirements
- Marketing requirements

Export Strategy

- Selection of service offerings or products
- Selection of primary and secondary target countries/regions
- Market entry strategy
- Pricing strategy
- Promotion strategy
- Payment/collection policies and procedures
- Distribution strategy
- Detailed marketing and implementation plan

In a Nutshell

The world economy is in a state of change, and change signals opportunity to the entrepreneur. Exporting is a whole new experience for many, and takes commitment, patience, and money. You'll have to learn about new markets, cultures, terms, rules, and behaviours. The purpose of this chapter was to get you started thinking about exporting opportunities. First, we asked you to take a hard look at your export readiness. Then, we suggested that you do an export SWOT analysis—an honest appraisal of the strengths and weaknesses of your business idea, and the market opportunities and threats. Next, we provided you with information on some key export issues. Finally, we encouraged you to draft an export strategy and think about incorporating this into your business plan.

Key Terms

agent
cash in advance
direct selling
documentary collection
domestic cost plus markup
export shock
foreign distributor
full-cost pricing
high-context culture
letter of credit
low-context culture
manufacturer's representative
marginal-cost pricing
open account transaction
SWOT analysis
trading houses

Think Points for Success

- ✓ Exporting can be a wonderful way to see the world and cultivate an understanding of various cultures.
- ✓ Use your government officials and agencies, especially at the federal level. Did you know, for example, that the Export Development Corporation (EDC) helped over 3000 smaller exporters in 1999? Smaller exporters now account for about 90 percent of the EDC's customers.
- ✓ Make the Internet a primary source of export information. Visit, for example, the websites listed in Box 15.2.
- ✓ If you find yourself balking at exporting because you don't know how to do it, analyze your initial feelings about operating your computer. You didn't know how to work it then, but now you probably couldn't do business without it.
- ✓ Use your "new eyes" all the time when you travel. It's amazing what opportunities lie in cultural differences.
- ✓ If you're going to export, do an export SWOT analysis. Then you'll need an exporting plan and a lot of advice.

NOTES

1. Based on a special supplement by the Department of Foreign Affairs and International Trade, CIBC, Export Development Corporation, and Bell Advantage. The supplement appeared in the "1996 Canada's Export Awards," *The Globe and Mail Report on Business*.
2. Louis E. Boone, David L. Kurtz, and Ronald A. Knowles, *Business* (Toronto: Dryden, 1998), p. 59.
3. Statistics Canada, "Imports and Exports of Goods on a Balance-of-Payments Basis," retrieved from www.statcan.ca/english/Pgdb/Economy/International/gblec02a.htm; and "Real Gross Domestic Product, Expenditure-Based," retrieved from www.statcan.ca/english/Pgdb/Economy/Economic/econ05.htm
4. Statistics Canada, "Imports and Exports of Goods."
5. Team Canada Inc., ExportSource.ca, Step-by-Step Guide to Exporting, retrieved from http://exportsource.gc.ca/heading_e.cfm?HDG_ID=2
6. Adapted from Rick Spence, *Secrets of Success from Canada's Fastest-Growing Companies* (Toronto: John Wiley & Sons Canada, 1997), pp. 115–116.
7. Information for much of this section came from Industry Canada, Entrepreneurship and Small Business Office, "Exporting for Competitiveness: Ten Steps for Small Business," *Report on Small Business in Canada*, 1992.
8. Patrick Brethour, "Software Company Lands in Tehran," *The Globe and Mail*, October 16, 1996, p. B15.
9. Boone, Kurtz, and Knowles, *Business*, p. 30.
10. Ibid., p. 236.

SUGGESTED READING

Acuff, Frank L. *How to Negotiate Anything with Anyone Anywhere Around the World*. Whitby, ON: McGraw-Hill Ryerson, 1996.

Campbell, Colin, with Carol Hood. *Where the Jobs Are: Career Survival in the New Global Economy*, 2nd ed. Toronto: Macfarlane Walter & Ross, 1997.

McInnes, J. David. "Will You Be Paid? International Sales." *Law Now*, October/November, 1995, pp. 15–16.

Osberg, Lars, Fred Wien, and Jon Crude. *Vanishing Jobs: Canada's Changing Workplace*. Toronto: James Lorimer & Company, 1995.

chapter 16

Pulling the Plan Together

BUSINESS PLAN BUILDING BLOCK

In this chapter, you do the final assembly of your business plan building blocks. Read your plan again and rewrite for maximum clarity and impact. Insert an executive summary, a table of contents, and an appendix, and put the completed plan in an attractive binder.

LEARNING OPPORTUNITIES

After reading this chapter, you should be able to:

- Pull all the information you have together into one coherent unit, which becomes a working showcase for your business.
- Study a sample business plan to see how one group of entrepreneurs defined and presented their business.
- Match or surpass the sample business plan in value-added information, research, and effectiveness.
- Put your finished business plan to work.

In the late 1900s, Herb Evans, a business promoter from Florida, presented an idea to Crila Plastics Industries Ltd. in Mississauga, Ontario. Evans claimed he represented someone by the name of Geoff House, who had invented a plastic called Extrudawood that looked and acted like a wood. The staff at Crila studied Herb's proposal and reported to their president, Peter Clark, that the concept looked intriguing. The staff knew that Clark was a man with a willingness to listen to innovative ideas and who had a passion for reading business plans. Fortunately, Herb had drawn up a plan. "Let me take that home," said Peter. He read the document over a weekend. It didn't take long before he signed a joint-venture deal with the inventor, Geoff House, for the North American rights to produce Extrudawood. "One million feet is a nice order in a year. The two companies are both looking at doing that much each month," says Peter. Today, Extrudawood has become the backbone of Crila Industries—largely because of a well-documented business plan.[1]

Chapter 16 tells you how to draw on all of the materials you have generated in the earlier chapters to create your finished business plan—a portable showcase for your business, as well as a personal road map to small business success.

ACTION STEP PREVIEW

65. Write a cover letter for your plan.
66. Write an executive summary.
67. Describe your product or service.
68. Describe the market and the target customer.
69. Describe your major competitors.
70. Describe your marketing strategy.
71. Show off your location.
72. Introduce your management team.
73. Introduce your personnel.
74. Project your cash flow.
75. Project your income statement.
76. Project your balance sheet.
77. Construct a PERT chart and go for it.

Your business plan could be the most important document you've created. It will help keep you focused while you're out there doing the work on your start-up, researching, finding the gaps, interviewing small business owners, profiling your target customers, and so on.

Staying focused is important because you're going to get a lot of distracting ideas for more new businesses while you're out there hunting.

A business plan will keep your creativity on track and help you work toward your vision. How? By being a constant reminder of who you are and where you are going.

When you've finished your plan, you've got something in writing to show the people who are important to your business: your banker, lenders, relatives, venture capitalists, vendors, suppliers, key employees, friends, and others. The plan is portable, and you can make as many copies as you need to show to the people who can help you succeed. You can even fax or e-mail it to contacts across the country.

Planning is hard work. You'll stay up nights over this, maybe lose some sleep, but with a plan, implementation is a lot easier. Just as a pilot would not consider a long flight without a flight plan, neither should you consider a business venture without a business plan.

How to Write Your Business Plan

TWO-PART STRUCTURE: WORDS AND NUMBERS

Your business plan tells the world what kind of business you're in. For ease of handling, divide your plan into two sections and provide the needed documentation in appendices at the end. In Section I, use *words* to briefly introduce your strategies for marketing, production, and management. (In this section, you also share your vision, mission, and goals.) Try to "hook" your reader with the excitement of creating a business, assessing the competition, designing a marketing plan, targeting customers, finding the right location, and building a team—all those human things that most people can relate to even if they're not in business.

In Section II present *numbers* such as an income statement, cash flow projection, projected balance sheet, and ratio analysis. This section is aimed primarily at bankers, credit managers, venture capitalists, vendors, and commercial credit lenders. At the same time, you've got to make it accessible to the casual reader who searches for the bottom line.

Support the two sections with *appendices*. This is where you put résumés, maps, diagrams, photographs, tables, reprints from industry journals, letters from customers, letters from vendors, credit reports, personal financial statements, bids from contractors, and other documentation that demonstrates the viability of your plan. Note that in most cases, material in the appendices comes from primary and secondary sources. You're not stating anything new here; you're just supporting what you've already said. (Appendices vary according to each business; for that reason, sample appendices are not included in this book.)

By following the Action Steps in this chapter, you will complete all the components you need to make a successful business plan. If you want to jump ahead for a quick overview of your plan, take a look at our sample table of contents in Box 16.2 (see page 327). Although this chapter provides one template for a business plan, not all plans will look the same. Your eventual plan will depend on your type of business and your reasons for preparing the plan. Other business plan templates can be found on the websites listed in Box 1.6 on page 11.

THE RELATIONSHIP OF YOUR PLAN TO THIS BOOK

You may be closer to producing your business plan than you think. If you have completed the Action Steps and Building Blocks in the preceding chapters, you already have the major components of your plan. The earlier chapters gave you the materials; this chapter gives you the structure.

When your entire business plan is assembled, you will notice weaker sections that need more attention. Much of the information that was developed in the Action Steps and Building Blocks will be useful in strengthening the plan and thus building the reader's confidence in it.

HOW TO START WRITING

If you're a creative thinker, chances are your thought processes don't always follow a linear sequence. That's great—it will help you as an entrepreneur! Nonetheless, the Action Steps in this chapter *do* follow a linear sequence, the sequence of the parts of a finished business plan. This is a matter of convenience: you get to see an example of each part as it would appear in the finished product. Bear in mind, however, that we don't expect you to write each part directly in sequence.

The best way to start writing a business plan is to begin with the material with which you feel most comfortable. For example, if you really enjoyed interviewing target customers, you might begin with Part B, "The Market and the Target Customer," referring to Chapters 3 and 4 for boosts. Once you have a foothold, the other parts will seem easier to reach.

In this chapter, the Action Steps can serve as a checklist for keeping track of which parts of the plan you have written. For example, in practice you would probably write the cover letter last, although that is the first Action Step we present. Think of the writing of this first cover letter as a valuable exercise. The more cover letters you write, the easier it becomes to write them effectively.

The Cover Letter

To aim your plan so that it will achieve the most good, you use a cover letter. Each time you send the plan to someone, you write a special cover letter addressed to that specific reader. The cover letter introduces the excitement of your plan, and it tells the person why you are sending it to him or her.

Read the sample cover letter in Box 16.1.

Let's summarize what's good about our sample cover letter. We can see that:

1. The writer is making use of a previous contact.
2. The writer tells the reader—the manager of a bank—that he is in the market for a loan. He does not put the manager on the spot by asking for money.
3. Instead, he asks for advice on where to find sources of capital.
4. The writer struck the right tone. (To do that, he rewrote the letter several times.)

You can do as well or better—and it's worth the effort! As you draft your cover letter, remember that the reader will pass judgment on your business plan (and on your business ability) on the basis of the letter. Do you want your small business to look bright, attractive, and welcoming? Your cover letter needs to give the same impression. A good cover letter will make its readers want to become involved in your venture.

Action Step 65 will help you write your cover letter.

ACTION STEP 65

Write a cover letter for your plan.

Address your letter to a specific person who can help your business. Be brief; aim for about 200 words.

State the reason you are sending the plan. If you are asking for money, tell the person what you want it for and how much you need. One well-written paragraph should be all you need to do this.

Your purpose in writing the cover letter is to open the door gently and prepare the way for further negotiations. The cover letter is bait on your hook.

If you are putting money into the business, or if you have already donated, indicate how much.

The tone you are after in this opening move is confident and slightly formal. You want to appear neat, bright, organized, and in control of your venture.

Be certain to explain briefly how you will repay the money.

Refer to the sample letter in Box 16.1.

Box 16.1 Sample Cover Letter

In this sample cover letter, The Software School's CEO introduces his company's business plan to a potential lender.

November 24, 20XX

THE SOFTWARE SCHOOL
47 Turbo Drive
Suites 108–110
Toronto, Ontario

Mrs. Deborah Wallis
Manager, Royal Bank
1400 Market Circle
Anytown, Canada

Dear Mrs. Wallis:
We at The Software School want to extend our appreciation for the advice and guidance you have provided on revising and updating the enclosed business plan. Your input was helpful in the marketing area and invaluable for the financial section. Everyone here at The Software School appreciates the care you took reading over those early drafts.

We're now in the market for a loan of $50 000 (the figure you suggested) to be used for capital expenditures—microcomputers, desks, chairs, and upgrading our curriculum—and we'd appreciate any guidance you could give us concerning sources of capital. (As I'm sure you'll recall, our venture was launched without any debt whatsoever, with each of our five principals putting up $20 000 apiece. And the present Turbo Drive location already has space available for the second classroom.)

We're planning to repay the loan out of new profit over the next three years. (For more information, please refer to the financial section of our plan, beginning on page 14.)

Again, thank you very much for your help and advice. We couldn't have done it without you.

Cordially,

Derek Campbell, CEO

Preliminaries

THE TABLE OF CONTENTS

Box 16.2 provides a sample table of contents to give you a quick overview of a finished business plan. In practice, the table of contents is prepared last.

THE EXECUTIVE SUMMARY

The executive summary serves as an introduction to the business plan. In function, it is similar to the preface of this book: it is written to acquaint the reader with the nature of the business, to direct the reader's attention to whatever

Box 16.2 Sample Table of Contents

The table of contents page of The Software School's business plan.

Table of Contents
Executive Summary 1

- I. Description of the Business 1
  - A. The Service We Provide 3
  - B. The Market and Our Target Customer 4
  - C. The Competition 6
  - D. Marketing Strategy 8
  - E. Our Location 10
  - F. Management 11
  - G. Human Resources 12
- II. Financial Section
  - H. Projected Cash Flow 16
  - I. Projected Income Statement 18
  - J. Projected Balance Sheet 19
  - K. Other Financial Information 21

Appendices*

1. Customer Surveys, First Six Months of Operation
2. Letters from Mass Merchandisers
3. Quote from IBM Supplier
4. Personal Résumés
5. Personal Financial Statements
6. Credit Reports
7. Letters of Reference
8. Bid from Contractor
9. Diagram of the Turbo Drive Location

*The need for specific appendices varies greatly from business plan to business plan. For that reason, this chapter does not include sample appendices. As you draft your plan, you will need to document and substantiate your business strategies; this kind of documentation is best included as appendices.

strengths the author (entrepreneur) wants to emphasize, and to make the reader want to turn the page and become involved. Because the executive summary gives perspective to the entire business plan, it needs to be written after the entire plan is completed. All the information should be condensed in one to three pages. Pay special attention to the *business description, current position,* and *future outlook, management, uniqueness,* and—if funds are being sought—*funds sought, how they will be used,* and *when they will be repaid.* This summary will appear right after the table of contents (and the confidentiality statement, if one is used).

As you write your executive summary, remember that lenders prefer "hard" numerical data and facts; they cannot take speculations about things seriously. Therefore, such phrases as "50 percent return on our original $100 000 investment" and "secured agreements from 17 retail computer stores" make the example in Box 16.3 a strong executive summary. They help to paint a picture of good management and solid growth potential for The Software School.

You, too, can write an effective executive summary. Action Step 66 will help you to decide which facts and numbers will portray you and your business venture as credible and promising and then to summarize them on paper.

ACTION STEP 66

Write an executive summary.

Imagine you had two minutes to explain your business venture to a complete stranger. This gives you an idea of what information you need to put into writing for your executive summary.

Practise explaining your venture to friends and strangers, limiting yourself to two minutes. Ask them to raise questions, and use their questions to guide you as you revise and hone your presentation.

When you are satisfied with your oral summary, write it down and type it up. It should not exceed three typed pages. (The Software School's executive summary that serves as our example was less than one page, single-spaced.)

This may constitute a very small portion of your business plan, but it could be the most important part of it.

Box 16.3 Sample Executive Summary

The Software School provides numerical data and hard facts in its executive summary.

Executive Summary

The Software School is a user-friendly, state-of-the-art microcomputer training centre. In our first six months of operation, we demonstrated our unique and profitable way of exploiting a strong and growing market within a fast-growing industry. The Software School's sophisticated electronic classroom provides "hands-on" education that teaches computer users how to use new software programs. By January 2, 20XX, we were operating at 92 percent capacity (50 percent is break-even) and had a waiting list of 168 students.

We plan to add a second classroom in order to double our capacity. This expansion will allow us to attain $400 000 in sales by the end of our eighteenth month. At that time, our pretax profits will have reached almost $50 000, representing a 50 percent return on our original $100 000 investment.

Our target customers seem to have insatiable appetites for software application knowledge, and The Software School anticipates an annual compound growth rate of 50 percent over the next five years. We have secured training agreements from 17 retail computer stores in the area and firm contracts for more than 700 employees from 84 industrial users.

Our competitors continue to train in the traditional style and currently show no sign of copying our unique instructional approach. Occasional price cutting by competitors has had no effect on our enrollment.

Management, led by Derek Campbell, has demonstrated how to offer superior training at competitive prices. Our plans for the future include developing additional profit centres by providing on-site counselling and training for firms throughout Southern Ontario. Research and customer surveys indicate that we have just begun to satisfy the ever-increasing need for software education.

ACTION STEP 67

Describe your product or service.

Excite your reader about your business. Excitement is contagious. If you can get your reader going, there's a good chance you'll be offered money. Investors love hot ideas.

If this is a start-up, explain your product or service fully. What makes it unique? What industry is it in? Where does the industry fit in the big picture?

Mention numbers wherever you can. Percentages and dollar amounts are more meaningful than words like lots and many.

If this is an ongoing business, your records of sales, costs, and profit and loss will substantiate your need for money.

Keep the words going and the keyboard smoking. You need to persuade the reader to keep reading.

Section I: Description of the Business

You know your business, but you need to prove it with words and numbers. By the time your reader finishes your business plan, you should have a convert to your side. To give you examples to follow, we reprint key sections from the business plan (newly revised and updated) for The Software School, an ongoing business that is seeking financing for acquiring more equipment. Regardless of whether your business is already in existence or just starting up, the goals of Section I are the same: to demonstrate that you know your business and that you're a winner.

PART A: BUSINESS DESCRIPTION

Box 16.4 shows how The Software School tackled this part of Section I.

The Software School will get its funding because the writer of the plan proves that the business is a winning concern. The writer has:

1. let the facts speak for themselves
2. supported all claims with numbers
3. avoided hard-sell tactics
4. refused to puff the product
5. projected a positive future

The writer does a terrific selling job without appearing to be selling at all. Now it's your turn. Do Action Step 67.

Box 16.4 Sample Business Description

The Software School effectively describes its business in Section I.

The Service We Provide

The Software School, a federal corporation, is a microcomputer training facility located in Toronto, between the Pearson International Airport and a high-density executive business complex. The area has a large number of microcomputer users. Now in its seventh month of operation, the school has a waiting list of 168 students (67 percent of whom have paid a deposit).

We train people in computer software systems from the "Top Ten" list of best-selling microcomputer and Internet software packages. Because of their power, these systems are complex. They provide a learning hurdle, especially at first.

Students are drawn to our teaching method because it gives them hands-on experience and because we have a very knowledgeable staff. Our teaching works. Working people are busy, and a student can upgrade a given software skill by 80 percent in eight hours. (Slower learners are guaranteed a second try, and a third, at no additional cost.) Most of our courses can be completed in one day or two evenings. In contrast, the average college course (which emphasizes concepts, rather than hands-on software systems) takes 12 to 18 weeks. Our price is $100 for most courses, and so far no one has complained about the cost.

The Software School achieves this space-age learning speed with a sophisticated electronic teaching system adapted from flight-simulation techniques used by airlines for training pilots. We are constantly streamlining and upgrading the system, using funds already allocated in our start-up budget.

One especially bright note: We have done far better than we had hoped. Our actual income figures average 24 percent above our original projections. Projected income for the first six months, with an assumed occupancy rate of 50 percent, was just over $10 000 a month. The actual occupancy has not peaked, and for the past two months we have operated at 92 percent capacity.

As a service business, we sell seats as well as skills and information, and as Appendix 1 shows, our promotion has generated a heavy demand for present courses such as Computer Fundamentals, Excel, and Windows 2000. At the same time, customers are asking for courses to meet their needs—for example, a course in Lotus Notes.

Until the end of our fifth month, we were open six days a week from 8 a.m. to 10 p.m. To meet demand with our current classroom facilities, we are now open on Sundays from 9 a.m. to 6 p.m., and the Sunday classes are full.

The demand increased dramatically when we contracted with some of Southern Ontario's large computer retailers to develop a training program. (See Appendix 2 for letters from specific sales managers.) These retailers sent us their salespeople for training; the salespeople, in turn, have referred their customers to us. Computer retailers quickly discovered they can sell better systems to buyers who are not afraid of computers, and they are in the business of selling, not training. We combat customers' fears in a logical way, with knowledge.

Our equipment (IBM Pentium PCs) is top-quality. Our staff combines excellent training skills and great practical experience with a focus on people and their needs. We have launched a solid start-up in a heated growth industry, and we plan to continue our growth and success.

PART B: THE MARKET AND THE TARGET CUSTOMER

Knowledge is power, especially in the information age. The Software School—an information business—capitalized on expert knowledge to define the marketplace. In the same way, if your research is sound, that knowledge will show up in your writing.

ACTION STEP 68

Describe the market and the target customer.

Bring all of your marketing research into this section and wow your reader with a picture of your target customer just sitting there waiting for your product or service.

Use data from secondary sources to give credibility to the picture you are painting.

As you continue to read The Software School's business plan, remember:

1. This is a revised business plan, so the writing flows well. You will need to do several revisions in order to smooth out your writing. (How many revisions are you planning?)
2. The reader of your business plan is a special kind of target customer. (How can you use your marketing abilities to look at this reader with new eyes? Have you developed a profile of this very special target customer?) Action Step 68 gives you a chance to show what you know about your market and target customer. If you need help getting started, review your work in Chapters 3 and 4. You can also review what the business plan for The Software School says about its market and TCs (see Box 16.5). Be sure to use secondary sources (like documents, tables, and quotes) to lend credibility to this portion of your plan.

PART C: THE COMPETITION

ACTION STEP 69

Describe your major competitors.

Briefly profile the businesses that compete with you directly. Try to be objective as you assess their operations.

What are their strengths? What are their weaknesses? What can you learn from them?

After you've described your competitors, indicate how you're going to outdistance them.

Obviously, if you know who your competitors are and how they fail to meet market needs, you are well on your way to strategic competition. You need to persuade your reader how great your competitive tactics are. (If you need a reminder, reread Chapters 4 and 5. Competition changes according to the life-cycle stage of the industry, so a good way to begin your section on competition is to place your industry in the proper life-cycle phase.)

How tough do your competitors look? As you read The Software School's assessment of its competition, note that the writer takes a cool, objective look at the competition. He does not belittle them, and he certainly doesn't underestimate them. (See Box 16.6 on page 332.)

How will you handle the competition in your business plan? Your readers will expect you to be cool and objective. Now you should be ready to complete Action Step 69.

PART D: MARKETING STRATEGY

ACTION STEP 70

Describe your marketing strategy.

Now that you've profiled your target customer and assessed your competition, take some time to develop the thrust of your market strategy. Which techniques will get the best and most cost-effective response?

Because pricing is such an important consideration, you might start with what your TC sees as a good value, and then develop your marketing mix.

Now it's time to describe your marketing strategy. Need a reminder? Look back at your work in Chapter 6.

The marketing strategy excerpt from The Software School's business plan (Box 16.7 on page 333) demonstrates a carefully reasoned approach. The excerpt describes conscious marketing policies that will help this small business be competitive. If you read a business plan in which the writer did not demonstrate this care and deliberation, how much faith would you have in the writer's business abilities?

Note that The Software School uses a three-pronged approach to reaching the public. This business understands the importance of finding a good promotional mix.

The entrepreneurs who run The Software School stay on top of the changing market picture. They have demonstrated this by:

1. dropping discount inducements from their ongoing print campaign,
2. looking ahead to radio and TV exposure,
3. logging calls and gathering information on the callers to maintain a base of up-to-date information on their target market, and
4. determining how they have gained their largest accounts, and planning to intensify their efforts in that area.

Action Step 70 will help you to refine your marketing strategy. Note that you must continue to focus on the target customer.

Box 16.5 Sample Marketing Strategy Description

The Software School clearly describes its market and target customer.

The Market and Our Target Customer

Industry Overview

Fifteen years ago, the personal computer (PC) did not exist in the marketplace. There were mainframes, of course, and terminals linked to invisible data banks—but nothing you could carry home in a suitcase.

Things are different today. Approximately 200 firms are making PCs. The lion's share of the market goes to IBM, Dell Computers, Compaq, and so forth, and yet someone brings out a new PC almost every day of the year. The microcomputer industry and the Internet are moving so fast that statistics can hardly keep pace. The growth in computer purchases tripled over the 1990s. A 2000 ACNielsen survey found that 69 percent of Canadian households own a computer, and 55 percent have web access. According to Statistics Canada, over 71 percent of businesses are connected to the Internet.

With all this sales flurry and emphasis on space-age speed and the Internet, some people are being left behind because they don't know how to use computers. A computer can be your best friend, but only if you learn how to use it. This makes training people to use computers a booming industry, and The Software School is on the leading edge of a major growth segment.

Target Market

Our potential total market is Southern Ontario, with a logical concentration in the Toronto Census Metropolitan Area (CMA), whose population is 4 682 897 according to the 2001 census.

Geographically, our target market or industry segment includes Mississauga, Brampton, the area north to Barrie, and those areas east to Oshawa.

For now, our focus is Metropolitan Toronto. Within this highly concentrated population area, our target customer is the small-business person.

Given the success we have projected, we plan by the third year to better service our clients in Brampton and Oshawa by opening offices in these locations.

Our Target Customer

Our primary target is the small business, profiled here:

Size: 1–30 employees
Annual sales: $250 000 to $500 000
Type of business: service industry
Major output: paper (reports, letters, documents, etc.)

Our secondary target is the home user:

Sex: 50% male, 50% female
Age: 18–45
Education: some college
Owns PC: 30%
Access to computer at work: 52%
Lives near computer store: 73%
Household income: $55 000+
Occupation: professional, managerial, executive, entrepreneurial

PART E: LOCATION

The next part of your business plan is the one on location. You may want to review your work in Chapter 7 now.

Read how The Software School shows off its location to advantage (Box 16.8 on page 334).

Box 16.6 Sample Competition Assessment

The Software School assesses its competition objectively.

The Competition

The Software School has four main competitors:

Traherne Schools. Our oldest, most entrenched competitor. Three locations in Metro: Etobicoke, North York, and Scarborough. Traherne conducts a six-hour course, Introduction to Microprocessors, for $95. They currently run a course on desktop publishing for the Mac, and they have been planning to introduce an Internet course, but to date have not done so.

Traherne operates within our geographic market. Their Scarborough operation is closed on Saturdays.

Big Micro Computer Instruction. Excellent classroom facilities, located in East York near the Don Valley Parkway. All instruction is tied to Macintosh machines, and is free if you buy your hardware from Big Micro. Otherwise, courses usually cost around $95 and take six to eight hours.

The instructors try hard, but Big Micro is really in the business of pushing hardware.

Micro Hut Computer Centre. Friendly salespeople with teaching skills double as teachers. Courses at Micro Hut are Microsoft-related. Prices range between $100 and $200 per student/day: VisiCalc, $89; Word Processing, $149.

Your Micro and You. Local facility developed by professional educators. The atmosphere of YMAY is excellent. They offer a normal range of programs and a course in using the computer in a small business, each course costing about $125. Their market seems to be divided between adults with casual interest in computers and children aged 10 to 15.

These people have done it right.

Other Competitors. Secondary competitors are colleges, which offer a range of six- to twelve-week courses. As well, more companies today are supplying in-house training for their employees.

Meeting the Competition

The Software School is in the computer education business. We do not sell hardware or software.

Our program of instruction is relevant. We teach software, and we are constantly on the lookout for trends that will lead us to new markets. For example, we have just added a course on how to create your own home page. Furthermore, our prices are competitive, and we teach classes seven days a week.

Our price per hour may be higher than the college courses, but time and results are important to our students. Therefore, we are seen as price-competitive.

ACTION STEP 71

Show off your location.

The great thing about a location is that it's so tangible. A potential lender can visit your site and get a feel for what's going on.

A banker will often visit your business site. That's good news for you because now the banker is on your turf.

Clean up the place before your banker arrives.

In this section, you want to persuade potential lenders to visit your site. Describe what goes on here. Use photographs, diagrams, and illustrations to make it feel almost like home.

You need to paint an attractive picture of your business site and, at the same time, keep your reader interested by inspiring confidence in your choice. Location takes a tremendous amount of analysis. The Software School writer gives himself a subtle pat on the back by describing the lease arrangements and by identifying the need for a second classroom. The reader who needs more is referred to the appendix. This is smart writing.

Your plan will become very real when you showcase your physical facility. Complete Action Step 71.

PART F: MANAGEMENT

Management will make or break your small business. You are a member of the management team, and you want this business plan to inspire confidence in your team.

Box 16.7 Sample Marketing Strategy Description

The Software School takes a carefully reasoned approach in its description of its marketing strategy.

Marketing Strategy

An analysis of our competitors indicates that our prices—$99 for a one-day course, $198 for a two-day course—are between two extremes. These prices are competitive but still maintain our image of quality.

We use a wide range of strategies to let our customers know where we are: mass-media advertising (newspapers, television, and radio), special promotions (press releases, brochures, newsletter, etc.), and personal selling (commissioned salespeople, networking, corporate contracts, trade shows, etc.).

Mass-Media Advertising

The Software School places ads in *The Toronto Star* and smaller area newspapers to keep a continuous presence in front of our target customers. In the beginning, we used inducement (two-for-one offers, 15 percent reductions, etc.), but that is no longer necessary as our waiting lists grow. As we continue to expand, we will develop advertising on radio and TV.

Creative Promotions/Ink/Free Ink

In our first month of operation, we sponsored a scholarship contest in the local high schools, which resulted in some very positive press. In addition, the school has been featured in several local newspapers.

We are in the information business, and toward that end we are developing three different publications: a computer handbook, a newsletter, and a brief history of the founding of The Software School. In time, we hope that this history (a how-to for computer educators) will become a guide for the industry. We have also developed our own website (www.software.com).

Our mailing list grows daily. We log all in-coming phone calls and e-mail with information on the callers and how they found out about us. This information helps us define our target market.

Personal Selling

Personal contact has gained us our largest accounts so far. (Please refer to letters from computer retailers in Appendix 2.) We intend to intensify our efforts along these lines. Fortunately, our directors have experience and talent in the area of personal selling.

We maintain a booth at the major computer trade shows in the area. Approximately 17 percent of our hobbyist/home-user business has been generated this way.

Writing this section will help you focus more closely on your management team members. (If you need a refresher, review your work in Chapters 11 and 12.)

Now let's see how The Software School introduces *its* management (Box 16.9).

Nothing is more important than the people who will make your business work. Present their pedigree and focus on their track records and accomplishments as you complete Action Step 72. It is also helpful to include résumés in the appendix.

PART G: HUMAN RESOURCES

Part G of your plan shows off your human resources. For a start-up business, you're peering into the future with confidence, conducting informal job analyses for key employees who will help you to succeed. For an ongoing business, you need to list your present employees and anticipate your future personnel needs. If you have

ACTION STEP 72

Introduce your management team.

Almost every study you read on small business failure puts the blame on management. Use this section to highlight the positive qualities of your management team.

Focus on quality first: their experience, accomplishments, education, training, flexibility, imagination, tenacity. Be sure you weave in experience that relates to your particular business.

Remember—dreamers make terrific master builders, but they make lousy managers. Your banker knows this, and potential investors will sense it. A great team can help you raise money.

The key to a great team is balance.

Box 16.8 Sample Location Description

The Software School paints an attractive picture of its location.

Our Location

The Software School is currently in the first year of a three-year lease at 47 Turbo Drive, Toronto, Ontario. The facility is all on the ground floor and occupies 210 square metres.

The area, which is zoned for business use, is a hotbed of high-technology activity. Within the immediate area, there are two computer stores, one computer furniture store, one software dealer, an electronics store, and two printers, one of which does typesetting directly from software diskettes. Within a seven-kilometre radius are 27 computer dealers.

During our lease negotiations, we persuaded the landlord to make extensive improvements in the interior, and to spread the cost out over the three-year term of the lease. The decor—blue carpet, white walls, orange furniture—gives the effect of a solid, logical, somewhat plush business environment in which our target customer will be comfortable and learn fast.

The building is divided into four areas: a reception area (30 square metres), a director's office (10 square metres), a classroom (75 square metres), and a storage area (90 square metres).

The principals envision the storage area as a second classroom. See diagram in Appendix 9.

The area is easily accessible by public transportation, and we offer free parking.

Box 16.9 Sample Management Team Description

The Software School shows off its winning management team.

Management

Derek Campbell. Mr. Campbell was born in Stratford, Ontario, in 19XX. He took a B.Sc. degree in Industrial Engineering from McGill University and then spent five years in the Armed Forces, where he was a flight instructor, a check pilot, and a maintenance officer. While in the service, Mr. Campbell completed an M.A. degree in Marketing Management and Human Relations.

Following military service, Mr. Campbell was employed as a pilot for Air Canada. He is currently the CEO of EuroSource, a software importing company. He is the author of several articles on computers and the information age.

Roberta Jericho. Ms. Jericho was born in Lethbridge, Alberta, in 19XX. She has a B.Sc. degree in Geology and Physical Sciences from the University of Calgary.

She has completed the Microsoft training program and has been the IT manager for EuroSource for the past five years.

Directors

C. Hughes Smith. Mr. Smith was born in Halifax, Nova Scotia, in 19XX. He has a B.A. degree in Political Science and Philosophy from Dalhousie University, an M.B.A. from Stanford, and a law degree from the University of Toronto.

Mr. Smith is a senior vice-president of Lowes and Lockwood, a residential home-building firm, and a partner in Graebner and Ashe, a Toronto law firm. He is the author of numerous articles in the field of corporate planning and taxes.

Philu Carpenter. Ms. Carpenter was born in Winnipeg, Manitoba, in 19XX. Her B.A. degree is from the University of Manitoba and her M.B.A., with a marketing specialty, is from the University of Western Ontario.

Ms. Carpenter spent 20 years in the corporate world (IBM, DEC, InterComp, etc.), where she worked in marketing and industrial sales. Currently a professor of Business at York University, Ms. Carpenter is the general partner in two businesses and a small business consultant. She has written and lectured widely in the area of small business.

Dan Masters. Mr. Masters was born in Mississauga, Ontario, in 19XX. His degrees (B.A., M.B.A.) are from the University of Western Ontario, where he specialized in marketing and finance. Mr. Masters has worked for Kodak and Nortel Networks (as senior account sales executive and sales manager, respectively) for a total of 25 years.

Mr. Masters is currently a professor of Business at Seneca College. He is active in several small businesses, lectures widely, and has published numerous articles in the field of small business.

Personal résumés of all personnel are provided in Appendix 4.

Other Available Resources

The Software School has retained the legal firm of Farney and Shields and the accounting firm of Hancock and Craig. Our insurance broker is Sharon Mandel of Fireman's Fund. Our advertising agency is George Friend and Associates.

five employees now and you want to indicate growth, try to project how many jobs you'll be creating in the next five years.

When you start thinking about tasks and people to do them, review your work in Chapters 11 and 12. Preparing a human resource plan is important because it gives you one more chance to analyze job functions and develop job descriptions before you start interviewing, hiring, and paying benefits—all of which are expensive.

You'll notice that The Software School gives a very brief overview of its human resource situation (Box 16.10).

In describing their lean operation, the entrepreneurs who run The Software School keep their description brief as well. They show good sense when they express a commitment to control operating costs. Their decision reflects business discipline and foresight. If you were a potential investor in this business, wouldn't you appreciate some purse strings?

Every person on your team is important. Action Step 73 will help you describe the kinds of people you will need and how you will help them be productive.

ACTION STEP 73

Introduce your personnel.

Describe the kinds of people you will need as employees and how they fit into your plan.

What skills will they need? How much will you have to pay them? Will there be a training period? How long? What benefits will you offer? How will you handle overtime?

If you haven't yet written job descriptions, do that now. Job descriptions will help you hire people who best match the skills required.

Box 16.10 Sample Human Resources Description

The Software School provides a brief overview of its human resources.

Human Resources

At the end of six months of operation, The Software School has three full-time employees and 14 part-time employees. The full-time employees include:

1. Manager, salaried at $3000 per month
2. Receptionist, salaried at $8 per hour
3. Training Director, salaried at $1500 per month

The part-time employees include three directors, who assist in the marketing function, three outside commissioned salespeople, and eight part-time instructors. According to our plan, one salesperson will become full-time at the end of the seventh month.

We will continue to hold down overhead with qualified part-time employees as long as it is feasible. We believe that running a lean operation is important to our success.

Section II: Financial Section

GOOD NUMBERS

The financial section is the heart of your business plan. It is aimed at lenders—bankers, credit managers, venture capitalists, vendors, commercial credit lenders—people who think in numbers. Lenders are professional skeptics by trade; they will not be swayed by the enthusiasm of your writing in Section I. Your job, therefore, is to make your numbers do the talking.

In Chapter 9 your drafted you financial plan. In Chapter 10 you investigated your financial options. Now you are ready to finalize your numbers into four standard categories.

1. the opening and projected balance sheets
2. the cash flow projection (also called a pro forma)
3. the projected income statement
4. other important financial information

Examples from The Software School will serve as models for you. You can adapt them to fit your business.

The idea is to know where every dollar is going. You need to show when you'll make a profit and you need to show you are efficient, conservative, and in control. You'll know you've succeeded when a skeptical lender looks up from your business plan and says, "You know, these numbers look good."

GOOD NOTES

One way to spot a professional lender is to hand over your business plan and watch to see which section is read first. Most lenders study the notes that accompany income and cash flow projections first. Knowing this allows you to be forewarned. Use these notes to list all assumptions and to tell potential lenders how you generated your numbers (for example, "Advertising is projected at 5 percent of sales") and to explain specific entries (for example, "Leased Equipment—monthly lease costs on IBM microcomputers").

Make these notes easy to read, with headings that start your readers off in the upper left-hand corner and march them down the page, step-by-step, to the bottom line. (Some sample projection charts use tiny footnotes, on the same page. We prefer *large* notes on a separate page. Notes are important, no less important than the rest of the plan.)

Creating your business plan takes a lot of time. It's only natural for you to hope that lenders will read it, get excited, and ask questions. These notes can help you accomplish that, even if you haven't started up and the numbers and assumptions are projections into the future.

PART H: PROJECTED CASH FLOW

Next, focus your attention on the projected cash flow, the lifeblood of your business. By projecting cash flow month by month, you get a picture of how healthy your business will be.

The Software School's cash flow projection is set out in Table 16.1. The notes for these numbers are reprinted in Box 16.11. If you compare the projected income statement (Table 16.2) with the cash flow projection, you will see that some items are treated differently in the tables. For example, expenses in the projected income statement are divided into monthly installments, whereas the same expenses in the

Table 16.1 The Software School's Cash Flow Projection

	Cash Flow: Software School												
	7th Month	8th Month	9th Month	10th Month	11th Month	12th Month	13th Month	14th Month	15th Month	16th Month	17th Month	18th Month	Total
Cash-Receipts													
Beginning of Month	$3 970	$7 365	$6 015	$51 575	$47 060	$35 275	$31 840	$28 645	$27 900	$33 115	$43 895	$47 800	$364 455
Sales	23 500	25 200	26 900	28 500	30 200	31 900	33 600	35 300	38 350	40 100	43 300	43 300	400 150
Less: Credit Card Expense	(295)	(315)	(335)	(355)	(380)	(400)	(420)	(440)	(480)	(500)	(540)	(540)	(5 000)
Loan			60 000										60 000
Total Sales	$27 175	$32 250	$92 580	$79 720	$76 880	$66 775	$65 020	$63 505	$65 770	$72 715	$86 655	$90 560	$819 605
Disbursements													
Books	$175	$190	$200	$210	$225	$235	$250	$305	$350	$370	$370	$385	$3 265
Inst./Materials		6 000			7 500			9 000			9 000		31 500
Salaries													
Instruction	2 000	2 000	2 040	2 080	2 120	2 160	2 200	2 240	2 280	2 320	2 360	2 360	26 160
Administration	2 640	2 640	2 640	3 120	3 600	3 600	3 600	3 600	3 600	3 600	3 600	3 600	39 840
Commissions	1 730	1 865	1 995	2 130	2 255	2 390	2 530	2 660	2 795	3 030	3 170	3 420	29 970
Payroll Taxes	2 045	2 195	2 250	2 435	2 690	2 755	2 805	2 870	2 925	3 025	3 075	3 170	32 240
Advertising	1 080	1 175	1 250	1 335	1 410	1 495	1 580	1 660	1 750	1 895	1 980	2 135	18 745
Leased Equip.	1 270	1 270	1 270	1 270	1 270	1 270	1 270	1 270	1 270	1 270	1 270	1 270	15 240
Licences/Fees	2 160	2 330	2 495	2 665	2 820	2 990	3 160	3 325	3 495	3 790	3 960	4 275	37 465
Accounting	500	500	500	500	500	500	500	500	500	500	500	500	6 000
Rent	3 890	3 890	3 890	3 890	3 890	3 890	3 890	3 890	3 890	3 890	3 890	3 890	46 680
Office Supplies	60	65	65	70	75	80	85	90	95	100	110	110	1 005
Dues/Subscript.	20	20	20	20	20	20	200	20	20	20	20	20	420
Repair/Maint.	235	250	265	285	300	320	335	355	385	395	435	435	3 995
Insurance	480						480						960
Telephone	325	355	380	405	430	455	480	505	530	575	600	650	5 690
Utilities	430	470	505	540	570	605	640	670	705	765	800	865	7 565
Interest				650	650	650	650	650	650	595	595	595	5 685
Loan Payback									5 000				5 000
Miscellaneous	705	755	805	855	905	955	1 010	1 060	1 150	1 205	1 300	1 300	12 005
Inc. Tax Reserve	65	265	435	200	375	565	710	935	1 265	1 475	1 820	1 820	9 930
Total Disbursements	$19 810	$26 235	$21 005	$22 660	$31 605	$24 935	$26 375	$35 605	$32 655	$28 820	$38 855	$30 800	$339 360
Net Cash Before Capital Invest.	$7 365	$6 015	$71 575	$57 060	$45 275	$41 840	$38 645	$27 900	$33 115	$43 895	$47 800	$59 760	$480 245
Capital Equipment			10 000										10 000
Contracted Course Development			10 000	10 000	10 000	10 000	10 000						50 000
	$7 365	$6 015	$51 575	$47 060	$35 275	$31 840	$28 645	$27 900	$33 115	$43 895	$47 800	$59 760	$420 245

ACTION STEP 74

Project your cash flow.

Get used to doing cash flow. Once a month is not too often to do it. If you prepared a cash flow for your business back in Chapter 9, bring those numbers forward. If you skipped that step, do it now. Here's how it's done:

1. Write down all the cash you will have for one year.
2. Add net profit.
3. Add any loans.
4. Figure your total cash needs for the year.
5. Spread these numbers out across the year. You may have a lot of cash at the start of the year; you want to make sure you have enough to get all the way through.
6. Now list all disbursements. Spread these out too.
7. Now examine the figures. Is there any time during the year when you will run short of cash? It's better to know the truth now, when you're still working on paper.
8. If your cash picture looks good, drop in a couple of what-ifs. (Let's say you've budgeted $300 for utilities, and the air conditioner goes out. It will cost $200 to repair it, and the lease says it is your expense. Or let's say you see an opportunity for a sale, but you would have to hire someone to handle it for you. Can your cash flow handle such surprises?)

cash flow projection are shown as bulk payment when due. Now look at insurance expense. In the projected income statement, we find a total expense of $960 shown as 12 monthly debits of $80 each. The same expense in the cash flow projection is shown as two payments of $480 each, falling due in the seventh and thirteenth months. If the entrepreneurs running the business had only $80 available to pay for insurance in the seventh month—that is what is shown in the income statement—they would be in trouble.

Profits don't pay the bills and the payroll; cash flow does. Potential lenders look at cash flow projections first. In Action Step 46, Chapter 9, you drafted your projected cash flow. Now it is time to revisit these estimates. Finalize your projected cash flow. Complete Action Step 74.

Box 16.11 Sample Cash Flow Projection Notes

The Software School's notes for its cash flow projection.

1. **Beginning of the Month.** Cash available as the month begins.
2. **Sales.** Includes all sales by cash, cheque, or credit card at the time the class is taken. Does not include accounts receivable.
3. **Credit Card Expense.** Fees of 2.5 percent paid to credit card companies. Approximately 50 percent of customers use charge cards.
4. **Loans.** Loan for new course development and audiovisual equipment.
5. **Total Cash Available.** Sum of all money available during the month.
6. **Books.** Books for sale are ordered and paid for one month in advance of projected sale.
7. **Instructional Materials.** Covers course materials purchased from licenser.
8. **Salaries.** Net salaries paid employees approximate 80 percent of gross salaries paid.
9. **Payroll Taxes.** Total of amount withheld from employees, plus Income Statement payroll tax item.
10. **Advertising.** Established as 30-day accounts with all media companies.
11. **Leased Equipment.** Lease payments are due the first of each month.
12. **Licences and Fees.** Licence fees are due the fifteenth of the following month.
13. **Legal and Accounting.** Due 30 days after bill is received.
14. **Rent.** Due the first of each month.
15. **Office Supplies.** Paid at time of purchase or with subscription. No credit.
16. **Insurance.** Paid every six months in advance.
17. **Telephone and Utilities.** Paid within 30 days of receipt of bill.
18. **Interest.** Interest only, paid each month.
19. **Loan Payback.** $5000 loan payment due every six months.
20. **Miscellaneous.** Paid in month when expense occurs.
21. **Income Tax Reserve.** Paid into a special tax account at the bank.
22. **Total Disbursements.** Total cash expended during the month.
23. **Net Cash Before Capital Investment.** Cash balance before capital investment payments.
24. **Capital Equipment.** Purchase of additional audiovisual equipment.
25. **Contracted Course Development.** Contract payment due for new course development.
26. **Monthly Cash Flow.** Cash balance after all payments at the end of the month.

Table 16.2 The Software School's Projected Income Statement

Cash Flow: Software School

	7th Month	8th Month	9th Month	10th Month	11th Month	12th Month	13th Month	14th Month	15th Month	16th Month	17th Month	18th Month	Total
Sales													
Instruction	$23 285	$24 950	$26 630	$28 215	$29 900	$31 580	$33 265	$34 945	$37 915	$39 600	$42 770	$42 770	$395 825
Books	215	250	270	285	300	320	335	355	435	500	530	530	4 325
Total Sales	$23 500	$25 200	$26 900	$28 500	$30 200	$31 900	$33 600	$35 300	$38 350	$40 100	$43 300	$43 300	$400 150
Cost of Instruction													
Clssrm. Matrls.	$1765	$1890	$2 020	$2 140	$2 265	$2 395	$2 520	$2 650	$2875	$3 000	$3 240	$3 240	$30 000
Inst./Personnel	2 500	2 500	2 600	2 600	2 700	2 700	2 800	2 800	2900	2 900	3 000	3 000	33 000
Books	150	175	190	200	210	225	235	250	305	350	370	370	3 030
Total Cost/Instr/Books	4 415	4 565	4 810	4 940	5 175	5 320	5 555	5 700	6080	6 250	6 610	6 610	66 030
Gross Profit	$19 085	$20 635	$22 090	$23 560	$25 025	$26 580	$28 045	$29 600	$32 270	$33 850	$36 690	$36 690	$334 120
Expenses													
Sales													
Commissions	$2 330	$2 495	$2 665	$2 820	$2 990	$3 160	$3 325	$3 495	$3790	$3 960	$4 275	$4 275	$39 580
Advertising	1175	1250	1335	1410	1495	1580	1660	1750	1895	1980	2135	2135	19 800
Credit Cards	295	315	335	355	380	400	420	440	480	500	540	540	5 000
Administrative													
Salaries	3 300	3 300	3 300	4 500	4 500	4 500	4 500	4 500	4 500	4 500	4 500	4 500	50 400
Payroll Taxes	570	580	600	695	715	725	745	755	785	795	825	825	8 615
Leased Equip.	1270	1270	1270	1270	1270	1270	1270	1270	1270	1270	1270	1270	15 240
Licences/Fees	2300	2 495	2 665	2 820	2 990	3 160	3 325	3 495	3 790	3 960	4 275	4 275	39 550
Accounting	500	500	500	500	500	500	500	500	500	500	500	500	6 000
Rent	3 890	3 890	3 890	3 890	3 890	3 890	3 890	3 890	3 890	3 890	3 890	3 890	46 680
Office Supplies	60	65	65	70	75	80	85	90	95	100	110	110	1005
Dues/Subscript.	20	20	20	20	20	20	200	20	20	20	20	20	420
Repair/Maint.	235	250	265	285	300	320	335	355	385	395	435	435	3 995
Insurance	80	80	80	80	80	80	80	80	80	80	80	80	960
Telephone	355	380	405	430	455	480	505	530	575	600	650	650	6 015
Utilities	470	505	540	570	605	640	670	705	765	800	865	865	8 000
Depreciation	1170	1170	1170	1335	1335	1335	1335	1335	1335	1335	1335	1335	15 525
Interest				650	650	650	650	650	650	595	595	595	5 685
Miscellaneous	705	755	805	855	905	955	1 010	1 060	1150	1 205	1 300	1 300	12 005
Total Expenses	$18 725	$19 320	$19 910	$22 555	$23 155	$23 745	$24 505	$24 920	$25 955	$26 485	$27 600	$27 600	$284 475
Net Profit	$360	$1315	$2 180	$1 005	$1 870	$2 835	$3 540	$4 680	$6315	$7 365	$9 090	$9 090	$49 645
Reserve for taxes	65	265	435	200	375	565	710	935	1265	1 475	1 820	1 820	9 930
Net Profit After Taxes	$295	$1 050	$1 745	$805	$1 495	$2 270	$2 830	$3 745	$5 050	$5 890	$7 270	$7 270	$39 715

PART I: PROJECTED INCOME STATEMENT

Your next task is to put together your projected income statement (sometimes called a profit and loss statement). With the information you've gathered so far, it shouldn't be too hard. In fact, it will be enjoyable—if the numbers look good.

The Software School's projected income statement is shown in Table 16.2, and the careful documentation of each item is reprinted here. For instance, if a lender wanted to know how the figures for commissions were generated, Note 6 explains that they are estimated as 10 percent of sales (Box 16.12).

Box 16.12 Sample Projected Income Statement Notes

The Software School's notes for its projected income statement.

1. **Instruction.** Based on 2.5 percent occupancy growth per month, starting at 35 percent (235 students) and growing to 69 percent. Students pay $99 per course.
2. **Books.** Revenue from books sold averages approximately 1 percent of instructional sales, rounded to bring total sales to an even $100 figure.
3. **Classroom Materials.** $7.50 per student.
4. **Instruction Personnel.** Instructor cost is $100 per eight-hour class, starting with 25 classes and growing to 30 classes by the end of the year.
5. **Books.** Cost of books is 70 percent of selling price.
6. **Commissions.** Average 10 percent of instructional sales.
7. **Advertising.** Projected at 5 percent of sales.
8. **Credit Cards.** Approximately 50 percent of sales are paid with credit cards. The cost is 2.5 percent of the sale.
9. **Salaries.** Start with three full-time employees. Bring on one additional person beginning the tenth month.
10. **Payroll Taxes.** The company's share of employee taxes averages 7 percent of commissions and salaries.
11. **Leased Equipment.** Monthly lease costs on IBM microcomputers.
12. **Licences and Fees.** Licence (right to use copyrighted material) costs 10 percent of instruction sales.
13. **Accounting.** Average accounting and bookkeeping costs for the area and size of the business.
14. **Rent.** Based on three-year lease.
15. **Office Supplies.** Estimated at 0.25 percent of sales.
16. **Dues and Subscriptions.** Estimated costs for magazines, newspapers, and membership in organizations.
17. **Repair and Maintenance.** Projected to be 1 percent of sales.
18. **Insurance.** Based on current insurance contract for next 12 months, payable every six months.
19. **Telephone and Fax.** Figured at 1.5 percent of sales.
20. **Utilities.** Figured at 2 percent of sales.
21. **Depreciation.** Schedule established by accounting firm.
22. **Interest.** Loan at 13 percent, with $5000 payments due every six months until paid off.
23. **Miscellaneous.** Figured at 3 percent of sales.
24. **Reserve for Taxes.** Local, provincial, and federal taxes estimated at 20 percent of net profit.

Refer to Table 16.2 as you predict your income.

PART J: PROJECTED BALANCE SHEET

The professionals will look at your balance sheet (sometimes called a statement of financial position) to analyze the state of your finances at a given point in time. They are looking at things like liquidity (how easily your assets can be converted into cash) and capital structure (what sources of financing have been used, how much was borrowed, and so on). Professional lenders will use such factors to evaluate your ability to manage your business.

Table 16.3 shows two balance sheets for The Software School. Note that the first one shows its actual position at the end of its first six months and the second is a projection of where it will be at the end of its first 18 months. If you're just starting up, *all* figures will be projections.

In Chapter 9, Action Step 47, you drafted a projected income statement. Now it is time to add the final touches. Complete Action Step 75.

ACTION STEP 75

Project your income statement.

What you're driving at here is net profit—what's left in the kitty after expenses—for each month and for the year.

First, you figure your sales. The first big bite out of the figure is the cost of goods sold. (In a service business, the big cost is labour.) Subtracting that gives you a figure called gross margin.

Now add up all your expenses (rent, utilities, insurance, etc.) and subtract them from the gross margin. This gives you your net profit before taxes. (Businesses pay quarterly installments.)

Subtract taxes. There's your net profit.

Table 16.3 The Software School's Balance Sheet

	Actual Balance Sheet of Software School as of September 30, 20xx (after first 6 months)			Projected Balance Sheet of Software School as of September 30, 20xx (after first 18 months)		
Assets						
Cash	$3 970			$59 670		
Inst. Materials & Books	2 500			4 495		
Total Current Assets			$6 470			$64 165
Leasehold Improvements	$41 000			$41 000		
Furniture	15 100			15 100		
Audio/Visual	10 600			20 600		
Office Equipment	3 600	$70 300		3 600	$80 300	
Less Depreciation		7 020	63 280		22 545	57 755
License Agreement			25 000	$25 000		
New Courses			–0–	50 000		75 000
Total Assets			$94 750			$196 920
Liabilities						
Instructors' Salaries	$1 250			$1 500		
Administrative Salaries	1 650			2 250		
Commissions	2 165			4 275		
Accounts Payable	4 495			9 020		
Current Liabilities		$9 560			$17 045	
Long-Term Debt		–0–			54 970	
Total Liabilities			$9 560			$72 015
Net Worth (Owner's Equity)						
Capital Stock	$100 000				$100 000	
Retained Earnings	(14 810)		85 190	24 905		124 905
Total Liabilities & Net Worth			$94 750			$196 920

OTHER IMPORTANT FINANCIAL INFORMATION

The ratios tell you a lot about the health of your business. They allow you to compare it with industry benchmarks and also to compare your results to your objectives.

ROI (RETURN ON INVESTMENT)

net profit to owner's investment

Let's talk for a minute about **ROI (or return on investment)**. It is a bottom-line figure that shows how much is earned on the total dollars invested in the business. You have this kind of information up front if you invest money in bonds. The interest tells you your ROI. Imagine that you had two funds, Bond A and Bond B, and Bond A paid you a 4 percent return and Bond B paid you 25 percent. Which bond would have the better ROI?

You compute ROI for a business by dividing the net profit by investing dollars. For The Software School, the profit after taxes is \$39 715 (from Table 16.2). Divide that by the owner's investment of \$100 000 (from Table 16.3):

$$\$39\ 715 / \$100\ 000 = 39.7\%$$

Could you get 39.7 percent from a savings account or a bond fund? It's not a bad ROI. It would dazzle lenders and probably draw the attention of a venture capitalist.

It is also helpful to include a comparison of your ratios to industry standards. Don't forget to include your break-even analysis as well.

The Software School did not provide notes to its balance sheets because, in this case, no notes are needed. In conjunction with the income statement and the cash flow projection, all the entries in the balance sheet will make sense to your professional readers. Under some circumstances, you would want to note unusual features of a balance sheet for an actual fiscal year, but in most cases—and in most projections—this won't be necessary.

Now project a balance sheet for your business. Action Step 76 will help you.

ACTION STEP 76

Action Steps

Project your balance sheet.

A projected balance sheet is simply a prediction, on paper, of what your business will be worth at the end of a certain period of time. This prediction allows you to figure your actual and projected ROI, which is the real bottom line.

1. Add up your assets. For convenience, divide these into current (cash, notes, receivables, etc.), fixed (land, equipment, buildings, etc.), and other (intangibles like patents, royalty deals, copyrights, goodwill, contracts for exclusive use, and so on). You'll need to depreciate fixed assets that wear out. For value, you show the net of cost minus the accumulated depreciation.
2. Add up your liabilities. For convenience, divide these into current (accounts payable, notes payable, accrued expenses, interest on loans, etc.), and long-term (trust deeds, bank loans, equipment loans, balloon payments, etc.).
3. Subtract the smaller figure from the larger one.

You now have a prediction of your net worth. Will you be in the red or in the black?

Epilogue: Act on What You Know

Well, do you feel like you're ready? You are. You have thoroughly researched your product or service, your market and target customer, your competition, your marketing strategy, and your location. You've discovered how to prepare for surprises you can't afford, how to handle numbers, how to pursue financing, when and why you should incorporate, how to build a winning team, and whether you should buy, franchise, or start on your own. You've surveyed the vistas that a small business computer training school can open up for you. And you've written it all up in a workable business plan that can be implemented.

Before you take off running, we want to give you one more tool that we think every entrepreneur should have—a tool to help you put your business plan to work. It's called **PERT,** an acronym for Program Evaluation and Review Technique, and it's often used to establish schedules for large projects.

PERT

acronym for Program Evaluation and Review Technique

A PERT chart is just the thing if you feel overwhelmed by the tasks of starting up and don't know where to begin. If you're a person who sometimes tries to do everything at once, PERT is also recommended. It will help you focus your energy on the right job at the right time. A sample PERT chart is provided in Table 16.4. Yours will need to be bigger and more detailed. You can use days, weeks, or months to plot the tasks ahead. (If you think you should use years, reassess your industry.)

Action Step 77 symbolizes the first one taken on your own as an entrepreneur. It's the end, yes, but also the beginning. All our best wishes go with you as you embark on your great adventure. We hope that this book and its Action Steps have persuaded you that you can achieve success—whatever it means to *you*—and have fun at the same time. Good luck! Work smart, and enjoy your adventure!

Table 16.4 A Sample PERT Chart

Task	Week 1	2	3	4	5	6
Befriend banker	X	X	X	X	X	X
Order letterhead		X				
Select site	X					
Get business name statement	X					
Register company			X			
Select ad agency	X					
Lunch, lawyer			X			
Appointment, accountant				X		
Prepare vendor statement					X	
Make utilities deposit					X	
Review promotional material					X	
Survey phone system			X	X	X	
Order phone system						X
Hold open house						X

ACTION STEP 77

Construct a PERT chart and go for it.

Rehearsal is over. Now it's time to step onto the stage and get the drama under way. One way to shift from planning into action is to develop your own personal PERT chart. A PERT chart will serve as a script for you. It also will tell you and the other members of your team how long certain jobs should take.

List the tasks you need to accomplish—befriending a banker, filing a fictional name statement, taking a lawyer to lunch, ordering business letterhead, selecting a site, contacting vendors, and so on—and set your deadlines.

As you already know, a successful package is made up of many details. If you take the details one at a time, you'll get there without being overwhelmed. The sample PERT chart in Table 16.4 can guide you.

In a Nutshell

It's been a long haul, and you're now ready to create your business plan. The business plan is a portable showcase for your business. When you visit vendors, bankers, and potential lenders, you can take along a copy of your business plan to speak for you, to show them you've got a blueprint for success.

Begin writing by starting with the material you feel most comfortable with. Once you have finished one part of the plan, the other parts will fall into place more easily. Fortunately, your work in earlier chapters has prepared you for each section. The executive summary will be written last.

You'll need to write a cover letter for each copy of the plan you send out. The cover letter will personalize the plan and target the prime interests of each reader.

Key Terms

PERT

ROI (return on investment)

Think Points for Success

✓ Section I should generate excitement for your business. Section II should substantiate the excitement with numbers.

✓ Be sure to use sufficient footnotes to explain the numbers in your financial statements—Parts H, I, and J.

✓ The executive summary should read like ad copy. Hone it till it's tight and convincing.

✓ Now that you have Plan A, have you thought about Plan B?

Checklist Questions and Actions to Develop Your Business Plan

PULLING THE PLAN TOGETHER

- ❑ How will your business idea contribute to society in general?
- ❑ In what way does your product or service differ from that of your competitors?
- ❑ What are the critical success factors for your business?
- ❑ How would your customers define your quality and level of customer service?
- ❑ In completing your business plan, ask yourself: Have I been consistent in my thinking that the quality of sales staff fits the image I wish to convey, and that money is set aside for appropriate training?
- ❑ What social responsibility practices do you intend to follow?
- ❑ What business-related ethical issue might surface about your business venture?
- ❑ If your business is successful, what is your long-term growth plan?
- ❑ Are you going to achieve your personal vision?

NOTES

1. Adapted from Rod McQueen, "Canada's 50 Best Managed Private Companies: Crila Plastics Industries Ltd.," *Financial Post*, December 13, 1997, p. 19. Reprinted by permission of The Financial Post.

SUGGESTED READING

Brodsky, Norm. "Why You Need a Personal Business Plan." *Inc.* January 1997, pp. 27–28.

Burstiner, Irving. *The Small Business Handbook*, 3rd ed. New York: Simon & Schuster, 1997.

Chang, Richard. *The Passion Plan at Work: Building a Passion-Driven Organization.* San Francisco: Jossey-Bass, 2001.

Dupree, James V. *A Business Plan for the Small Business with Software.* Saddle River, NJ: Prentice Hall, 1996.

Good, Walter S. *Building a Dream: A Comprehensive Guide to Starting a Business of Your Own.* Whitby, ON: McGraw-Hill Ryerson, 1997.

Gunther McGrath, Rita, and Ian McMillan. *The Entrepreneurial Mindset* Boston: Harvard Business School, 2000.

Ross, L. Manning. *Business Plan.com: How to Write an E-Commerce Business Plan.* Central Point, OR: Oasis Press, 2000.

Royal Bank of Canada. *Starting a Business: A Guide for Independent Business.* 1998.

Sherman, Andrew J. *Running and Growing Your Business.* New York: Times Business, 1997.

chapter 17

Fast-Start Business Plan

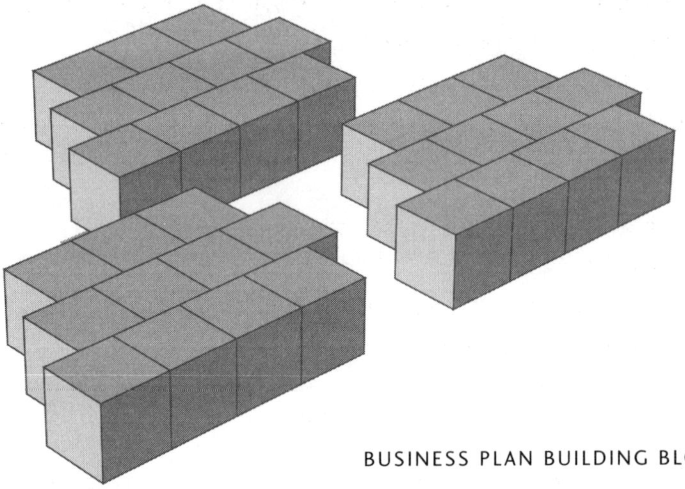

BUSINESS PLAN BUILDING BLOCK

If your business concept is very simple or short-term, perhaps you don't need a fully developed business plan. This chapter was developed to allow you to respond quickly to a narrow window of opportunity, and to demonstrate to yourself that the venture is viable.

LEARNING OPPORTUNITIES

After reading this chapter, you should be able to:

- Admit that you're in a hurry.
- Launch a start-up without getting financial help from bankers.
- Capitalize on a hot opportunity in the marketplace.
- Start small while you explore the possibilities of growing larger.
- Work with numbers so that you can keep going when the going gets tough.
- Make some money now.
- Plan as you work in your new business.

ACTION STEP PREVIEW

78. Describe your new business.
79. Describe the business you are really in.
80. Describe what your competitors look like.
81. Describe your pricing strategy.
82. Describe your target customer and your main market area.
83. Describe your advertising and sales program.
84. Calculate what it will cost you to open your doors.
85. Determine how much you will sell in your first month and how much you will spend.
86. Make a "things to do" list.

George Finklestein had a lot of experience in window cleaning over the three summers he was attending university. As a matter of fact, it paid for his education. After graduating, and after a fruitless job search that involved sending out over 100 résumés, Finklestein decided that he could have a career in business. He knew that there was money to be made in window cleaning, and so he decided that this is where he would start. He wasn't looking for financing and wanted to get going right away. When he registered his business name, "Yes, We Do Windows," he knew he had to have some kind of plan. He created a fast-start plan. It took him only about a month to fill in the details since he already knew the business quite well.

Did the plan work? Here is George's response. "In February of my first year, I took three weeks off and did some deep sea fishing. Turned out window cleaning was quite profitable. While on vacation, I made a decision: when I got home I would spend my spare hours developing a detailed plan and a franchise package for my student

Chapter 17 hands you a "Fast-Start Business Plan" that is almost ready to fly.

employees." The next summer, he had 12 student franchisees, and was making plans to go biking in Europe during his off-season.

Many of you, like George Finklestein, may not need an exhaustive business plan. You are in a hurry. You probably won't need to go to the bank. You just want to get started. If the business doesn't work, fine, you'll dream up something else. If this is your situation, Chapter 17 will help. But first, you need to make sure the fast start is the right start for you. In this chapter, we help you give thought to your big decision. We also provide a model "Yes, We Do Windows" business plan based on George Finklestein's experience.

The Big Decision

If you're going it alone with money you can afford to lose ($500, $1000, even $5000), and if the loss of that money won't jeopardize your loved ones and make wolves howl at your door, use the fast-start business plan.

If other people are involved—investors, bankers, advisers, company officers—then return to Chapter 16 and write a comprehensive plan.

The comprehensive plan gives you a blueprint to follow month by month through the first year. It gives you the framework to go for a four-year projection following that first year. It tracks your business through seasonal ups and downs. It allows for contingencies.

The fast-start business plan lets you get going now. It's great if you've been in business before and know the footwork of entrepreneurship. With the fast-start business plan, you're using the business as a probe into the marketplace. You can start quickly because you have an instinct for what to expect and where you are going. You have a market sense. You also have a good sense of the business you are starting.

The fast-start business plan is quicker to write than the more detailed plan. Marketing, pricing, and advertising employ a low-key approach. As you gain experience, you fold that experience into a rolling projection. You can write the fast-start plan in one to three months. The full business plan, because of the extensive data gathering and need to pass through many hands, can take six months to a year.

QUICK CHECKLIST

Here's a quick checklist for implementing the fast-start business plan:

- ☐ Can you afford to lose your dollar investment? How much money can you afford to lose at the slots in Reno or Las Vegas or Windsor, Ontario? Can you lose $100? $1000? $5000? More? What's your deductible on your car insurance? Your boat? Your major medical? Write down the amount you can afford to lose. If you have excess money to speculate with, then the fast-start business plan is for you.
- ☐ How easy is it to enter this business? Are there barriers to entry low? Is it easy to talk to owners? Are role models in great abundance? Do the prospective customers have a clear understanding of the goods and services provided? Examples of business with wide doors: window washing, auto detailing, landscape maintenance, pet-sitting, house-sitting, consulting.
- ☐ Can you start this business on a part-time basis? Starting part time lessens your risk. You have a chance to prove the business. You see how much you really like it. You keep a running tally of customer responses. You keep your other job.

- ❑ How tough is it to gather the data needed to formulate a fast-start business plan? In breaking new ground, be careful. In a venture like this, the market is not clearly defined. There are very few competitors. Pricing is not clear. Remaining part-time is essential. You must make certain you've got a market out there.
- ❑ Can you start using only your own funds? Bill Gates, the founder of Microsoft, could use the fast-start business plan for a business start-up costing $50 000 to $1 000 000. A single parent of two with rent and a car loan to pay might afford much less. Be honest with yourself. Be honest with your family.

STRUCTURING YOUR PLAN

Use these questions to structure your fast-start business plan:

1. How do you describe your business?
2. What business are you really in?
3. Who is your main and secondary competition? How are they doing?
4. What is your entry strategy?
5. What is your pricing strategy?
6. Who is your target customer? Why should they buy from you?
7. How will you advertise?
8. What are your start-up costs?
9. What are your sales goals for the first three months?
10. What are your operating expenses for the first three months?
11. If you crash and burn, what can you salvage for cash?

Business Description

It's night. The family's gone to bed. The house is quiet. The pets are snoozing.

It's time to sit back in your favourite chair, time to relax, time to dream about your new business. Think about your vision, and then write down your dream:

> You step out of your van. It's a handsome vehicle, spotless, white, and gleaming. On the side, in red letters, is your sign: My Carpet Cleaners—Quality and Service Is Our Number One Job. Your company phone number is underneath. You are all in white, white jumpsuit, white shoes. The starched look gives you the image of being the best carpet cleaner in town. You catch your reflection in the mirror. The jumpsuit makes you look taller. The company logo stitched on your breast pocket makes you proud.
>
> The house of your prospective customer is large. Three stories, well-kept lawn, a three-car garage, a curved driveway. The walkway leading to the front door is paved. The doorway is large enough to drive a truck through. Out back, you can hear the happy shrieks of children as they splash in the pool.
>
> Cut to the job. You're in a big room with wall-to-wall carpet. Your machine sucks up the dirt. The customer enters, walking on a drop cloth you laid down for your equipment. Pointing to a transparent tube attached to your super-steam vacuum, you show the customer the dirt coming out of her carpet. The carpet sparkles in the sunlight as you go

ACTION STEP 78

Describe your new business.

What will your business look like to your customers? To your competitors? To yourself?

Write quick descriptions of your products and/or services. What do they look like? How do they feel? How much time do they take? How much do they cost? Next, describe them in terms of benefits to your customers. How will Target Customer A benefit from buying your product or service?

Keep going.

What is unique about your product or service? What separates you from your competitors?

Research the marketplace. Is your type of business growing? If so, how fast? Where are you on the life-cycle chart? Is your market area growing?

Try to describe your business in 50 words or less. When you tell people about your business, you want to have a clear, crisp picture. You want to use the right words.

This is your business. You want to know exactly what it is.

after those drapes. The customer, overwhelmed with such service, hands you the biggest cheque you've ever seen.

This cheque is two metres long and one metre high. The customer smiles. You read the amount—fantastic money for a fantastic job—and dance your way out of the house and down the walkway to your van.

GREAT DREAM EQUALS GREAT BUSINESS

A business dream separates your business from everyone else who's out there trying to clean carpets.

You're clean and you're in the cleaning business. You're proud of being in business. You care. The customer, owner of expensive things, cares that you care. We like to do business with people who care about what they're doing. Such people take pride in a job well done.

By being spotless when you enter this home, you show the customer respect. Your equipment is spotless. You're not dragging someone else's dirt into the place. The drop cloth is a nice touch.

You look like a carpet cleaner. You act like a carpet cleaner and are very knowledgeable about carpet cleaning. Your dream gives you a jump start. Now you add in details.

What products and services will you offer? Will you limit yourself to carpets? Or will you clean chairs and drapes? Will you specialize in homes? Or will you do offices? Will you provide a simple service? Or will you also sell spot remover, touch-up cleaners, other extras?

Complete Action Step 78.

WHAT BUSINESS ARE YOU REALLY IN?

Are you selling clean carpets? Are you selling a better-looking home or office? Are you selling better health? Are you helping the customer preserve an investment? Remember, in the eyes of the customer you are selling benefits.

To help you get an appreciation of this, let's profile two different businesses in the same industry.

Business A is a family restaurant. It's open 24 hours a day. There's nothing on the menu over $9.95. The menu for children is extensive. On each table is a digital clock and a sign that says you eat free if your meal is not on the table within 10 minutes of being ordered. The clock invites the customer to set it, invites the waiter to beat the clock.

Business B is a restaurant with limited hours. Weekdays it's open from 11 a.m. to 2 p.m. and from 5 p.m. to 10 p.m. Weekends it's open from 5 p.m. until midnight. Each table features large, comfortable chairs. The lighting is soft. The china is fine, the silverware first class. The waiters wear tuxes, and their manners are impeccable. The wine list contains fine vintages from Europe and California. If you can stump the bartender by requesting a drink she cannot mix, your drink is served free by the mâitre d'hotel. The cheapest entrée on the menu is $25 (this restaurant rounds prices off).

Both A and B are in the food service business. You can find both in the restaurant section in the Yellow Pages. But are they both in the same business?

For your answer, look at the customers.

Customers go to Business A for fast service. Their desire is to feed the whole family without going broke. They don't want a long travel time, so Business A is close to home. The food is good. Not wonderful, not divine, but good.

Customers go to Business B for excellent food and superior service. They go to relax, to enjoy a perfect moment over a rare vintage. They may be driven by fantasy or romance or escape. They may go just to watch the staff perform. That's entertainment.

What business is A in? What business is B in?

Business A is in the family-feeding business. But B is in the entertainment business. While A provides nourishment at affordable prices, B provides more than food—it provides a dining experience. If you were the manager of Business A, you would do these things:

- purchase good food in quantity
- get it at the lowest price
- control waste in the kitchen
- develop a fast and efficient delivery system
- turn those tables

If you were the manager of Business B, you would do these things:

- hire and train employees to fit the upscale image
- provide ambience
- select top-quality food, rare food, specialty food, and top-quality wines
- find a bartender who knows the latest mixes and has excellent human relations skills

To figure out what business you're in, take a couple of steps back. Look at your business from the viewpoint of the customer. Complete Action Step 79. Then plan your course of action.

ACTION STEP 79

Describe the business you are really in.

This is a tough task.

Start by interviewing customers of your competitors. Why do they buy what they buy? Why do they shop here instead of somewhere else? What are they after? What are they trying to satisfy? What itch does this business scratch?

Stimulate your thinking by analogy. What, for example, do you get when you have your car washed? It costs you anywhere from $2 to $25, and for what? A clean car? A savings in time? Pride of ownership? A car your customer will ride in? Does washing the car make you feel clean? Or maybe it's maintenance. Do you live near the beach, where the salt air eats your chrome?

Where do you buy clothes? Why? Where do you buy gas? Why? Who cleans your carpet? Why?

Probe your own buying habits. Probe the buying habits of your friends. Keep an open mind. Gather data. All this will lead you to discover what business you're really in.

WHO ARE YOUR COMPETITORS?

This is a good time to try out your new eyes. How much can you learn from your competitors?

How do you find them? If you're hunting for retailers or restaurant owners, you hop in your car and drive around. But how do you find a home-based word-processing business? How do you find a home-based cleaning service? How do you find a mobile auto detailer?

You know this: in order to stay in business, a business must communicate with potential customers. So you tune in your entrepreneurial radar. Check your Yellow Pages. Check area newspapers. Look for business cards in copy services. Check the Internet and visit your competitors' websites. Look in trade magazines.

Once you find your competitors, take a closer look. Were they easy to find? How visible was their advertising? As you study their advertising strategy, what kind of a customer profile can you draw? Are they spending a lot on their advertising? Are they working on a shoestring?

What can you tell from their pricing? Are prices firm? Are they negotiable? Are they high, low, or competitive? What kind of customer will go for these prices? Who will get shut out? Do your competitors understand the marketplace? Is their pricing structure positioned properly? Where is their pricing in the product life cycle?

Are your competitors zeroed in on a specific target customer, or are they using the shotgun approach? Just for practice, profile the target customer of your competitors.

Which of your competitors are successful? Can you tell why? Which are just hanging in there? Why? If a business has been operating for some time, there's a good chance the owner's doing something right. What is your competitors' market niche? What is their marketing strategy? What customer benefits do they offer? Fast service? Quality work? Free delivery and pickup? Low prices? Better use of technology?

ACTION STEP 80

Describe what your competitors look like.

Are they winners? Losers? Why? What things are they doing right? What are they doing wrong?

How many competitors do you have? What customer groups are they serving? Whom are they overlooking? Where do they advertise? Where do they promote? What do you think of their location? What market area do they cover?

If you owned a competitor's business, what would you change?

What can you learn from studying your competitors? After you have opened your business, do some more marketplace detecting as you study your competitors. You'll learn more because you know more. A veteran entrepreneur knows what to look for.

Even the most successful business overlooks something. Find out what they missed. Did they overlook a market segment? Did they get sloppy with their advertising? Is their range of services actually limited? Is their inventory sparse? Thousands of businesses have been built on the weaknesses of competition.

Take the time to chat with the customers of your competitors. Are they satisfied? If not, why not? How do they see the competition? What image does the competition project? How do customers feel about price, quality, timeliness, and so on?

Take the time to chat with competitors outside your area. Is there a gap no one has thought to close? Complete Action Step 80.

HOW MUCH SHOULD YOU CHARGE?

Pricing is key. Don't be misled by thinking you can whisk customers away from established competitors by charging less for the same thing. It didn't work for now bankrupt department stores. It won't work for you. Price should never be your only strategy.

Find out what is important to the customers. Is it time? Dependability? Quality? Convenience? Once you find out what it is, learn to see the value of your product or service through your customers' eyes.

For example, when you eat lunch at a fast-food restaurant, you buy french fries, coffee, tea, a soft drink. You pay a dollar or more for each of these items. The cost to the seller is a quarter or two per item. Within limits, these items are not price-sensitive. The question is, what is the customer's perception of value?

When you shop, train yourself to make price comparisons. You might notice, for example:

Newspapers at the newsstand	
The Globe and Mail	$0.85
local paper	$0.70
Coffee	
at local doughnut shop	$1.00
at a luxury hotel	$2.00
Car wash	
high-school students' Saturday special	$3.00
do-it-yourself	$3.00
done for you	$12.00
Transportation	
Ford	$23 000
Mercedes	$75 000
Bentley	$275 000
Education	
one year at university	$8 000
one year at college	$3 000

Almost everyone has a price limit for every product or service. What is the maximum that people will pay for your product? Take a look at Action Step 81.

ACTION STEP 81

Describe your pricing strategy.

What does your target customer see as good value?

What is most important to your target customer? Convenience? Quality? On-time delivery? Image? Price?

What stage of the product or service life cycle are you in? How many competitors do you have? How close are they?

If price is the main decision factor, try to add a little extra something. What's unique about your product? Is it sufficient to let you charge a little extra?

PROFILE YOUR TARGET CUSTOMER

Who will receive the biggest benefit from your business? Who can afford your product? Who are your main, secondary, and invisible target customers? Where do they live? What's their income range? What do they need? What benefits do they want? What work do they do? Are they married? Single? Divorced? Retired?

To profile your customers, become a marketplace detective. To practise, study the customers that buy from your competitors.

Do the women outnumber the men? What's the average age? What cars do they drive? What make? Price range? How are the customers dressed? How expensive are their shoes? Can you tell what methods of payment they use? Cash? Cheques? Credit? Debit? How expensive are the items they're buying?

Practice trains your eyes to consider the person as a prospect. The bottom line: what are the three or four critical success factors that characterize your target customer? Now complete Action Step 82.

ACTION STEP 82

Describe your target customer and your main market area.

Who is your primary target customer? Do a profile: sex, age, income, occupation, residence, vehicle driven—anything that gives you a picture of needs and wants. What do they read? What do they watch? What do they listen to?

When you have profiled your primary customer, do the same thing for secondary customers.

How large is your main market area? Will you sell in one section of town? The whole town? The province? The region? The country? If you're driving around to service accounts, how far will you have to drive?

HOW DO YOU MAKE THAT CUSTOMER CONNECTION?

Before you spend a bundle on a TV ad, or three months knocking on doors of houses along Golf Course Drive, take some time to put together a message.

What image do you want to project? How do you want the marketplace to perceive your product or service? What position do you want to assume among your competitors? What are the key benefits your business will offer customers? How soon do you want to start? How many autos can you detail—or homes can you clean—in one day?

Once you answer these questions, develop your overall marketing strategy. Start by designing your business card. Use a logo that offers an insight into your business. If you're starting a computer training business, use something along the lines of "Computer Training That Works for You Tomorrow." If you're thinking of house cleaning: "Only Sparkle—Not a Speck of Dust." Always carry lots of business cards. They're inexpensive memory seeds, handy reminders, and often your most cost-effective advertising.

Once your business cards are done, research ways of reaching customers. Do they gather at church? At school? At football games? At little league baseball? What do they read? Watch? Listen to? Could you reach them best through the Yellow Pages? Through radio? On a billboard? The Internet? What can you afford? Match that up with the most effective communication channel.

Stay visible. If your target customers gather in groups, try to reach them there. Attend their meetings. Get on their list of speakers. Give a demonstration. Hand out business cards. Offer a freebie.

If you must find your customers one at a time, spend a few hours each day knocking on doors. Telephone prospects. Work your mailing list. If you use mail or e-mail contacts, be sure you do phone follow-ups.

Join the local chamber of commerce. If you're lucky, your chamber will run a short piece about you, the newcomer, in its newsletter. Stay visible at chamber meetings. Don't get pushy with your business cards, but have them handy.

While you're connecting with customers, don't overlook organizations that might act as your sales force. For example, let's say you've found a school where the parents' group is trying to raise funds to support an athletic endeavour. Put together a flyer for students to take home. In return for each sale from the flyer, your business will donate 10 to 25 percent to the fund-raising group. Consider the donation a part of your promotional budget.

Try your hand at Action Step 83.

ACTION STEP 83

Describe your advertising and sales program.

How will you let potential customers know that you are open for business? How will you let them discover the benefits of buying from you?

Start with the budget. How much money can you spend on promotion? Once you know what you can afford, select the advertising to match your budget.

As part of your plan, set up an evaluation procedure. You want to know how well each promotion works.

What Are Your Start-up Costs?

At your local office supply store, make these purchases: a travel log, an expense journal, and a folder to hold receipts. You can deduct travel and expenses related to your business start-up.

List everything that you need to get started. Don't worry whether the list would cost a bundle. You're brainstorming at this point. The key here is not to overlook anything. A visit to your competitors will add ideas to your list. An interview with an owner will trigger new items. When you're chatting with businesspeople, ask questions: What kind of cash register or computer system and software do you use? What kind of bookkeeping system do you have? What's the cost of a start-up inventory? When your list is fat, add price tags.

When you start purchasing, check the large discount stores. Also investigate mail-order houses. If one company in your area can supply most of your needs, try to make a package deal and develop a long-term relationship.

On equipment items, save by buying used. Used equipment might be scratched or dented, but you stand to save 50 to 90 percent. Check the newspaper classifieds under "Equipment for Sale" or "Office Furniture." Talk with potential suppliers—they usually know someone who's going out of business. You can find good deals from an owner who's folding.

You should also consider leasing your equipment. Leasing costs more in the long run, less when you're getting started. As your business grows, and your leases expire, you can decide whether to replace by buying new or used. Leasing provides you a lot of flexibility up front.

Divide your start-up list into two columns. Column 1 should contain items that are absolutely necessary. Column 2 should contain "nice-to-haves."

Check Column 1. Is there anything you can borrow from home, parents, friends? Scrape to the bottom of the barrel here. Your goal is to cut costs so that you'll have cash to run the business. Whatever the case, allow for a cash contingency of at least 10 percent of your first three months' expenses, as you will likely forget something.

Take a look at Action Step 84.

ACTION STEP 84

Action Steps

Calculate what it will cost you to open your doors.

List your expenses, equipment, rentals, inventory—everything you'll need to start your business. Start your list with business cards. End with the key for the front door. What comes in between?

When you have listed all the items, give each one an estimated cost. On equipment, buy used. If you can't buy used, try leasing. On inventory, negotiate with each supplier to see whether you can get credit terms right from the start. If you can't get credit, find out how you can get quality.

When the list is complete—items and costs—go through it with a black marker, deleting items you can do without for a month or so. You are trying to keep your up-front cash outlay to a minimum.

CHARTING YOUR SALES GOALS FOR THE FIRST THREE MONTHS

How much would you like to sell the first month? The second? The third? How much can you afford to sell? What is a realistic target for your business?

Sales goals provide the information you need to forecast your variable expenses—those expenses forced to change in relation to sales volume. If you are selling a product, sales goals will allow you to estimate the cost of goods sold.

Sales goals provide the driving force for your team. They help you focus on your target for the month. When the month is finished, compare how you did with your initial sales goals. Did you make it? If not, why not? Did you exceed your goal by 25 percent? Why? What worked well? What didn't? As you evaluate, decide how to improve next month, and how to keep improving.

To chart a reasonable sales goal, focus on three factors:

1. *The weight of your advertising program.* Do you plan a wide-area campaign? Or will you start by calling on friends and neighbours, counting on them to spread the word slowly? How much energy are you putting into this? Will you start full-time? Will you keep your job? If you're in school, will you stay enrolled?
2. *The experience of entrepreneurs in business like yours who operate in a non-competing area.* How much effort does entrepreneur A have to put out to make a $100 sale in his or her area?
3. *The capacity you have to deliver the product or service.* What do you need to make this venture go? If it costs you $500 for materials to build one computer cabinet and you only have $500 worth of capital, then you will be limited to building one cabinet at a time. You have to get paid before you can build a second cabinet.

Or let's say you're starting a part-time business detailing, or cleaning, autos. Detailing one auto takes three hours. Driving time takes almost a half hour per auto. Your maximum sales activity per week will be based on the number of hours you can devote to your business after you put in your hours at your full-time job. If you can devote 20 hours a week, then your sales would be 20 hours, divided by time, multiplied by your charge. Let's try that:

20 divided by 3.5 = 6 autos per week.
Your charge per auto is $60.
6 times $60 = $360 per week.

Make a list of your friends and relatives. Find out how many of them have their autos detailed. Add the repeat factor: how often do they want detailing? Once a month? Once every quarter? Once a year? When your list is finished, suppose you have 24 prospects. Let's say you have a realistic shot at 18 of those prospects. You are then going to have to determine if that's enough for a start-up.

As a wise entrepreneur, you know that your first few jobs will take longer than later ones. You're new. You're learning the business. You want to make sure you do a super job. You have four prospects who want monthly detailing. You have six who want it quarterly. Start with these 10 prospects and lay out a chart. (See Table 17.1.)

Make these assumptions:

1. Assume that the first and second months contain four weeks and the third month has five weeks.
2. Assume sign-ups of four monthly detailing prospects from your list of 24. Add one new monthly prospect out of every six new customers from the "need-to-find" group.
3. Assume a sign-up of six quarterly customers from your list of 24 prospects. Add one new quarterly customer out of every six new customers from the "need-to-find" group.
4. Assume a sign-up of eight one-time prospects from your list of 24 prospects.
5. Action: Must find new customers from the remaining six prospects on the list of 24 names. Other sources are referrals, sales calls, and advertising.
6. We plan only for the first three months, but continue to update the plan every month. The fourth month is easy to start building from monthly and quarterly customers.

Table 17.1 First Sales Forecast

	1	2	3	4	5	6	7	8	9
1									
2	First Sales Forecast								
3									
4		1st Month		2nd Month		3rd Month		4th Month	
5	Monthly Detailing (2)	$240	(4)	$240	(4)	$300	(5)	$360	(6)
6	Quarterly Detailing (3)	180	(3)	180	(3)	0		180	(3)
7	Rest of 18 Prospects (4)	180	(3)	300	(5)	0			
8	Need to Find (5)			360	(6)	1500			
9	Sales	600		1080		1800			
10									
11									
12									

EXPENSE FORECAST

List everything you'll need to pay for on a regular basis to operate your business—for example, phone, cell phone, fax, supplies, truck, and advertising/promotion. Next, list everything you can think of under each heading. Here's a partial example:

Supplies	**Truck**
rags	gas
soap	oil/maintenance
wax	insurance
cleaner	
Q-Tips	

Now consider each specific item. Which ones can you tie to the detailing job? For example, for each auto detailing job, you use two packages of rental rags, one-half can of wax, one-quarter can of cleaner, 10 Q-Tips, $2 for gas, and so on.

Add these expenses to your first sales forecast. Also add expense items that don't change. (See Table 17.2.)

Table 17.2 First Income Statement Forecast

	1	2	3	4	5	6	7
1	First Income Statement Forecast						
2							
3		1st Month	2nd Month	3rd Month			
4	Sales						
5	Monthly	$240	$240	$300			
6	Quarterly	180	180				
7	Original Prospects	180	300				
8	Need to Find		360	1500			
9							
10	Sales Total	600	1080	1800			
11							
12	Expenses:						
13	Phone (1)	20	20	20			
14	Gasoline (2)	30	38	50			
15	Oil/Maint. (3)	15	19	25			
16	Insurance (4)	100	100	100			
17	Supplies (5)	100	180	300			
18	Ad./Promotion (6)	50	75	75			
19	Depreciation (7)						
20	Miscellaneous (8)	50	50	50			
21							
22	Expense Total	365	482	620			
23	Profit (9)	235	598	1180			
24							
25							

Assumptions:

1. Monthly basic rate, plus pager.
2. $20 per month plus $1 per job.
3. $10 per month toward oil change, tires, and maintenance, plus 50 cents per job.
4. $1200 a year, $100/month expense paid quarterly for insurance.
5. Estimated at $10 per job.
6. Yellow Pages ad at $35 a month, plus $15 a month for four-line ad in weekly paper for the first month and $125 for flyers and business cards in the second and third months.
7. Depreciation should be factored in for truck and buffer.
8. Set aside: contingency (surprise) expenses.
9. Profit before depreciation (a non-cash expense). In time, you should get an estimate from your accountant for depreciation.

Now we want you to get started on your sales and expense forecast. Complete Action Step 85.

ACTION STEP 85

Determine how much you will sell in your first month and how much you will spend.

Your aim in this Action Step is to set realistic goals. To do that, you need to know your maximum capacity. For example, how many houses with an area of 1500 to 2000 square feet can you clean in one day? One week? One month? This will give you the top sales figure you could reach. That's your ideal.

Fixed expenses don't change with sales volume. List those first. Then list the variable expenses.

For fixed expenses, check with people who can give you answers: public utility companies (water, gas, electricity, natural gas); a leasing agent for rental rates; an insurance agent for estimated insurance costs.

For variable expenses, those that change with sales volume, figure out how far they go up relative to some fixed unit of change—for example, $100 of sales per house cleaned. If you can establish a percentage relationship between sales and each individual variable expense, then it will be easy to fill in your projections each month.

Final Pass

Out of the 24 prospects, you manage to sign up 15 for auto detailing. That's good. Six of those who want monthly detailing bargained you down to $50. Two of those six agreed to a weekly hand wash at $12. Five prospects agreed to a quarterly detailing, and one of those five agreed to a weekly hand wash. Five prospects decided on a one-time trial. You'd like to snag 25 new customers by the third month. A more reasonable estimate, however, is 15 new customers.

New expenses include $5 a week for a Leads Club breakfast; $75 to join the chamber of commerce; $2 for the car washes; $1 for gas. The new numbers go into your forecast. (See Table 17.3.)

"THINGS TO DO" LIST

Now that your plan is complete; act on it. Your first step is to write up a list of things that need doing. You need this list for at least three reasons:

1. It gives you easy steps to follow.
2. It keeps you on target.
3. It gives you a sense of getting there at last.

Following is a sample "things to do" list from a catering service started by Doris and Mike.

List of Necessities Before Opening Day

1. Talk with experienced caterers.
2. Prepare fast-start business plan.
3. Stay focused on the business.
4. Choose a business name.
5. Make arrangements with food service kitchen.
6. Determine what market area to service.
7. Have business phone installed with voice mail. Purchase office supplies.
8. Set up business bank accounts and establish relationship with banker.
9. Locate suppliers: refrigeration, cooking, baking, utensils, cash register, tables, chairs, other.
10. Check business licence regulations.
11. Get PST and GST numbers.

Table 17.3 Start-up Income Statement Forecast

	1	2	3	4	5	6	7
1	Start-up Income Statement Forecast						
2							
3		1st Month	2nd Month	3rd Month			
4							
5	Sales						
6	Monthly	250	250	300			
7	Car Washes	108	120	156			
8	Quarterly	180	120				
9	Rest of 15	120	180				
10	Need to Find		360	900			
11							
12	Sales Total	658	1030	1356			
13							
14							
15	Expenses:						
16	Phone	20	20	20			
17	Gas	39	41	54			
18	Oil/Maint.	19.5	23	27			
19	Insurance	100	100	100			
20	Supplies	100	180	236			
21	Ad./Promotion	145	95	95			
22	Depreciation						
23	Miscellaneous	50	50	50			
24							
25	Expense Total	473.5	509	582			
26	Profit	184.5	521	774			
27							

12. Select an insurance agent and appropriate insurance policy.
13. Develop job descriptions and application forms.
14. Hire employees. Full-time or part-time? How many? Make sure to get all information.
15. Complete marketing plan and advertising for the opening.
16. Join a discount-price warehouse.
17. Choose food suppliers.
18. Establish support business contracts:
    a. Rental tents, equipment
    b. Florists
    c. Entertainment
    d. Service staff
    e. Other bakeries, specialty suppliers, ice carvers, props, lighting, etc.

19. Order business cards and get ready to hand them out.
20. Order preprinted billing statements for customers who do not pay on receipt (but preferably get money up front).
21. Record all income and expenses daily in a ledger.
22. Find a bookkeeper to prepare financial statements. Check out computerized accounting systems.
23. Contact a lawyer for all lease and legal agreements.
24. Network with friends, relatives, other caterers.
25. Join chamber of commerce. Good place to meet potential customers.
26. Do projected profit and loss statement for three months.

It's your turn. Complete Action Step 86. Make up your "to do" list.

Now it's time to take a look at the model business plan for "Yes, We Do Windows," created by George Finklestein.

ACTION STEP 86

Make a "things to do" list.

Use lists—they work for you. When you write down things to do, do them and cross them off. You'll feel good. As you move from item to item, you'll feel even better.

Set up a pre-start list and continue right on into your business. You'll find that you are more in control of your time and business by keeping lists.

In a Nutshell

The fast-start business plan is not a substitute for preparing a full-fledged plan. Use the fast-start for a specific venture that is easy to start, carrying minimal risk. Also use it for a business that's breaking new ground, where there is little information available.

The key to any business, and to any business plan, is how well you understand the needs of your target customer. Find an itch that isn't being scratched and you can ace your competitors.

Write your own fast-start business plan. Keep it handy. Refer to it often. Use it to keep your business on track in those early months of operation. When you've been in business for three months, use your fast-start business plan as a launching pad for your next nine months of operation. For your second year, write a full-fledged business plan.

Think Points for Success

- ✓ Your business plan, fast-start or full-fledged, is your pathway to success.
- ✓ Looking at your competition helps you see your target customer. Seeing your target customer clearly helps you position your business strategically in the marketplace.
- ✓ Building a plan builds confidence. Confidence breeds excitement. If you don't feel excited and confident about your business, bail out now.
- ✓ Once you get started heading around the track, don't forget to keep your new eyes on the marketplace.

Model Business Plan: Yes, We Do Windows

1. Definition of your business
2. What business am I really in?
3. Competition
4. Pricing
5. Target customer
6. Ad/sales program
7. Start-up costs
8. Sales goals and expenses—first three months
9. "Things to do" list

1. DEFINITION OF YOUR BUSINESS

I have been a window washer for three years. For two years I worked for Windowlite Ltd., a large organization with over 250 satellites across three provinces. For the next year, I worked for a local operator who owned a truck and three squeegees. I feel that I know the business from both ends.

My idea—and the subject of this plan—is to do window washing and house cleaning.

Window washing: I will clean windows, screens, and window casings.

House cleaning: I will vacuum, dust, polish/wash, and mop. I will do bathrooms, mirrors, kitchens, range tops, and ovens.

A customer may contract for one or more services. House cleaning will be offered on a once-a-week or once-every-two-weeks basis. Window washing will be offered monthly, quarterly, twice a year, or as needed.

2. WHAT BUSINESS AM I REALLY IN?

I have determined the answer by identifying the following customer benefits:

1. Pride of ownership—a home is a person's most expensive investment. Keeping it clean makes the customer proud.
2. Time-saving—homeowners work hard to pay for their investment; many homes today are supported by double incomes; few homeowners have the time to do their own cleaning.
3. Preserving the value of the investment—dirt and grime damage the home. Cleaning on a regular basis enhances and preserves the value of the home.
4. Comfortable, healthy living area—a clean home is a healthier home. Who wants to live with dirt?

The business I am really in: "Providing a clean and healthy environment, while at the same time preserving the value of an investment and deepening pride of ownership."

3. COMPETITION

At this writing, there are 77 window cleaning services and 102 house-cleaning services listed in my metropolitan area's Yellow Pages.

Taking the time to make phone calls to these competitors made me feel even better about my idea for a business. Their phone skills need retooling. The clerks who answered were impolite. They didn't seem interested in the prospect of making money. Out of 59 businesses polled, a hefty 68 percent charged for an on-site estimate.

The phone bids were vague. When pressed, the people who answered the phone said they would have to call me back. Very few did call back.

I can see two "musts" for the business. (1) My bids must be firm. (2) My phone skills must be customer-oriented. If I can't answer the phone, I must find a phone person who can fulfill these two musts. The image we're presenting here is "We aim to please. We're interested in servicing your home."

One question I asked was: "Will the same person be in my home every time?" A mere 6 percent said yes. The other respondents were vague. That indicated a problem in scheduling.

Measuring the competition has given my start-up a real advantage. Since I'll be doing all the work myself, I can gather customer data as I work. As I expand, I shall match employees to homeowners. A home is a private place. It's a place where you go to escape from the day. You don't want it invaded by different strangers every week. My plan is to expand only when I find the three right employees.

4. PRICING

My strategy is to price my services just slightly higher than the current competitors' rates. Every three months, to stay current, I will survey the competition.

Basic Rates for Cleaning:

First Cleaning

Square Feet	Price	
1000	$ 50	
1000–1500	75	
1500–2000	100	
2000+	100	+ $25 per 1000 sq. ft.

Weekly Cleaning

Square Feet	Price	
1000	$ 35	
1000–1500	55	
1500–2000	75	
2000+	75	+ $15 per 1000 sq. ft.

Bimonthly Cleaning

Square Feet	Price	
1000	$ 45	
1000–1500	70	
1500–2000	90	
2000+	90	+ $20 per 1000 sq. ft.

Window Washing

One-storey house

up to 15 windows	$ 25
each additional 5 windows	10

Two-storey house

up to 25 windows	$ 60
each additional 5 windows	10

5. TARGET CUSTOMER

I can classify three types of target customers for my business.

Customer A—Family Dwelling
A married couple with one or more children. The household income is $75 000 or more. Two vehicles. Both parents work. Reason for the service: spare time is at a premium for child care, recreation, and entertainment. Parents cannot spare the time to do windows or other cleaning.

Customer B—Single-Person Condo
Customer B is a single or divorced person living alone, usually in an apartment or waterside condo. Age range from 28 to 40. The income here runs from $32 000 to $50 000. Time is at a premium. Customers are seldom at home on nights or weekends.

Customer C—High Roller
Customer C is distinguished by income in the six-figure range. Home values start at $400 000 and move up the scale to $1 million. Customer C has high standards, zero desire to perform menial tasks, wants a spotless home. If work is excellent and customer feels there is no rip-off, price is mainly no object.

6. ADVERTISING AND SALES PROGRAM

1. I will maintain an image of high visibility. My truck is washed daily. The colour is white. If there is mud on the tires after a job, the mud is washed off before the next job. I wear a white jumpsuit that bears the company logo. My employees wear similar jumpsuits. Our footgear is white sneakers. They're easy on the feet and look professional, almost a sporty image.
2. My business cards are white with blue lettering. On the reverse side is a list of my services. I make it a habit to get a business card whenever I hand one out. Data from these cards are entered into a computer. Names are added to a master list.
3. Flyers will be placed door to door in target neighbourhoods. I plan to do one neighbourhood of 100 to 200 homes, and then evaluate the response. I ask questions of each person who calls about the flyer: What did they like? What was missing? From this marketing survey, I'll redesign the flyer before approaching a second neighbourhood.

I make a habit of leaving flyers and business cards at all daycare centres in the area. In exchange for each customer I gain, I donate to a fund for school books or toys.

7. START-UP COSTS

Truck	$10 000*
Paint truck white	1 000
Ladder rack (custom-made)	350
Ladders	412
Supplies—window washing	400
Supplies—house cleaning	500
Signs for new truck	195
Advertising	250
Answering machine	75
Phone and pager installation	200
Post office box per month (first and last month)	40
Chamber of commerce	200
Business name	65
Business licence	55
Used desk and chair	275
Desk calendar	6
Date book, home	65
Date book, truck	15
Rolodex, supplies, file system	50
Bank account and accounting system	125
Total Estimate for Start-up Expenses	$14 278*

*I should be able to buy a used truck for $1000 down and $175 to $200 per month for 36 months. Thus, start-up cash may be as low as $5078.

8. SALES GOALS AND EXPENSES—FIRST THREE MONTHS

My plan is to work six days per week. Until I gain experience, I can work a maximum of three jobs per day. As an incentive for customers, I will do windows at half price with the first house cleaning. I will devote two full weeks to marketing my new business. On the schedule at present, I have four weekly customers and two bimonthly scheduled for the third week. When not on the job, I plan a strong marketing effort so that I can add one customer per week until I'm up to 18 customers, my maximum for the week. At that time, I will evaluate my ability to add additional customers and/or hire a part-time employee. (See Table 17.4.)

Table 17.4 Sales Goals and Expenses

	1	2	3	4	5	6	7
1	First Income Statement Forecast						
2							
3		1st Month	2nd Month	3rd Month			
4							
5	Sales[1]	$1 087.50	$2 580	$4 580.50			
6							
7	Expenses:						
8	Gas[2]	73	91	115			
9	Maintenance[3]	25	25	25			
10	Insurance[4]	125	125	125			
11	Phone[5]	45	45	45			
12	Advertising[6]	80	80	80			
13	Supplies[7]	65	155	275			
14	Truck Loan Interest	60	60	60			
15	Expense Total	473	581	725			
16	Profit	$614.50	1 999	3 855.50			
17							

Notes for Table 17.4

1. Average customer will own a one-storey house of 2000 square feet with 15 windows. Month 1 = four weeks. Month 2 = four weeks. Month 3 = five weeks. Every other new customer bimonthly. All window washing contracts on a quarterly basis.
2. Gas: $15 per week plus $1 per job.
3. Maintenance—mainly a reserve for tires, repairs, oil changes, $25 per month.
4. Auto insurance and bonding, $1500 per year.
5. Basic phone, pager, post office box.
6. Approximately 400 flyers per month comes to $55, plus $25 for distribution.
7. Approximately $5 per job.

9. "THINGS TO DO" LIST

- File for business name.
- Design business logo, cards, and flyer.
- Order phone installation.
- Purchase phone.
- Lease pager.
- Set up bank account.
- Order one-write cheque system.
- Order business cards.
- Set up post office box.
- Locate source of supplies.
- Purchase supplies.
- Purchase truck.
- Obtain quotes and arrange for truck painting.
- Order signs for truck.
- Purchase answering machine.
- Buy ladder rack for truck.

- Buy ladders.
- Join chamber of commerce.
- Purchase desk, chair, and office supplies.

Copyright Acknowledgments

Page 1, chapter epigraph ("If life is a tree . . ."): From Networking interviews, October 2002, with Adrienne Armstrong, owner, Arbour Environmental Shoppe (www.arbourshop.com).

Pages 5–6, Box 1.2 (Test Your Entrepreneurial Quotient): Adapted from Rick Spence, *Secrets of Success from Canada's Fastest-Growing Companies* (Toronto: John Wiley & Sons Canada, Ltd., 1997), p. 228.

Page 8, Table 1.1 (Business Establishments by Firm Size, December 2000): Adapted from Statistics Canada's Business Register, December 2000, National Income Accounts, 2000, and Estimates of Population by Age and Sex for Canada, the Provinces and Territories, July 2000. Reprinted with permission.

Page 23, Figure 2.2 (Canadian Households Purchasing over the Internet): Adapted from Statistics Canada web page http://ecom.ic.gc.ca/english/research/b2c/regional/sld002.htm. Accessed January 7, 2003.

Page 24, Figure 2.3 (Types of Internet Usage Among SMEs): From Canadian Federation of Independent Business, http://e-com.ic.gc.ca/english/research/b2b/connectivity/sld003.htm.

Page 26, Table 2.1 (Canada's Changing Population Profile): From Statistics Canada, "Canada's Changing Population Profile," adapted from "Population Projections for Canada, Provinces, and Territories, 1996–2011," Cat. No. 91-520. Reprinted by permission.

Page 45, Box 3.2 (The Power of Vision): From Rod McQueen, "Canada's 50 Best Managed Private Companies: CHC-Working Well," *The Financial Post*, December 13, 1997, p. 17.

p. 50, Box 3.1 (Internet Commerce—10 Key Metrics): From Industry Canada (Electronic Commerce Branch) web page http://e-com.ic.gc.ca/english/research/rep/e-comstats.pdf, accessed January 7, 2003.

Page 52, Table 3.2 (Small Business Gets Wired): Adapted from Statistics Canada, "Small Business Gets Wired," *The Daily*, Cat. No. 11-001. Reprinted with permission.

Page 56, Figure 3.5 (Context in Which Competitive Strategy Is Formulated): Adapted with the permission of The Free Press, an imprint of Simon & Schuster Adult Publishing Group, from *Competitive Advantage: Creating and Sustaining Superior Performance*, by Michael E. Porter. Copyright © 1985 by Michael E. Porter.

Page 66, Figure 4.1 (Goldfarb's Psychographic Segments as a Percentage of the Canadian Population): From Goldfarb Consultants, www.goldfarbconsultants.com/psycho/index.html. Reprinted with permission of Millward Brown Goldfarb.

Pages 66–68, Box 4.3 (Key Characteristics of the Nine Goldfarb Psychographic Segments): From the Goldfarb web pages that follow "What is your psychographic profile? Take our test to find out who you are," www.mbgoldfarb.com/who_are_you/index.htm. Reprinted with permission of Millward Brown Goldfarb.

Page 72, Box 4.6 (Ten Tips for Joint Ventures and Strategic Alliances): From Rick Spence, *Secrets of Success from Canada's Fastest-Growing Companies* (Toronto: John Wiley & Sons Canada, Ltd., 1997), pp. 117–118.

Page 87, Box 5.3 (What Drives Your Strategy?): From Michael Robert, *Strategy Pure and Simple II* (New York: The McGraw-Hill Companies Inc., 1998). Reprinted by permission of The McGraw-Hill Companies.

Pages 97–98 (introductory vignette): Courtesy of JustWhiteShirts.com.

Page 105, Box 6.5 (Direct Sales Is Alive and Thriving): Data reprinted with permission of Direct Sellers Association of Canada (www.dsa.ca/english.html).

Pages 114–115, Box 6.10 (Your Entrepreneurial Know-Who): From Rein Peterson, "How Is Entrepreneurship Different in Canada?" in *Mastering Enterprise, Part One* (sponsored by Doane Raymond, Compaq, and Bank of Montreal), *Financial Post* and *Financial Times*. Reprinted by permission of Rein Peterson, Professor and Director of Entrepreneurial Studies, Schulich School of Business, York University, Toronto.

Page 116, Box 6.1 (Sample Promotional Plan—Flower Warehouse): Adapted from Barbara Lambesis and Margaret Swine, *101 Big Ideas for Promoting a Business on a Small Budget* (Toronto: Pierce Communications Press, 1990), p. 90. Reprinted by permission.

Page 126, Box 7.1 (Dispelling the Myths About Home-Based Businesses): From Barbara Orser and Ted James, *Home Business: A Report Prepared for the Home-Based Project Committee*, Industry, Science and Technology Canada and Employment and Immigration Canada, p. 8. Reproduced with the permission of the Minister of Public Works and Government Services Canada, 1998.

Page 129, Box 7.4 (Census of Population): From Statistics Canada, "Census of Population," adapted from *Labour Market and Income Data Guide,* April 1992, Cat. No. 75F0010XPB.

Page 131, Figure 7.2 (Census Metropolitan Growth Rates, 1996–2001): From the Statistics Canada web page Census Metropolitan Growth Rates, http://geodepot2.statcan.ca/Diss/Highlights/Page8/Chart1_e.jpg, accessed January 7, 2003.

Page 132, Box 7.6 (www.statcan.ca): From the Statistics Canada web page "First Visit to Our Site," www.statcan.ca/english/about/first.htm, accessed January 7, 2003.

Pages 153–159 (Patents, Copyrights, and Trademarks section): Adapted from the Canadian Intellectual Property Office web page http://strategis.gc.ca/sc_mrksv/cipo/welcome/welcome-e.html). Reproduced with the permission of the Minister of Public Works and Government Services, 2002.

Pages 190–192, Appendix 9.1 (Definitions of the Ratios): Adapted from "Do It Yourself Business Planning Package," from Analyzing Financial Statements, © Business Development Bank of Canada, 1984. Reprinted by permission of the Business Development Bank of Canada.

Page 194, Box 10.1 (Sources of Financing): Adapted from Rick Spence, *Secrets of Success from Canada's Fastest-Growing Companies* (Toronto: John Wiley & Sons Canada, Ltd., 1997), p. 161.

Pages 198–199, Table 10.3 (Personal Financial Cash Budget—Monthly Expenses): Adapted from Human Resources Development Canada, *Working Solutions: Preparing a Realistic Budget,* Take Charge Self-Help Series, No. 6. Reprinted with the permission of the Minister of Public Works and Government Services Canada, 2002.

Pages 237–238, Ten Things You Should Know About Bankruptcy: Adapted from Industry Canada, Office of the Superintendent of Bankruptcy, "Dealing with Debt: A Consumer's Guide" (http://strategis.ic.gc.ca/SSG/br01035e.html#Introduction). Reproduced with the permission of the Minister of Public Works and Government Services, 2002.

Pages 242–243, numbered list (five types of behaviour): From "The Leverage of Leadership," by Jane Howard and Bruce Avolio, in *Managing for Success,* a special supplement to *The Globe and Mail,* May 15, 1998, prepared by the Richard Ivey School of Business. Copyright © 1998 Ivey Management Services.

Page 243, Box 12.1 (Leadership from Within): From Peter Urs Bender, *Leadership from Within* (Toronto: Stoddart Publishing, 1997), pp. 7–11. Reprinted by permission of Stoddart Publishing Co. Limited, Toronto, Ontario.

Page 244, Table 12.1 (Organic versus Mechanistic Organizational Structure): Adapted from Dr. Pradip N. Khandwalla, *The Design of Organization* (New York: Harcourt Brace Jovanovich, 1977), p. 411. Reprinted by permission of the author.

Page 246, Figure 12.2 (The Shamrock Model): Adapted from Charles Handy, *Age of Unreason,* 2nd ed. (London: Century Business Books, Ltd., 1991). Reprinted by permission of the author.

Pages 247–249 (the Founding Team section): Much of the information in this section adapted from the Royal Bank of Canada, Business Plans, "The Team" (www.royalbank.com/sme/bigidea/team.html).

Page 254, Table 12.2 (Characteristics of Mentors): From Ronald A. Knowles and Debbie White, *Issues in Canadian Small Business* (Toronto: Dryden, an imprint of Harcourt Brace & Company, Canada, 1995), p. 78. Reprinted by permission.

Pages 260–264, Appendix 12.1 (The Personality Analysis): From Peter Urs Bender, *Leadership from Within* (Toronto: Stoddart Publishing, 1997), pp. 60–65. Reprinted by permission of Stoddart Publishing Co. Limited, Toronto, Ontario.

Pages 285–286 (introductory vignette): Prepared by Doug Tam, franchise owner, Second Cup, St. Laurent Mall, Ottawa, Ontario. Reprinted by permission.

Pages 293–295, Box 14.2 (Franchise Evaluation Checklist): Adapted from C.R. Stigleman, *Franchise Index/Profile,* Small Business Management Series, No. 35 (Washington, DC: Small Business Administration, 1973), pp. 31–41.

Page 319, Figure 15.1 (eleven global regions): From Gene Boone and David Kurtz, *Contemporary Business Communication,* 2nd ed. Copyright © 1994. Reprinted by permission of Prentice-Hall, Inc., Upper Saddle River, NJ.

Page 323 (introductory vignette): Adapted from Rod McQueen, "Canada's 50 Best Managed Private Companies: Crila Plastics Industries Ltd.," *Financial Post,* December 13, 1997, p. 19. Reprinted by permission of The Financial Post.

Index

Sept 13, 2004 Jim